AN INTRODUCTION TO HUMAN RIGHTS
AND THE COMMON LAW

D1612296

An Introduction to Human Rights and the Common Law

Edited by
ROSALIND ENGLISH
and

PHILIP HAVERS QC
1 Crown Office Row

·HART·
PUBLISHING

OXFORD – PORTLAND OREGON
2000

Hart Publishing
Oxford and Portland, Oregon

Published in North America (US and Canada) by
Hart Publishing c/o
International Specialized Book Services
5804 NE Hassalo Street
Portland, Oregon
97213-3644
USA

Distributed in the Netherlands, Belgium and Luxembourg by
Intersentia, Churchillaan 108
B2900 Schoten
Antwerpen
Belgium

Hart Publishing Ltd is a specialist legal publisher based in Oxford, England.
To order further copies of this book or to request a list of other
publications please write to:

Hart Publishing Ltd, Salter's Boatyard, Oxford OX1 4LB
Telephone: +44 (0)1865 245533 or Fax: +44 (0)1865 794882
e-mail: mail@hartpub.co.uk
www.hartpub.co.uk

British Library Cataloguing in Publication Data
Data Available
ISBN 1 84113–032–X (cloth)

Typeset in Sabon 10pt
by Hope Services (Abingdon) Ltd.

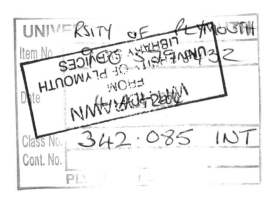

Foreword

LORD ALEXANDER OF WHEEDON QC

When we joined the European Community lawyers were slow to appreciate the potential of Community law on our domestic system. It took Lord Denning to highlight that the "incoming tide" would flow so strongly.

In sharp contrast the legal profession has been quick to realise the effect that the incorporation of the European Convention on Human Rights will have on so many aspects of our legal system. Our primary legislation will have to be compatible with the Convention; so will statutory instruments and administrative decisions of central and local government. And public authorities will have to act in conformity with the Convention since otherwise they may be sued under the new cause of action introduced by the Human Rights Act.

The courts are public authorities, so they will have to comply with the Act both procedurally and substantively. Not only will they have to take it into account in the interpretation of statutes, they will also need to have regard to it in shaping the development of our common law.

Most of the authors of this work are practitioners at 1 Crown Office Row, which has long been a leading common law set of Chambers. Lord Woolf, who has contributed so much to the development of public law, is one of a formidable list of senior judges that have come from these Chambers. So it is not surprising that they should now be contributing to our understanding of the way in which the Convention would impact upon the common law. They have already lectured widely to the profession, both in conjunction with Justice and individually in this area. The way in which the law will develop is far from predictable, but the authors have identified in this book and cogently discussed many issues which are of key contemporary importance.

All this is an illustration of the excellence of the Bar at its best. I commend this thoughtful, but practical book which should be of real value to all who have to grapple with human rights issues.

Contents

Table of Cases   xi

Table of Legislation   xxi

List of Contributors   xxvii

1. Introduction   1
   William Edis

2. The Convention and the Human Rights Act: A New Way of
   Thinking   5
   Philip Havers QC and Neil Garnham
   1. The Mechanics of Incorporation   5
   2. The Impact of Incorporation   9
   3. Conclusion   26

3. Costs, Conditional Fees and Legal Aid   29
   Guy Mansfield QC
   1. Introduction   29
   2. Article 6: The Right to a Fair Hearing   32
   3. The Right to Legal Aid in Civil Cases   40
   4. Conditional Fee or Speculative Fee Agreements – Relationship
      with Legal Aid   45
   5. The High Cost of Proceedings   47
   6. Costs   48
   7. Article 5: The Right to Liberty   51
   8. Conclusion   52

4. Horizontality: The Application of Human Rights Standards in
   Private Disputes   53
   Jonathan Cooper
   1. Introduction   53
   2. Defining the Terms   54
   3. Vertical Application of Human Rights Standards: State Actors   55
   4. Horizontal Application of Human Rights Standards: Non-State
      Actors   55
   5. Applying the Act to State Actors   55
   6. Extending the Scope of the Act Horizontally   57
   7. The Approach of the Strasbourg Authorities   61
   8. Comparative Law   64
   9. Conclusion   68

5. Remedies   71
   Rosalind English

   1. New Remedies   71
   2. Article 13   72
   3. Declarations of Incompatibility   74
   4. Damages   76

6. General Common Law Claims and the Human Rights Act   89
   Richard Booth

   1. Introduction   89
   2. Landlord and Tenant   90
   3. Contract   94
   4. Trespass   94
   5. Unlawful Interference with Goods   95
   6. Economic Torts   97
   7. Civil Actions against the Police   97
   8. Conclusion   101

7. Bringing and Defending a Convention Claim in Domestic Law:
   A Practical Exercise   103
   Philippa Whipple

   1. Introduction   103
   2. Case Study   104

8. The Impact of the Convention on Medical Law   119
   Philip Havers QC and Neil Sheldon

   1. Introduction   119
   2. Prolonging Life   119
   3. Enforced Medical Treatment   122
   4. Funding Treatment   124
   5. Medical Records   125
   6. Medical Tribunals   127
   7. Inquests   129
   8. Right to Found a Family   130
   9. Aids   131

9. Clinical Negligence and Personal Injury Litigation   135
   Robert Owen QC, Sarah Lambert and Caroline Neenan

   1. Introduction   135
   2. The Relevant Articles   135
   3. Practice and Procedure in Medical Negligence and Personal
      Injury Litigation   145
   4. Conclusion   157

10. Environmental Rights   159
    David Hart
    1. Introduction   159
    2. The Victim Requirement   161
    3. Substantive Rights   162
    4. Procedural Rights   175
    5. Conclusions and Predictions   183

11. Confidentiality and Defamation   185
    Rosalind English
    1. Confidentiality and the Protection of Privacy   185
    2. Confidentiality and Privacy under Article 8   189
    3. Defamation and Freedom of Expression   201

12. Mental Health   209
    Jeremy Hyam
    1. Introduction   209
    2. The Detention of Patients   212
    3. The Detention of Patients under the Mental Health Act   216
    4. Detention without Treatment   217
    5. Emergency Confinement and Treatment   224
    6. Likely Areas of Challenge   225
    7. Capacity and Consent   232
    8. Conclusions   235

13. Bibliography and Guide to Sources   237
    Owain Thomas
    1. General Textbooks and Reference Books   237
    2. Court Reports   238
    3. Commission Reports   238
    4. Other Reports   239
    5. Other National and International Jurisdictions   239
    6. Travaux Preparatoires   240
    7. Journals   240
    8. Citations   240
    9. Precedent   241

Index   243

Table of Cases

A v United Kingdom (1999) 27 EHRR 611..62, 110
A v United Kingdom [1998] 5 BHRC 137, [1998] FCR 597 10
A.B. v South West Water [1993] QB 507 170
Aerts v Belgium (1998) 5 BHRC 382...40, 42, 220
Airedale NHS Trust v Bland [1993] AC 789...............................119, 121, 136
Airey v Ireland (1979) 2 EHRR 305 ....11, 32, 36, 40, 41, 42, 47,
                                                            73, 125, 146, 147
Ait-Mahoub v France, judgment of 28 October 1998
   (unreported) 40, 41, 42, 49
Aksoy v Turkey (1997) 1 BHRC 625; 23 EHRR 553 12
Albert and Le Compte v Belgium (1983) 5 EHRR 533 ....35, 129
Armstrong v Attorney-General of NZ [1995] 1 ERNZ 43..........................93
Arrondelle v United Kingdom 26 DR 5 (1982) 91, 165
Artico v Italy (1980) DR 73 32
Ashingdane v United Kingdom (1985) 7 EHRR 528 ....31, 37, 47, 146, 216,
                                                            221, 222
Asselbourg & Greenpeace Luxembourg v Luxembourg, 29 June 1999
   (unreported)..161, 162
Association of General Practitioners v Denmark 62 DR 226 (1989)................96
Association X v United Kingdom Application No 7154/75 14 DR 31
   (1978) 120, 132
Attorney-General v Guardian Newspapers Ltd (No.2) [1990]
   1 AC 109 .... 9, 186, 187, 188, 199
Aydin v Turkey (1998) 25 EHRR 251 ....73, 79

B (a minor) (Wardship:Sterilisation), Re [1988] AC 199.............................. 123
Baggs 44 D & R (1990) 250..165
Baigent's case, see Simpson v Attorney General (Baigent's case)
Balmer-Schafroth v Switzerland (1998) 18 EHRR 175 ....176, 177, 183
Baner v Sweden (1989) 60 DR 128..172
Barbera, Messegue and Jabardo v Spain (1988) 11 EHRR 360.....................77
Barclay v United Kingdom, No 35712/97, 18 May 1999 199
Barrett v Enfield LBC [1999] 3 WLR 79 .... 101, 147, 180
Beatham v Carlisle Hospitals NHS Trust TLR 20 May 1999 153
Bendreus v Sweden, 8 September 1997 (unreported) 169
Bentham v Netherlands (1986) 8 EHRR 1 175
Bergland v Sweden, 16 April 1998 (unreported)..169
Bernstein v Skyways & General [1978] 3 WLR 136 186

Biguzzi v Rank Leisure PLC, 27 July 1999 (CA) 54
Bladet Tromso and Stensaas v Norway, 20 May 1999 (unreported) 206
Blood, ex parte [1997] 2 ALL ER 687 130
Bolam v Friern Hospital Management Committee [1957]
    1 WLR 582...140, 213, 215
Bolitho v City & Hackney HA [1998] AC 232..140
Booker Aquaculture [1999] Eur LR...173
Boyle and Rice v United Kingdom (1988) 10 EHRR 425...........................43, 72
Bozano v France (1986) 9 EHRR 297..79, 111
Bramelid and Malmstrom v Sweden 29 DR 64 (1982)...................................96
Bruggeman and Sheuten v FRG No 6959/75 10 DR 100..............................123
Bryan v United Kingdom (1995) 21 EHRR 342.................129, 178, 179, 229
BSC v Granada Television Ltd. [1981] 1 All ER 417 187
Buckley v United Kingdom (1997) 23 EHRR 101, CD 129............30, 141, 169
Bugdaycay v Secretary of State for the Home Department [1987]
    AC 514 ....12, 136

Campbell v United Kingdom (1992) 15 EHRR 137......................................50
Canea Catholic Church v Greece (1997) 27 EHRR 521................................29
Carter v United Kingdom, No 3541/97, 29 June 1999 (unreported) 190
Chahal v United Kingdom (1997) 23 EHRR 413..........................19, 79, 87, 229
Chappell v United Kingdom 53 (1989) 53 DR 241; 12 EHRR 1................17, 91
Chassagnou v France, 29 April 1999 (unreported) 171, 181
Coco v A.N. Clark Engineers Ltd [1969] RPC 41 ....186, 187, 199
Commission v Germany [1989] ECR 1263 90
Cossey v United Kingdom (1990) 13 EHRR 622..........................30, 45, 60, 92
Costello-Roberts v United Kingdom (1995) 19 EHRR 112 ....13, 62
Cyprus v Turkey Nos 6780/74 and 6950/75 (1976) 4 EHRR 482..................91

D v United Kingdom (1997) 24 EHRR 423 ....13, 121, 132, 144
Darnell v United Kingdom (1993) 18 EHRR 205 153
David John Baron v Brian Lovell TLR, 14 September 1999 (CA) 147
De Cubber v Belgium (1984) 7 EHRR 236...32
De Haes and Gijsels v Belgium (1998) 25 EHRR 205, 206
Delta v France (1990) 16 EHRR 574 80
Demicoli v Malta (1991) 14 EHRR 47...33
Dickinson, Re, [1992] 2 NZLR 43 93
Diennet v France (1995) EHRR CD 491...127, 228
Director Mineral Development v Save the Vaal Environment, 12 March 1999
    (unreported)...160
Dombo Beheer v Netherlands (1993) 18 EHRR 213.........................39, 52, 204
DPP v Jones (1992) 2 WLR 625 ....18, 183
Du Plessis v De Klerk [1997] 1 LRC 637...66
Duchess of Argyll v Duke of Argyll [1967] 1 Ch 302........................... 186, 187

Dudgeon v United Kingdom (1983) 4 EHRR 149 ....30, 123

E v Norway (1994) 17 EHRR 30..109, 227, 229, 233
Edwin John Stevens v R J Gullis, judgment of 27 July 1999 (CA)................147
Engel v Netherlands (1976) 1 EHRR 647 ....51, 98, 128
Eriksson v Sweden (1990) 12 EHRR 183 83
Erkalo v Netherlands (1999) 28 EHRR 509 227

F (Mental Patient: Sterilisation) [1990] 2 AC 1.......................108, 123, 212, 231
F.G. v United Kingdom, Application No 39552/98, April 20 1999
     (unreported)...36
Fayed v United Kingdom (1993) 18 EHRR 393 ....14, 15, 25, 30, 37, 42,
                                                                                      45–6, 146, 201
Feldbrugge v Netherlands (1986) 8 EHRR 425 34
Findlay v United Kingdom (1997) 24 EHRR 221 128
Fitzpatrick v Sterling Housing Association 93
Forbes v Smith [1998] 1 All ER 973 152
Francome v Williams, 30 October 1998 (unreported) 155
Fredin v Sweden (1991) 13 EHRR 784 ....81, 172, 181
Fressoz and Roire v France (1999) 5 BHRC 692 196
Funke v France (1993) 16 EHRR 297 82

G & E v Norway (1983) 35 DR 30 169
Gartside v Outram 26 LJCh 113 187
Gaskin v United Kingdom (1990) 12 EHRR 36 ....82, 194, 195
Gautrin v France (1998) 28 EHRR 1996..35, 229
General Medical Council v British Broadcasting Corporation [1998]
     1 WLR 1573 127
General Mediterranean Holdings FA v (1) Ramanbhai Manibbai Patel
     (2) Kirit Kumar Ramanbhai Patel, QBD [1993] 3 All ER 673;
     The Times, 3 August 1999..49, 50, 52, 200
Gibson v Chief Constable of Strathclyde Police TLR 11 May 1999 101
Gillow v United Kingdom (1986) 11 EHRR 335 91
Glass v United Kingdom, 3 January 1997 (unreported)..............................180
Golder v United Kingdom (1975) 1 EHRR 524 ....29, 39, 146
Goodwin v United Kingdom (1996) 22 EHRR 123 ....94, 198
Greenpeace Schweiz v Switzerland (1997) 23 EHRR CD 116...............161, 176
Groppera Radio A.G. v Switzerland (1990) 12 EHRR 245...........................62
Guerra v Italy (1998) 26 EHRR 357 ....120, 143, 163, 167, 168, 169, 183
Guzzardi v Italy 3 EHRR 333 221

H v Belgium (1987) 10 EHRR 339..36
H v France (1989) 12 EHRR 74 ....40, 147
H v Norway, No 17004/90 73 DR 155...233

H.S. and D.M. v United Kingdom, No 21325/93 201
Hadjianastassiou v Greece (1992) 16 EHRR 219 197
Hakansson v Sweden (1990) 13 EHRR 1 151
Halford v United Kingdom (1997) 24 EHRR 523 ....99, 137, 191
Handyside v United Kingdom (1976) 1 EHRR 737 ....17, 22, 23, 24, 25, 31, 99
Hauer v Land Rheinland-Pfalz [1979] ECR 3727 173
Helmers v Sweden (1991) 15 EHRR 285 81
Hentrich v France (1994) 18 EHRR 440 95
Herczegfalvy v Austria (1992) 15 EHRR 437..109, 219, 229
Het Parool v Van Gasteren, HR 6 Jan 1995, NJ 1995 nr 442.......................67
Hill v Chief Constable of West Yorkshire [1989]
    AC 53 ....15, 85, 100, 146, 189
Hipwood v Gloucester Health Authority [1995] PIQR 447...................156, 157
Hodgson v Imperial Tobacco 1 WLR 1056 152
Holy Monasteries v Greece (1994) 20 EHRR 1 ....61, 96
Hong Kong Polytechnic University v Next Magazine Publishing Ltd [1996]
    2 HKLR 260..64
Hopu v France (1997) 3 BHRC 597..169
Howard v United Kingdom (1987) 52 DR 198 ....90, 91
Huber v France (1998) 26 EHRR 457 ....34, 36
Hughes v United Kingdom (1986) 48 DR 259 141
Hunter v Canary Wharf [1997] AC 655 ....169, 182, 186
Hurtado v Switzerland (1994) Series A 280-A...145

Immobiliare v Italy, 28 July 1999 (unreported)..174
Ireland v United Kingdom (1978) 2 EHRR 25...13, 98
Italy (1995), 80-A, MR 14..48

J.S. v United Kingdom, No 21220/93 194
J.T. v United Kingdom, No 2694/95 230
James v United Kingdom (1986) 8 EHRR 123 ....37, 91, 95
John v Mirror Group Newspapers [1996] 2 All ER 35 57
Johnson v UK (1997) EHRLR 105 ....217, 218, 226, 227
Jones v Miah (1992) 24 HLR 578..92

K v UK 40 BMLR 20 226
K.L. v United Kingdom No 29392/95, May 26 1998 72
Kanthak v FRG No 12474/86, 58 DR 94 (1988) 90
Karakaya v France Series A 269-B..133
Kaufman v Belgium No 10938/84 (1986) 50 DR 98.............................38,147
Kaye v Robertson [1991] FSR 62..188
Keegan v Ireland (1994) 18 EHRR 342..83
Khan v United Kingdom Application No 35394/97 (unreported) 99
Khatun v United Kingdom 26 EHRR CD 212 ....169, 182

Kirkham v Chief Constable of Manchester [1989] 2 KB 283......................... 217
Klass v Germany (1994) 2 EHRR 214...72, 99, 129
Koendjbihare v Netherlands (1990) 13 EHRR 820............................109, 227
Konig v FRG (1978) 2 EHRR 170...34, 80
Kopp v Switzerland, 25 March 1998 (unreported) 191
Kroon v Netherlands (1994) 19 EHRR 263 90
Kumar v State of Bihar AIR (1991) 420 162

L v Sweden, No 10801/84 222
L v United Kingdom, No 34222/96 (unreported) 193
L.C.B. v United Kingdom (1998) 27 EHRR 212 ....137, 142, 163, 164, 168
L.K. v Netherlands CERD Communication no. 4/1991 64
Lam v Brennan & Torbay Council [1997] PIQR 488 169
Lange v Atkinson [1997] 2 NZLR 32 67
Larkos v Cyprus, 18 February 1999 (unreported) 181
Lawless v Ireland (1961) 1 EHRR 15...23
Le Compte v Belgium (1981) 4 EHRR 1..32, 35
Leander v Sweden (1987) 9 EHRR 490 ....72, 195
Lithgow v United Kingdom (1986) 8 EHRR 305...................................147, 174
Lopez Ostra v Spain (1994) 20 EHRR 277 ....83, 164, 165
Luberti v Italy (1984) 6 EHRR 440...217, 218
Lustig Prean v United Kingdom Applications No 33985/96 and 33986/96,
   27 September, 1999...74

Maharaj v Attorney General of Trinidad and Tobago (1979) AC 385...........86
Malone v United Kingdom (1987) 7 EHRR 14 ....21, 215
Maltez v Lewis, 4 May 1999 TLR 148
Manning v Hill [1995] 2 SCR 1130 65
Mantovanelli v France (1997) 24 EHRR 370...38, 42
Marcx v Belgium (1979) 2 EHRR 330 210
Mark Intern and Beerman v Germany (1989) 12 EHRR 161....................62, 97
Matnard v West Midland Regional Health Authority [1984]
   1 WLR 634..140
Matts Jacobssen v Sweden (1990) 13 EHRR 79..77
Mayor and Burgesses of LB Hounslow v Perera, 3 November 1982
   (unreported)..93
Mayor and Commonality and Citizens of London v Prince, 6 June 1995
   (unreported) 93
MB (an adult: medical treatment), Re [1997] 2 FCR 541 ....232, 233, 234
Mbatube v Secretary of State for the Home Department (1996)
   Imm AR 184 24
McCann v United Kingdom (1995) 21 EHRR 97............................12, 129, 136
McFeely v United Kingdom (1981) 3 EHRR 161 13
McGinley & Egan v United Kingdom (1998) 27 EHRR 1 ....34, 168

McTear v United Kingdom No 40291/98, judgment of September 7 1999
 (unreported)...42
Megyeri v Germany (1992) 15 EHRR 584 ....44, 51, 228
Mellacher v Austria (1989) 12 EHRR 391 96
Mentes v Turkey (1998) 26 EHRR 595 91
Meskell v Coras Iompair Eireann [1973] IR 121 68
Metropolitan Property Realizations v Cosgrove, 27 January 1992
 (unreported) 93
Moore v United Kingdom, 15 June 1999 (unreported) 174
Moriera de Azeved v Portugal (1990) EHRR 721 32
Moustaquim v Belgium (1991) 13 EHRR 802......................................83
MS v Sweden (1997) 27 EHRR 91 ....26, 125, 126, 155, 194
Muller v Switzerland (1988) EHRR 212..30
Munro v United Kingdom No 10594/83, 52 DR 158 (1987) 40, 201
Musial v Poland, 25 March 1999 (unreported) 224

N v Switzerland, 11 September 1997 (unreported)............................177
National Provincial BS v United Kingdom (1997) EHRR 127......................171
Neumeister v Austria (1968) 1 EHRR 91...147
New York Times v Sullivan 376 US 254..65, 204
Niederost-Huber v Switzerland (1997) 25 EHRR 709................................39
Nielsen v Denmark, Comm. Report 12 March 1987;
 (1988) 11 EHRR 175...222, 230
Niemitz v Germany (1992) 16 EHRR 97...............17, 50, 82, 97, 190

O v United Kingdom (1988) Series A No. 136A...................................80
Oberschlick v Austria (No.2) (1998) 25 EHRR 357....................................205
Olssen v Sweden (1988) 11 EHRR 259 83
Open Door Counselling v United Kingdom (1992) 15 EHRR 244..........68, 122
Osman v Ferguson [1993] 4 All ER 344...101
Osman v United Kingdom (1999) 5 BHRC 293 ......15, 31, 37, 40, 41, 52, 85, 86,
                                  100, 120, 138, 139, 141, 146, 164, 180, 201, 216, 217

P v France No 10412/83, 52 DR 268..49
P.N. v Switzerland, 11 September 1997 (unreported) 177
Papamichalopoulos v Greece (1995) 21 EHRR 439...............................84
Paton v United Kingdom (1980) 3 EHRR 408...........................122, 233
Pelling v United Kingdom No 35974/97, September 14 (unreported) 149
Pepper v Hart (1993) AC 593 ....6, 74
Perks v United Kingdom, 12 October, 1999 (unreported) 81, 147
Pine Valley Developments v Ireland (1991) 14 EHRR 319 ....172, 181
Poku v United Kinghdom No 26985/85 (unreported)..................122, 138
Powell & Rayner v United Kingdom (1986) 4 DR 5 ....160, 165, 179, 181
Preden v Sweden (1991) 13 EHRR 784 176

Preto v Italy (1983) 6 EHRR 182..151, 153
Prince Albert v Strange (1849) 1 Mac & G.25..186
Putz v Austria (1996) RJD 1996-1, No 4...33

R v BCC ex parte Barclay, 2 October 1996...186
R v Bournewood Community Mental Health Trust ex parte L [1998]
  3 WLR 106 ....211, 214, 215, 234, 236
R v Bow County Court ex parte Michael John Pelling, TLR
  18 August 1999...149
R v Broadcasting Standards Commission ex parte BBC, 9 July 1999
  (unreported) 166, 191, 199
R v Cambridgeshire Health Authority, ex parte B [1995] 1 FLR 1055;
  [1995] 1 WLR 129 (CA) 124, 139
R v Canons Park Mental Health Review Tribunal, ex parte A [1994] 2 All ER
  659; [1995] QB 60 (CA)...217
R v Collins, ex parte S (1998) All ER 673 122
R v Derby JJ ex parte B [1996] AC 487 50
R v Derbyshire CC ex parte Noble [1990] ICR 808......................................106
R v Director of Public Prosecutions ex parte Kebeline [1999]
  3 WLR 175 (DC); [1999] 3 WLR 972 (HL)...........................7, 23, 75, 92, 170
R v Legal Aid Board ex parte Hughes (1992) 24 HLR 698 (CA) 43
R v Lord Chancellor ex parte Lightfoot *The Times*, 18 August 1999............. 35
R v Lord Chancellor ex parte Witham [1998] 2 WLR 849...............................47
R v MHRT ex parte Hall, *The Times* 5 October 1999....................................218
R v Ministry of Defence, ex parte Smith (1996) QB 517...................................25
R v N Lincolnshire Council ex parte Horticultural Sales (Humberside) Ltd
  [1998] Env LR 295 173
R v North Humberside Coroner ex parte Jamieson [1994] 3 All ER 972 129
R v Rochdale MBC ex parte Brown [1997] Env LR 100 179
R v Secretary of State for Health ex parte Eastside Cheese Company CA,
  July 1 1999 (unreported)...96, 173
R v Secretary of State for the Environment ex parte Standley [1999]
  3 WLR 744 173
R v Secretary of State for the Home Department ex parte Brind (1991)
  1 AC 696...9, 18, 24
R v Secretary of State for Wales ex parte Emery [1996] 4 All ER 1 179
R v Secretary of State of the Environment ex parte Greenpeace [1994]
  Env LR 76 161
R v Stratford JJ ex parte Imbert *The Times* 25 February 1999 DC.................30
Rantzen v Mirror Group Newspapers [1994] QB 670...................................57
Reed v United Kingdom (1981) 3 EHRR 136..13
Reed v United Kingdom (1981) 3 EHRR 136..13
Reeves v Commissioner of Police for the Metropolis [1999] 3 WLR 363 217
Reid v Secretary of State for Scotland [1999] 1 All ER 481 217

Retail, Wholesale and Department Store Union Local 580 v Dolphin
  Delivery (1987) 33 DLR (4th) 174 ....65, 66
Reynolds v Times Newspapers [1993] 3 WLR 862 ....202, 203, 204
Ribitsch v Austria (1995) 21 EHRR 573 79
Ringeisen v Austria (1971) 1 EHRR 455...35
Robins v United Kingdom 23 September 1997 RJD 1997-V, No 49........48, 153

S v France 65 D & R (1990) 250 165
Saif al Islam Gaddafi v Telegraph Group Limited, 28 October 1998............203
Salesi v Italy (1998) 26 EHRR 457 34
Saunders v United Kingdom (1997) 23 EHRR 313...................................77
Schonenberger v Switzerland (1989) 11 EHRR 202....................................99
Schuler-Zgraggen v Switzerland (1993) EHRR 405 ....36, 204
Seager v Copydex Ltd [1967] 1 WLR 923 187
Sheffield and Horsham v United Kingdom (1998) 27 EHRR 163....................30
Shelley v Kraemer 334 US 1 65
Sidaway v Governors of Bethlem Royal Hospital [1985] AC 571 140
Silver v United Kingdom (1983) 5 EHRR 347 ....43, 129, 215
Simpson v Attorney General (Baigent's case) (1994) 1 HRNZ 42 ....55, 86
Smith & Grady v United Kingdom, 27 September 1999 (unreported)...........170
Smith Kline and French Laboratories v Netherlands 66 DR 70 (1990)............96
Smith v Secretary of Trade and Industry *The Times*, 11 October 1999........178
Soering v United Kingdom (1989) 11 EHRR 202 ....13, 31, 79
Soobramoney v Minister of Health 4 BHRC 308.................................124, 125
Spencer v United Kingdom (1998) 25 EHRR CD 113 ....62, 198
Sporrong and Lonnroth v Sweden (1982) 5 EHRR 35..................25, 77, 96, 174
St George's Healthcare NHS Trust v S [1998] 3 WLR 936
  (CA) 136, 214, 220, 232
Starrs v Procurator Fiscal, Linithgow 11 November 1999, *The Times*,
  17 November 1999 (unreported) 128
Steel v United Kingdom (1998) 5 BHRC 339 182
Stephan v UK (1998) 25 EHRR CD 130 ....127, 228, 229
Stewart v United Kingdom (1984) 39 DR 162............................136, 137
Stiching Greenpeace v European Commission [1998] All ER (EC 620) 161
Stockton v United Kingdom, 15 January 1998 (unreported).........................170
Stovin v Wise [1996] AC 923...163
Stran Greek Refineries and Statis Andreadis v Greece (1994)
  19 EHRR 293 96
Stuart v United Kingdom No 41903/98 (unreported) 150
Stubbings v United Kingdom (1996) 23 EHRR 213............................150, 151
Sullivan v Co-operative Insurance Society 19 May 1999 TLR (CA).............148
Sunday Times v United Kingdom (1979) 2 EHRR 245......21, 57, 58, 62, 97, 196
Sunday Times v United Kingdom (1992) 14 EHRR 229 196
Sur v Turkey October 1997 RJD-VI No 5 79

Swinney v Chief Constable of Northumbria Police (No.2) *The Times*, May 25 1999 189

T v Surrey County Council [1994] 4 All ER 577 142
Tam Hing-yee v Wu Tai-wai [1992] 1 HKLR 185 64
Tanko v Finland No 23634/94 DR 77-A 144
Tapling v Jones (1815) 4 Camp 219 186
Tauiria v France (1995) D & R 83-A 113..161
Taylor v United Kingdom No 23412/94 (unreported) 140
Telnikoff v Matusevitch [1991] 4 All ER 817 (HL) 202, 206
Thorgeirson v Ireland (1992) 14 EHRR 843 205
Timmer v Netherlands, 22 October 1997 (unreported) 166
Tinelley & Sons Ltd v United Kingdom (1999) 27 EHRR 249 ....31, 32
Tolstoy Miloslavsky v United Kingdom (1995) 20 EHRR 442 ....49, 200
Tomasi v France (1993) 15 EHRR 1..13
TP and KM v United Kingdom Application No 28945/95..............................85
Tre Traktorer Aktiebolag v Sweden (1984) 13 EHRR 309 96
Turner v W H Malcolm Ltd (1992) 136 *Sol Jo*...153
TV v Finland No 21780/93 76 DR 140 (1994) 131, 193
Tyrer v United Kingdom 91978) 2 EHRR 1................................10, 13, 60

United Kingdom (1990) 64 DR 232 48
Unterpertinger v Austria (1986) 13 EHRR 175 38

Vallee v France Series A 289-C..133
Van der Leer v Netherlands (1990) 12 EHRR 567 50
Van Droogenbruck v Belgium (1981) 4 EHRR 443 218
Van Marle v Netherlands (1986) 8 EHRR 483 ....35, 127
Van Orshoven v Belgium (1997) 26 EHRR 55 38
Vereniging Weekblad "Bluf" v Netherlands (1994) 20 EHRR 189................197
Vernon v United Kingdom, No 38753/97, 7 September 1999 (unreported)....193

W v Egdell [1990] 1 Ch 359..187
W v Sweden No 12778/87 59 DR 158 223
W v United Kingdom (1983) 32 DR 190 137
W v United Kingdom, No 10871/84 201
Waltons & Morse v Dorrington [1997] IRLR 488 (EAT)............................141
Webb v United Kingdom No 9353/81, 33 DR (1983) 42, 43
Weber v Switzerland (1990) 12 EHRR 508 33
Weeks v UK (1987) 10 EHRR 293 218
Whitehouse v Jordan [1981] 1 WLR 246 140
Wickramsinghe v United Kingdom (1998) EHRLR 338 129
Widmer v Switzerland No 20527/92 (1993) (unreported) 121
Wiggins v United Kingdom No 7456/76, 13 DR 40 (1978)............................91

Winer v United Kingdom (1985) 45 DR 291 ....41, 192
Winnipeg Child and Family Services (North West Area) v G
    3 SCR 925 ....123, 234
Winterwerp v Netherlands (1979) 2 EHRR 387 ....108, 109, 110, 223, 224,
                                                                            225, 226, 228
Woolgar v Chief Constable of Sussex Police and UKCC [1999] Lloyd's Rep
    Med 335 188
Worm v Austria (1998) 25 EHRR 454 196

X (Minors) v Bedfordshire County Council [1995] 2 AC 633 ....71, 84, 85, 163
X and Y v Germany (1976) 5 DR 161 160
X and Y v Netherlands (1985) 8 EHRR 235, No 6202/73,
    1 DR 66 ....16, 47, 61, 62, 82, 110, 148, 155, 190
X and Y v Switzerland (1981) 4 EHRR 139 231
X v Belgium 12 Yearbook HR 174..98
X v Commission of the European Communities C-404/92P [1995]
    IRLR 320 194
X v Denmark (1983) 5 EHRR 27, (1983) 32 DR 282...............................92, 144
X v Denmark, *see* X v France
X v France (1992) 14 EHRR 483, 9993/82 31 DR 241 (1992) 133, 153
X v France, No 9993/82 31 DR 241 (1992)..133
X v FRG (1956) 1 YB 202 90
X v Morgan-Grampian (1991) 1 AC 1..197
X v United Kingdom (1978) 14 DR 31..138
X v United Kingdom (1981) 4 EHRR 188..224, 228
X v United Kingdom No 6564/74 2 DR 105..123
X v United Kingdom No 8158/78, 21 DR 95 (1980) 42
X v United Kingdom, Coll HR 90..99
X v United Kingdom, No 9702/82 30 DR 239 (1982)................................192
X v Y [1988] 2 All ER 648..187

Y v UK (1977) 10 DR 37 230
Y v United Kingdom (1977) 10 DR 37 230
Y v United Kingdom (1994) 17 EHRR 238..13
Yagci and Sargin v Turkey (1995) 20 EHRR 505 79
Yilmax-Dogan v Netherlands CERD Communication no. 1/1984
Young, James and Webster v United Kingdom (1982) 4 EHRR 38................62

Z v Austria, No 10392/83 56 DR 13 (1988) 195
Z v Finland (1997) 25 EHRR 371 ....23, 126, 131, 192
Zamir v United Kingdom (1983) 40 DR 42..40
Zander v Sweden (1994) 18 EHRR 38..81, 176

Table of Legislation

EUROPEAN

European Convention on Human Rights and Fundamental
   Freedoms 5, 103, 159, 209, 212
Art. 1 29
Art. 2...........................10, 11–12, 13, 15, 19, 97, 119, 120, 121, 122, 123, 125,
                   129, 130, 132, 135, 136, 137, 138, 140, 141, 142, 143,
                   144, 151, 159, 162, 163, 164, 167, 168, 183, 216, 233
   (1)..120, 123, 136, 210, 233
   (2) 136
Arts. 2–12 5
Art. 3, 12–13...........................19, 87, 97, 98, 99, 109, 110, 115, 121, 132, 135,
                   136, 142, 144, 145, 150, 164, 210, 219, 220
Art. 4..13, 19
Art. 5 ....13–14, 29, 50, 51, 97, 98, 115, 220, 221, 223, 224, 225, 226, 227
   (1)...........................14, 97, 98, 108, 114, 168, 220, 224, 225, 226, 229
    (b) 50, 51
    (e) 108, 218, 219, 221, 222, 223
   (2) 98
   (2)–(5) 14
   (3) 98
   (4)...............51, 87, 109, 114, 116, 220, 221, 223, 224, 225, 227, 228, 229
   (5) 97, 111
Art. 6.....................8, 14–16, 29, 32, 33, 35, 37, 39, 40, 41, 43, 45, 49, 50, 51,
        57, 74, 75, 77, 80, 81, 84, 85, 93, 94, 99, 111, 127, 128, 131,
        132, 133, 139, 145, 146, 149, 152, 153, 154, 157, 188,
        193, 196, 197, 200, 201, 203, 206, 207, 212, 228, 229
   (1) 14, 15, 16, 29, 31, 32, 33, 34, 35, 36, 37, 38, 40, 41, 43, 46,
        47, 51, 77, 81, 95, 101, 127, 129, 145, 146, 147, 149, 150, 151,
        159, 162, 175, 176, 177, 178, 179, 180, 183, 201, 210, 228, 229
   (2) 8, 14, 32, 127
   (3)...14, 32, 127
    (c) 40, 45, 81
Art. 7 ....16, 19, 92, 93
Art. 8 ....15, 16–17, 20, 21, 22, 50, 80, 81, 82, 83, 84, 85, 90, 91, 92,
      93, 97, 98, 99, 110, 115, 116, 121, 123, 125, 126, 131, 132, 139, 141,
      142, 143, 149, 150, 154, 155, 156, 159, 162, 163, 164, 165, 166, 167,
      168, 169, 170, 171, 175, 182, 185, 186, 187, 188, 189, 190, 191,
      192, 193, 194, 195, 196, 198, 199, 200, 223, 229, 230, 233

(1) 16, 17, 90, 92, 155, 157, 164, 165, 166, 169, 170, 195

(2) 17, 20, 65, 92, 115, 137, 155, 164, 165, 166, 169, 170,
183, 192, 193, 195, 198

Arts. 8–10 20

Art. 9..17, 20

Art. 10.................17, 20, 68, 125, 143, 152, 159, 167, 182, 185, 195, 196,
198, 199, 200, 201, 203, 204, 205, 206, 230, 231

(2) 17, 183, 196, 198, 200, 205, 206, 231

Art. 11..17–18, 20, 97, 159, 182, 183

(2) 183

Art. 12 ....18, 19, 123, 130, 131, 231

Art. 13....................5, 43, 72, 73, 74, 75, 85, 87, 97, 111, 129, 130, 142, 149,
150, 159, 171, 180, 181, 199, 207, 210

Art. 14 ....5, 18, 60, 93, 110, 111, 125, 130, 131, 150, 159, 172,
181, 182, 231, 232, 233

Art. 15 19

(2) 135

Arts. 16–18.. 5

Art 34 (ex 26) 105, 161, 162, 176, 180, 199

Art 35...162

Art. 41...8, 71, 76, 84, 111, 166

Protocol No. 1

Art. 1 ....18, 19, 37, 83, 84, 91, 94, 95, 96, 97, 99, 159, 171, 172, 174, 175

Arts. 1–3 5

Art. 2 19

Art. 3 19

Protocol No. 4

Art. 1 51

Art 2 222

Protocol No. 6 Arts. 1–2 5

Treaty of Rome 27

Directives

Nitrates Directive 91/676/EEC...173

INTERNATIONAL

International Convention on the Elimination of all forms of Racial
Discrimination 63

International Covenant on Civil and Political Rights, Art. 26 ....63, 66

United Nations Economic Commission for Europe Convention on Access
to Information, Public Participation in Decision-Making and Access
to Justice in Environmental Matters...159, 168

NATIONAL

Canada
Canadian Charter of Rights and Freedoms 1982, s 32 65
Bill of Rights Ordinance No 59 of 1991 64
Offences Against the State Act 23

Hong Kong
Bill of Rights...58, 66, 67
  s 3...66, 67
  s 21 86

South Africa
Constitution of South Africa 1996 66
  s 11 124
  s 24 160
  s 27(3) 124
Interim Constitution, s 7,
  (i) 66
  (ii)...66

United Kingdom
Abortion Act 1967 ....123, 233
Access to Justice Act 1999..44, 51
Broadcasting Act 1990, s 143 186
Broadcasting Act 1996, s 110(1)(b) 191
Children Act 1989 193
Civil Aviation Act 1982, s 76(1) 180
Civil Procedure Act 1997...48, 200
Civil Procedure Rules 1998..48, 52, 103, 148, 154
  Pt 1 147
    r 1..47
      (1)(d) 154
      (2)(a)..147
      (2)(c)..147
      (4)(1)..154
    r 2..148
  Pt 3..
    r 3 ....
      (1)(m) 153
      (4)(c) 153
  Pt 27, r 1(2)..148
  Pt 35, r 1(2)..147

Pt 39

    r 2(1) 152

    r 2(3) 152

    r 2 16

Pt 44

    r 3 47

    r 4 47

    r 5 47

Pts 44–48 48

Pt 47, r 7(3) 200

Pt 48

    r 7 49

    (3) 49

Practice Direction 2.1–2.4 105

Practice Direction 7, para 2.1 111

Practice Direction 39, para 1.6 152

Consumer Protection Act 1987 150

Contempt of Court Act 1981

    s 10 197

    s 19 127

County Courts Act 1984, s 53 157

Data Protection Act 1984 1

Data Protection Act 1998 ....185, 191

Defamation Act 1996 201

Environment Act 1995, Sch 13 173

Environmental Pollution Act 1990 177

Food Safety Act 1990, s 13 96

Harassment Act 1977 156

    s 1 186

Housing Act 1988

    s 8 92

    s 27 ....92, 93

    s 28 ....92, 93

Housing Grants' Construction and Regeneration Act 1996, s 108 94

Human Fertilisation and Embryology Act 1990, s 13(5) 130

Human Rights Act 1998 ....1, 3, 4, 5, 8, 15, 17, 25, 26, 27, 53, 54, 55,
                            59, 60, 68, 69, 71, 73, 74, 76, 89, 94, 97, 101, 103, 105,
                            106, 109, 113, 116, 139, 161, 199, 209, 210, 211, 212

    s 1 5

    s 2 ....6, 135, 181, 216

    (1) 74, 108, 111

    s 3 ....5, 6, 8, 10, 75, 86, 97, 154

    (1) 58, 59

    (2)(b) 76

s 4 ....8, 59, 75
  (2) 76
  (6) 75, 76
s 5 116
s 6 ....56, 68, 105, 114, 137, 151, 154, 163, 170, 212
  (1) 56
  (2) 137
  (3)
    (a) 57, 58, 66, 137, 145
    (b) 56, 68, 106, 109, 137
  (5) 56, 68, 106, 109, 137
  (6) 61, 75, 142
ss 6–8 6
s 7 ....7, 163
  (1) 56, 161
    (b) 7
  (3) 161
  (5) 8, 151
    (a) 110, 116
    (b) 110, 116
  (7) 105, 161, 162
s 8 ....8, 16, 73, 74, 76, 84, 87, 111
  (1) 56, 181
  (4) 166
s 10 ....8, 75
s 11(b) 76
s 12 ....75, 199
Sch 180
Interception of Communications Act 1985 22
Limitation Act 1980
  s 2 150
  s 11A 150
  s 33 ....116, 150
Mental Health Act 1983 ......103, 105, 106, 110, 112, 116, 209, 212, 219, 225, 230, 235
  s 1 221
  s 3 ....104, 106, 107, 109, 113
  s 12(3) 109
  s 29 ....110, 116
  s 42(3) 226
  s 62 225
  s 63 ....108, 109, 110, 114, 115
  s 66 224
  s 68 ....115, 116
  (1) 104, 109, 116

s 131(1) 211, 236
s 134...230
s 139...111
  (1) 113
  (2) 104, 111
Police and Criminal Evidence Act 1984 ....98, 99, 221
Prevention of Terrorism (Temporary Provisions) Act 1989.......8, 75
Protection from Eviction Act, s 5...92
Protection from harassment Act 1996 185
Rent Act 1977, Sch 1, ...177
  para 2(2) 93
  para 3(1) 93
Scotland Act 1998 128
Supreme Court Act 1981
  s 35A...111
  s 51...48
  s 67 152
Torts (Interference with Goods) Act 1977....................................95
Water Resources Act 1991 177

United States

Bill of Rights...65

List of Contributors

[in order of Chapters]

William Edis, Barrister, specialises in professional indemnity litigation, clinical negligence, and environmental law. His cases include major group litigation in relation to pharmaceutical products, the Court of Appeal decision in *R v CPC* (liability for escape of polluting matter from factory premises) and acting for Nuclear Electric plc in the prosecution of a major UK nuclear installation. He has written for a variety of legal publications and is a regular lecturer to professional bodies and associations.

Philip Havers QC is a Barrister whose areas of practice include administrative law, human rights, environmental law, media law and professional and clinical negligence. He has acted in many cases involving human rights including *Spycatcher* (freedom of speech), *Findlay v United Kingdom* (fair trial), *Wingrove v United Kingdom* (freedom of speech and the English law of blasphemy), *Ex parte S* (the rights of an unborn fetus) and in a wide range of public law and media contempt of court cases, including *Ex parte Page* (university law), *AG v Blake* (fiduciary duties of a spy) and *AG v Associated Newspapers* (publication of a jury's deliberations).

Neil Garnham, Barrister, specialises in judicial review, professional and clinical negligence and human rights law. Previous cases include a number of decisions concerning Convention rights before incorporation, such as *R v Secretary of State for the Home Department, ex parte McQuillan* (1995). He has also represented the United Kingdom before the European Court of Human Rights in *Gregory v United Kingdom* (1997), *D v United Kingdom* (1998) and *ADT v United Kingdom* (1999).

Guy Mansfield QC specialises in professional negligence and personal injury. He has acted in legal professional negligence cases including *Spencer v Family Law Consortium* (divorce proceedings), *Carr-Glynn v Frearsons* (duty of care owed by a solicitor to beneficiary under a will) and *Tolstoy-Miloslavsky v Aldington* (wasted costs order in pro bono case). He has been vice-chairman (1995–7) and chairman (1998–to date) of the Bar Council's Remuneration/ Legal Aid Committee.

Jonathan Cooper is the Director of the Human Rights Project at the law reform organisation Justice. He is also an Associate Tenant at Doughty Street Chambers. He has taken several cases to the European Court of Human Rights and has written many articles and spoken extensively on the Human

Rights Act and the European Convention on Human Rights. He is co-editor of a guide to the Parliamentary Debates on the Human Rights Act published by Hart Publishing.

Rosalind English is Visiting Research Fellow at Queen Mary and Westfield College and Associate Tenant of 1 Crown Office Row. She is a former college lecturer at Merton College, Oxford. She specialises in human rights law and has co-written a textbook on public law (*Principles of Public Law*, Cavendish, 1999) as well as articles on public law (*Modern Law Review*). She has also published articles on environmental law (*Journal of Environmental Law and Planning*), tort and comparative law (*Cambridge Law Journal*), in the case law of the Constitutional Court of South Africa (*South African Journal of Human Rights*).

Richard Booth is a Barrister practising in employment law, sports law, clinical negligence and personal injury. He has been involved in a number of cases with an EC or ECHR dimension, including *Plenderleith v Royal College of Veterinary Surgeons* (1996) (Privy Council – freedom of establishment/freedom to provide services) and *R v Secretary of State for Health ex parte Eastside Cheese Company* (1999) (cheese ban – Food Safety Act 1990 – proportionality – Article 1, First Protocol, ECHR).

Philippa Whipple is Barrister practising in clinical and professional negligence, medical law, personal injury, employment, public law and tax. She has appeared in the European Court of Justice for the Government of the United Kingdom (*Institute of the Motor Industry v Commissioners of Customs and Excise* – resolving conflict between different language versions of an EC Directive). She appears regularly in the higher domestic courts for the Commissioners of Customs and Excise and others. Before coming to the Bar she was a solicitor at Freshfields. She has lectured widely, in particular on the Civil Procedure Rules and on human rights legislation, and is a member of the Bar Pro Bono Unit.

Neil Sheldon is a Barrister practising in professional negligence, personal injury, employment and administrative law. He is the holder of Prince of Wales, Karmel and Senior Scholarships from Grays Inn, and in 1999 he was the Inn Mooting Champion and World Debating Champion.

Robert Owen QC is a Barrister specialising in clinical and professional negligence. He has been involved in a number of major multi-party actions including the human growth hormone litigation, the benzodiazepine litigation and the tobacco litigation. He was instructed in the House of Lords in *Bolitho v City and East Hackney Health Authority* on causation and the *Bolam* test, and the triple appeal of *Wells, Thomas and Page* on multipliers and the discount rate. Robert Owen is a former Chairman of the Bar and sits as a Deputy High Court Judge.

Sarah Lambert, Barrister, practises in clinical negligence, personal injury, employment law, family law and professional negligence (including wasted costs). She has lectured on the Civil Procedure rules and on the impact of human rights legislation on clinical negligence and personal injury litigation. She is the author, together with Guy Mansfield QC, of "Wasted Costs and Costs against Non-Parties" in the *Personal Injury Handbook*. She is a member of the Bar Pro Bono Unit.

Caroline Neenan, Barrister, practises in professional negligence, personal injury, human rights, administrative law and employment law. She has contributed several articles to the *Judicial Review Journal*.

David Hart, Barrister, specialises in environmental law and clinical and professional negligence. He has acted in a number of environmental cases involving points of administrative and European law, including *R v Falmouth Port Health Authority ex parte South West Water* (1999) and *Bowden v South West Water* (1998), (environmental *Francovich* claims). He was also involved in other significant environmental cases such as *Cambridge Water v Eastern Counties Leather* (House of Lords 1994), the *Coalite, Loscoe Tip, Chatham Dock* and *Orimulsion* cases. He has published articles in the *Journal of Planning and Environmental Law* (on human rights) and in the *Journal of Environmental Law* (on environmental damages).

Jeremy Hyam, Barrister, practises in clinical and professional negligence, personal injury, environmental law and human rights law. He has taken on employment and public law pro bono work for the Bar Pro Bono Unit.

Owain Thomas, Barrister, practises in clinical negligence, personal injury, construction law and VAT. He is a contributor to *Professional Negligence: Law and Practice* and co-author of Archbold Practical Research Papers on Contempt of Court. He has lectured and written articles on various aspects of human rights law, most recently on "Bias after *Pinochet* and under the Convention" (1999) *Judicial Review*.

1

Introduction

WILLIAM EDIS

It is inevitable and right that every proposal for substantial reform in the law should be tested against a requirement that it be beneficial and necessary. A country which managed to pass forty six statutes into law in 1998 (to say nothing of secondary legislation) cannot be expected to ask this very important question too often, but the incorporation of the Convention into English and Welsh law was very definitely an occasion when it might be thought appropriate.

In Britain we have, of course, a long-cherished the view that a happy amalgam of the common law and occasional parliamentary action provides the best safeguard of essential rights, even if our direct and indirect lawmakers have not always been entirely sure what those rights are or should be or how best to devise a coherent strategy for their protection. The native suspicion that codification precludes flexibility and rapid adaptation is as enduring as it is misconceived.

A good illustration of why it is that the Human Rights Act 1998 is so welcome comes from a case fought out in June 1944, only two weeks after D-Day and at a period when great sacrifice and hardship were at last beginning to bring an end to a war proclaimed then and now as necessary for the defence of civilised values against barbarism.

Leary Constantine, later Lord Constantine, could be considered one of the great figures of Caribbean history. Born in the West Indies, he lived in Lancashire for a considerable time, playing cricket in the Lancashire leagues as well as for the West Indies. During the Second World War he was a Welfare Officer looking after West Indian workers on Merseyside. After the war he became Minister for Transport in the Federal Government of the West Indies and enjoyed a distinguished career in public life.

In 1944 he obtained special leave from his post with the Ministry of Labour to travel to London to captain the West Indies in a cricket match at Lords, the proceeds of which would go to charity. He sought a room in the Imperial Hotel, having earlier inquired about availability, but when he arrived he was turned away. According to his account, supported by a colleague and unreservedly accepted by the judge, the refusal to accommodate him was accompanied by crude and racist language. The hotel did not deny that Constantine had been turned away solely because he was black but denied the use of offensive language and argued that its actions were reasonable. For even though it accepted that Constantine had enough money to pay for his room, had duly booked it and was a man of unimpeachable character, it claimed that it nevertheless had the right to exclude him given that it also accommodated very large numbers of (white) Americans. Whilst the hotel itself had no objection to accommodating Constantine it asserted that its American guests undoubtedly would object to sharing the building and its facilities with him. The hotel therefore chose, it said, the easier course. The heavy irony that Constantine, a British subject, was being excluded to cater to the prejudices of foreign visitors was not lost on him at the time or later. It is striking that the hotel's attitude before trial and in cross-examination of Constantine was that its staff were perfectly entitled to take into account, indeed to pander to, the quite possibly violent emotions of its American guests when faced with a single black family under the same roof.

There are several interesting features of the case. The first, reflecting the attitudes of the times, is that Constantine had felt it wise to contact the hotel in advance to ensure that it had no objection to him as a "man of colour". The second surprise is that the hotel took the matter to trial at all. That is particularly true since it accepted that sufficient accommodation was available for Constantine and his family, that he was a man of the highest character and that its only justification was that his presence may cause a riot amongst other guests.

But the most notable feature for present purposes is that the case is not at all concerned with unlawful discrimination on the grounds of race. Although Constantine secured judgment he recovered but five guineas in damages and the case is reported only on whether the wrong done to him was actionable without proof of damage. The reported judgment[1] omits all mention of the findings of fact and concentrates exclusively on the points of law raised by the hotel. The rather pedestrian headnote reads:

> "An action by a traveller against an innkeeper for wrongfully refusing to receive and lodge him is for the violation of a right at common law so that the action, although sounding in case, can be sustained without proof of special damage".

True to this summary, the majority of the judgment concentrates on whether the action was maintainable at all, given that Constantine and his family were accommodated in the Imperial's sister hotel that very night and that no special damage was claimed. Relying on cases from the sixteenth century and referring to the practice in the Court of the Star Chamber, the judge ruled that the claim was actionable without proof of damage. The only reference to the affront suffered by the family comes in a passage when Birkett J, having found that the hotel's staff did indeed use grossly offensive language, went on to refuse any award of "exemplary or substantial damages" though accepting that

---

[1] [1944] 1 KB 693.

Constantine had suffered "much unjustifiable humiliation and distress". The judgment contains far more Latin than it does discussion of the gross insult visited upon Constantine by the hotel and its offensive discrimination. Nor does the judgment contain any discussion of the need for a common law protection against discrimination. Had there been no existing common law right for a traveller in funds to obtain lodging from a common innkeeper, Constantine would have been entirely without remedy at English law.

Constantine was represented by perhaps the leading civil trial lawyer of his day, Sir Patrick Hastings, who had been Attorney-General in the first Labour Government of 1923. He was assisted in the case by the future Mrs Justice Heilbron. Nevertheless, the researches which we can confidently assume they and their solicitors made turned up no more reliable protection against what had occurred than the resurrection of an eighteenth century cause of action. Even the skilful manhandling of that cause of action to enable Constantine to litigate his grievance left open significant questions of damage and proof.

Birkett, of course, went on to be this country's nominated alternate judge at the Nuremberg trials, which played a significant part in establishing the need for human rights standards. It is tempting to wonder whether the inadequate relief afforded to Mr Constantine by English law ever struck him as showing the need for a new approach in English law.

One can, of course, look elsewhere in the common law for the articulation of rights and mechanisms for their protection and the search is not always in vain. It would be at the same time churlish to deny any achievements to the judiciary in past protections of human rights and unjustifiable to claim that they have proved adequate in resolving the tension between conflicting rights, for example the rights to privacy and to free speech.

The second element of the traditional approach to rights protection involves consideration of the historical role of Parliament as bulwark of freedom. Here one encounters what ought to be one of the most important influences on rights law, namely that the body which is overwhelmingly most likely to be in a position to, and for that matter to want to, infringe an individual's human rights is the government of the day. The power of the legislature and the executive to influence all our lives exceeds massively that enjoyed by any other body, and history provides us with numerous examples of the enactment of legislation in accordance with established democratic processes which nevertheless grossly infringes what would or should be considered core rights of individuals or communities. Parliament can also be slow to act. It was not, after all, until 1976 that Parliament legislated to provide redress for those who might have found themselves in Constantine's position.

The most obvious example of this phenomenon this century would have been fresh in the minds those who drafted the Convention in 1948 and would have emphasised the need to have overarching standards to which, they may have hoped, even the doctrine of parliamentary sovereignty would be subordinate. This purpose is not entirely realised by the Human Rights Act, for it is not entrenched against repeal and may be set aside in the future in the same way as any other statute, but the Act nevertheless represents a significant advance in the recognition of rights which are inviolable or which may be infringed upon only in extraordinary circumstances.

The other reason not to be satisfied that Parliament alone can be trusted to protect our rights and freedoms is that the complexion of Parliament, and its attitude to that task, can depend on considerations utterly divorced from a discussion of human rights. Our electoral system gives almost unrestricted power to those who secure but a minority of the votes cast in any general election and if, indeed, "it's the economy, stupid" which governs how we cast those votes, a government which is inimical to the concept of enshrined rights could nevertheless well be in power for a considerable time either because of sound fiscal management or sheer luck. Political and legal historians can gain some slight amusement from compiling a list of statutes, divided into those which generally protect and those which generally infringe upon human rights, and trying to guess the party in power when the Act was passed. It would surely have been unsatisfactory to have continued to have the framework of rights protection at the mercy of, amongst other things, the economic cycle.

Finally, though it remedies many of the failings of the common law and of the legislature, it would be wrong to conclude that the 1998 Act represents the last word in the protection of rights. There is still a significant role for the statutory additions to purely Convention rights, in particular, perhaps, to protect against discrimination on grounds which are, or ought to be, unacceptable. The Convention and the Act are both valuable and admirable additions to the armoury of those who fight for a freer and safer society but they do not stand alone.

2

The Convention and the Human Rights Act: A New Way of Thinking

PHILIP HAVERS QC and NEIL GARNHAM

1. THE MECHANICS OF INCORPORATION

The Human Rights Act 1998 became law on 9 November 1998, some forty-seven years after the Convention for the Protection of Human Rights and Fundamental Freedoms was ratified. The Government's portrayal of the Act as "bringing human rights home" or "the domestication of human rights" seeks to suggest that the Act will achieve a delicate balance between formal acknowledgement of fundamental freedoms and the sovereignty of the United Kingdom Parliament. Such sovereignty is maintained by, for example, not entrenching the Act against repeal (it may be repealed or amended in the usual way) and by preserving the immunity of primary legislation against being struck down by the Court, as to which see below.

The Government has presented the Act as conferring no new rights upon UK citizens; it simply gives, in the words of the preamble, "further effect to those rights which we already enjoy under the Convention". The first part of this chapter will look at the the techniques employed by the draftsman to weave the Convention into the fabric of English law and at the remedies the Act provides. The second part will consider the impact of the Convention on existing common law rights, which will be addressed individually and in more detail in succeeding chapters.

Section 1 defines as "Convention rights" the rights set out in Articles 2–12 and 14 of the Convention, Article 1–3 of the First Protocol, and Article 1–2 of the Sixth Protocol, as read with Articles 14 and 16–18 of the Convention. Article 13, which entitles individuals to an effective remedy before national authorities for breach of their Convention rights, has not been incorporated, the Government's justification for the exclusion being that incorporation of the main Convention rights fulfilled its obligations under Article 13.[1]

The relevant provisions of the Convention are "drip fed" into English law by three routes: First, by Section 3 and the introduction of a new technique of

---

[1] The exclusion of Article 13 has precipitated much debate; some of the arguments are explored in chapter 5 on Remedies

interpretation, which alters the approach which must be taken by the courts when considering primary or subordinate legislation. Secondly, by the creation of a new cause of action in Sections 6 to 8. Thirdly, the Act provides new mechnisms by which pressure is placed on Government and Parliament to bring existing and future legislation into line with the Convention.

1.1. Statutory Construction

Pursuant to Section 3, primary and secondary legislation must be interpreted so far as that is possible in a manner which is compatible with the Convention. This is an innovation. It displaces several principles of statutory construction, which must all take second place to this new overriding objective. So, for example, even where resort to *Hansard* under the rule in *Pepper v Hart*[2] would suggest that Parliament meant something very different, if it is possible to construe the words of the legislation in accordance with the Convention that is how they must be construed.

Section 3 has a second interesting effect. It neatly sidesteps the doctrine of implied repeal. The courts are to interpret past legislation so far as possible in accordance with the Convention. But if it is not possible to do so, the legislation survives. Parliamentary sovereignty prevails in that primary legislation which unequivocally offends against Convention rights will live on, subject to remedial measures, and subordinate legislation too will survive if there is no room under the primary or enabling legislation to remove the offending parts. This means that just because pre-1998 legislation has received authoritative interpretation, it does not follow that that interpretation will be followed after the relevant provisions of the Act are brought into force. The legislation may be subject to fresh interpretation in the light of the new Act.

The effect of Section 3 is to give extra power and responsibility to all courts, which must (and the provision is mandatory) interpret legislation consistently with the Convention so far as it is possible. This is to be contrasted with the power to make a declaration of incompatibility, which is only open to the House of Lords, the Privy Council, the Court of Appeal, the High Court and the Courts-Martial Appeal Court. Although Section 3 does not affect the continued operation and validity of incompatible primary legislation, the courts will have the power to strike down subordinate legislation which is inconsistent with Convention rights, in much the same way as at present they can strike down secondary legislation which is ultra vires.

In interpreting Convention rights the courts will be obliged to take into account decisions of the European Court and Commission of Human Rights and of the Committee of Ministers (Section 2). Note that the court is obliged to "take into account" the earlier decisions, not follow them. This is consistent

[2] [1993] AC 593

with the idea that the Convention is a "living instrument"; a concept that would be stultified by a doctrine of binding precedent. The meaning of this term in relation to Strasbourg case law itself is explored more fully in the second part of this chapter.

Equally, though not specifically referred to in the Act, the views of the Courts of other Contracting States will be directly relevant because they are considering the same Convention. Judgments of courts in countries with similar constitutional provisions like South Africa, Canada, New Zealand and India may also be highly persuasive.[3]

1.2. A New Cause of Action: Sections 6, 7 and 8

Section 6 makes it unlawful for a public authority to act in a way which is incompatible with a Convention right, unless primary legislation gives the public authority no choice but to do so. The definition of a "public authority" has given rise to considerable debate. The current view is that Section 6 contemplates three categories of authorities:

(i) "*obvious*" public authorities like government departments and local authorities;
(ii) hybrid bodies, i.e. those who have some public functions and some private ones; and
(iii) bodies with no public functions.

Obvious public authorities are liable in respect of all their actions, public and private. Hybrid authorities are liable provided that the nature of the act of which complaint is made is not private and private bodies are not affected at all.

Public bodies are defined to include courts and tribunals.[4] It is likely that the comparatively informal procedures of various professional disciplinary bodies will come under close scrutiny if a court can be persuaded to view them as public bodies or hybrid bodies acting, in their disciplinary capacity, publicly.

Section 7 gives a right to sue for such unlawful acts provided the claimant is a victim of the unlawful act. If a person is likely to be a victim he or she can bring proceedings whether for an injunction or under the terms of the Act itself. Note that Section 7(1)(b) is already in force, allowing "victims" of potentially offending actions to bring this to the attention of the courts. This happened in *R v Director of Public Prosecutions, ex parte Kebilene*[5] where the Divisional Court ruled that the applicants were entitled to a declaration that the DPP had acted

---

[3] The following chapters on individual areas of common law practice explore the extent to which comparative case law from other jurisdictions will bear on national courts' interpretation of the rights under the Human Rights Act; see, for example, Jonathan Cooper's discussion of the impact of rights in private law in chapter 4 on Horizontality

[4] The implications of this inclusion are explored more fully in chapter 4 on Horizontality

[5] [1999] 3 WLR 175; overturned by the House of Lords [1999] 3 WLR 972

unlawfully by failing to take into consideration the likelihood that their convictions under the reverse onus provisions of the Prevention of Terrorism (Temporary Provisions) Act 1989 would be overturned once Article 6(2) with its presumption of innocence came into force. The decision was overturned on appeal to the House of Lords, who ruled that before the passing into force of the Human Rights Act, applicants should not be allowed to challenge by way of judicial review acts of public authorities which would be unchallengeable once the Act came into force (because the DPP's decision was made in accordance with primary legislation).

It is worth noting that Section 7(5) means that the limitation period for bringing any proceedings under the Act is one year. This is an interestingly short time limit, given that many claimants' lawyers in personal injury cases are already limbering up to challenge the three year primary limitation period, which is of course extendable at the discretion of the Court, as being a denial of Article 6.[6]

Section 8 entitles a court which has found a public authority's actions to be in breach of Convention rights, to grant any remedy or relief in its powers. Remedies will include the public law remedies of certiorari, mandamus and prohibition; they will also include declarations and injunctions. Perhaps most importantly, Section 8 covers damages, providing that in determining quantum the Court is to take account of the principles applied by the Strasbourg Court in making awards under Article 41.[7]

1.3. Political Pressure on Government

If it is not possible to read primary legislation in a way compatible with the Convention, as required by Section 3, so that there is a frank conflict between the Convention and the statute, the statute prevails. The Court cannot strike down primary legislation. But faced with such a conflict the Court can make a declaration of incompatibility under Section 4. The declaration has no effect on the legislation under scrutiny and the Court will decide the case according to that domestic legislation. Thus the effect of such a declaration will be political and will depend upon the resolve of the Government and its immunity (or sensitivity) to criticism. The fact of a declaration, however, will enable the fast track amendment procedure provided for by Section 10 to be used. By this route an amendment to the statute can be made by what is called a Remedial Order. The Remedial Order procedure will thus enable the Government to remove offending parts from legislation quickly.

---

[6] Limitations in respect of Convention claims in medical negligence proceedings are discussed in chapter 9 on Practice and Procedure in Medical Negligence and Personal Injury Litigation
[7] See chapter 5 on Remedies

2. THE IMPACT OF INCORPORATION

2.1. Introduction

It is difficult to overstate the importance of the incorporation of the Convention. Lord Woolf has already agreed that it will revolutionise our legal world and Professor Wade has described incorporation as "one of our great constitutional milestones" which will introduce "a new legal culture of fundamental rights and freedoms".[8] It is important to appreciate, at the outset, precisely why our legal world will be revolutionised. Whether they appreciate it or not, English lawyers tend to view the law through the eyes of Dicey. A citizen may do what he likes unless what he proposes to do has been made unlawful either because Parliament has deemed it to be a criminal offence or because it amounts to a civil wrong or because it can be prohibited by administrative action. In each case, however, it is for he who complains of what the citizen proposes to do or has done, to prove that it is unlawful. Thus, the prosecution must prove the offence, the plaintiff must prove the civil wrong, the public body must prove the prohibition. Once the Convention has been incorporated, the position will be altogether different. The starting point will no longer be the freedom of every citizen to do what he wishes, but the rights which every citizen will enjoy under the Convention. Subject to proving an interference with those rights, the enjoyment of those rights will prevail unless the interference can be justified. And because the incorporation of the Convention has come so late, the actions of those directly bound by the Convention, i.e. public authorities, will constantly require to be tested against the relevant Convention rights. In other words, whereas at present the question which may arise is whether the citizen is in the wrong, post-incorporation the question will be whether the public authority is in the wrong for having breached the citizen's rights.

The Convention has already had some effect on English law. Where the common law is either ambiguous or undecided the courts may have regard to the Convention, see for example *AG v Guardian Newspapers (No 2)*[9] where Lord Goff considered the Court to be under a duty to interpret the common law in line with Convention rights where possible. Equally, it has informed administrative and executive decisions, for example as to immigration and deportation issues. Where a decision infringes what the Convention regards as fundamental rights the Court will apply much narrower limits to *Wednesbury* reasonableness.

But essentially a treaty is not part of the law until incorporated. Thus in *R v Secretary of State for the Home Department ex parte Brind*[10] the House of Lords warned against "incorporation by the back door", and held that the Convention

---

[8] JSB Annual Lecture 1998, "Human Rights and the Judiciary"
[9] [1990] 1 AC 109
[10] [1991] 1 AC 696

was not part of English domestic law although the court could consider the Convention in order to resolve an ambiguity or uncertainty in a statutory provision. This falls far short of the Section 3 position where the court must interpret in accordance with the Convention wherever semantically possible.

2.2. The Convention as a "Living Instrument"

It is also important to understand that the Convention is a "living instrument" to be interpreted, as the Court has stated, in the light of present day conditions and so as to reflect changing social attitudes.[11] It has been suggested that this will revolutionise well-established canons of interpretation in English law. In one sense, of course, this is true in that English courts have applied, albeit increasingly more flexibly, strict canons of interpretation to English statutes. On the other hand, such an approach represents the bedrock on which the English common law has been developed by lawyers and judges. Thus the approach is entirely familiar albeit its application to a written document will be novel. It will also be important to bear in mind the high importance placed by the Court on construing Articles of the Convention so as to give them their presumed legislative intent. Given the very general terms in which the Articles of the Convention were drafted, this approach provides very considerable scope for the judges to develop the reach of the Convention and one of the features of the Strasbourg case law is the extent to which the Convention has been dynamically developed by both the Commission and the Court. Such an approach, again, is not unfamiliar to English lawyers and judges who have increasingly sought to give a purposive effect to legislation. The Convention provides even more scope for such an approach. Indeed, it will be surprising if English lawyers and judges do not develop the Convention even more dynamically and creatively than has been achieved hitherto by their often more conservative continental counterparts. They now have the opportunity to extend the scope of the rights protected by the Convention and to build imaginatively upon the existing Strasbourg jurisprudence.

For example, the Strasbourg Court has thus far construed Article 2, which guarantees the right to life, so as to restrict it to physical life only. But courts in other jurisdictions have gone much further.[12] For example, the Constitutional Court of India has held that under the Constitution of India, the right to life includes the right to enjoy pollution-free water and air for the full enjoyment of life. English lawyers and judges will now be able to decide for themselves what should be the reach of the Convention and at long last thereby contribute directly to it. Indeed, theirs will now be the primary role in safeguarding the rights embodied in the Convention.

[11] *Tyrer v United Kingdom* (1978) 2 EHRR 1 at 10
[12] See in particular David Hart's comparative analysis of the right to life in other jurisdictions in Chapter 10 on Environmental Rights

2.3. The Strasbourg Jurisprudence

The starting point in any case where a Convention right is in play will be the Convention and the relevant Strasbourg case law. And because the Court has given an autonomous interpretation to many of the terms of the Convention, the English courts will in practice usually be obliged to follow and adopt that interpretation because if they fail to do so, the ultimate appeal to Strasbourg (which will, of course, remain in place) may otherwise lead to a finding of a breach. But even absent such specific case law, the overarching interpretive approach laid down by the Court (to be followed by the English courts) is that the Convention must be interpreted and applied in such a way that the safeguards it provides are practicable and effective.[13]

Because the Convention is a living instrument, the Court does not regard itself as bound by its earlier decisions if conditions, such as social attitudes, have changed in the meantime. Indeed, in a recent article, a former judge of the Strasbourg Court, Judge Martens, described the Court's case law as "like a living body of water, continuously open to changing currents".[14] If this approach is adopted by our domestic courts, then this will represent yet another important departure from traditional principles of statutory interpretation.

2.3.1. The Protected Rights

The rights set out in the Convention which are to be incorporated into our domestic law will have an immediate impact in the fields of public law and criminal law, which are outside the scope of this book. The less obvious potential impact of the Convention is on the common law, both in terms of the public functions of public authorities which find their legal basis in the common law, and in the potential horizontal reach of the Act, which includes judicial bodies in its definition of "public authority".[15] The brief outline of the incorporated rights below therefore touches on their potential influence on common law rights and obligations.

Article 2: The Right to Life
The first point to note about this right is that it is an absolute right. For example, it cannot be derogated from in times of war or other public emergency. The Court has recently stated that Article 2 "ranks as one of the most fundamental provisions in the Convention" and that "together with Article 3, it enshrines one of the basic values of the democratic societies making up the Council of Europe".[16] In fact, it scarcely needed the European Court to say so. Some years

---

[13]   *Airey v Ireland* (1979) 2 EHRR 305 at 314
[14]   (1998) EHRLR 5 at 6
[15]   See chapter 4 on Horizontality
[16]   *McCann v United Kingdom* (1995) 21 EHRR 97

ago Lord Bridge had already said that "The most fundamental of all human rights is the individual's right to life . . ."[17]

But note that deprivation of life is only permissible where it results from the use of force which is (1) no more than absolutely necessary and (2) in pursuance of one of the three stated objectives.

Later in this chapter the doctrines of pressing social need and proportionality will be explained but they are brought into Article 2 by the expression, "absolutely necessary".

Article 2 is routinely upheld in relation to acts of agents of the state against Khurdish minorities in Turkey. The only adverse ruling the Court has reached against the United Kingdom under Article 2 – albeit by a majority of only 10 votes to 9 – was confined to the particular facts of the case.[18] Three Provisional IRA members who were suspected of having planted a car bomb in Gibraltar were shot dead by SAS members when they made sudden movements as if to trigger the bomb as they were approached. At the inquest in Gibraltar the jury returned a verdict of lawful killing. The applicants, who were representatives of the IRA members, brought an application under the Convention alleging a breach of Article 2. The Court held that in assessing whether the use of force had been absolutely necessary, particularly where deliberate lethal force is used, the Court must subject the deprivation of life to the most careful scrutiny taking into consideration not only the actions of the agents of the state who actually administer the force, but also all the surrounding circumstances including such matters as the planning and control of the actions under examination. The Court concluded that the actions of the soldiers who shot the terrorists did not, in themselves, give rise to a violation of Article 2 but, to the surprise of many, went on to find a violation of that Article as regards the control and organisation of the operation as a whole even though the majority accepted that the terrorists had been intending to plant a bomb in Gibraltar, and for that reason refused to award any damages. This decision, which did not bite on government policy as such, may nevertheless have implications as to operational negligence by the police and the security services when Article 2 comes into force.

Article 3: Freedom from Torture or Inhuman or Degrading Treatment or Punishment

This Article provides an absolute guarantee of these rights. It cannot be derogated from in time of war or other public emergency, even an emergency which threatens the life of the nation.[19] And it is unqualified in its terms. The reason, of course, is obvious. The worst excesses almost always take place under cover of war or public emergency: see the Nazis during the Second World War and, more recently, the Serbs in Bosnia and Kosovo.

[17] *Bugdaycay v Secretary of State for the Home Department* [1987] AC 514
[18] *McCann v United Kingdom* (1995) 21 EHRR 97
[19] *Aksoy v Turkey* (1997) 1 BHRC 625

"Torture" has been defined by the Court as "deliberate inhuman treatment causing very serious and cruel suffering". "Inhuman treatment" covers ". . . at least such treatment as deliberately causes severe suffering, mental or physical, which in the particular situation is unjustifiable" and "treatment of an individual may be said to be degrading if it grossly humiliates him before others or drives him to act against his own will or conscience".[20]

Article 3 has arisen in cases involving the treatment of terrorist suspects,[21] the infliction of corporal punishment,[22] detention in seclusion,[23] assault,[24] the application and operation of immigration controls, the refusal to grant political asylum and extradition to face the possible death penalty.[25] These decisions are discussed in more detail in the following chapters; suffice it to say here that the importance of the rights under Article 3 is such that the Strasbourg Court has repeatedly ruled that the state's responsibility may be engaged even when the treatment contrary to Article 3 is carried out, or threatened, by a third party over which the respondent state has no control. For example, in *D v United Kingdom*[26] the Court held that, consistent with its obligations under Article 3, the United Kingdom could not deport an illegal immigrant suffering from the final stages of a terminal illness (AIDS) to a country where the medical treatment and social support were "grievously inadequate" since to do so would lead to inhuman and degrading treatment . It is therefore conceivable that both Articles 2 and 3 will be relied upon in future in medical negligence actions, for example where it is alleged that experimental treatment has been carried out against the claimants' wishes, even if the state is not directly engaged.[27]

Article 4: Freedom from Slavery, Servitude or Forced or Compulsory Labour

Only a handful of cases have been brought under this Article and no breach of it has yet been found.

Article 5: The Right to Liberty and Security of the Person

This right is clearly most relevant to criminal procedure and the detention of mental patients and applicants pending decisions on deportaion and extradition. However, Strasbourg case law under Article 5 will have some relevance to the common law actions for false imprisonment and malicious prosecution, as well as to allegations of police ill-treatment in custody amounting to assault.

Under Article 5(1), deprivation of liberty is authorised in six separate categories of cases. Circumstances which do not fall under one of these categories

---

[20] *Ireland v UK* (1979–80) 2 EHRR 25
[21] *Tomasi v France* (1993) 15 EHRR 1 *Ireland v UK*
[22] *Y v UK* (1994) 17 EHRR 238; *Tyrer v UK* (1979–80) 2 EHRR 1 *Costello-Roberts v UK* (1995)19 EHRR 112
[23] *McFeely v UK* (1981) 3 EHRR 161
[24] *Reed v UK* (1981) 3 EHRR 136
[25] *D v United Kingdom* (1997) 24 EHRR 423; *Soering v United Kingdom* (1989) 11 EHRR 202
[26] *Ibid*
[27] See chapter 8 on Medical Law

are not therefore justified. Articles 5(2)–(5) apply whether the deprivation of liberty falls under one of the categories in paragraph 1 or not. There is a very considerable amount of case law as to the procedural rights set out in paragraph 2 which is more pertinent to criminal proceedings and police powers than it is to common law claims for false imprisonment, and therefore lies outside the scope of this chapter.

As to the circumstances set out in Article 5 (1), (a) is self-explanatory; (b) covers, for example, imprisonment for contempt of court; (c) covers the remand in custody of those accused of having committed a criminal offence; (d) is self-explanatory; (e) covers, for example, the compulsory admission of patients to mental hospital;[28] and (f) covers illegal immigrants and those whom the courts or the Home Secretary find should be deported or extradited.

Article 6: The Right to a Fair Trial

This is one of the fastest developing areas of Strasbourg jurisprudence, and, as will be evident from the following chapters, one of the most useful channels for bringing the common law under Convention scrutiny. This is because it has been relied upon in Strasbourg to circumvent the verticality of the Convention at an international level (the Strasbourg Court only admits claims against state respondents) and therefore a substantial body of case law has built up where Article 6 has been invoked – in many cases successfully – against the state's failure to provide a fair hearing for essentially private disputes.

Only the first paragraph of Article 6 applies to civil rights and obligations. Paragraphs 2 and 3 are concerned with criminal offences alone and therefore will not be considered here. The Court has construed the expression "civil rights and obligations" as referring only to rights and obligations in private law with the result that Article 6 does not apply to the determination of rights and obligations in public law (for example, the right to vote). So decisions whether to grant or refuse immigrants the right to enter and the proceedings by which such decisions are reached fall outwith Article 6, although it is important to note that a deportation decision may impinge on the right to family life which is recognised as a civil right under the Convention and thus, by that route, the procedural guarantees of Article 6 will apply.

Article 6 may not be used as a vehicle for the creation of "civil rights" which are not recognised in the existing legal system. In *Fayed v United Kingdom*[29] the Court rejected the applicant's argument that the defence of privilege for company inspectors' reports prevented him from exercising his right to take defamation proceedings. The fact that the report was covered by this immunity meant that it was not dispositive of any legal right or obligation and therefore Article 6 could not apply. However, the Strasbourg authorities have recently moved some way from the position in *Fayed*, by extending the reach of Article 6 to a

---

[28] See chapter 12 on Mental Health
[29] (1994) 18 EHRR 393

rule of immunity in English law which is imposed in some areas of negligence but not in others.

Osman v United Kingdom[30] was arguably a decision with more potential impact on the common law than any previous ruling under Article 6 or indeed any other of the rights under the Convention. Here the applicants were the widow and son of a murder victim. The police had been notified of the obsessive and potentially dangerous behaviour of the man charged with the murder towards the victim and one of the applicants, but failed to prevent the murder and the assault on the son taking place. The applicants were prevented from taking action in negligence against the police by the rule of immunity in *Hill v Chief Constable of West Yorkshire*.[31] They claimed breach of their right of access to court under Article 6 and the Strasbourg Court upheld their claim[32] ruling that the dismissal of their action for negligence for reasons of public policy amounted to a restriction on their right of access to court guaranteed by Article 6(1). The Court distinguished its position from *Fayed* by holding that here the applicants enjoyed a right, derived from the general law of negligence, to request the domestic court to rule on their arguable claim that they were in a relationship of proximity to the police, that the harm suffered was foreseeable and that in the circumstances it was fair, just and reasonable not to apply the rule excluding liabiltiy of the police for alleged negligence in respect of the investigation of crime. The assertion of that right by the applicants was sufficient in itself to ensure the applicability of Article 6, and the failure of the national courts to consider that claim because of *Hill* was a disproportionate interference with their right of access to a court.

This decision has considerable implications for the development of new causes of action under the Human Rights Act, as well as the rolling back of many long-established areas of common law immunity.[33]

The right to a fair hearing also involves the principle of *"equality of arms"*, that is to say that every party to civil (and criminal) cases must have a reasonable opportunity of presenting his case to the court under conditions which do not place him at a substantial disadvantage vis-à-vis his opponent. Many common law rules of evidence, such as the "newspaper rule" which allows publisher defendants to refuse to disclose their sources of information in legal proceedings, may come under Article 6 attack, the point of entry for the Convention being Section 8 of the Human Rights Act, which includes judicial bodies, and therefore their decisions, as "public authorities".

Article 6 also requires that a court gives reasons for its judgment, at least to the extent of indicating with sufficient clarity the grounds on which its decision

---

[30] (1999) 5 BHRC 293
[31] [1989]AC 53
[32] Separate claims under Article 2 (right to life) and Article 8 (right to family life) were rejected
[33] See chapter 5 on Remedies p 85 for the implications of *Osman* in relation to the damages liability of public bodies

is based. Article 6(1) also provides that everyone is entitled to a public hearing,[34] the right to trial within a reasonable time, and the right to an independent and impartial tribunal established by law.[35]

Finally, it is to be noted that Article 6(1) does not guarantee a right of appeal from a decision by a court which complies with the requirements of Article 6 but if a right of appeal is provided, then Article 6(1) will apply to proceedings before the Appellate Court. Moreover, where a breach of Article 6(1) has occurred at first instance, it may be remedied on appeal provided that the defect in question may be corrected by the Appellate Court. Even if the first instance proceedings do not satisfy the requirements of Article 6(1) (for example, because they comprise disciplinary proceedings held in private), provided that an appeal is available to an appeal body with full jurisdiction, no breach of Article 6(1) will occur since what matters is the proceedings as a whole.

Article 7: Freedom from Retroactive Criminal Offences and Punishment

Since this Article is exclusively concerned with criminal law, we say no more about it.

Article 8: The Right to Respect for Private Family Life, Home and Correspondence

This is one of those Articles where both negative and positive obligations are involved, that is, public authorities will not only have to respect the rights guaranteed by Article 8, but must protect them and this may involve taking positive measures to do so.[36]

What is covered by the four interests referred to in Article 8(1)? This question has to be asked since, as has been pointed out, none of the four interests is entirely self-explanatory in meaning and each has thus been interpreted by the Court and the Commission. For example, the Court has held that the right to respect for private life comprises to a certain extent ". . . the right to establish and to develop relationships with other human beings, especially in the emotional field for the development and fulfilment of one's own personality" and that ". . . to this effect (everyone) must have the possibility of establishing relationships of various kinds, including sexual, with other persons".[37] Family life has been held to extend well beyond formal relationships. The Court has recently decided that "home" may extend, in some circumstances, to a professional person's office.[38] The right to respect for one's home includes the right of

---

[34] See now Rule 39.2 of the Civil Procedure Rules
[35] This latter right is particularly relevant to administrative and disciplinary tribunals such as the GMC and is explored in greater detail in chapter 8 on Medical Law
[36] The scope of Article 8 in environmental claims is explored in chapter 10 on Environmental Rights; and its relevance to the tort of breach of confidence is discussed in chapter 11 on Confidentiality and Defamation
[37] *X and Y v The Netherlands* (1985) 8 EHRR 235
[38] *Niemitz v Germany* (1992) 16 EHRR 173

access to and occupation of that home and a right not to be expelled or evicted from it.[39] The right to respect for one's correspondence is essentially a right not to have one's correspondence interfered with. There may be some overlap between the right to respect for one's correspondence provided for by Article 8(1) and the right to freedom of expression in Article 10.

Note the qualification to these rights set out in paragraph 2. Similar qualifications apply to Articles 9, 10 and 11. The balancing of these qualifications against the guaranteed rights will play a central part in human rights litigation and practitioners will need to acquaint themselves thoroughly with the related doctrines of "margin of appreciation" and "proportionality" in order to formulate and defend claims under the Human Rights Act. These doctrines will be explored in detail below.

Article 9: Freedom of Religion

In a world where religious views are in some quarters held at least as passionately as ever before, often by minorities, Article 9 plainly has very considerable potential importance although very few cases have been brought before the Commission or the Court. We propose to say no more about it.

Article 10: Freedom of Expression

The relevance of this right to the common law actions for defamation and confidentiality is explored in chapter 11 and so it will not be discussed further at this stage other than to emphasise the importance attached to it by both the Commission and the Court. Time and again the Court has stressed that freedom of expression constitutes, as the Court has put it, "one of the essential foundations of a democratic society, one of the basic conditions for its progress and for the development of every man. Subject to paragraph 2 of Article 10, it is applicable not only to 'information' or 'ideas' that are favourably received or regarded as inoffensive but also to those that offend, shock or disturb the State or any sector of the population. Such are the demands of that pluralism, tolerance and broad-mindedness without which there is no 'democratic society' ".[40]

Article 11: Freedom of Assembly and Association

We propose to say little about the rights protected by Article 11 since, to a large extent, they are self-explanatory, at least for present purposes. Most of the cases in Strasbourg involving the UK have concerned trade union membership, as one might have expected.[41] Common law restrictions on the right of public assembly (in so far as that "right" could have been said to exist before incorporation of the Convention) have frequently been challenged under this Article,

---

[39] As David Hart explains in chapter 10 on Environmental Rights, it also includes the right to peaceful enjoyment of residence in one's home and thus directly links in with the law of nuisance

[40] *Handyside v UK* (1976) 1 EHRR 737

[41] Although one of the cases involved the claimed right of Druids to celebrate the summer solstice at Stonehenge: *Chappell v UK* 53 DR 241

and, despite the rule in *Brind* that interpretation of unambiguous rules of law in accordance with Convention rights amounted to incorporation "by the back door", the right to assemble, like the right of free speech, has been accepted as something of a common law "given" right in the national courts. Some two years before the Convention was due to come into force in this country, the House of Lords reconsidered the common law position on the legal use of the highway to accord with the right of assembly under Article 11.[42]

Article 12: The Right to Marry and to Found a Family

The scope for potential development of this article in relation to advances in medical reproductive technology is discussed in chapter 8 on Medical Law.

Article 14: Freedom from Discrimination

Again, this Article will not be discussed in any detail here since actions for discrimination, per se, are governed by legislation rather than the common law. However, it is worth noting that Article 14 does not protect against discrimination in isolation but only as regards the rights and freedoms protected by the Convention. For example, where a right falls outside the Convention, for example the right of access to civil service employment, Article 14 does not apply. It is also important to remember that Article 14 imposes a positive obligation to secure the non-discriminatory enjoyment of the rights and freedoms protected by the Convention. Post-incorporation, therefore, all public authorities will be required to comply with that obligation.

First Protocol, Article 1: Protection of Property

Article 1 protects the right to the peaceful enjoyment of one's possessions: as Harris has explained it,[43] the right to have, to use, to dispose of, to pledge, to lend, even to destroy one's possessions. It is, as the Court has said, in substance guaranteeing the right of property. Possessions are not limited to physical goods; provided the right or interest has some economic value, or is of a pecuniary nature, it will come within the scope of this Article. Company shares, patents, goodwill in a business and ownership of a debt have all been held to qualify as "possessions" under Article 1 Protocol 1.

But one may be lawfully deprived of one's possessions if deprivation is in the public interest, if there is some basis in law for the deprivation and the law provides protection against arbitrary deprivation of property and subject to the general principles of international law. "Control" of property is permitted under this Article unless such control imposes an "excessive burden" on the individual.[44]

---

[42] *DPP v Jones* [1999] 2 WLR 625

[43] In Harris, Boyle and Warbrick (eds), *Law of the European Convention on Human Rights* (Butterworths, London 1995) 516

[44] This, and other aspects of Article 1 Protocol 1 are explored more fully in chapter 10 on Environmental Rights

At this stage, the precise structure of Article 1 becomes more than a little complex and it is sufficient if we simply indicate that what in practice the Court does in cases where someone has been deprived of his possessions is to apply a "fair balance" test, namely, was a fair balance struck between the demands of the general interests of the community and the requirements of the protection of the individual's fundamental rights? However, it will be interesting to see if this right to property can be used as a defence to freezing and search orders (formerly known as Mareva and Anton Pillar orders) and, if so, in what circumstances.

First Protocol, Article 2: The Right to Education and First Protocol, Article 3: Right to Free Elections

These rights relate to the legislative activities of Contracting States and are therefore outside the scope of this book.

2.4. Absolute and Qualified Rights

It will have been at once apparent that the rights protected by the relevant Articles fall, broadly, into two categories.

2.4.1. Absolute Rights

First, those which are absolute (i.e. unqualified), namely Articles 2, 3, 4, 7, 12 and 14. It is important to understand just what this means in practice. This is best illustrated by reference to the case of *Chahal v UK*.[45] The case concerned a Sikh believed by the UK Government to have engaged in terrorist activities designed to undermine the lawful government of India. The Home Secretary sought to deport him on the grounds that his continued presence in the United Kingdom was a danger by reason of his terrorist activities in the United Kingdom. He resisted deportation on the basis that if returned to India there was a real risk that he would suffer ill-treatment. Thus, he argued, he was entitled to asylum. The decision of the Home Secretary was upheld both at first instance and by the Court of Appeal but a very different result was reached by the Strasbourg Court. The Court stated that:

> "... Article 3 makes no provision for exceptions and no derogation from it is permissible under Article 15 even in the event of a public emergency threatening the life of the nation. The prohibition provided by Article 3 against ill-treatment is equally absolute in expulsion cases. In these circumstances the activities of the individual, however undesirable or dangerous, cannot be a material consideration".

There will be some who will regard such a conclusion, in the case of a man whose continued presence in this country will represent a danger to national security, as incomprehensible since it appears to involve giving a higher priority

[45] (1997) 23 EHRR 413

to the interests of the terrorist than to those of the innocent citizens of the state. Yet the decision represents a graphic illustration of the practical effect of those Convention rights which are unqualified.

2.4.2. Qualified Rights

Articles 8–10: Although expressed in slightly different language, these rights are qualified in essentially the same way. Take, for example, Article 8. Paragraph 2 provides, in effect, that the right protected by paragraph 1 may be interfered with provided that the interference is:

(a) in accordance with the law;
(b) is necessary in a democratic society in the interests of national security, public safety, or the economic well-being of the country, for the prevention of disorder or crime, for the protection of health or morals, or for the protection of the rights and freedoms of others.

Article 9 qualifies the right to freedom of thought, conscience and religion by reference only to such limitations as:

(a) are prescribed by law (cf Article 8, "in accordance with the law");
(b) are necessary in a democratic society in the interests of public safety, for the protection of public order, health or morals, or for the protection of the rights and freedoms of others (cf Article 8 which includes, in addition, the interests of national security, the economic well-being of the country and the prevention of disorder or crime).

Article 10 qualifies the right to freedom of expression by reference to such formalities, conditions, restrictions or penalties as:

(a) are prescribed by law;
(b) are necessary in a democratic society, in the interests of national security, territorial integrity or public safety, for the prevention of disorder or crime, for the protection of health or morals, for the protection of the reputation or rights of others, for preventing the disclosure of information received in confidence, or for maintaining the authority and impartiality of the judiciary.

Article 11 qualifies the right to freedom of assembly and association by reference to restrictions which:

(a) are prescribed by law;
(b) are necessary in a democratic society in the interests of national security or public safety, for the prevention of disorder or crime, for the protection of health or morals or for the protection of the rights and freedoms of others.

It follows, therefore, that in each case, in order to be justified, the interference must be either in accordance with or prescribed by law and be necessary in a democratic society in one of the interests identified. These qualifications have been the subject of considerable interpretation by the Commission and the Court and the Court has held that it is for the Contracting States to satisfy all the criteria necessary to justify the interference in question. There is no reason to suppose that our domestic courts will not, likewise, hold that it is for the public authority in question to do so.

2.4.3. *"in accordance with the/prescribed by law"*[46]

The Court has held that in order to show that the interference was in accordance with or prescribed by law, the respondent state (for which now read public authority) must satisfy three criteria:

(i) They must be able to point to some specific legal rule or regime which authorises the interference. It need not be a rule of domestic law but may be a rule of international law or Community law so long as it purports to authorise the interference.
(ii) The law in question must be adequately accessible, i.e. (as the Court has said) "The citizen must be able to have an indication that is adequate in the circumstances of the legal rules applicable to a given case".[47]
(iii) The law must be formulated with sufficient precision to enable the citizen to foresee the circumstances in which the law would or might be applied. The Court has held that the availability of legal advice is relevant to these criteria.

There are countless illustrations of this requirement to be found in the European Human Rights Reports, but the one that exemplifies it most clearly in relation to the common law is the telephone tapping case of *Malone v United Kingdom*.[48] At the time in question there was no specific statutory authorisation for telephone tapping in the UK. Instead, it was regulated by administrative practice, the details of which were not published. The English Court held that telephone tapping was lawful because it was not prohibited by law. Looked at under the Convention, however, the starting point was Article 8 and the right to respect for private and family life. In order to justify the interference with that right, it was necessary for the United Kingdom to demonstrate that the telephone tapping in question had been carried out in accordance with the law. However, as has been pointed out, there was no specific statutory authorisation for telephone tapping and the Court held that an administrative practice, however well adhered to, did not provide the guarantee required by law. The Court also held that there was insufficient clarity about the scope or the manner

---

[46] Note that although somewhat different language is used on this point, it has been established by the Court that both formulations are to be read in the same way (and the French text of the Convention is, in fact, identical), *Silver v UK* (1983) 5 EHRR 347, 371
[47] *Sunday Times v UK* (1979) 2 EHRR 245
[48] (1984) 7 EHRR 14

in which the discretion of the authorities to listen secretly to telephone conversations was exercised. Details of the administrative practice were never published and, because it was an administrative practice, it could be changed at any time. As the Court said:

"... Apart from the simple absence of prohibition, there would appear to be no legal rules concerning the scope and manner of the exercise of the discretion enjoyed by public authorities".

As a result, a breach of Article 8 was found and the Government was compelled to introduce legislation providing a statutory basis for telephone tapping, namely the Interception of Communications Act 1985.

The second question is whether the interference, or the restriction or limitation said to justify the interference, served one of the aims or objectives set out in the relevant Article. Again, it will be for the public authority to identify the aim or objective in question (sometimes there may be more than one in play). Unless the public authority can point to one such aim or objective, and show that the interference was carried out in pursuance of that aim or objective, then it will have acted in breach of the applicant's rights.

2.4.4. *"Necessary in a democratic society"*

It will not, however, be enough for the public authority to show that the interference was in accordance with the law and pursuant to one of the stated aims or objectives since it must also show, finally, that the interference was "necessary in a democratic society". This is a phrase described by one commentator as "heavy with uncertainty"[49] and it was inevitable that the Court would be called upon to explain and interpret it. This indeed it has done and it has held that the notion of necessity implies that the interference corresponds to a pressing social need and, in particular, that it is proportionate to the legitimate aim pursued. A democratic society, the Court has said, involves "pluralism, tolerance and broad mindedness".[50]

However, in deciding whether any interference has been necessary in this sense, the Court has allowed the Contracting States what it has described as "a margin of appreciation". This principle was explained by the Court as follows:

"By reason of their direct and continuous contact with the vital forces of their countries, State authorities are in principle in a better position than the international Judge to give an opinion on the ... 'necessity' of a 'restriction' or 'penalty' ... It is for the national authorities to make the initial assessment of the reality of the pressing social need implied by the notion of 'necessity' in this context. ... Consequently Article 10(2) leaves to the Contracting States a margin of appreciation. This margin is given both

---

[49] Harris, Boyle and Warbrick, *Law of the European Convention on Human Rights*, N. 43, pp 290–1
[50] *Handyside v United Kingdom* (1976) 1 EHRR 737 at 754

to the domestic legislator ('prescribed by law') and to the bodies, judicial amongst others, that are called upon to interpret and apply the laws in force".[51]

In this way, the Court and Commission have been able to accommodate the different ways in which Member States have sought to protect the rights set out in the Convention and the general superiority of the domestic courts and tribunals of the Member States in finding the facts in each case and in assessing what local circumstances demand by way of any limitation of those rights.

The case in which the first detailed exposition of the doctrine was given by the Court, *Lawless v Ireland*,[52] provides an example of the application of the doctrine in practice. The applicant had been detained without trial for five months under emergency measures (the Offences Against the State Act). The Commission held that once the Court was satisfied that the Government's appreciation of the circumstances which constituted an emergency was at least on the margin of the powers conferred by the relevant Article, then the public interest in effective government and the maintenance of order justified and required a decision in favour of the Government's appreciation. More recently, it is to be noted that all the trans-sexual cases brought against the United Kingdom in Strasbourg have failed on the application of the doctrine of the margin of appreciation.

The question now arises as to what, if any, role this doctrine will have domestically once the Convention has been incorporated[53] (it should be pointed out, in passing, that in any event there are those in the Court who think that the time has come to reconsider the doctrine, for example, Judge de Meyer).[54] It has already been explained how the doctrine has allowed the Court to accommodate the different approaches of the Contracting States to the protection of human rights within those states. Thus it has been asserted by some commentators that the doctrine is simply an interpretative tool specific to the international supervision of human rights and has no place in domestic arrangements for the protection of human rights.[55] Others argue that it is analogous to the doctrines of justiciability that limit domestic adjudication of policy matters or decisions relating to allocation of scarce public resources, and that the adoption of a "margin of appreciation" doctrine is merely a change in form rather than substance. Such an approach has received the support of the House of Lords, in the words of Lord Hope in *R v DPP ex parte Kebilene*:[56]

---

[51] *Handyside v United Kingdom*. See McBride, "Proportionality and the European Convention on Human Rights" in Evelyn Ellis (ed.), *The Principle of Proportionality in the Laws of Europe* (Hart Publishing, Oxford, 1999)

[52] *Lawless v Ireland* (1961) 1 EHRR 15

[53] See Feldman, "Proportionality and the Human Rights Act 1998" in *The Principle of Proportionality*, N. 51, pp 117–18 and 124–7

[54] In *Z v Finland* (1997) 25 EHRR 371

[55] See, for example, Pannick, "Margin of Appreciation and the Discretionary Area of Judgment" in Lester and Pannick (eds), *Human Rights Law and Practice* (Butterworths, London, 1999) pp 73–6

[56] [1999] 3 WLR 972, 994

". . . in the hands of the national courts also the Convention should be seen as an expression of fundamental principles rather than as a set of mere rules. The questions which the courts will have to decide in the application of these principles will involve questions of balance between competing interests and issues of proportionality.

"In this area difficult choices may have to be made by the executive or the legislature between the rights of the individual and the needs of society. In some circumstances it will be appropriate for the courts to recognise that there is an area of judgment within which the judiciary will defer, on democratic grounds, to the considered opinion of the elected body or person whose act or decision is said to be incompatible with the Convention".

Whether or not this view accurately predicts the approach of national courts to the margin of appreciation, it is submitted that it has no place in domestic litigation. It must surely be for our domestic courts to decide whether there was a pressing social need for the public authority in question to interfere with an applicant's rights, and whether the interference was proportionate to the aim or objective which the public authority was pursuing. There should be no need to defer to the public authority's greater proximity to the issues in question along the lines of *Handyside*. And if this proves to be the better view, this may well provide a means of distinguishing some of the Strasbourg case law on similar facts where the decisions in question were based on the application of this doctrine.

Mention should be made, however, of one area where specific concern has been expressed, namely the area of public law where it has been suggested that the doctrine of the margin of appreciation may be conflated with the doctrine of Wednesbury unreasonableness so as seriously to undermine the incorporation of the Convention by allowing public authorities when acting as decision-makers a margin of appreciation where human rights are in play.[57] There are two objections to this approach.

First, the latitude allowed by the English courts to decision-makers by the *Wednesbury* approach (namely, the court will not intervene unless the decision was perverse) is very different to the latitude allowed by the Strasbourg Court to respondent states as to how they have sought to guarantee Convention rights. Indeed, the concepts are quite different.[58] The Strasbourg Court has never adopted the *Wednesbury* approach: on the contrary, it scrutinises the decisions in question much more closely than the *Wednesbury* approach would permit, albeit always subject to the quite separate margin of appreciation.[59]

---

[57] As the Court of Appeal has already done in *Mbatube v Secretary of State for the Home Department* [1996] Imm AR 184 at 189

[58] See *R v Secretary of State for the Home Department, ex parte Brind* [1991] 1 AC 696 per Lord Ackner at 62E–763B and Lord Lowry at 763C and 766C–767G

[59] See Singh, Hunt and Demetriou, "Is there a Role for the 'Margin of Appreciation' in National Law after the Human Rights Act?" (1999) EHRLR 15 and David Pannick QC, "Principles of Interpretation of Convention Rights under the Human Rights Act and the discretionary area of judgment" (1998) *PL* 545

Secondly, this is surely to misunderstand the true basis of the doctrine of the margin of appreciation. The enforcement of human rights is too important to leave to the very authorities who may be accused of failing to respect them. This is for our domestic courts to rule on. True it is that questions as to whether there was a pressing social need for the interference and whether the interference was proportionate will call for value judgments and, as will sometimes be the case, where there are rights and freedoms which pull in opposite directions, a difficult and delicate balancing exercise may be required. This will be amply demonstrated in the chapters to follow. But the making of value judgments and the carrying out of balancing exercises are part of the stock in trade of the modern English judge. In any event, as we have seen, the courts themselves are obliged by the Human Rights Act to act in conformity with the Convention.

2.4.5. *"Pressing social need"*

All that the Strasbourg Court has said thus far as to this requirement is that it must decide, on the basis of the material available to it, whether the reasons given by the national authorities to justify the interference in question are relevant and sufficient. Clearly, the domestic courts will be able to go much further and decide in terms whether there was a pressing social need for the interference in question. The more important the right in play, the more difficult it will be for the public authority to show a pressing social need to interfere with it.[60] On the other hand, the less significant the interference, the easier it should be to show a pressing social need for it. These considerations, of course, go not only to the question whether there is a pressing social need for the interference, but also to the question of proportionality, namely whether the interference was "proportionate to the legitimate aim pursued".[61]

2.4.6. *Proportionality*

"There must be a reasonable relationship of proportionality between the means employed and the legitimate objectives pursued by the contested limitation".[62] This doctrine of proportionality is central to the general principle which applies to the interpretation and application of the Convention, namely that the Convention is seeking to strike a "fair balance . . . between the demands of the general interest of the community and the requirement of the protection of the individual's fundamental rights".[63]

An example of how the doctrine of proportionality has been applied by the Court is a decision with obvious relevance to the common law right to

---

[60] cf *R v Ministry of Defence, ex parte Smith* [1996] QB 517
[61] *Handyside v United Kingdom* (1976) 1 EHRR 737 at 754
[62] *Fayed v United Kingdom* (1994) 18 EHRR 393 at 432
[63] *Sporrong and Lonnroth v Sweden* (1982) 5 EHRR 35 at 52

confidentiality of medical records, *MS v Sweden*.[64] The applicant suffered from
a painful spine condition which she claimed had been caused by an injury at
work. On this basis she tried to claim compensation from the Social Insurance
Office and it subsequently transpired that the Office had requested the head of
the clinic who had treated her for the back injury to supply it with her medical
records without her knowledge or consent. The records suggested that an abortion had been performed due to previous back problems, making no reference
to her alleged injury at work. The Office rejected her claim finding that her sick
leave had not been caused by an industrial injury and successive appeals were
unsuccessful. She then applied under the Convention contending that the submission of her medical records to the Office constituted an unjustified interference with her right to respect for her private life under Article 8. The Court held
that the disclosure had involved an interference with that right because of the
highly personal and sensitive data contained in the medical records in question.
However, the interference was in accordance with Swedish law and served the
legitimate aim of the protection of the economic well-being of the country as it
was potentially decisive for the allocation of public funds. As to proportionality, since disclosure of such records was limited by Swedish law to the extent
that the information was deemed material to the application of the compensation legislation, and was also accompanied by adequate safeguards of civil
and/or criminal liability for failure to observe the conditions of the legislation,
the interference was not disproportionate to the aim pursued.

3. CONCLUSION

The Human Rights Act is to be brought into effect on 2 October 2000. It is difficult, if not impossible, to exaggerate its importance and significance. It is self-
evident that it will have an immediate impact on public law and criminal law.
But it will also have a very significant impact on the common law as we hope to
demonstrate in the chapters which follow. Common lawyers will now need to
consider whether a private law dispute which involves a public authority
involves any question of human rights, because if it does, then it may be possible to use the Convention either to support a free standing cause of action for
breach of a Convention right or to reinforce an existing domestic cause of
action. It follows that common lawyers (as much as public lawyers and those
who practise in criminal law) will need to understand the Convention and famil-
iarise themselves with its jurisprudence. In particular, they will need to famil-
iarise themselves with some of the essential principles which underpin the
operation of the Convention, for example the doctrine of proportionality which
hitherto has only been familiar to domestic lawyers in public law or as part of

---

[64] (1999) 27 EHRR 91, also considered in chapter 11 on Confidentiality and Defamation and in
chapter 8 on Medical Law

the jurisprudence of the Treaty of Rome. The Human Rights Act is surely the most important legal development in the United Kingdom since the Treaty of Rome, now a quarter of a century ago. In the common law, as elsewhere, the legal landscape is about to change for ever.

3

Costs, Conditional Fees and Legal Aid[1]

GUY MANSFIELD QC

1. INTRODUCTION

This chapter addresses the issue of legal representation and funding in the context of non-criminal cases, that is cases involving civil rights and obligations and matters ancillary thereto. Costs, legal aid and conditional fees arise essentially in the context of the procedural rights guaranteed by the Convention, namely the rights under Articles 5 and 6, in particular the right of access to court provided under Article 6 (1). But issues relating to funding of litigation cannot be looked at in isolation. It is necessary to have in mind at all times the underlying rationale of the Convention and in particular in this context the principles governing Article 6. So, Article 1 declares the Contracting States' agreement to secure to everyone within their jurisdiction the rights and freedoms defined in Section 1 of the Convention. The Contracting States have the task of seeing that this is achieved.

Article 6 is a qualified and not a fundamental right, a distinction explained in full in chapter 2 above. Article 6 is concerned to guarantee fairness in all aspects of a trial or hearing. It achieves this by seeking to ensure procedural fairness, in other words hearings in public, within a reasonable time, before an independent and impartial tribunal which pronounces judgment publicly. The proceedings as a whole (taking into account the effect of any appeal procedure) must be fair. Going further still, the Strasbourg Court, since *Golder v UK*[2] has held that the right of access to a court is inherent in the right declared in Article 6(1). Nevertheless this right, which is not an absolute one, by its very nature calls for regulation by the state. It may be subject to limitations although these must not restrict or reduce access in such a way or to such an extent that the very essence of the right is impaired.[3] This is the context in which to consider specific aspects of access to court, and in particular costs and legal aid. Finally, it is essential to note that no question of a possible entitlement to legal aid for civil proceedings can arise if the proceedings in question do not concern a private civil right within the terms of the Convention.

[1] "Legal Aid" is used by the ECtHR. It is used in this chapter to cover all support for proceedings from the Legal Services Commission

[2] (1975) 1 EHRR 524

[3] *Canea Catholic Church v Greece* (1997) 27 EHRR 521

As with all the rights in the Convention, the twin doctrines of margin of appreciation and proportionality are relevant. These principles have been explored in some detail in chapter two and therefore they will only be touched upon here.

In the absence of a European consensus the Strasbourg Court accommodates variations in state practice through the doctrine of margin of appreciation.[4] Thus no breach will be found if it reflects a practice followed in a number of other European states: the same approach is adopted where practice varies widely. So in *Muller v Switzerland*[5] the Court held that the national measure pursued the legitimate aim of protecting public morals which aim is naturally linked to the rights of others. A margin of appreciation was recognised in this area. It was not possible to find in the legal and social order of the Contracting States a uniform European conception of morals. The state authorities were in principle in a better position than the international judge to give an opinion on the exact content of these requirements. Similarly in *Cossey v UK*,[6] the Court held that the reports revealed continuing diversity of practice between national governments. Accordingly this was still, having regard to the existence of little common ground between the Contracting States, an area in which they enjoyed a wide margin of appreciation. Note the similar approach in *Sheffield and Horsham v UK*.[7] As to proportionality, the Court in *Cossey* continued,[8] that "the notion of proportionality was already encompassed within that of the fair balance that has to be struck between the general interests of the community and the interests of the individual".

The permitted scope of the margin of appreciation differs according to its context. It is wide in planning matters, where the authorities may properly have regard to a wide range of local factors.[9] However, if the matter involves interference with an intimate area of private life there must be "particularly serious reasons" for interfering.[10] This is reflected in the statement of principle in *Fayed v UK*[11] that while in laying down regulations which limit the right of access to court "according to the needs and resources of the community and of individuals", the state enjoys a certain margin of appreciation, the final decision rests

---

[4] An English judge cannot himself apply or have recourse to the doctrine as implemented by the ECHR. He must however recognise the impact of the doctrine on the Strasbourg Court's analysis of the meaning and implications of the broad terms of the provisions, *R v Stratford JJ, ex parte Imbert*, [1999] 2 Ct. App. R. 276, DC

[5] (1988) 13 EHHR 212, para 35

[6] (1990) 13 EHHR 622, para 40, concerning the UK's refusal to allow a trans-sexual to obtain a certificate of birth stating she was female or legally to marry a man in the UK

[7] (1998) 27 EHRR 163, the Court could not conclude that the state could not rely on a margin of appreciation

[8] Para 41

[9] *Buckley v UK* (1997) 23 EHRR 101, para 75

[10] *Dudgeon v UK* (1983) 4 EHRR 149 – Breach of Article 8 in respect of the Northern Irish legislation making it a criminal offence for one man to commit an act of gross indecency or buggery with another man

[11] (1994) 18 EHHR 393, para 65

with the Court which must be satisfied that the very essence of the right is not impaired.

In the context of the right to a fair hearing under Article 6(1), there is a wide diversity in trial practice arising from the differences between the civil law and common law systems of justice. This of course applies particularly to the approach to costs and the grant of legal aid in civil cases. It widens the scope of what will be held compatible.

Proportionality involves the search for a fair balance between the demands of the general interest of the community and the requirements of the protection of the individual's fundamental rights.[12] The state may restrict a qualified right to the extent necessary in a democratic society. From this it follows that any restriction must be proportionate to the legitimate aim pursued.[13] In *Osman*[14] the Strasbourg Court held that while the aim of the exclusionary rule to protect the police from actions alleging injury and loss from negligent policing might

> "be accepted as legitimate in terms of the Convention, as being directed to the maintenance of the effectiveness of the police service and hence to the prevention of disorder and crime, the court must nevertheless, in turning to the issue of proportionality have particular regard to its scope and especially its application *in the case in issue*" (emphasis added). "The application of the rule . . . without further enquiry into the existence of competing public interest considerations only serves to confer a blanket immunity on the police . . . and amounts to an unjustifiable restriction on an applicant's right to have a determination on the merits of his . . . claim against the police in deserving cases".

In other words, if the right which would otherwise exist to have the claim heard by the courts was to be excluded, the restriction must in every case be proportionate to the aim. In *Tinelly & Sons Ltd v UK*[15] the Secretary of State, under Northern Irish legislation which did not permit any review of his decision by the national courts, had issued a Section 42 Certificate declaring that his decision not to grant a contract for public works to the applicant was "an act done for the purpose of safeguarding national security or the protection of public safety or order". The Court found a breach of Article 6(1); a complaint could properly be submitted for an independent judicial determination even if national security considerations were present and constituted a highly material aspect of the case. The issue of the Certificate was a disproportionate restriction on the right of access to court. The restriction must not impair the very essence of the right.[16]

---

[12] *Soering v UK* (1989) 11 EHRR 439, para 189
[13] *Handyside v UK* (1976) 1 EHRR 737
[14] (1999) 5 BHRC 293, para 150
[15] (1999) 27 EHRR 249
[16] See, in the context of access to court, *Ashingdeane v UK* (1985) 7 EHRR 528, para 57

2. ARTICLE 6: THE RIGHT TO A FAIR HEARING

Article 6 is the most important provision for the points addressed in this chapter. Before coming directly to the questions of costs, conditional fees and legal aid, I must first address the rationale of the Convention. Some of this ground has already been covered earlier in this book. However it is vital to an understanding of the Convention. I shall seek to put it into a very specific context, namely Article 6.

2.1. Practical and Effective Rights

The Convention is intended to guarantee not rights that are theoretical or illusory, but rights that are practical and effective.[17] Most violations of the Convention have been found under Article 6(1), the most frequent of these being related to delay, which is a violation of the requirement that individuals be guaranteed a trial within reasonable time. Other breaches involve the right to legal aid (criminal procedures only) and the right to an independent and impartial tribunal. The summary which follows is intended simply to provide the relevant context in which to consider costs and other aspects of the funding of civil litigation. Of necessity it is not comprehensive. It is the necessary point of reference from which discussion of these topics can follow. Only paragraph 1 of Article 6 applies expressly to civil proceedings. But the civil and criminal aspects of Article 6 (1) are not mutually exclusive. The provisions of Article 6 (2) and (3) are aspects of the notion of a fair trial contained in Article 6(1) in the civil context.[18]

For convenience I set out the essential parts of Article 6(1) :

> *"In the determination of his civil rights and obligations . . . everyone is entitled to a fair and public hearing within a reasonable time by an independent and impartial tribunal established by law. Judgment shall be pronounced publicly but the press and public may be excluded from all or part of the trial in the interest of morals, public order or national security in a democratic society. . . Juveniles. . . protection of the private life of individuals or to the extent strictly necessary. . . in special circumstances where publicity would prejudice".*

The right to a fair trial holds a "prominent place . . . in a democratic society"[19] such that "there can be no justification for interpreting Article 6(1) of the Convention restrictively".[20] The state must provide courts, legal aid (where appropriate) and translators in connection with this right. The right includes

---

[17] *Artico v Italy* (1980) 8 DR 73, where there was a breach of the right to legal aid because the legal aid lawyer was wholly ineffectual; see too *Airey v Ireland* – n.41 below and *Tinnelly & Sons Ltd v UK* – above n.15

[18] *Le Compte v Belgium* (1981) 4 EHRR 1

[19] *De Cubber v Belgium* (1984) 7 EHRR 236

[20] *Moriera de Azevedo v Portugal* (1990) EHRR 721

generally the right to an oral hearing and equality of arms. But as we shall see below the fact that an individual has civil rights which are under challenge and which bring him or her within the ambit of Article 6(1) does not lead inexorably to an entitlement to legal aid in proceedings concerned with such rights.

2.2. The Civil/Criminal Divide

It is necessary to have in mind what proceedings are considered "criminal" other than the obvious categories of crime. For if a matter is properly categorised as criminal then the fuller and more generous express scope of the rest of Article 6 will apply. If it is a "civil" matter only the first paragraph of the Article will apply. In determining whether a matter is "criminal", the *Engel*[21] criteria must be applied. These are threefold: (1) the classification of the offence in domestic law, (2) the nature of the offence, (3) the severity of the penalty. So if domestic law classifies it as criminal that is conclusive. But the fact that domestic law does not so classify it is not conclusive. The Court will look at the nature of the "offence"; in particular, is the offence one which potentially affects the population at large? So proceedings for contempt of court against a journalist[22] who was not a party to the proceedings, and proceedings against a journalist for breach of privilege of the legislature[23] were held to be criminal. But sanctions on litigants to ensure the orderly conduct of proceedings are not likely to be criminal.[24] However, even if application of the first two criteria would not render a matter criminal, the severity of any penalty can. If it is punishable with imprisonment this will generally define the proceedings as criminal unless "the nature, duration or manner of execution of the imprisonment" is not "appreciably detrimental".[25] Disciplinary proceedings by professional bodies charged with regulating the professions, such as the General Medical Council, do not carry the risk of imprisonment. They are not therefore likely to be held to be criminal and such proceedings will fall outside the wider "criminal" ambit of Article 6. Courts martial are of course different; here the test will be the substance of the offence alleged and the possible or actual penalty.

2.3. "Civil" as opposed to "Public" Rights

The origin of the term "civil" lies in the civil (not common law) system of law. So it does not mean civil in the broad sense that we understand it. Article 6 applies only to private rights; only private rights can be "civil". It does not apply

---

[21] (1976) 1 EHRR 706
[22] *Weber v Switzerland* (1990) 12 EHRR 508
[23] *Demicoli v Malta* (1991) 14 EHRR 47
[24] *Putz v Austria* (1996) RJD 1996–1, No 4
[25] *Engel*, para 82

to the determination of public rights such as nationality. So if the right concerned falls within the definition of a "public" right which is not "criminal" and does not have that private element to make it a "civil" right, no ancillary right to legal aid will arise.

2.3.1. Civil Rights

In the context of provision of legal aid the question whether a private civil right is involved is plainly crucial. The fact that a state may treat a particular right as a "public" law right is not determinative.

In *Feldbrugge v Netherlands*,[26] domestic law defined the right to health insurance benefits as a public law right, but the Court held that it was a civil right within Article 6(1). "Only the character of the general right at issue is relevant".[27] The existence of any "uniform European notion" is influential.[28] The national "municipal" law necessarily determines the content of the right or obligation to which the Convention concept of civil rights and obligations is applied. For example, the question whether medical services are part of a public service or contractually provided, albeit subject to state regulation, will need to be determined before the question of applicability of the Convention rights, e.g. access to court, will arise.

Generally speaking Article 6(1) is now held to apply to matters of social insurance[29] even when the benefit is non-contributory and wholly independent of a contract of employment. So too in *McGinley and Egan v UK*[30] the applicants, who had served on or near Christmas Island at the time of nuclear testing, applied for pension increases based on illnesses alleged to be attributable to that service. The Court held that the claim involved a determination of their civil rights and so Article 6(1) applied. In the context of the employment of civil servants, the Court has retained a more restrictive approach. In *Huber v France*[31] a civil servant alleged breach of Article 6(1) on account of the length of the proceedings in the administrative courts which he had brought to quash the decision to send him on leave and suspend payment of his salary. The Court held that Article 6(1) did not apply; it was not a civil right which was in issue. A dispute relating to the recruitment, career and termination of service of a civil servant was generally outside Article 6(1). It was different where the claim related to a purely economic right, e.g. payment of a pension or salary. His dispute, it held, primarily concerned his career, the fact that the consequence was pecuniary did not make it civil proceedings. It remains to be seen whether the new court will continue to uphold this view.

---

[26] (1986) 8 EHRR 425
[27] *Konig v FRG* (1978) 2 EHRR 170
[28] *Feldbrugge v Netherlands* (1986) 8 EHRR 425
[29] *Salesi v Italy* (1993) 26 EHRR 187
[30] (1998) 27 EHRR 1
[31] (1998) 26 EHRR 457

The Court looks at the private and personal nature of the right, its basis – whether from a contractual relationship, a property right, the exercise of commercial, business or professional activity or a pecuniary claim or for the infringement of a pecuniary right (including a claim arising from detention prior to acquittal in criminal proceedings). The rights and obligations of private persons between themselves are in all cases civil rights and obligations.

For Article 6(1) to apply, civil rights or obligations must be *at issue* in the dispute. The "*contestation*" (dispute) must be of a "genuine and serious nature".[32] Such dispute may relate to the existence of a right and also to the manner in which it may be exercised or to its scope.[33]

The crucial question is whether the proceedings are decisive for private rights and obligations. Article 6 applies to proceedings which, even though they do not have as their purpose the determination of civil rights and obligations, will in fact be determinative of such rights or obligations.[34] The requirement is that the proceedings must be "directly decisive", i.e. not too remote in effect. An example of such proceedings arose in *Le Compte v Belgium*.[35] This concerned temporary suspension from medical practice by the disciplinary bodies. The proceedings were directly decisive of the private law right to practice medicine; the suspension of that right was a direct result of the tribunal's decision that breaches of the rules had occurred. Article 6 (1) applied. See too *Gautrin v France*.[36]

Conversely Article 6 has been held not to apply to a dispute that is for example concerned with the assessment of the applicant's competence to be registered as professional, e.g. an accountant.[37] The Court in *Van Marle* found that there was no true dispute. There were no claims that there had been procedural irregularity, and assessments of the knowledge and experience required to carry on a profession were akin to university examinations and thus removed from normal judicial functions. Recently the Court of Appeal in this country have sought to follow this approach. In *R v Lord Chancellor ex p Lightfoot*[38] the Court held that a debtor's right to petition the Court for his own bankruptcy was not a constitutional right, since the required deposit of £250 was not for access to the courts but for the costs of services provided by others for the petitioner's benefit. A debtor did not petition the Court for the adjudication of general disputes, but rather so that he might be relieved of his debts under a "benign self-standing

[32] *Le Compte v Belgium* (1981) 4 EHRR 1, para 49
[33] *Le Compte*
[34] *Ringeisen v Austria* (1971) 1 EHRR 455
[35] (1981) 4 EHHR. See too *Albert et al. v Belgium* (1983) 5 EHHR 533 "civil rights and obligations" were being determined, e.g. the right to practise and the risk of being struck off
[36] (1998) 28 EHRR 1996 imposing an obligation on the French equivalent of the General Medical Council to sit in public and to be impartial, its members having no competing or conflicting interests with those on trial before it
[37] *Van Marle v Netherlands* (1986) 8 EHRR 483
[38] [1999] 2 WLR 1126, CA

administrative scheme". Since Article 6(1) only applied in relation to a dispute whose outcome would decide rights and obligations, and there was no such dispute in the present case, the petitioner could not invoke the Article. Article 6 is concerned with judging in the true sense. The issue must be justiciable in that there must be a dispute involving civil rights.

2.3.2. Public Rights

For cases involving the individual's relations with the state the position is less clear cut. Action which determines property rights is "civil" and subject to the right to a fair trial. This extends to planning applications. So too is the right to conduct commercial activity, e.g. a public service licence or the right to practise a profession.[39] The right to compensation for unlawful acts by the state is a "civil" right to which the Article applies. But for persons employed by the state, disputes relating to appointment, dismissal or conditions of service are not necessarily within the Article. If what is truly sought is a non-pecuniary remedy, such as reinstatement, the Court usually concludes that a civil right is not in dispute.[40]

2.4. The Right of Access to a Court

It is to this right in particular that the possible right to legal aid is relevant. The right of access to a court is not absolute and the state has a margin of appreciation in making regulations to limit it. However, any limitations must not so restrict or reduce the access that the "very essence of the right is impaired".[41] It must have a legitimate aim and be proportionate.[42] The Convention protects primarily civil and political rights rather than economic and social rights, although this distinction is becoming blurred. So as we have seen above the general rule is that Article 6(1) applies in the field of social insurance, including even welfare assistance. In *Schuler-Zgraggen v Switzerland*[43] despite the existence of public law features affecting the applicant's relations with the administrative authorities, the applicant had "suffered an interference with her means of subsistence; she was claiming an individual economic right flowing from specific rules laid down in a federal statute".[44] This is an example of a growing tendency to protect economic and social rights, although the position of employment of

---

[39] e.g. *H v Belgium* (1987) 10 EHHR 339 [the legal profession]
[40] see *Huber v France*, N. 30 above, for details of the judgment and reasoning
[41] *Airey v Ireland* (1979) 2 EHRR 305
[42] A Chamber of the Court has, for example, recently found that dismissal for want of prosecution is such a proportionate limitation on individuals' right of access: see *F.G. v United Kingdom* Application No 39552/98, April 20 1999, unreported
[43] (1993) EHRR 405
[44] *Schuler-Zgraggen v Switzerland*, para 46

civil servants remains outside the scope of Article 6.[45] The proper approach to construction is one which achieves its object and purpose: the protection of individual human rights and the maintenance and promotion of the ideals and values of a democratic society.[46]

As we have seen, for Article 6 (1) to apply there must be a "dispute" at the national level between two private persons or the applicant and the state, whose outcome determines the applicant's civil rights and obligations. The test is whether he has a tenable argument that the decision will have such a determinative effect. However, Article 6 is only a procedural guarantee to the right to a fair hearing of those substantive rights and the obligations which the state provides.

The absence of a remedy under national law does not mean that there is always a breach of Article 6 see e.g. *James v United Kingdom*.[47] Here the statute conferred the right to long leaseholders to acquire freeholds. It was of the essence of the legislation that if given criteria were met the deprived landlord had no remedy. The Court refused to order the restoration of the landlord's rights. The Statute was found to conform with Article 1 of the First Protocol (right to peaceful enjoyment of possessions)[48] so it was sufficient that the aggrieved landlord could go to court to secure compliance with the Act.

Nonetheless it is not permissible for the state to remove from the jurisdiction of the courts a whole range of civil claims or confer immunities from civil liability on large groups or categories of persons.[49] But that is different from ordering the provision or restoration of the landlord's rights as in the *James* case. It will be a matter of degree. Restraint can be exercised over the state by the right of access to court. A restriction on the right of access would have to be justified as having a legitimate aim and being proportional to the attainment of that aim.

2.4.1. Effective Access

The right of access to a court means a right to access in fact, i.e. effective access. In *Ashingdane v UK*[50] it was held that limitations to the right of access to a court may be permissible where they do not restrict or reduce access to the extent that the very essence of the right is impaired (important in the context of availability of legal aid), where they pursue a legitimate aim and they disclose a reasonable relationship of proportionality between the means employed and the aim to be achieved. Effective access to justice does not import a right to appeal. But where

---

[45] *Huber v France*, N. 30 above
[46] Thus, for example, the monetary award made by the Court in *Osman v United Kingdom* (1999) 5 BHRC 293 has been criticised for confusing a public right to an investigation with a civil, tort-based, right to compensation: see chapter 5 on Remedies, pp 71–88
[47] (1986) 8 EHRR 123
[48] Explored more fully in chapter 9 on Environmental Rights
[49] *Fayed v UK* (1994) 18 EHRR 393, a point made forcibly by *Osman v UK* (1999) 5 BHRC 293
[50] (1985) 7 EHRR 528

there is a right to appeal there must be no unjustifiable restrictions on its exercise. In *Garcia Manibado v Spain*,[51] an appellant as a condition of leave had been ordered to pay into court the substantial damages under appeal. The Court held that while it was not for to substitute itself for the national jurisdiction, the right of access was not absolute and the national jurisdiction had the legitimate aim of avoiding excessive clogging of the Court of Appeal, yet if there was a right of appeal there must be an *effective* right of access and the condition imposed prevented access and breached Article 6(1). An order deeming the applicant a vexatious litigant so that he could not commence proceedings without leave did not offend because he had abused his right of access, wasting the resources of the court and defendants, and in a new matter he could apply for leave so it was not a total bar.[52] It is suggested however that this will not be so if the decision to make such order is not itself sustainable on the facts.

2.5. The Right to a Fair Hearing

The Contracting States have a greater latitude when dealing with civil cases concerning civil rights and obligations than they have when dealing with criminal cases.[53] The strongest established rights are those to an oral hearing in person and to equality of arms. The test will be the effect on the trial as a whole, which may not assist the applicant where prejudice cannot be shown to have resulted.

2.6. Equality of Arms

In adversarial proceedings the procedural right to "equality of arms" arises:

"Everyone who is a party to proceedings shall have a reasonable opportunity of presenting his case to the court under conditions which do not place him at a substantial disadvantage vis à vis his opponent".[54]

This applies to all aspects of the proceedings and includes "civil" cases. This covers for example the right to cross-examine or to be allowed access to facilities on equal terms. The court is concerned with the process, not the result. "What is essential is that the parties should be able to participate properly before the 'tribunal' ".[55]

"The requirement of 'equality of arms' – in the sense of a fair balance between the parties applies in principle in civil cases. That principle in litigation involving opposing

[51] 15 February 2000, [decision of the chamber]
[52] *H v UK*, (1986) 45 D.R.281
[53] (1993) 18 EHRR 213
[54] *Kauffman v Belgium* No 10938/84, 50 DR 98 at 115 (1986)
[55] *Mantovanelli v France* (1997) 24 EHRR 370, para 33

private interests implies that each party must be afforded a reasonable opportunity to present his case, including his evidence, under conditions that do not place him at a substantial disadvantage vis à vis his opponent. It is left to the national authorities to ensure that in each individual case the requirements of a fair hearing are met".[56]

In *Dombo Beheer v Netherlands* the applicants sought to prove an oral agreement. The effect of domestic law was to bar them from calling as a witness the relevant person present at the meeting in issue but to permit the other side to call their witness. The Court held that this placed *Dombo Beheer* at a substantial disadvantage and violated Article 6(1).

Another example of violation of Article 6(1) involving inequality of arms is to be found in the decision of *Unterpertinger v Austria*[57] where a conviction had been based mainly on statements made by two witnesses to the police which were treated as truth of the accusations made by these witnesses. The applicant had not been permitted to question the witnesses. So in *Van Orshoven v Belgium*[58] concerning a civil appeal, the court stressed that there must not be infringement of the applicant's right to adversarial proceedings, namely the parties' right to have knowledge of and comment on all evidence advanced or observations filed with the court.

Finally, in *Niederost-Huber v Switzerland*[59] the Court brought together a number of principles. (1) The principle of equality of arms required each party to be given a reasonable opportunity to present this case under conditions that did not place him at a disadvantage vis à vis his opponent. (2) There was hence *no* infringement of equality of arms where the fact that the lower court had filed observations with the Appeal Court was not communicated to *either* party (para 23). (3) However, the concept of a fair trial required the parties to have knowledge of and comment on all evidence adduced or observations filed (para 24). (4) Although national authorities enjoy wider latitude in the civil than criminal sphere, the requirements derived from the right to adversarial proceedings are the same in both civil and criminal cases (para 28). (5) Only the parties to a dispute might properly decide whether observations filed presented an argument which had not appeared in the decision under appeal (para 29). (6) Although the Court attached great importance to the objective of saving time and expediting proceedings, this did not justify disregarding such a fundamental principle as the right to adversarial proceedings. Article 6(1) was intended above all to secure the interests of the parties and those of the proper administration of justice (paras 30–32).

However, as will be seen below, decisions on whether legal aid should have been available have not been made under the principle of equality of arms but rather under the wider head of effective access to the Court. That is because the refusal of legal aid does not of itself affect the manner in which the hearing is

---

[56] *Dombo Beheer v Netherlands* (1993) n. 53, para 33
[57] (1986) 13 EHRR 175
[58] (1997) 26 EHRR 55
[59] (1997) 25 EHRR 709

conducted. It does not mean that evidence cannot be called or a witness cross-examined; the rights of the opposing parties before the Court remain equal. Rather the absence of legal representation and funding for the ancillary costs of litigation such as expert witnesses and preparation of documents goes to the ability *effectively* to bring or conduct or defend a claim at all.

3. THE RIGHT TO LEGAL AID IN CIVIL CASES

3.1. Applications for Legal Aid

Article 6 usually applies from the time when the proceedings are instituted. But in a civil case it may begin to run before the claim is issued. In the leading case of *Golder v UK* [60] the Home Secretary had refused a convicted prisoner permission to write to his solicitor concerning possible libel proceedings against a prison officer. There was an issue under Article 6 because it affected the right to institute proceedings. Thus, for a claimant any right to legal aid is likely to be contemporaneous. It remains an open question whether the guarantee of "reasonable time" applies to a pre-trial application for legal aid in civil litigation, [61] but it is submitted that the principle must apply.

3.2. Relevant Criteria

In *Airey v Ireland* [62] a needy wife had been refused legal aid to bring proceedings for judicial separation. The Court took into account the complexity of the proceedings raising complicated points of law and requiring proof of adultery and unnatural practices of cruelty; there was the need to examine witnesses and possibly experts; the subject matter entailed an emotional involvement of the parties scarcely compatible with the objectivity required to present a case in court. It held that to be effective access she needed legal representation. For a needy person this meant legal aid. But the Court stated that it was not holding that the right of access in Article 6(1) provided a full right to legal aid in civil cases comparable to the rights under Article 6(3)(c) in all criminal cases where "the interests of justice so require".

So legal representation is subject to a qualified guarantee in civil cases – viz. the right of effective access to the courts so that the applicant can take effective advantage of remedies available at law. Where there is established a right to legal assistance, this involves the provision of legal aid where the party has

---

[60] (1975) 1 EHRR 524
[61] *H v France* (1989) 12 EHHR 74
[62] (1979) 2 EHRR 305

insufficient means.[63] So we must ask what creates that right and whether it exists in a given case. Legal aid is required in civil cases as a consequence of the right to effective access where a person cannot plead his case effectively by himself or the law makes representation compulsory. Historically that has not had as far-reaching an effect as might be imagined, although the Court's approach may be changing.[64]

3.3. Excluded Categories

In determining whether legal aid should be available, what is at stake may be important. The Commission in *Munro*[65] made the distinction between judicial separation (which attracts the entitlement to legal aid) and defamation (no breach of Article 6 disclosed by its unavailability). The Commission in *Munro* recognised the difficulties facing a lay person in defamation. But defamation proceedings, although complex, involved a person's reputation which was not as important as the family relationship involved in *Airey* (judicial separation), so the absence of legal aid was held not to be a breach. The Commission has paid particular attention to the individual circumstances of such cases. It observed in *Munro* that when the applicant's claim for unfair dismissal had been before the industrial tribunal, that body had considered associated complaints about the alleged malice of the employer; in its indirect assessment of the merits it observed that there was in fact nothing to indicate that he would have succeeded any better in the defamation action. In *Winer v UK*[66] it was held legitimate to exclude certain categories of legal proceedings altogether from legal aid by reference to financial criteria and the inherent riskiness of such cases. However, given the importance which the Court in *Osman*[67] attached to the applicants' right "to seek an adjudication on the admissibility and merits of an arguable claim" (para 139), and "to have the police account for their actions and omissions in adversarial proceedings" and the obvious complexity of such proceedings (leaving aside the emotional involvement of the applicants who were seeking redress for the death of their son), it is surely well arguable that if, for example, there had been a failure to grant legal aid in *Osman*, this would have been held to violate Article 6(1).

---

[63] *Zamir v UK* (1983) 40 DR 42: free legal aid was required for an illegal immigrant detained pending deportation in view of the complexity of the proceedings and his limited English. Note that this decision was not under Article 6, because extradition proceedings involve "public" rights, but under Article 5, which guarantees procedural safeguards for persons detained pending deportation

[64] See below *Ait Mahoub v France*, judgment of ECHR 28 October 1998 unreported, *Aerts v Belgium* (1998) 5 BHRC 382 and, by inference, *Osman v UK* (1998) 5 BHRC 293

[65] *Munro v UK* No. 10594/83, 52 DR 158 (1987). See also the discussion of Article 6 in defamation cases in chapter 11 on Confidentiality and Defamation

[66] No 11564/85, 45 DR 291 (1985)

[67] (1998) 5 BHRC 293

Further support for the view that change is afoot may be found in the contemporaneous decision of the Court in *Ait Mahoub v France*.[68] In this case the applicant, a convicted armed robber, had lodged two sets of criminal complaints alleging subornation of perjury, forgery and other like matters against gendarmes said to be responsible for his conviction. He had in each case made civil party applications, in one expressly and in the other by implication, mentioning financial loss. In neither case (the second complaint was lodged after dismissal of his outstanding appeal against the original conviction) had he been granted legal aid. But his means were assessed as nil. The investigating judge had then directed the applicant, because he was not in receipt of legal aid, to pay 80,000 French francs (some £8,000) into court as a condition of being allowed to proceed. This was notwithstanding the nil assessment of means and the discretion in any event to "exempt the civil party from paying security". The Court held (para 45) that the complaint was designed "to secure a conviction that would have enabled him to exercise his civil rights in regard to the alleged offences, and in particular to obtain compensation for financial loss". It continued (para 57) "It is not for the court to assess the merits of the complaint lodged by the applicant . . . It considers, however, that the settling of such a large sum . . . was disproportionate seeing that Mr Ait Mahoub . . . had no financial resources whatsoever. Requiring the applicant to pay such a large sum amounted in practice to depriving him of his recourse before the investigating judge" (citing *Aerts v Belgium*).[69]

3.4. Other Restrictions on the Right to Legal Aid

In further considering the application of the *Airey* principles the Commission has tended to confine them and given weight to the reasons for the refusal of legal aid. The Commission has held that limited resources are a legitimate ground for restricting the grant of legal aid and requiring the payment of contributions.[70]

Where there was no reasonable prospect of success its refusal "would not normally constitute a denial of access to the Court unless it could be shown that the decision of the administrative authority was arbitrary".[71] So it has been held

---

[68]   (1998) 28 October, unreported

[69]   (1998) 5 BHRC 382, see 3.4 below. See also *McTear v United Kingdom* (Application No 40291/98, September 7 1999, unreported). Here the Court rejected a claim that the refusal of legal aid for the applicant's negligence action against a tobacco company in respect of the illness and death of her husband from smoking denied her effective access to court. The finding of inadmissibility was based on the fact that the applicant's legal representatives had agreed to act for her on a *pro bono* basis, so it could not be said she had been deprived of her right of access to court

[70]   No 8158/78, July 10 1980, 21 DR 95; and see also the reference in *Fayed v UK* (1994) 18 EHRR 393, para 65, to the state's margin of appreciation in laying down regulations which limit the right of access to court "according to the needs and resources of the community and of individuals" provided the very essence of the right is not impaired

[71]   *X v UK*, No 8158/78, 21 DR 95 (1980)

legitimate to require a case to have reasonable prospects of success and be well-founded, not frivolous or vexatious. For the applicant should still enjoy reasonable access to the Court having the opportunity to be heard under the proper and effective control of the fairness and conduct of the proceedings by the court.[72] But the assessment by the legal aid authority must not result in an arbitrary refusal. In this respect existing English public law remedies would seem to parallel the standards of the Court.

Two recent decisions suggest however that the Court may be softening its approach. First in *Mantovanelli v France*[73] the Court reiterated that "what is essential is that the parties should be able to participate properly before the 'tribunal'". Secondly in *Aerts v Belgium*,[74] cited with approval in *Ait-Mahoub v France* (above), the applicant had not the means to instruct a lawyer and could legitimately apply to the Legal Aid Board with a view to an appeal on points of law, since domestic law required representation by counsel before the Court of Cassation[75] in civil cases. The Court held that it was for the national court and not the Legal Aid Board to assess the proposed appeal's prospects of success. The Board's refusal of aid on the ground that the appeal was not well-founded impaired the very essence of the applicant's right to a tribunal. There had been a breach of Article 6(1). This decision might be said to have at its heart the requirement to appear by counsel. Nonetheless in a complex case the absence of representation may *effectively* impair the right of proper access. That will be all the more so where the other party is an organ of the state or even a corporate or insured party.

The fact that the applicant's opponent is in receipt of legal aid does not necessarily render the refusal of legal aid incompatible with Article 6(1) (*Webb v United Kingdom* above). This is because the party still has the same opportunity to put his case before the Court, which will regulate the procedures. However, although there will not thereby be a breach of the principle of equality of arms, in a more complex case wider considerations are likely to obtain – see the discussion above. Further, if the refusal of legal aid is not absolute, there will not be a breach of Article 6: the Commission has upheld an order which prohibited an applicant from seeking legal aid where he had made repeated applications. His remedy was to apply for the five year ban to be lifted.[76]

3.5. Legal Aid for Human Rights Act Cases

The Legal Services Commission will have to consider how to assess the merits of an application for legal aid in human rights cases. Assessment will have to be

[72] *Webb v UK* , No 9353/81, 33 DR 133 (1983)
[73] (1997) 24 EHRR 370, para 33
[74] (1998) 5 BHRC 382
[75] A not unimportant distinction from the UK
[76] Application No. 27788/95 January 27, 1996

carried out so far as consistent with the Convention by the Legal Services Commission in accordance with the principles laid down by the Access to Justice Act 1999 and the Funding Code to be brought in thereunder – see below. As we have seen above, subject to qualification arising from the effect of recent decisions, the Court has held that it is legitimate to require a case to have reasonable prospects of success and be well-founded, not frivolous or vexatious.

Brief reference should be made here to Article 13, which is discussed fully by Rosalind English in chapter 5 on Remedies. In the context of Article 13 (which of course is not to be expressly incorporated) the Court has held that provision of an effective remedy means that a remedy must be guaranteed to anyone who has an "arguable claim" that his rights have been violated, i.e. that he is a victim of a violation.[77] The complaint must not be manifestly ill-founded or inadmissible for it would not then be arguable. This suggests that the proper test for the LSC should be that which is applied in considering whether the applicant has reasonable grounds for bringing proceedings for judicial review, namely whether or not the applicant has a prima facie arguable case.[78] The test set by the Funding Code is that the prospects of success in a claim against a Public Authority involving breach of human rights must be at least "borderline", i.e. better than "poor". That would seem appropriate.[79]

3.6. Legal Aid for Tribunal Hearings

Legal aid has not previously been available for Industrial Tribunals or indeed many other similar bodies notwithstanding the importance of the issues to the individuals concerned. No doubt the rationale is that legal aid resources are finite and the state enjoys a margin of appreciation in deciding how and where to make them available. However, "help" short of advocacy at a tribunal hearing will now be available.[80] Support for advocacy will be available in the EAT. This is all to the good. Similar considerations apply to disciplinary tribunals. In such cases, the hearing is at least theoretically more informal and the tribunal will usually have specialist members who will understand the factual and related legal issues. In the context of professionals, members of the medical profession almost invariably have membership of a Defence Union, which will provide legal representation. Lawyers called before their professional bodies can usually obtain the free assistance of a fellow practitioner. If such is not available they have the intellectual weapons to understand and deal with the issues.[81]

---

[77] *Silver v UK* (1983) 5 EHRR 347 and *Boyle and Rice v UK* (1988) 10 EHRR 425

[78] *R v Legal Aid Board ex parte Hughes* (1992) 24 HLR 698 (CA)

[79] See *The Funding Code*, Part 1, para 8.3.2

[80] See *The Funding Code* defiition of "Proceedings"

[81] The position is otherwise in the case of specialist public tribunals who have power to order the release of people in detention such as mental patients: *Megyeri v Germany* (1992) 15 EHRR 584, where the Court held that the psychiatric patient applicant was unlikely to be able to address the medical and legal points arising before the tribunal; further, what was at stake for him (detention) was important; legal aid was needed

4. CONDITIONAL FEE OR SPECULATIVE FEE AGREEMENTS — RELATIONSHIP
WITH LEGAL AID

The Access to Justice Act 1999 creates the Legal Services Commission (LSC) to replace the Legal Aid Board (LAB). Subject to the power provided to the Lord Chancellor to add services by direction, certain services are excluded and may not be funded. The most significant change in terms of volume is the exclusion of the provision of help in bringing or defending any proceedings for negligence where the alleged damage is to property or the person other than for clinical negligence.

The Lord Chancellor has given Guidance explaining the intentions underlying the excluded services.[82] The personal injury exclusion[83] does not exclude deliberate injury, e.g. by public servants, nor claims for intangible property. Claims for professional negligence for failure properly to commence or conduct a claim are not excluded. It is not clear whether this applies where the underlying claim was excluded, e.g. personal injuries. The Schedule excludes claims arising out of carrying on a business, on the premise that businessmen can insure. That seems reasonable. But it would extend claims by the self employed contractor who cannot always bring himself within an Industrial Tribunal's jurisdiction. Those within the jurisdiction will be eligible for support. The law in such matters can be complex and the consequences serious. It remains to be seen whether refusal of support will deny effective access in a deserving case.

The Lord Chancellor has made directions[84] authorising the LSC to fund in specific cirumstances services generally excluded from scope. This brings back in "cases that have a significant wider public interest and cases against public authorities alleging serious wrongdoing, abuse of position or power, or significant breach of human rights". This meets much of the criticism when the proposal was initially made to exclude from scope virtually all claims for damages.

The Funding Code sets out the criteria for decisions to fund. These will include new factors such as:

1. the availability to the individual of services not funded by the LSC and the likelihood of his being able to avail himself of them, and
2. the public interest.

The premise is that it is not a high priority for the Commission to provide funding where CFAs can provide satisfactory access to justice. This will create problems in cases where the LSC believes the person should be able to get a CFA but is told he cannot. How is the problem to be addressed? By way of further elaboration, in discussions with the Bar Council, the LAB has said that it starts from a premise of risk sharing with the lawyers in publicly funded civil claims for damages. Personal injury claims will only come into the scheme where they would be

---

[82] See *The Funding Code – Decision making Guidance*, para. 3.2
[83] See Schedule 2 of the Access to Justice Act 1999 for this and other exclusions
[84] See *The Funding Code – Decision making Guidance*, para. 3.3

difficult to take on a CFA. Three classes of cases have been identified as potentially entering the scheme: but – see below – even then only on a very limited basis.

1. cases with very high investigative costs, which may well then be expected to
   proceed on a CFA basis if favourable prospects emerge;
2. public interest cases: i.e. where individually the cost/benefit test is not met,
   but there is a range of other claimants who stand to gain;
3. cases with very high overall costs – because the commercial risk is too high
   for CFAs.

For cases with very high investigative costs the LAB accept they cannot expect
lawyers to take them on a CFA until they know the risk. If after an opinion in
favour of continuing, the case is then too costly to be a viable commercial risk
for the lawyers, the case can then continue within the scheme under the High
Cost Cases exemption.

However, the LSC will not give support unless investigative costs exceed a
given threshold. So unless the likely cost of investigating exceeds such threshold,
the lawyers will be expected to finance the investigation just to get to the starting gate. It remains to be seen whether in practice adequate support will be
available in needy cases. If the client cannot find lawyers prepared to take on his
case for the purpose of investigation, then it is submitted that he has arguably
been denied effective access to court.

A further difficulty is that the Lord Chancellor has said there will be an overall
budget for the provision of all legal services, criminal, family and civil. There will
be no cap on the criminal funding which will be demand led. The civil budget will
not be ring-fenced. How will services be provided if, as is likely, the criminal budget expands? Will priorities be revised mid-year, or funding for a deserving case
held over to the next year? Will this cause unreasonable delay? Will this lead to an
arbitrary and impermissible denial of effective access to justice?

Nonetheless we must not lose sight of the fact that Article 6 is a qualified
right, there is no express right to legal aid in civil cases in contrast to criminal
matters (Article 6(3)(c)) and this is an area where different states are more or less
generous in the provision of civil legal aid. We have seen that the notion of proportionality encompasses the fair balance to be struck between the general interests of the community and the interests of the individual.[85] Further, in *Fayed v
UK*,[86] the Court acknowledged that in laying down regulations which limit the
right of access "according to the needs and resources of the community and of
individuals", the state enjoys a certain margin of appreciation. Conversely,
however, the limitation must not impair the very essence of the right, nor will it
be compatible if there is not a reasonable relationship of proportionality
between the means employed and the aim sought to be achieved. In the light of
the Strasbourg position that permits economic resources of the state to be taken
into consideration, and which holds that the grant of legal aid to one party does

---

[85]   *Cossey v UK* (1990) 13 EHRR 622, para 41
[86]   (1994) 18 EHRR 393

not give a like entitlement to the other, it seems unlikely that changes in the scope of legal aid which exclude many but not all claims for damages but leave it for defendants whose means qualify them, will in *all* cases be held to be a breach of Article 6(1). But in individual cases the new criteria will fall to be tested on their merits against the Article.

For claimants for whom no legal aid is available in a damages claim there will still be the possibility of a lawyer funded by way of a CFA. It is now permissible for a lawyer to agree that he will not to seek to recover any fees unless an enforceable order for costs is obtained against the unsuccessful opponent. When the new provisions are in force which make any insurance premium and success fee recoverable from the unsuccessful defendant, then in straightforward cases with reasonable prospects of success, the claimant should be able to obtain legal assistance and not suffer undue deduction from his damages award. That would likely be held compatible with the procedural guarantees in the Convention.

It must be less certain however that widespread withdrawal of legal aid in damages claims will always be compatible. Consideration must also be given to the position of the individual of full capacity who has an apparently reasonable but expensive and complex claim for damages against, for example, a bank or a lawyer and whose predicament and impecuniosity are attributable to the negligence alleged. Such a claim may well be in the excluded category if it is deemed to arise out of the carrying on of a business so even a measure of litigation support will be unavailable. The Guidance[87] suggests that in individual cases support for an excluded case is most unlikely. What will he do if he cannot find lawyers to act who are prepared to risk not being paid? Can it not be argued that he has no *effective* access to the Court and is effectively unable to seek an adjudication or have a defendant account for his actions and omissions in adversarial proceedings. It may be said by the Government that he should have been insured. That may be reasonable in future, although most legal expenses policies impose limits on the amount and type of action they will underwrite, but someone whose disaster happened before the new legislation and who is uninsured will find that no comfort. The poor will never have been able to afford insurance in the first place. Might not *Airey* come to be extended in practical application? Life and litigation have become much more complex. The balance may be found to have tipped too far in favour of the institutional or corporate party.

The Government has said that it believes its long-term aim to remove legal aid from all damages claims will not breach the Convention. This surely remains open for debate.

5. THE HIGH COST OF PROCEEDINGS

No case has been admitted yet on the basis that the high cost of the proceedings may infringe the right of access but that does not mean that it will not.[88] The

---

[87] See *The Funding Code – Decision making Guidance*, para. 3.4.1
[88] *X and Y v Netherlands* No 6202/73, 2 *Digest Supp* 6.1.1.4.3.2.1., p.2 (1982)

English courts in *R v Lord Chancellor ex parte Witham*[89] have directly recognised in the context of court fees and the position of the needy that "Access to Justice" is a fundamental requirement of the rule of law and its imperative rests on the need for objective and independent adjudication of disputes between man and man, and man and the state. If therefore an applicant has a genuine dispute which he wishes to air before the courts the old saying that the courts, like the Ritz Hotel, are open to all will not suffice, at least not without qualification.

It must be remembered that the above cases apply to the level of lawyers' fees as well as the costs of the proceedings. It is questionable that the high cost of proceedings may affect the right of effective access if it deprives the applicant of the very essence of the right under the *Ashingdane* principle – see too *Airey*. This has implications for civil procedure and legal aid. The "overriding objective" (Civil Procedure Rules; CPR Part 1.1) and the new costs rules (CPR Part 44.3, 44.4, 44.5) are intended to improve access, but see the discussion below as to whether this will work to the advantage of the less well off.

6. COSTS

6.1. General Costs Rules

Where the substantive proceedings involve civil rights and obligations, the costs procedures must be seen as a continuation of the substantive litigation and hence within Article 6(1) even where they are decided separately. So the four years taken in the proceedings on the issue of costs disclosed a violation of the requirement that the state ensures that proceedings be concluded in a reasonable time.[90] There is no right to free proceedings or to a repayment of costs or fees in civil cases.[91]

Section 51 of the Supreme Court Act 1981, coupled with the Civil Procedure Act 1997, is the statutory basis for the courts' jurisdiction to make costs orders; the rules of court (CPR Parts 44 to 48) are made under the latter. The provisions and their implementation will fall to be considered in the context of compliance with the Convention. It seems likely that the courts in this country will continue along existing principles and if appealed to the Court will get the benefit of a margin of appreciation in an area where national practices vary widely. The Commission has held compatible the rule that costs ordinarily follow the event because it acts as a disincentive to unnecessary litigation and provides for the recovery of some of the successful litigant's costs.[92] The CPR encourage assessment and the making of orders for the immediate payment of interlocutory orders for costs. Whether orders for the immediate payment of costs will assist those with limited resources litigating against more powerful opponents is an

[89] [1998] 2 WLR 849
[90] *Robins v UK* 23 September 1997, in R.J.D., 1997-V, No 49 (1997) (costs)
[91] Italy No 15488/89, 80-A, MR 14
[92] 15434/89, UK (1990) 64 DR 232

open question. The rationale behind CFAs is that the client should not have to pay costs *during* the litigation. The CPR and relevant Practice Directions at the time of writing make no allowance for this. So a claimant on a CFA will have to meet any order for assessed costs regardless of ability to pay. It should be observed that the fact that an order might be made in favour of a party on a CFA is no comfort because his lawyers cannot look for payment of their costs until the case is successfully concluded. So there is no balancing factor in such cases. This opens up another area for Article 6 to be invoked.

6.2. Costs in Convention Cases

In the context of applications which raise directly a claim that there has been a violation the courts may tread more cautiously so as not to be seen to be deterring arguable and meritorious points from being taken. Thus there may well be a public interest in obtaining in a piece of litigation a declaration of incompatibility to prevent repetition and to lay down the law on a matter of wider importance. On the other hand, historically our courts have shied away from awarding the costs of an issue to someone who has nonetheless lost the substantive litigation. However the new CPR expressly provide for awards of costs on an issue by issue basis in appropriate cases. The best that can be suggested at the moment is that in the context canvassed above the Court may be reluctant to make an order for costs against the party whose rights were violated unless the issue was plainly otiose.[93]

6.3. Security for Costs

The requirement for security for costs at first instance has been upheld by the Commission.[94] But see *Ait-Mahoub v France*[95] for a contrary decision of the Court. In the context of appeals, an order for security is permitted where the purpose is the legitimate one of protecting a party from being faced with an irrecoverable bill of costs if the prospective appellant fails in his appeal, provided there has been a full and fair hearing at first instance and the court hearing the application for security has given the appellant the opportunity to argue his case for appealing. Thus in *Tolstoy*[96] a requirement for the appellant to put up £124,900 as security for the costs of the appeal was not held to infringe the right of effective access. The applicant had had a full hearing on the merits to which the Court of Appeal had paid regard when making the order.

[93] The Constitutional Court of South Africa has said that its Courts should be slow to make orders for costs against litigants seeking to enforce such rights: *Matsope v IRC* (1997) 6 BCLR 692 at 705
[94] *P v France* No 10412/83, 52 DR 268 (1990)
[95] (1998) 28 October, unreported, discussed at 3.3 above
[96] *Tolstoy Miloslavsky v United Kingdom* (1995) 20 EHRR 44

6.4. Wasted Costs Orders

Wasted costs orders have not been held in principle to concern the determination of civil rights or obligations and so not to obtain the protection of Article 6. Nor are they "criminal". The Commission has held such costs to be disciplinary in the context of the administration of justice and not to involve a "criminal" charge.

CPR Part 48.7(3) makes a radical inroad into the doctrine of privilege, the confidentiality of legitimate communications between lawyer and client and the client's right to privacy therein. It provides that when the Court is considering whether to make a wasted costs order, "for the purposes of this rule, the court may direct that privileged documents are to be disclosed to the court and, if the court so directs, to the other party to the application for an order". The rule change directly raises a Convention issue. This has already been addressed by the High Court and the rule has been struck down in *Mediterranean Holdings*.[97] There the defendants' solicitors applied for a direction under CPR 48.7(3) that privileged documents containing statements made by the defendants be disclosed to the Court, and if so directed to the claimant. The defendants' solicitors were respondents to an application by the claimant for a wasted costs order against them. The defendants resisted the application on the grounds, inter alia, that (i) CPR 48.7(3) was ultra vires; (ii) CPR 48.7(3) infringed Articles 6 and 8 of the European Convention on Human Rights, such that even if intra vires the Court should exercise its discretion by declining to make any order under it. Toulson J held (i) that rule 48.7 was ultra vires; (ii) he would not have exercised any discretion to order disclosure since the defendants had a right to confidentiality under Article 8 of the Convention in respect of their communications with their solicitors; the right to a fair trial conferred by Article 6 did not give the right to interfere with another person's right to legal confidentiality; moreover, it was doubtful whether an order for the disclosure of privileged material for purposes of wasted costs application was a necessary and proportionate measure for the purposes of doing justice to the legal profession. There will be no appeal in *Mediterranean Holdings*.

6.4.1. Article 8[98]

In this context the Court has stressed the importance of legal professional privilege – *Campbell v UK*.[99] In *Niemitz v Germany*[100] the Court expressly linked a lawyer's professional secrecy with the proper administration of justice under

---

[97] *General Mediterranean Holdings FA* (Claimant) v (1) *Ramanbhai Manibhai Patel* (2) *Kirit Kumar Ramanbhai Patel* (Defendants), [1999] 3 All ER 673

[98] See also chapter 11 on Confidentiality and Defamation for a full discussion of lawyer/client confidentiality in Strasbourg case law

[99] (1992) 15 EHRR 137

[100] (1992) 16 EHRR 97

Article 6. The House of Lords has recently held that the right to privilege is a substantive right, not just a matter of procedure.[101]

7. ARTICLE 5: RIGHT TO LIBERTY

7.1. Detention in a Civil Context: Entitlement to Legal Aid

Article 5 is concerned with detention. Detention can arise in civil proceedings in the context of committal for non-compliance with a court order. The right to liberty under the Convention is not absolute. But any deprivation must be effected in accordance with a procedure prescribed by law. This includes the procedure followed by a court when ordering detention.[102] In this context legal aid becomes relevant because of what is at stake for the individual – the loss of liberty which can arise in a civil context, e.g. committal. The list of exceptions to the right to liberty is exhaustive; because it is a list of restrictions to a right, it is given a narrow interpretation. Limitations must be lawful. This applies both to procedure and substance, which two requirements run together.

Article 5 (1) (b):

Detention is lawful "for non-compliance with a lawful order of the court". This makes it lawful to detain for civil contempt or failure to pay a maintenance order. But detention for non-compliance with a court order for the enforcement of a contractual obligation merely because the person has been unable to comply because of lack of funds would be in breach of Article 1 of the Fourth Protocol: "No one shall be deprived of his liberty merely on the ground of inability to fulfil a contractual obligation".[103]

Detention is lawful "in order to secure the fulfilment of any obligation prescribed by law". This covers detention to compel performance of a specific and concrete obligation which the person has failed hitherto to satisfy.[104] Such obligation must of course be consistent with the Convention, e.g. the obligation to make a tax return which is plainly necessary and appropriate in a democratic society.

In each of these two limbs of Article 5 (1) (b) there is a right to legal assistance; that is, when the application for detention is being sought and (per Article 5(4))[105] when application is made for release; these will give rise to a possible right to legal aid so that the right to legal assistance is an effective right.

---

[101] *R. v Derby JJ ex parte B* [1996] AC 487

[102] *Van der Leer v Netherlands* (1990) 12 EHRR 567

[103] Article 1 of the Fourth Protocol will not be incorporated under the Act. So if there is a breach the remedy will lie in Strasbourg before the Court and not in the domestic courts of the United Kingdom

[104] *Engel v Netherlands* (1976) 1 EHRR 647. Note: Article 5 (1)(b) does not extend to an obligation to comply with the law generally. It is not enough that the party is in breach of a civil obligation alone

[105] *"Everyone who is deprived of his liberty by arrest or detention shall be entitled to take proceedings by which the lawfulness of his detention shall be decided speedily by a court and his release*

By interaction with Article 6 legal assistance must be available when this is necessary for the remedy under Article 5 to be effective, for example a minor. Thus although proceedings to detain do not of themselves involve the determination of a person's civil rights and obligations under Article 6 (1), a person being detained in accordance with Article 5, e.g. on the grounds of mental disorder, is entitled to legal aid unless there are special circumstances to the contrary.[106]

8. CONCLUSION

Following the enormous changes wrought by the Access to Justice Act 1999 the precise nature of the categories of case to be excluded from Legal Aid altogether and the manner in which discretion as to its grant will be exercised, and the extent of the assistance provided, have yet to be worked out in practice. The Legal Services Commission will have to tread carefully. What might even a year or two ago have been thought to be "acceptable" might now be found to be violations of Article 6(1) following developments in the Court's greater readiness to examine the way in which states operate the grant of civil legal aid. Modern legislation is complex, the judges are heavily dependent on specialist advocates to keep them abreast of developments. The litigant in person, quite apart from often impeding and slowing the proceedings, often cannot, as the Court of Appeal has recognised with its *pro bono* support unit, be expected to put cases properly.

On the procedural front, the Civil Procedure Rules which require compliance with protocols and time limits are not, outside Fast Track, ideal for the litigant in person. The extent to which courts may legitimately cut down what one or both parties feel is necessary to a fair hearing will fall to be tested. The Court has historically allowed national courts a considerable margin in deciding what evidence may or may not be called[107] but recently have emphasised the right of the parties and not the Court to address what they reasonably believe to be in issue, so that saving time and expediting proceedings while of great importance do not justify disregarding the *fundamental* principle of the right to adversarial proceedings.[108] The incorporation of the Convention will likely have unexpected effects. The decision of the High Court in *Mediterranean Holdings*[109] already shows that the brand new Civil Procedure Rules are not sacrosanct. The full impact of the decision in *Osman* remains to be worked through. For those interested in access to justice and funding of litigation to achieve this aim, the way ahead is interesting and full of challenges.

ordered if the detention is not lawful". So there must be a right of recourse to the Court where a person has been deprived of liberty

[106] *Megyeri v Germany* (1992) 15 EHRR 584, see too 3.6 above
[107] *Dombo Beheer*, n. 53
[108] *Van Orshoven v Belgium* (1997) 26 EHRR 55
[109] N. 97 above

4

Horizontality: The Application of Human Rights Standards in Private Disputes

JONATHAN COOPER

1. INTRODUCTION

As has been made clear in the opening chapter, the Human Rights Act (HRA) will mark a watershed in the United Kingdom's constitutional framework and the relationship between the government and the governed. For the first time individuals in the United Kingdom will be able to rely upon positive and pre-scribed rights. As the Lord Chancellor, Lord Irvine of Lairg QC, has acknowl-edged, the Act is,

> "a constitutional change of major significance: protecting the individual citizen against erosion of liberties, either deliberate or gradual. It will promote a culture where positive rights and liberties become the focus and concern of legislators, admin-istrators and judges alike".[1]

The theoretical consequence of the Act's subtle balance between enforceable human rights standards and the guarantee of parliamentary sovereignty should be that the United Kingdom develops a rights-based culture, with all aspects of government engaging in their promotion. However, if civil society is also to embrace the full benefits of human rights, it too must be held to be accountable under the Act. An essential question which remains unresolved is the extent to which the Human Rights Act will apply in the regulation of affairs between pri-vate parties. Will the Act have horizontal as well as vertical application? In other words, will private individuals and/or companies be able to enforce their human rights against other private individuals and/or companies? Will the Act's scheme permit the rights contained within it to be enforced in private litigation? The concepts of horizontal and vertical application should be considered as the two extremes on a continuum, with a variety of approaches in between.

---

[1] Lord Irvine, "The Development of Human Rights in Britain under an Incorporated Convention on Human Rights" (1998) PL 221

These questions evidently raise profound philosophical issues. They go to the heart of what the application of human rights is all about. Are human rights principally concerned with limited and accountable government, or do they go beyond the individual's relationship with the state and require universal application? If human rights are an attempt to codify human psychology into law and, as such, are representative of the essential features of human identity and human dignity, surely the latter principle applies, and those standards should be applicable against any potential violator. Why then should it make a difference whether it is a private party who is interfering with defined human rights standards, or a representative acting on behalf of government? Human rights standards should of course be an essential safeguard against the abuse of state power, however, entities other than the state can undermine human dignity, and in a liberal democracy it is not only the state that holds power. Should multi-national corporations and the media, for example, also be held directly accountable?

If there is to be universal application of the HRA, beyond emanations of the Government, then additional questions need to be addressed. These are beyond the scope of this chapter, but would include the nature and level of scrutiny to be applied. The courts, for example, would probably be unwilling to interfere with the right to respect for correspondence in the home setting and would therefore apply nominal scrutiny, whereas an interference with prisoners' right to correspondence, particularly with their legal advisers, does require the strictest scrutiny.

This chapter will explore the practical potential for the HRA to be used in the regulation of conduct between private parties. It begins by seeking to define the relevant terms applicable to this horizontal application of human rights. After exploring the HRA's scheme and the statutory cause of action against public authorities, it then examines the scope of the Act and identifies how the Act might be used directly in private litigation. To support these arguments, the approach adopted by international tribunals, with particular reference to the Strasbourg Court, in their application of human rights standards is investigated. Finally, a brief survey of comparative jurisdictions is carried out to identify common themes.

2. DEFINING THE TERMS

The language used in this chapter, the horizontal and vertical application of human rights standards, is the traditional language of public international law. This geo-metric approach has been criticised as being inappropriate and unhelpful in the context of the HRA.[2] However, whilst those criticisms are valid, in

---

[2] In particular see Stephen Sedley in The Second Hamlyn Lecture, "Public Power and Private Power", *Freedom, Law and Justice* (London, Sweet & Maxwell, 1999), and Murray Hunt's paper to the JUSTICE/UCL seminar series, "Fundamental Human Rights Principles: Defining the Limits to Rights", to be published by Hart Publications

considering the practical application of human rights standards against private parties the stark language of horizontal and vertical application can be helpful. Therefore for the purposes of this chapter, which is principally concerned with how to apply the Act in those circumstances, the traditional language will be retained. The two terms can be broadly defined in the following way.

3. VERTICAL APPLICATION OF HUMAN RIGHTS STANDARDS: STATE ACTORS

A primary purpose of the HRA is to define the relationship between the government and the governed. It is a general principle of the enforcement of human rights standards that government, government agencies and agencies acting on behalf of government are required to act in a manner which conforms to those standards. Government actions or omissions are regulated to avoid abuse. Government is held accountable. This is generally termed the vertical application of human rights standards where a state actor is involved. Such emanations of government can be called to account in public law or private law proceedings. The vertical application of human rights can be defined in the following way: human rights govern relations only between the state, including public bodies and bodies exercising a public function, and the individual.

4. HORIZONTAL APPLICATION OF HUMAN RIGHTS STANDARDS: NON-STATE ACTORS

The principles underlying human rights also engage in situations beyond the relationship between those who govern and those who are governed. For example, following incorporation it will be unlawful for a local housing authority to discriminate against tenants or would-be tenants on grounds of their religion. However, what about the private landlords who refuse to house people they believe to be of a certain religion? Will those prospective tenants be able to sue successfully relying on the HRA? Will the Act create a new cause of action? Will a constitutional tort emerge?[3] Can a plaintiff rely upon the horizontal application of human rights between private parties, or non-state actors? The horizontal application of human rights can be defined as follows: human rights also govern all relations between private individuals and bodies.

5. APPLYING THE ACT TO STATE ACTORS

Without question, the HRA will apply to all public authorities, with the exception of the Houses of Parliament (except for the judicial committee of the House

---

[3] See discussion of *Simpson v Attorney General (Baigent's case)* (1994) 1 HRNZ 42 in chapter 5 on Remedies

of Lords). Section 6 of the Act clearly states the responsibilities of all public authorities to act in compliance with the Act and creates a statutory cause of action against them. This obligation of public authorities to act compatibly with the Act covers all the activities of those institutions from their employment practices to the public functions they carry out.

The definition of public authority is broad and Section 6(3)(b) includes agencies "certain of whose functions are functions of a public nature." Section 6(1) asserts "it is unlawful for a public authority to act in a way which is incompatible with a Convention right". Section 6(5) states that "In relation to a particular act, a person is not a public authority by virtue only of subsection (3)(b) if the nature of the act is private". Section 6(5) therefore defines the scope of the statutory cause of action.

It would appear plain that it is the Government's intention that Section 6 of the Act should bite against them, and the public actions, or omissions, of all state actors. Furthermore Section 7(1) and Section 8(1) of the Act which relate to proceedings and remedies respectively only refer to public authorities. The Government's White Paper, *Rights Brought Home*,[4] also only makes reference to new requirements for public authorities. It would appear, therefore, from a cursory glance at the Act that, on its face, it is intended, principally, to have vertical effect.

The Lord Chancellor at Second Reading acknowledged this. He said,

> "a provision of this kind should only apply to public authorities, however defined, and not to private individuals. That reflects the arrangements for taking cases to the Convention institutions in Strasbourg. The Convention had its origins in a desire to protect people from the misuse of power by the State, rather than from actions of private individuals . . . Clause 6 does not impose a liability on organisations which have no public function at all".[5]

The parameters of Section 6 raise abundant and fascinating arguments in relation to who, or what, is a public authority, or state actor – contracting out and privatisation may have blurred traditional distinctions. Similarly the nature of the function, power or duty which is under review will have increased importance in seeking to establish whether the section applies. However, whilst these considerations are essential in broadening, or limiting, the scope of Section 6 and the statutory duty to act compatibly with a Convention right, they do not settle the issue in hand which is the extent to which the HRA could be used to settle, when applicable, disputes between private parties.

---

[4] Cmd 3782, October 1997
[5] HL Deb, 13 November 1997, cols 1231–2

6. EXTENDING THE SCOPE OF THE ACT HORIZONTALLY[6]

It is well-established that the courts in the United Kingdom have already shown a willingness to develop private law, and the law of defamation in particular, in light of the Convention.[7] Once the Human Rights Act is in force, these principles will be strengthened. It was open to the Government in drafting the legislation specifically to attempt to exclude private parties from the scope of the Act. Other jurisdictions when introducing human rights legislation have sought to do this.[8] Whilst too much weight should not be attached to this omission, aspects of the Act indicate that it is intended to have, at the very least, some horizontal application.

6.1. Defining Courts as Public Authorities

What is likely to be decisive in ensuring that the Act is not limited to actions involving state actors is the definition of public authority. Section 6(3)(a) includes in its definition of a public authority "a court or tribunal". During the debates in the House of Lords, the Lord Chancellor explained the Government's understanding of the provision. He said:

> "We also believe that it is right as a matter of principle for the courts to have a duty of acting compatibly with the Convention not only in cases involving other public authorities but also in developing the common law in deciding cases between individuals . . ."[9]

A minimalist interpretation could be limited simply to requiring the courts to act in compliance with Article 6, the right to a fair trial, of the Convention. However, if this is the correct meaning, the inclusion of Article 6 (ECHR) in the schedule of the Act renders the sub-section redundant. A less restrictive interpretation of Section 6(3)(a) could be that the courts' obligations under the Act are limited only to the fact that they are not entitled to breach the Convention. For example, in the *Sunday Times v United Kingdom*,[10] the Strasbourg Court found against the United Kingdom because the domestic court had breached the Convention by granting an injunction.

---

[6] For a comprehensive analysis of the theory of horizontality, which includes an examination of the Human Rights Act, see Hunt, "The Horizontal Effect of the Human Rights Act" (1998) PL Autumn, 423

[7] *Rantzen v Mirror Group Newspapers* [1994] QB 670 and *John v Mirror Group Newspapers* [1996] 2 All ER 35. See chapter 11 on Confidentiality and Defamation for further discussion of constitutional rights in defamation cases

[8] See for example the section on Hong Kong p XXX below

[9] 6 HL Deb, 24 November 1997 col 783

[10] *Sunday Times v UK* (1979) 2 EHRR 245

The *Sunday Times case* concerned an article written in that newspaper which highlighted the situation of families affected by the Thalidomide drug. At the time the article was published, litigation was still on-going, but principally concerned quantum. In order to prevent the newspaper publishing a further article on the subject matter, the courts granted an injunction against the newspaper. They held that the injunction was to prevent contempt of court. The Strasbourg Court considered that under the circumstances such an interference with freedom of expression could not be justified.

Yet, if this interpretation of Section 6(3)(a) is accepted, in practice it could appear impossible to draw a distinction between, on the one hand, a breach of the Convention by one non-state actor against another and the Court subsequently upholding that breach or condoning it by failure to find a violation, and, on the other, the courts being asked to resolve a dispute between parties where as a result of its actions the Convention is breached.

Again, some assistance can be gleaned from *Hansard*. The Lord Chancellor has stated that

> ". . . We have taken the view that . . . excluding Convention considerations altogether from cases between individuals . . . would have to be justified. We do not think that would be justifiable; nor indeed do we think that it would be practicable".[11]

If a broad definition of Section 6(3)(a) is given and that section is interpreted to require the courts to decide all cases, where possible, in compliance with the HRA, what remains unresolved is the approach that the courts will take to this duty. Will the effect of Section 6(3)(a) be the creation of a common law cause of action, amounting, in effect, to a constitutional tort? Or will the HRA be limited to informing the existing common law only where a cause of action is already extant? Help in interpreting Section 6(3)(a) can be found in the case law of other jurisdictions with comparable provisions. For example, in relation to the New Zealand Bill of Rights, the courts have held that:

> ". . . the Bill of Rights also makes it clear that the Act applies to acts done by the Courts. The Act is binding on us, and we would fail in our duty if we did not give an effective remedy to a person whose legislatively affirmed rights have been infringed".[12]

6.2. The Interpretative Obligation

Further support that the Act is likely to have application to litigation between private parties comes from Section 3(1). That section requires that legislation (both primary and subordinate) is to be read to give effect, where possible, to Convention rights. Section 3(1) is not restricted to the actions of public authorities and therefore it is intended to have universal effect regardless of the parties

---

[11] 9 HL Deb, 24 November 1997 col 783
[12] See N. 3 above

involved. As such the law governing private actors is caught by the HRA, even if those actors themselves may not have a statutory duty to act in a way which is compatible with the Convention.

There should be no dispute that the Act will apply to all law, including the common law. As a matter of constitutional principle, the Act is governed by the doctrine of implied repeal; although the Act is unique in that it permits, under prescribed and limited circumstances, for it to be both extended and side-stepped. In his second Hamlyn lecture, Sir Stephen Sedley described the HRA as spreading through our laws like a dye though cloth.[13] This metaphor is particularly graphic and illustrative in explaining the way the Act will infuse the legal system. The specific reference to giving effect to primary and subordinate legislation in Section 3(1) relates only to the Act's scheme and the intention to preserve the principle of parliamentary sovereignty.

At a minimum, therefore, the Act will mean that all law will be required to be interpreted in the light of the Act. Inevitably there will be a radiating effect as rights permeate both the common law and legislation and litigation involving private parties. If this is correct, the inescapable conclusion must be that in private litigation where an appropriate court cannot give effect to a statute to comply with the Convention, it would be empowered to make a declaration of incompatibility under Section 4 of the Human Rights Act.

This self-evident tension was captured by the Lord Chancellor during the parliamentary debates. He acknowledged,

> "In my opinion, the court is not obliged to remedy the failure by legislating via the common law either where a convention right is infringed by incompatible legislation or where because of the absence of legislation – say privacy legislation – a convention right is left unprotected. In my view, the courts may not act as legislators and grant new remedies for infringement of convention rights unless the common law itself enables them to develop new rights and remedies. I believe that the true view is that the courts will be able to adapt and develop the common law by relying on the existing domestic principles in the laws of trespass, nuisance, copyright, confidence and the like, to fashion a common law right to privacy".[14]

It is not seriously in doubt that the Lord Chancellor's prediction will come true in relation to certain aspects of privacy law, where the English courts already appear "pen-poised" in their preparedness to develop a defined cause of action and consequent remedy for breach.[15] The incremental development of the common law, under such circumstances, as it is informed by Convention standards, is not therefore really contentious. However the Lord Chancellor's statement does not settle the issue when the courts are faced with a breach of Convention rights by a non-state actor where there is no apparent common law to develop. The obvious examples where such a lacunae in English law may exist being the

---

[13] Sedley, N. 2 above
[14] 10 HL Deb, 24 November 1997 col 785
[15] Lord Bingham of Cornhill, "Protecting the Right to Personal Privacy" EHRLR , 1996, p 450

right to freedom of thought, conscience and religion and, or, protection from discrimination.[16]

Under these circumstances if a state actor were engaged a cause of action (and remedy) would be available. The implication being that the HRA may end up providing differing levels of protection, including the untenable situation of offering illusory rights, but no remedy, which is, of course no right at all. For example, what if an aggrieved individual considers her or his rights have been interfered with by another private party, but that interference has no legal basis outside the Human Rights Act? Under these circumstances, all that individual could hope for is that the common law could be sufficiently flexible and then be adapted and developed to fashion a remedy, without giving the impression of legislating by way of the common law.

Pragmatically, it may be that the courts will feel that they have no choice but to approach the development of the common law and the application of the Convention in private law litigation step by step. This may involve developing new causes of action and remedies. Under these circumstances, the nature and extent of scrutiny that the courts will provide is likely to depend upon the seriousness of the violation of the right in issue. Whilst the principle is accepted that the courts should not assume the role of legislators, when they are faced with upholding rights guaranteed by Parliament or maintaining a deficiency in the common law, their duties under the HRA will require them to be pro-active. If they do not rise to this challenge, that responsibility will then remain with the human rights institutions in Strasbourg.

6.3. Positive Obligations

Additional arguments supporting horizontal application of human rights standards can be found in the Strasbourg jurisprudence. The case law of the Court and Commission lends further support for a wide application of human rights standards. The Strasbourg Court requires that all law is given a purposive and teleological interpretation.[17] This means that not only will the intention behind the legislation become more relevant, its interpretation by the courts will be examined in context and in light of the object and purpose of the law. As such, the Convention demands that, where possible, law is given an interpretation consistent with its principles. This approach to construction will inevitably create obligations in private litigation once the HRA is in force.

Positive obligations under the Convention can be found in the following circumstances: the duty to put in place a legal framework which provides effec-

---

[16] Although the right to protection from discrimination under the ECHR (Article 14) is not a free-standing right. Protection from discrimination is only guaranteed in relation to the substantive Convention rights

[17] *Cossey v UK* (1990) 13 EHRR 622. See also *Tyrer v UK* (1980) 2 EHRR 1 which recognised that the Convention should be seen as a "living instrument"

tive protection for Convention rights; the duty to prevent breaches of Convention rights; the duty to provide information and advice relevant to the breach of Convention rights; the duty to respond to breaches of Convention rights and the duty to provide resources to individuals to prevent breaches of their Convention rights.[18] As will be developed below, the Convention has also been interpreted by the Strasbourg Court as imposing positive obligations which includes regulating behaviour between private parties. Because of this positive obligation under the Convention to ensure access to rights, Section 6(6) of the HRA, which states that an "act" includes a failure to act but does not include a failure to introduce legislation, may, in due course, be found to be in breach by the Strasbourg Court. Section 6(6) of the Act is again more concerned with retaining the Act's scheme and not interfering with parliamentary sovereignty.

Furthermore, as the Lord Chancellor points out, human rights standards have their origin in the need to protect people from the misuse of state power. This does not, however, preclude their application between parties. If government has ultimate responsibility for all law, the logical extension of this argument must be that the HRA is relevant where any law or its application would result in a breach of a Convention standard, and not only where a state actor is involved.

7. THE APPROACH OF THE STRASBOURG AUTHORITIES

As a matter of public international law, only State Parties to the European Convention on Human Rights can be challenged before the Convention institutions. By definition, therefore, the possibility of applying the Convention between private parties is limited. However, this does not mean that the Convention should be considered as having no horizontal application. In reality, due to the status of the Court as a tribunal of public international law, the relationship between positive obligations and horizontal effect is blurred. There are however a number of ways in which the private abuse of human rights can and does apply.[19] These include when the state is held responsible for a private violation, due to its failure to legislate or take other preventative action,[20] where the Commission or Court decides that a particular body is an organ of the state or a private body,[21] where other Council of Europe human rights treaties are relevant. For example the European Convention on Transfrontier Television has resulted in the Strasbourg organs indirectly imposing duties on broadcasters and

---

[18] Starmer K., "European Human Rights Law", LAG, 1999
[19] These, and others, are identified by Andrew Clapham in *Human Rights in the Private Sphere* (Oxford, Clarendon Press, 1993) ppp 91–2
[20] *X & Y v Netherlands* (1986) 8 EHRR 235
[21] *Holy Monasteries v Greece* (1994) 20 EHRR 1

journalists,[22] and where the state is held responsible due to a domestic court sanctioning or failing to compensate a private violation.[23]

Strasbourg clearly recognises a positive obligation on the part of the state to guarantee Convention standards and if an applicant has no remedy due to a deficiency in domestic law, Strasbourg will find a violation. The Court made its position clear in relation to private parties in the case of *X and Y v The Netherlands*.[24] That case involved the lack of opportunites in the national law for mentally handicapped individuals in the position of the applicant to bring criminal proceedings for sexual abuse, although civil remedies existed. The Court categorically stated that, "these obligations may involve the adoption of measures designed to secure respect for private life even in the sphere of the relations of individuals between themselves".[25]

The Court developed their case law in this area in *A v United Kingdom*.[26] In that case the Court found that the United Kingdom had violated the applicant's right to freedom from inhuman and degrading treatment under Article 3 of the Convention. A child had complained that he was repeatedly hit with a stick by his stepfather with whom he lived. The stepfather was prosecuted and he successfully pleaded the defence of reasonable and moderate parental punishment to the charge of assault occasioning actual bodily harm. The Strasbourg Court found that the punishment reached the level of severity prohibited by Article 3, and concluded that the domestic law of the United Kingdom failed to provide adequate and effective protection against corporal punishment. Further examples of this approach by the Court is that they have not felt inhibited from dealing with rules governing membership of trades unions.[27] Neither have they shied away from dealing with issues involving private schools.[28] Under these circumstances the private body, i.e. the school, is considered to be carrying out a function that is properly the responsibility of the state.

A further example of the approach of Strasbourg to regulating conduct between private parties can be found in the Commission decision of *Spencer v the United Kingdom*.[29] Earl Spencer and Countess Spencer sought to argue an interference with their right to respect for private life following press reports concerning the Countess's health. In the event the Commission declared the application inadmissible because they found that the applicants did have a remedy for breach of confidence. However, they stated that

[22] See for example *Markt Intern and Beermann v Germany* (1989) 12 EHRR 161 and *Groppera Radio A.G. v Switzerland* (1990) 12 EHRR 321
[23] *Sunday Times v United Kingdom* (1979) 2 EHRR 245
[24] (1986) 8 EHRR 235
[25] Para 23
[26] (1999) 27 EHRR 611
[27] *Young, James and Webster v United Kingdom* (1982) 4 EHRR 38
[28] *Costello-Roberts v United Kingdom* (1993) 19 EHRR 112
[29] (1998) 25 EHRR CD113. See also discussion of this decision in chapter 11 on Confidentiality and Defamation

"the Commission would not exclude that the absence of an actionable remedy in relation to the publications of which the applicants complain could show a lack of respect for their private lives. It has regard in this respect to the duties and responsibilities that are carried with the right of freedom of expression guaranteed by Article 10 of the Convention and to Contracting States' obligation to provide a measure of protection to the right of privacy of an individual affected by others' exercise of their freedom of expression (see, mutatis mutandis, No. 10871/84, Dec. 10.7.86, D.R. 48, p.158 and no. 31477/96, Dec. 15.1.97, unpublished)".

Support for the approach adopted in Strasbourg can be found in the case law of other tribunals responsible for implementing international human rights treaties. For example, Article 26 of the International Covenant on Civil and Political Rights (ICCPR),[30] which guarantees a free-standing right to equality and protection from discrimination, almost certainly applies to private parties.

The UN Human Rights Committee, which interprets the ICCPR, has included in its definition of discrimination, ". . . any distinction, exclusion, restriction or preference which is based on any ground such as race, colour, sex, language, religion, political or other opinion, national or social origin, property, birth or other status, and which has the purpose or effect of nullifying or impairing the recognition, enjoyment or exercise, on an equal footing, of all rights and freedoms".[31] The Committee has then gone on to hold that the prohibition of discrimination and the obligation to protection refers to every form of discrimination. This has been interpreted as requiring the State Party to take affirmative action designed to ensure the positive enjoyment of rights.[32] States in their reporting procedure are frequently asked which positive measures, statutory and other, have been taken to counter existing discrimination.

Article 26 almost certainly requires protection and prohibition of the horizontal effects of discrimination. The General Assembly has pointed out that State Parties are obligated by Article 26 to stop discriminatory practices among private parties in the quasi-public sector of employment, schools, transportation, hotels, restaurants, theatres, parks, beaches etc. This means that when certain groups of people are persistently denied access to private restaurants, schools or transportation services on account of their race, colour or religion, then the State Party must ensure, by legislation or other measures, that such discrimination is stopped and prevented.

The International Convention on the Elimination of all forms of Racial Discrimination (CERD) makes specific reference to the horizontal application

---

[30] Article 26 states: "All persons are equal before the law and are entitled without any discrimination to the equal protection of the law. In this respect, the law shall prohibit any discrimination and guarantee to all persons equal and effective protection against discrimination on any ground such as race, colour, sex, language, religion, political or other opinion, national or social origin, property, birth or other status"

[31] GAOR/45/40 p 173, para 7

[32] GenC 18/37

of its provisions.[33] The Committee for the Elimination of Racial Discrimination (CERD) has also made it clear that it feels competent to decide questions of private discrimination.[34]

8. COMPARATIVE LAW

The response of other jurisdictions to applying human rights to non-state actors gives an indication of the approach which the courts in this country may take. The United States, Ireland, Hong Kong, Canada, The Netherlands, Germany, New Zealand and South Africa have all tackled the issue differently. This difference of approach is not surprising given the variations in the legal and constitutional bases for the enforcement of rights in each country. The following is a snapshot, a brief introduction and overview to the way in which the courts in each country have responded to the question of horizontality. It is not intended to be a definitive, or comprehensive examination. The analysis looks first at countries which apply a more traditional, vertical approach and then explores jurisdictions which have, to varying degrees, recognised that human rights have some horizontal application.[35]

8.1. Hong Kong

The Hong Kong Bill of Rights Ordinance 1991[36] provides as follows:

> 7(1) This Ordinance binds only –
> the Government and all public authorities; and
> any person acting on behalf of the Government or a public authority.
> (2) In this section –
> "person" includes any body of persons, corporate or unincorporate.

The Hong Kong Court of Appeal has held that the Ordinance cannot be used in litigation between private parties,[37] although more recently the High Court has interpreted "Government" to be the "legislative, executive and judicial organs of the State".[38] The fact that the courts are considered bound may extend the scope of human rights to private actors in due course.

---

[33] Article 2
[34] *Yilmax-Dogan v Netherlands* (CERD Communication no.1/1984), *L.K. v Netherlands* (CERD Communication no.4 /1991)
[35] The approach of the European Court of Justice and domestic courts to the horizontal application of European Community law and human rights principles has not been analysed. Whilst the importance of this area of law should not be under-estimated, it is too specialised and complex to begin to do it justice in a few paragraphs
[36] Ordinance No. 59 of 1991. This is based upon the ICCPR
[37] *Tam Hing-yee v Wu Tai-wai* [1992] 1 HKLR 185
[38] *Hong Kong Polytechnic University v Next Magazine Publishing Ltd* [1996] 2 HKLR 260

8.2. Canada

Section 32 of the Canadian Charter of Rights and Freedoms 1982 states that the Charter only applies to Parliament and the Government of Canada and to the legislatures and Government of each province. In the landmark decision of the Supreme Court, known as *Dolphin Delivery*,[39] it was held that the Charter applied to the common law and statute, but not between private parties. The Court held that for the purposes of the Charter the actors to whom it applied were the legislative, executive and administrative branches of government. They explicitly excluded a court order from the scope of government action.

Following the decision in Dolphin Delivery it is possible to identify the following applications of the Charter:

(a) A Charter argument can be properly raised if the party to private litigation bases their claim (or defence) on legislation, or an executive act;
(b) The Chapter applies to the common law in a dispute between the government and a private litigant;
(c) The Charter applies to the State in contract or commercial transactions; but
(d) In litigation between private parties no inconsistency between the Charter and the common law can be relied upon.

The impact of the decision in *Dolphin Delivery*, which has been re-affirmed,[40] is that whilst the common law must be interpreted in a manner which is consistent with the principles of the Charter and the values it enunciates, the courts must be cautious when amending the common law. In private litigation the Charter should be taken into account only on a case by case basis.

8.3. The United States

It is an accepted principle of United States constitutional law that the Constitution and Bill of Rights can only be enforced against state action. However, in a case involving a racist restrictive covenant on property, the US Supreme Court held that as the courts constituted state action, they could strike down the covenant on the basis that it offended against the Fourteenth Amendment.[41] It was this principle that enabled the Supreme Court to open up the law of defamation and free speech in the historic decision of *The New York Times v Sullivan*.[42] Of relevance to the approach adopted in the United States is

---

[39] *Retail, Wholesale and Department Store Union Local 580 v Dolphin Delivery* (1987) 33 DLR (4th) 174
[40] See *Manning et al v Hill* [1995] 2 SCR 1130, a case involving the common law cause of action of defamation
[41] *Shelley v Kraemer* 334 US 1
[42] 376 US 254

that their comprehensive civil rights framework is applicable against both state and non-state actors.

8.4. South Africa

The South African Constitutional Court, when deciding a case under the Interim Constitution, adopted a similar line of reasoning to the Canadian Supreme Court. In the leading decision on this question, *Du Plessis and Others v De Klerk and Another*,[43] the majority of the Court held that issue of horizontality was too important a matter to be left to be implied. Despite the fact that Section 7(i) of the Interim Constitution bound the legislative and executive organs of the state at all levels of government and that Section 7(ii) applies the Constitution to all law in force, the lead judgment by Kentridge J found that the failure of the Interim Constitution to make a specific reference to the judiciary could not be an oversight. He felt unable to equate a court judgment with state action. Kentridge adopted the reasoning of *Dolphin Delivery* and found that human rights standards should be taken into account, on a case by case basis, when dealing with private litigation under the common law. Kentridge too held that the constitution could not be used to strike down the common law, rather human rights should influence its development, but have no general horizontal application. To go beyond this interpretation, he considered, would extend the scope of the Constitution to virtually all private litigation.

Kriegler J, dissenting, held that the Interim Constitution governed not only the relationship between the state and the individual, but also governed relations between private individuals *wherever* (my emphasis) law is involved.[44]

Of significance is that the final Constitution of South Africa (which was adopted in 1996) was deliberately amended so as to give effect to Kriegler J's dissent in *Du Plessis*. The final Constitution makes it clear that it applies to all law and the judiciary is expressly bound.

8.5. New Zealand

The New Zealand Bill of Rights incorporates the substantive rights of the International Covenant on Civil and Political Rights (ICCPR). Section 3 applies the Bill of Rights "only to acts done (a) By the legislative, executive, or judicial branches of the government of New Zealand". The use of the word "only" in Section 3 would seem to seek to limit the Bill of Rights application. There has been a paucity of case law on the interpretation of Section 3, although it is clear

---

[43] [1997] 1 LRC 637

[44] The effect of the decision in *Du Plessis v De Klerk* was to lead the draftsmen of the Final Constitution to include the judiciary as one of the organs of state against whom constitutional challenges can be taken, a provision analogous to Section 6(3)(a) of the Human Rights Act

from *Baigent's case* that the courts consider themselves bound to act compatibly with the Convention, which can include fashioning new remedies.[45]

One High Court decision involving defamation held that the Bill of Rights was applicable to the common law.[46] The judge stated: "The application of the Act to the common law seems to me to follow from the language of Section 3 which refers to acts of the judicial branch of the government of New Zealand". The case was appealed and the Court of Appeal would appear to have approved this principle. In the absence of a judgment on point, the Bill of Rights is probably considered to have horizontal effect.

8.6. Germany

The German Constitutional Court has adopted the principle of *Drittwirkung* or the indirect application of human rights standards found in the German Basic Law. The theory of *Drittwirkung* is that although the Basic Law is not available in private law disputes, it does permeate or influence relations between individuals.[47] As such the German courts are obliged to take the Basic Law into account without searching for an element of state action. In applying constitutional norms to private law, the ordinary courts are expected to carry out a balancing act. The German Constitutional Court will only review a decision of a court if it gives a seriously wrong interpretation of constitutional rights guaranteed by the basic law.

8.7. The Netherlands

The theory of the Dutch Constitution is that there is a sliding scale concerning the application of human rights to private litigation depending upon the rights in question. However, in reality, the horizontal application of constitutional rights appears now to be taken for granted. In recent cases concerning the free press and privacy rights, the courts have not even sought to discuss the theory behind horizontal effect and their jurisdiction. Instead they have dealt straight with the substantive issues.[48]

8.8. Ireland

In relation to constitutionally protected rights, where appropriate to the rights concerned, the Irish Constitution has been interpreted to provide a direct cause

---

[45] See n. 3 above

[46] 24 *Lange v Atkinson* [1997] 2 NZLR 32

[47] See Markesinis, "Privacy, Freedom of Expression and the Human Rights Bill: Lessons from Germany" for a detailed exposition of *Drittwirkung* and a persuasive analysis of how such a concept should influence national courts under the Human Rights Act (1999) 115 *LQR* 47

[48] *Het Parool v Van Gasteren*, HR 6 Jan 1995, NJ 1995 nr 442

of action, or a constitutional tort. As such full horizontal application of constitutional rights which can be enforced between private parties exists, enabling individuals in private litigation to invoke directly constitutional rights as the source of their claim.[49] So, for example, when a (private) pregnancy counselling service advised women about abortion services in mainland Britain, it was injuncted under the constitutional provision concerning the right to life, the basis for the injunction being a constitutional tort. This was later challenged successfully in Strasbourg under Article 10 of the Convention.[50]

9. Conclusion

Adopting a strict construction of the HRA, it would seem unlikely that courts in the United Kingdom will, initially at least, recognise a private law cause of action under the Act. However, once the implications of the Act's scheme are more closely analysed and the approaches of other jurisdictions and the Strasbourg jurisprudence are taken into consideration, the Act's horizontal application becomes increasingly plausible and, arguably, inevitable. The case for limiting horizontal application rests principally upon traditional notions that human rights are there to constrain government and also that HRA Section 6(5) seeks to define the scope of Section 6(3)(b). However, these provisions only relate to Section 6 and the acts of public authorities. Beyond this, in terms of restraining the Act's application, it is silent. The Act does not attempt to limit its application as the Hong Kong, and even the New Zealand legislation has sought to do.

The HRA is to be used to interpret all law and only where a statute is blatantly inconsistent with it does responsibility fall on the executive and the legislature to review and amend legislation. Instrumentally, the HRA also specifically requires courts and tribunals to act compatibly with the Convention. The consensus from other jurisdictions with similar provisions is that such an application means that private law and private litigation are, as a consequence, governed by human rights standards. The South African experience is worth emphasising here. To make sure that constitutional human rights protection was not limited solely to the acts or omissions of government, without specific reference to the courts, the interim Constitution was amended in 1996 to ensure that the courts were also bound. Thus avoiding the Canadian system, where only the legislature and the executive are required to act compatibly and thereby limiting the Canadian Charter's application.

Additionally, as part of their duty to act compatibly with the Convention, courts may be required to carry out positive obligations to ensure compliance. This may mean that the common law is developed to give effect to the rights

---

[49] See *Meskell v Coras Iompair Eireann* [1973] IR 121
[50] *Open Door Counselling v United Kingdom* (1992) 15 EHRR 244

which Parliament has sanctioned. What is perhaps more persuasive is that the European human rights institutions, even within the constraints of their jurisdiction, have recognised principles of horizontality. As the HRA requires that United Kingdom courts take into account that jurisprudence, it would seem unlikely that they will not endorse the principle. The consequence if they do not, is that such cases will continue to be heard in Strasbourg and that Court will, under those circumstances remain the court of first instance.

Therefore, if the Human Rights Act is to have a degree of horizontal application between non-state actors, what remains uncertain is the nature of that application. Following the Dutch example, it may be that it will be an incremental process and in years to come full horizontality, including the creation of a new cause of action, will simply be taken for granted. What is probable, in the initial stages of its interpretation, is that the HRA will be used to inform private law and the common law in much the same way that the German Basic Law is considered relevant to all private litigation.

If horizontal application of the Act is limited, this in turn may prove to be highly unsatisfactory and could identify a fundamental flaw in its scheme. Although intending to give further effect to the Convention, the Act may not be guaranteeing effective access to rights. Returning briefly to the earlier example of the private landlord who refused accommodation on the grounds of religion, in the absence of an existing cause of action or a direct cause of action under the Act, the would-be plaintiff may have no opportunity to require the courts as public authorities to examine his or her claim of discrimination on the basis of religious freedom. In any event the courts cannot oblige Parliament to legislate. Our would-be plaintiff's only remedy may remain the long and slow road to Strasbourg.

However what would happen if our prospective tenants took possession of the property? Could they use the HRA as a defence to any claim against them? If the Act could be used as a defence, why not a cause of action? It is self-evident that this situation would be unsatisfactory. A bolder approach may be to argue that by accepting incorporation and the positive obligations that flow from it, that we have, in effect, created a de facto common law cause of action, or a constitutional tort, and that to argue otherwise is an unsustainable fiction.

5

Remedies

ROSALIND ENGLISH

1. NEW REMEDIES

When the Human Rights Act comes into force, it will be much applauded (as it already has been) as an enlightened move for our legal system, an enforceable obligation on us to be nice to each other. But really the question on everybody's lips will be: what is there in it for me? Will the Human Rights Act be a new source of tax-free windfalls for happy claimants, or will it simply serve to bolster pre-existing common law claims, in which case, why bother? The following pages set out to explore the potential for novel remedies, drawing on the committee debates during the legislative process and some of the Strasbourg jurisprudence on remedies – in so far as these can provide any guidance to litigants and their lawyers, calculating the financial benefits of running a Convention claim.

The Human Rights Act provides for two main remedies for violations of Convention rights. In respect of primary legislation which is inconsistent with the Convention, it is possible for a court to grant a declaration of incompatibility. This applies where the public authority, by obeying Convention-incompatible primary legislation, has acted in breach of Convention rights.

Subordinate legislation, decisions or acts of a public authority that are unlawful because they breach Convention rights may lead to a range of awards already available in public law, such as declarations and injunctions. In addition, the courts have the jurisdiction to grant damages, where appropriate, notwithstanding the fact that the unlawful activity in question did not sound in damages before the Human Rights Act came into force.[1]

For compensating victims of this unlawful activity national courts are required to have regard to the remedial jurisdiction of the Strasbourg Court under Article 41 (formerly Article 50) of the ECHR. As will be evident from the following pages, Strasbourg damages awards tend to be modest. The Government clearly does not want Convention rights to be seen as a *milchcow* for lottery style damages awards, and by directing the national judiciary to take

---

[1] By virtue of the rule in *X (Minors) v Bedfordshire County Council* [1995] 2 AC 633

Strasbourg figures into account in their calculations, the draftsmen of the Bill
have sought to thwart such a development.[2]

There is also evidence that the proponents of the Bill hoped to neutralise any
judicial temptation to forge new remedies under the Act by excluding Article 13
from the incorporated rights.[3] The decision not to incorporate Article 13 has
been much debated in Parliament and in the academic literature following
Royal Assent, and a quick perusal of the select committee debates provides a
clue as to what the Government hoped incorporation of the Convention would
achieve, or rather not achieve, by way of new remedies. Before looking into
Hansard, however, it is worth considering the scope and reach of this Article as
it is analysed by the Strasbourg Court.

2. ARTICLE 13

If the claim of a violation is "arguable", Article 13 requires that the applicant
must have an opportunity to have it decided by an appropriate competent body,
and if necessary, redress should be available. The tests for "arguability" is the
same as that applied by the Commission to determine whether a claim is "manifestly ill-founded".[4]

The authority which hears the complaint need not be judicial, but it must be
competent to guarantee respect for that particular right. So, for example, the
opportunity of complaint to the Chief Ombudsman in Sweden was held to satisfy the requirements of Article 13 even though his recommendations are not
binding.[5] That is because the ombudsmen's decisions are held in high esteem
in Scandinavian jurisdictions. The same cannot be said of decisions of the
Parliamentary Commissioner for Administration and the local government
ombudsmen in this country; indeed, a complaint that local authorites' immunity
from suit under the rule in *X v Bedfordshire* which has been ruled admissible by
the Commission, includes a claim that the availability of a complaints procedure
to the local government ombudsman does not fulfil the requirements of Article
13.[6]

Article 13 does not require any specific remedy, although an aggregate of
remedies available at a national level may satisfy it.[7] But this remedy, or accu-

---

[2] See the Lord Chancellor's comments in "Address to the Third Clifford Chance Conference on
the Impact of a Bill of Rights on English Law" in *The Impact of a Bill of Rights on English Law* (ed.
Markesinis) (1998) Chapter 2

[3] Article 13 provides that anyone who has suffered a violation of their Convention rights "shall
have an effective remedy before a national authority notwithstanding that the violation has been
committed by persons acting in an official capacity"

[4] *Boyle and Rice v United Kingdom* (1988) 10 EHRR 425. However, the Court is not bound by
the Commission's finding that a claim is manifestly ill-founded, to find that that claim is unarguable;
it will apply its own test

[5] *Leander v Sweden* (1987) 9 EHRR 490

[6] *K.L. v United Kingdom* Application No 29392/95, May 26 1998

[7] *Klass v Germany* (1994) 2 EHRR 214

mulation of remedies, must be effective. In a group of judgments concerning human rights violations by agents of the state in Turkey, the Court has held that Article 13 imposes an obligation on states to provide individuals with an opportunity, through proper investigative proceedings, to determine whether there has been a violation of their rights under the Convention.[8]

The Government claims that it has fulfilled all these Article 13 obligations by incorporating the Convention into domestic law. In any event, if Article 13 were to be included in the Schedule to the Act, said Lord Irvine,

> "The courts would be bound to ask themselves what was intended beyond the existing scheme of remedies set out in the Bill. It might lead them *to fashion remedies other than the Clause 8 remedies*, which we regard as sufficient and clear".[9]

It was pointed out in the committee debates that Section 8 does not cover all situations that might be addressed by Article 13. The exclusion of Article 13 means for example that there will be no basis for complaint before domestic courts under the incorporated Convention where primary legislation is at stake, the Court has granted a declaration of incompatibility, but the minister responsible has failed to take any, or adequate action.

Article 13 also has implications for the Access to Justice reforms. Although the Strasbourg Court has hitherto refused to rule directly on the compatibility with the convention of civil legal aid systems in Contracting States,[10] if Article 13 had been incorporated it might have been used as a basis for the argument that the Government was under an obligation to do away with various obstacles in the way of litigants coming to court to seek a remedy at all. This matter was also raised during the committee stages of the Human Rights Bill. Such obstacles, it was suggested, would include crippling court fees and the substitution of contingency fees in most cases for legal aid. The question of funding for human rights cases has not yet been settled, although the Access to Justice Bill and the Draft Funding Code propose a test for "public interest cases" which will qualify for assistance. The threshold is a high one and public funding will only be provided for the sorts of actions which are likely to produce real benefits for a significant number of other people, or cases which raise "an important new legal issue". Proposed Human Rights Act points which do not reach this threshold will have to be litigated under the contingency fee system, the application of which, suggested Lord Ackner,

---

[8] *Aydin v Turkey* (1998) 25 EHRR 251. The implications of this ruling for environmental law are explored in chapter 10 on Environmental Rights; and in chapter 8 on Medical Law Philip Havers and Neil Sheldon consider its implications for inquests

[9] 18 November 1997, *Hansard* HL debates col 472

[10] *Airey v Ireland* (1981) 2 EHRR 305: although the Court has frequently reiterated that there is no right as such in the Convention to receive legal aid in cases concerning civil rights and obligations, this case is one of the rare instances where the Court has found that the lack of legal aid did amount to an unlawful denial of the applicant's right of access to court. This principle has been confined by the Strasbourg authorities in subsequent cases to the particular facts of the case; it involved complex separation proceedings, only available via a High Court action, and therefore the applicant could not in reality have taken action as a litigant in person

" is totally absurd to this litigation which will be uncertain and which will not in many cases ask for damages, but if they are obtained, they are so small that with the cap applied to them they will attract no solicitor".[11]

In any event, if the exclusion of Article 13 was meant to limit the development of new remedies under the Act, there is no reason to suppose this ruse will work. In committee, Lord Irvine suggested that the obligation under Section 2(1) of the Human Rights Act on courts to "take into account" relevant Strasbourg jurisprudence includes the Court's jurisprudence under Article 13.[12] He may come to regret these words, disclosable under the rule in *Pepper v Hart*, when a claimant alleges that in addition to suffering a violation of some incorporated Convention right, he or she has also been deprived of a proper remedy under Article 13. Such a scenario has already been foreshadowed by *Lustig Prean and others v United Kingdom*.[13] Here the applicants, servicemen who had been dismissed from the armed forces on the grounds of sexual orientation, argued successfully that not only had they suffered a violation of private life under Article 8, but that the judicial review proceedings which provided the only redress for their claim in English law, fell short of "an effective remedy" under Article 13. The Court upheld this reasoning, declaring that judicial review does not enable the domestic court to consider the merits of the complaint that Convention rights have been breached, as Article 13 requires. So in future domestic cases, where claimants allege, for example, that they have been denied a fair trial (contrary to Article 6) in conjunction with some other Convention right, the court hearing these conjoined claims will be bound to consider, did the intitial proceedings provide an adequate remedy according to the Strasbourg jurisprudence under Article 13? If it reaches the conclusion that they did not, the remedy granted will take into account the breach of Article 13, as well as the other rights, notwithstanding the fact that it has not been incorporated.

Article 13 aside, the broad equitable jurisdiction granted to the courts by Section 8 of the Human Rights Act to award damages is likely to extend to wrongs hitherto unrecognised by the common law, or claims where no injury has been caused other than the applicant's distress at the violation of his or her rights by a public authority.

3. DECLARATIONS OF INCOMPATIBILITY

The Human Rights Act does not permit direct challenges to Convention-incompatible provisions of primary legislation. In the White Paper "Rights Brought Home"[14] the Government explained that it had:

---

[11] Lord Ackner, loc.cit., above text at 2. Article 13
[12] See Lord Irvine's response to Lord Lester at *Hansard* HL debates, 18 November 1997 col 475: ". . . the courts may have regard to Article 13. In particular, they may wish to do so when considering the very ample provisions of [s.8(1)]."
[13] Applications No 33985/96 and 33986/96, 27 September, 1999
[14] Cm 3782, para 2.13

"reached the conclusion that courts should not have the power to set aside primary legislation, past or future, on the ground of incompatibility with the Convention. This conclusion arises from the importance which the government attaches to Parliamentary sovereignty".

Instead, they came up with a compromise. Section 3 of the Act obliges courts to interpret primary as well as secondary legislation in a way that is compatible with the Convention. Where this is not possible, an application may be made under Section 4 for a "declaration of incompatibility". The Crown will be notified of any such application and may join as a party to the proceedings to contest the claim. A declaration of incompatibility, if granted, may lead to a "remedial order" under Section 10 by which the minister responsible for the legislation in question will pass subordinate legislation to override the offending clause. A "fast track" procedure of sixty days followed by a positive resolution of both Houses of Parliament is provided for by Section 12 of the Act.

However, Section 6(6) states that no liability will arise under the Act for failure to introduce in, or lay before, Parliament a proposal for legislation, make any primary legislation or remedial order. In addition, Section 4(6) provides that a declaration of incompatibility does not affect the validity, continuing operation or enforcement of the offending provision, nor is it binding on the parties to the proceedings in which it is made.

However artfully these provisions appear to sidestep the problem of parliamentary supremacy, it is evident that the procedure relating to declarations of incompatibility is replete with uncertainties and potential injustices. Successful litigants, armed with their declarations, may have to wait for an unpredictable length of time for the legislation to be amended in this way, particularly where the challenge to primary legislation is controversial and may not enlist sufficient crossbench support to win the necessary approval from both Houses of Parliament (after all Section 10 of the Act imposes on the minister only a power, not a duty, to introduce remedial legislation). This might have grounded an Article 13 claim and could still form the basis of a complaint to Strasbourg.

In any event, it seems that even before the operative provisions of the Human Rights Act were due to come into force, lawyers had found ways to circumvent the bar on direct challenges to primary legislation. In *R v Director of Public Prosecutions ex parte Kebilene*[15] a declaration was granted against the DPP in respect of his decision to continue with prosecutions under the Prevention of Terrorism (Temporary Provisions) Act 1989. He was said to have acted unlawfully by disregarding a legally relevant consideration when considering the public interest in pursuing the prosecution, the consideration being that the convictions would in all likelihood be overturned when the Human Rights Act incorporates the presumption of innocence under Article 6. The Divisional Court's ruling on this issue was overturned by the House of Lords,[16] who ruled

[15] [1999] 3 WLR 175
[16] [1999] 3 WLR 972

that such challenges in satellite litigation to primary legislation should not be allowed, since the Human Rights Act, when it is in force, would prevent such attack. As Lord Hobhouse observed,

> "The scheme of the Human Rights Act is that no decision of the courts can invalidate an Act of Parliament. Under s.4(2) a court . . . may, if satisfied that a provision of an Act of Parliament is incompatible with a Convention right, make a 'declaration of that incompatibility'. But, by s.4(6), such a declaration '(a) does not affect the validity, continuing operation or enforcement of the provision in respect of which it is given; and (b) is not binding on the parties to the proceedings in which it is made'. S.3(2)(b) contains a similar reservation of validity. *Thus, incompatibility does not found any right under the Act*".

Notwithstanding the lukewarm response they received in the Lords, Kebilene's arguments which proved so successful in the Divisional Court foreshadow many future challenges, via judicial review, to the *vires* of a public authority pursuing a course of action under primary legislation, without the need to seek a declaration of incompatibility. If the enforcement of primary legislation can be thus stopped in its tracks, the primary legislation itself is effectively rendered a nullity.

4. DAMAGES

The Human Rights Act does not impose any general damages liability for violations of the Convention. Instead, Section 8 enables a court to grant such relief as it considers "just and appropriate". In exercising their broad remedial discretion under this section, national courts must take into account the principles applied by the Strasbourg Court in relation to the award of compensation under Article 41 of the Convention, which provides that the Court may order "just satisfaction to the injured party" if the internal law of the offending Member State only allows "partial" reparation to be made. This of course will not prejudice an appropriate personal injury or other award, which would be available before British courts otherwise than under the Human Rights Act (Section 11(b)).

4.1. Strasbourg Awards under Article 41

Compensation may be awarded both for "pecuniary" damage, in other words financial loss consequent on a breach of a Convention right that can be quantified; and for "non-pecuniary loss", known in civil law systems as "moral damage" and in this country as "general damages".[17] In all the other cases the Court said that a finding of a violation constituted sufficient redress.

---

[17] A recent survey has shown that from 1991–5 pecuniary damages were sought in 22 cases and only awarded in 8. Non-pecuniary damages were sought in 24 cases, but awarded only in 10

4.1.1. Awards for Pecuniary Damage

If the loss is proven and quantifiable, the Court will grant an appropriate figure. Where the projected loss is conjectural or hypothetical, the Court is reluctant to allow compensation. There is no principled loss of chance jurisprudence to Strasbourg. It is not therefore foreseeable whether the Court in a 30 per cent chance case will grant 30 per cent damages or nothing at all.

So, for example, in *Matts Jacobssen v Sweden*[18] the applicant complained that he was unable effectively to challenge administrative changes which affected his building interests. The Court held that although lack of such rights violated Article 6 of the Convention it did not follow that if he had had such rights he inevitably would have been able to preserve his building interests. Therefore no award was made.

In contrast to *Matts Jacobssen*, in an earlier planning case, also against Sweden,[19] the Court accepted that a planning restriction which had prohibited development for twenty years had affected the applicants' ability to raise loans by way of mortgages, and during that time they had been unable to refurbish or develop the buildings. They had therefore sustained a loss of opportunity – even though the restriction had been lifted at the time of the hearing and the value of the land had not decreased. Above all, the applicants were left in prolonged uncertainty as they did not know what the fate of their properties would be. To those factors had to be added the non-pecuniary damage occasioned by the violation of Article 6(1) – the applicants' case could not be heard by a tribunal competent to determine all the aspects of the matter. The applicants thus suffered damage for which reparation was not provided by the withdrawal of the expropriation permits, and they were awarded a rule of thumb figure of £100,000.

It is important to note, however, that that element of the award was non-pecuniary. It is rare that the procedural failing is seen as causative of pecuniary loss following on the subsequent conviction or sentence, or from the decision affecting civil rights or obligations. In *Saunders v United Kingdom*[20] for example, a claim for the loss of £3,668,181.37 in salary by the applicant who said he had lost his job as a consequence of the denial of his privilege against self-incrimination was rejected. The Court underlined that the finding of a breach of the Convention could not be taken to carry any implications as regards the likely outcome of the trial, had it not breached the presumption of innonence guaranteed by Article 6.

On the other hand, in *Barbera, Messegue and Jabardo v Spain*[21] following a finding of a violation of the applicants' fair trial rights due to a number of

(although all these were successful on the merits). See Mowbray's analysis of the case law on damages in Strasbourg "The European Court of Human Rights Approach to Just Satisfaction" [1997] *PL* 647

[18] (1990) 13 EHRR 79
[19] *Sporrong and Lonnroth v Sweden* (1984) 7 EHRR 256
[20] (1997) 23 EHRR 313
[21] (1988) 11 EHRR 360

defects in criminal proceedings against them, the Court accepted their claim for loss of earnings whilst they had been in prison, based on the minimum salary for their respective fields of employment plus one million pesetas (approximately £4,100) for loss of career prospects, plus increase by retail price index.

In *Open Door Counselling and Dublin Wellwoman v Ireland*[22] the applicant had been forbidden, in breach of Article 10, from providing pregnancy counselling. Although it was a non-profit making organisation it claimed loss of earnings of IR £62,172 for the period January 1987 to June 1988 due to the discontinuance of the service. The Court considered that even a non-profit making company such as the applicant can incur losses for which it should be compensated. It awarded IR £25,000 under Article 50.

There must be a direct causal link between the damage and the particular Convention right that has been violated. A woman who was forced to move out of her house because of threatened molestation by her husband could not claim the financial loss she had suffered (she might otherwise have been able to buy out her former home. Her move was not a consequence of the denial of her access to court to obtain judicial separation (which had been held to be a breach of her rights under Article 6). Even if she had obtained a separation decree she remained at risk of molestation. Therefore her loss was not related to the breach of her Convention rights.[23]

4.1.2. Awards for Non-Pecuniary Damage

Sometimes the Strasbourg Court awards a global figure under Article 41 without distinguishing between pecuniary and non-pecuniary loss. Before looking at some of the awards made under individual Convention rights, a couple of points are worth noting. The Court tends not to make non-pecuniary damage awards to companies[24] and claims for non-pecuniary damage by the press in consequence of a finding that their rights to freedom of expression have been violated are usually rejected. Awards are also not usually made to applicants whom the Court finds to be unsympathetic, such as terrorists or convicted criminals.

Article 2: Right to Life

In the first case to reach the Court on the right to life where the claim was upheld (albeit by a narrow majority of ten votes to nine) the Court found that Article 2 had been violated by an SAS anti-terrorist operation in Gibraltar, resulting in the deaths of three suspected IRA terrorists. Although the Court ordered the Government to pay some of the applicants' legal costs, it refused compensation for the victims' families stating that the finding of a violation was sufficient.[25]

---

[22] (1993) 15 EHRR 244
[23] *Airey v Ireland* (1981) 3 EHRR 305
[24] *Manifattura v Italy* February 27, 1992 Series A No. 230-B. Here the Court expressed doubts that a company could suffer moral damage
[25] *McCann v United Kingdom* (1996) 21 EHRR 97

Article 3: Inhuman and Degrading Treatment

Successful claims under this Article do not often raise difficult issues of causation. So for example, in *Sur v Turkey*[26] 100,000 francs were awarded plus legal costs for lesions inflicted during custody, from blows from sticks and electric shocks. Even if the ill-treatment has not been proved before the national courts, the Strasbourg Court will make an award for non-pecuniary damage if it finds that the alleged treatment satisfies the high threshold required by Article 3; so in *Aydin v Turkey*[27] £25,000 was awarded in respect of alleged rape and ill-treatment of the applicant while she was being detained by the gendarmerie, leading to a finding of a violation under Article 3.

The Court tends not to award damages for extradition and deportation cases where the applicant risks treatment in breach of Article 3 in the receiving state, stating that the finding of a violation is just satisfaction in itself.[28] This is because these applications tend to be anticipatory and the Court can make an interim order suspending the proposed government action. If the deportation has already taken place, damages may well ensue.

Article 5: Interference with Liberty of the Person

Compensation for non-pecuniary damage has been awarded to applicants who have been subject to excessive periods of detention[29] and to the victims of physical assault whilst in police custody.[30] Although national awards for false imprisonment often include an element for exemplary damages, this is a concept which is alien to the Strasbourg Court, since its remedial jurisdiction is drawn from the systems of most Contracting States which do not recognise exemplary damages. However, it is not impossible to discern a punitive or deterrent element in some of the awards made under Article 5; for example *Bozano v France*,[31] where the Court awarded 100,000 French francs (approximately £11,000) for only twelve hours' detention. The majority held that the respondent state had violated the applicant's rights to liberty and security under Article 5(1) by using their deportation procedures as a disguised form of extradition designed to circumvent a negative ruling by a French court. In the light of this abuse of procedure and the seriousness of consequence for the applicant (he faced the death sentence in Italy), the Strasbourg Court held that the compensation awarded him by the respondent government of 1,000 French francs had been inadequate.

---

[26] October 1997 RJD 1997-VI No 5
[27] (1998) 25 EHRR 251
[28] *Soering v United Kingdom* (1989) 11 EHRR 439; *Chahal v United Kingdom* (1997) 23 EHRR 413
[29] *Yagci and Sargin v Turkey* (1995) 20 EHRR 505
[30] *Ribitsch v Austria* (1995) 21 EHRR 573
[31] (1986) 9 EHRR 297

Article 6: Denial of Due Process

Awards are routinely made for prejudice suffered as a result of overlong legal proceedings in breach of Article 6. In *Konig v Germany*[32] the applicant had been forced to suspend his medical practice pending proceedings concerning his qualifications which ran on for more than ten years. He was forced to defer unduly the search for an alternative career; the anxiety and inconvenience merited an award of DM 30,000 (approximately £3,000). Another applicant was "detrimentally affected" by having to wait nine years for his divorce proceedings to go through in breach of his Article 6 rights and the Court awarded him £4,000.[33]

There are a number of cases concerning breach of Article 6 in respect of claims for compensation, largely made against France by patients who have contracted AIDS as a result of state sponsored blood transfusion schemes. Compensation proceedings have been found to concern the determination of civil rights within the meaning of Article 6, as the outcome would be decisive for private rights to damages for injuries. Where the claims have taken over two years to process, the Court has ruled the delay unreasonable (because particular expedition is required in the case of a terminally ill patient) and it has ordered the payment of compensation of up to 200,000 French francs to the victims or their families, if the victim has since died.[34]

Compensation has been awarded to persons who have experienced a loss of opportunity to represent their interests fully because the bodies determining their cases did not comply with the procedural safeguards under Article 6, particularly where parents have been denied participation in care proceedings. Even if the Court is doubtful as to whether the denial of due process has made any difference to the applicant's affairs, it will sometimes grant an award on the speculation that the applicant might have enjoyed a more favourable outcome. It is easier to claim non-pecuniary damages in speculative cases than it is to obtain a pecuniary award. So, in *O v United Kingdom*,[35] the Court considered that if the applicant had been able to have the question of his access to his children reviewed by a court, he might have obtained some degree of satisfaction. The Court also accepted that the applicant had suffered from feelings of frustration and helplessness warranting monetary compensation. Damages of £5,000 were awarded. (See also awards made under Article 8 in this context, below). In *Delta v France*[36] the applicant, who was imprisoned for six years as a result of a trial where he was deprived of an opportunity to cross-examine his accusers in breach of Article 6, was awarded non-pecuniary damages of £12,000 even though the Court "could not speculate as to the outcome of the trial if [the applicant] had had the benefit of all the guarantees of Article 6" . In *Perks and Others*

---

[32] (1978) 2 EHRR 170
[33] *Bock v Germany* (1989) 12 EHRR 247
[34] *X v France* (1992) 14 EHRR 483; *Vallee v France* (1994) 18 EHRR 549 and *Karaka v France* (1994) Series A No. 289-B
[35] *O v United Kingdom* (1988) Series A No. 136A
[36] (1990) 16 EHRR 574

v United Kingdom[37] the Court awarded £5,500 to an individual who had been sentenced to imprisonment for non-payment of the Community Charge in magistrate's court proceedings where, in the Court's opinion, he should have been legally represented, thus suffering a breach of Article 6(1) and (3)(c) together.

In *Zander v Sweden*,[38] the applicants were held to have suffered a breach of their Article 6 rights when the respondent state refused to allow them to challenge the grant of a permit to dump refuse. They each claimed 250,000 Swedish kronor for non-pecuniary damage. They maintained that, through fear of pollution of the well, they had to collect drinking water elsewhere; they feared that the value of their property had fallen considerably and they also claimed that being denied access to a court aggravated the distress which they had suffered for over ten years as a result of fear of pollution. The Court considered that sufficient just satisfaction would not be afforded solely by the finding of a violation. The applicants were awarded 30,000 Swedish kronor (about £2,300) each.

The Court is readier to grant non-pecuniary damages in these speculative cases than it is to accept pecuniary claims. In *Fredin v Sweden*[39] a claim for pecuniary loss of 28 million Swedish kronor (approximately £215,000) for revocation of a gravel exploitation licence, when there was no recourse to a judicial authority to dispute the lawfulness of the revocation in breach of Article 6, was rejected. The revocation of the permit did cause the applicants "considerable loss" but the Court refused to speculate as to what result they would have achieved had they been able to bring their case before a court. The Court did accept that the absence of an adequate court remedy had caused non-pecuniary loss and awarded a global figure of 10,000 kronor (about £800).

Sometimes the lack of a public hearing may provide a basis for an award even where the applicant's substantive claims fail; in *Helmers v Sweden*[40] the applicant, a university lecturer, claimed damage to his reputation under Article 8 and discriminatory treatment under Article 14. These were rejected but he was awarded 25,000 kronor (approximately £2,000) for the lack of opportunity to air these claims in court, having regard to the effect of these issues on his career.

These Article 6 cases illustrate an important aspect of Strasbourg remedial case law which is bound to have some effect on the domestic approach to such questions. As we have seen, the Court is reluctant to uphold claims for loss of opportunity where the link between the denial of a fair trial and the loss is speculative. But it is all too willing to grant non-pecuniary damages for feelings of frustration and despair suffered by the applicant when deprived of Article 6 rights. This contrasts vividly with the British position under which the courts, unless specifically enjoined to do so (for example, by discrimination legislation), do not allow damages for feelings of frustration and anger. So, for example, damages for wrongful dismissal cannot include compensation for the manner of

---

[37] October 12, 1999, unreported
[38] (1994) 18 EHRR 38
[39] (1991) 13 EHRR 784
[40] (1991) 15 EHRR 285

the dismissal, or for the employee's injured feelings.[41] After incorporation of the Convention, it may well be open to the applicant in such a situation to point to breach of a relevant Convention right, and to guide the national court through pertinent Strasbourg decisions where damages have been awarded for just such an "injury".

Article 8: Interference with Private Life

Private life may be violated by physical abuse. In *X and Y v Netherlands*,[42] the mentally handicapped applicant claimed that a procedural rule in Netherlands legislation which prevented her from lodging a complaint in relation to sexual abuse she had suffered in a mental institution, breached her right to privacy. The Court ruled that the Netherlands authorities had a degree of responsibility resulting from the deficiency of the legislation which gave rise to a violation of Article 8, and therefore they should pay her just satisfaction of 3,000 Dutch guilders even though the injury itself had been inflicted by a private third party.

The right to a private life includes the right of access to personal information.[43] In *Gaskin v United Kingdom*[44] the Court upheld G's argument that his rights under Article 8 had been breached by the refusal of the local authority to disclose documents relating to his upbringing in care. The Court rejected his claim for future earnings since they doubted that even if the documents had been released, this would have had a favourable effect on his future earnings. However, they acknowledged that he may have suffered some emotional distress and anxiety by reason of the absence of any independent procedure such as that mentioned above. They awarded him £5,000.

Private life may sometimes include business premises and confidential business information. In *Niemitz v Germany*[45] the applicant sought compensation for the damage to his business reputation which he alleged he incurred as a result of an unlawful search of his office. The Court did not consider that he had established that the breach of Article 8 had caused him pecuniary damage. If, and in so far as it may have occasioned him non-pecuniary damage, the Court considered that its finding of a violation constituted sufficient just satisfaction.

However in *Funke v France*[46] the Court did not think that the finding of a violation afforded sufficient satisfaction for the breach of the applicant's privacy when his home was searched by customs and excise officials in connection with alleged exchange control irrelgularities. Funke was awarded 50,000 French francs (approximately £5,500).

---

[41] *Johnson v Unisys* [1999] 1 All ER 854
[42] (1985) 8 EHRR 235
[43] This aspect of Article 8 is explored fully in chapter 11 on Confidentiality and Defamation
[44] (1990) 12 EHRR 36
[45] (1993) 16 EHRR 97
[46] (1993) 16 EHRR 297

Article 8: Interference with Family Life

This right generally arises in relation to deportation and asylum decisions. The Court will not in general acknowledge a link between deportation which amounts to a breach of Article 8 and the speculative earnings the deportee might have enjoyed if he had been allowed to stay: *Moustaquim v Belgium*.[47] However, non-pecuniary damages are sometimes awarded, particularly (as in this case) if the applicant has been exiled from his family and friends to a foreign country. M was awarded 100,000 Belgian francs or £2,000.

The right to family life is of course often engaged in care and adoption proceedings. In *Eriksson v Sweden*[48] a mother and daughter's Article 8 rights were held to have been violated by an order prohibiting the mother from removing her five year old daughter from a foster home and restricting the contact between them. The Court took into account the distress and embarrassment felt by the mother and daughter and awarded them 200,000 and 100,000 Swedish kroner (about £15,400 and £7,700) respectively.

The failure by the authorities to consult the natural father of a child before placing the child for adoption has also led to a finding of violations of Articles 6 and 8 and an award of £10,000 for the trauma, anxiety and feelings of injustice he had suffered as a result.[49]

Article 8: Invasion of the home

The right to a private life includes the peaceful enjoyment of the family home, which may be disturbed by environmental hazards. In *Lopez Ostra v Spain*[50] the applicant complained that the operation of a liquid and solid waste management plant operated by a group of tanneries twelve metres from her home violated respect for her home guaranteed by Article 8. She claimed damages under a number of specific heads, such as distress caused by fumes and smells, anxiety about her child's illness caused by toxic fumes and the inconvenience of moving. The Court considered that these heads of damage did not lend themselves to precise quantification and instead awarded her a global figure of ESP 4,000,000 (about £16,000).

Article 1, First Protocol: Inteference with Property Rights

Most of the awards made under this Article are pecuniary in nature; however the Court also assesses awards "on an equitable basis" for non-pecuniary damage in relation to deprivation of land. Where, for example, the Greek Government permitted the occupation of private property by the navy without

---

[47] (1991) 13 EHRR 802

[48] (1990) 12 EHRR 183. See also *Olssen v Sweden* (1988) 11 EHRR 259. Here the applicants were awarded the sum of 200,000 Swedish kroner for the inconvenience and distress of having their children removed from them for seven years

[49] *Keegan v Ireland* (1994) 18 EHRR 342

[50] (1994) 20 EHRR 277. Claims for remedies for environmental wrongs are explored more fully in chapter 10 on Environmental Rights

allocating substitute lands to the applicants or providing some sort of compensation for six years, the Strasbourg Court found a breach of Article 1 of the First Protocol. Each of the applicants was awarded £1,000.[51]

4.1.3. Reasons for Rejecting a Claim for Pecuniary or Non-Pecuniary Loss

As noted above, a claim for compensation will be rejected when there is nothing to suggest with reasonable certainty that without the violation the result would have been different, although non-pecuniary damages will sometimes be forthcoming.

If the Court finds that by holding the violation has occurred, its judgment has already furnished sufficient satisfaction for the purposes of Article 41, it will not award any compensation

Compensation will be denied if it is concluded that the applicants did not suffer any real damage. This approach shows that there is no deterrence objective behind the Court's calculations under Article 41.

In applications brought under Article 6, if the domestic court imposes a sentence identical to that given before the judgment of the Court, but after a trial attended by all the guarantees laid down by the Convention, compensation will be refused for the past due process violations.

No compensation will be awarded if the applicant has supplied insufficient evidence or information in support of his claim.

4.2.3. Damages under the Human Rights Act and State Liability

The position is straightforward as regards most potential breaches of the incorporated Convention rights; damages will be payable under Section 8, even if no existing tort has been developed. An obvious example is privacy. The absence of any available action in tort will not inhibit the courts from making an award under Section 8 based on the remedies provided by the Strasbourg Court for breaches of Article 8. More difficult questions arise where, Convention rights apart, the public authority would otherwise enjoy a statutory or common law immunity.

The present position is that liability in damages is simply excluded when the courts find that the relevant statute which the public body is said to have breached does not impose a duty. Where there is no duty, no action can lie in tort for damages.[52] Statutory duty is thus limited to legislative provisions that are clearly intended to be enforceable by a private action in tort. The

---

[51] *Papamichalopoulos and Others v Greece* (1995) 21 EHRR 439. The Court does not explain how it calculates these figures, a lack of transparency criticised by Mowbray , above N. 17

[52] *per* Lord Browne-Wilkinson in X *(Minors) v Bedfordshire* CC (1995) AC 633: ". . . statutory provisions establishing a regulatory system or a scheme of social welfare for the benefit of the public at large (do not) give rise to a private right of action for damages for breach of statutory duty"

Commission has recently referred applications arising out of the *Bedfordshire* case for judgment by the Court.

In *TP and KM v United Kingdom*[53] the applicants were respectively mother and child, who were separated when the London Borough of Newham took the child into care on the mistaken assumption that the mother was still cohabiting with the man who had abused the child. The Commission held that there had been violation of the applicants' right to family life under Article 8 of the Convention, that the child had been denied its right of access to court to complain of the local authority's negligence, and that the applicant had also been denied a remedy under Article 13. In a separate application, *Z v United Kingdom*, the Comission expressed the opinion that five siblings, all severely neglected and mistreated by their parents, had suffered a violation of the right to be protected against inhuman and degrading treatment under Article 3, and their right of access to court under Article 6, when the rule of immunity articulated in *X v Bedfordshire* prevented them from taking negligence proceedings against the County Council. This case has also been referred to the Court.

In the absence of any relevant statute, the common law duty of care in negligence is excluded from certain areas of public activity, such as the steps taken by the police in the investigation and prevention of crime.[54] This specific immunity has been held by the Court to constitute a violation of an individual's right of access to justice under Article 6 of the Convention.[55] In one of its most controversial rulings under Article 6, the Court granted £10,000 to each member of a murder victim's family. This was compensation, not for the loss of the victim's life, but "by way of compensation for loss of opportunity" because they had been deprived of a chance to proceed to an actual trial of their claim that the police were negligent. Although there are plenty of precedents for the award of damages for denial of a fair hearing, the Court has been criticised here for misinterpreting the nature of the applicants' claim, which was essentially a fact finding investigation into police mismanagement, not a tort suit:[56]

"The one thing leads to money, the other, being by its nature a public inquiry, simply doesn't".[57]

What then was the precise basis for the award of damages? The answer must be that the applicants could not go uncompensated for the breach of their Convention rights, however inappropriate a monetary award may have seemed for the original breach. A related difficulty about free standing "constitutional" rights has been dealt with by the New Zealand Court of Appeal, which may have some bearing on the way judges will approach similar cases in this

---

[53] Application No. 28945/95
[54] *Hill v Chief Constable of West Yorkshire* [1989] AC 53
[55] *Osman v United Kingdom* (1999) 5 BHRC 293
[56] In *X v Bedfordshire* Lord Browne-Wilkinson cited the availability of procedures to investigate grievances under the relevant statute as one of the reasons for not imposing civil liability leading to financial compensation
[57] Weir, "Down Hill all the Way?" (1999) 58 CLJ 4

country. In *Baigent's Case*,[58] the plaintiffs sought to pursue an action for damages for an unreasonable search of premises in violation of Section 21 of the New Zealand Bill of Rights Act 1990 (which provides that "Everyone has the right to be secure against unreasonable search or seizure, whether of the person, property or correspondence or otherwise"). But the Crown (vicariously liable for the police officers) sought to rely on certain statutory immunities which provided exemption from liability for negligence, trespass and misfeasance. The plaintiffs argued that the violations of their rights gave rise to a public cause of action separate from any other cause of action under the domestic law, and for which the courts were to accord an effective remedy, including monetary compensation. The Crown contended that the Bill of Rights Act conferred no new right to remedies beyond those available under the existing law, modified where necessary to ensure consistency with the Act.

The New Zealand Court of Appeal ruled for the plaintiffs, holding that their common law claims in neglience, trespass and misfeasance could not be defeated by the immunity provisions, because it was felt that none of the immunities covered "Bill of Rights liability". Enactments should be given a meaning consistent with the rights and freedoms in the Bill of Rights and that the protection it afforded against unreasonable search on behalf of the executive could not be eroded by Crown immunity. The proposed action for constitutional damages was also reinstated, despite the absence of an express provision for damages in the New Zealand Bill of Rights. Reliance was placed on Lord Diplock's analysis in *Maharaj v Attorney General of Trinidad and Tobago*[59] that liabilty for public wrongs was an independent liability, not to be confused with vicarious exposure to claims for wrongdoing by public servants, and the level of damages would depend partly on "the gravity of the breach and the need to emphasise the importance of the affirmed rights and to deter breaches".[60]

The Court endorsed the *Maharaj* principle of a *sui generis* public law remedy; in other words, the liability of the Crown itself rather than vicarious liability arising out of the acts of its servants.

We have yet to see whether English courts will take a position similar to that of the New Zealand Court of Appeal, either by reading down common law and statutory rules of immunity to conform with the Convention, as they will be obliged to do by Section 3 of the Human Rights Act, or by extending exemplary damages to cover Convention violations.[61]

In any event, the Strasbourg Court, whose lead the local courts are enjoined to follow, has awarded financial compensation for a range of wrongs including distress and anxiety caused by the failure of public officials to observe the requirements of the Convention. It would therefore be disingenuous to predict

---

[58] *Simpson v A.G.* 1994 3 NZLR 667
[59] (1979) AC 385,399
[60] *Baigent's Case*, p 677, 50
[61] At present exemplary damages are applicable only to causes of action which arose before the House of Lords judgment in *Rookes v Barnard* (1964) AC 1129

that the present broad immunity of public authorities from damages claims will remain intact.

On the other hand, it must be remembered that the obligation on national courts to "take account" of Strasbourg jurisprudence works both ways; in some cases, this might yield damages in situations where no award would otherwise have been available under national law; but in others the refusal by the Strasbourg Court to grant an award may lead the national court to the same position. This happened recently when Mr Chahal had succeeded in persuading the Strasbourg Court that his threatened deportation breached Articles 3, 5(4) and 13 under the Convention. He consequently sought an ex gratia payment by way of compensation from the Home Office, and judicially reviewed their refusal to pay out. The Court of Appeal[62] referred him to the Strasbourg decision, saying, bluntly, that "The fact was that the human rights court did consider the question of compensation and held that no financial award was called for". In the circumstances, then, the Strasbourg Court's attitude endorsed the rationality of the Home Office's decision.

---

[62] *R v Secretary of State for the Home Office, ex p. Chahal* Court of Appeal, November 4 1999, unreported

6

General Common Law Claims and the Human Rights Act

RICHARD BOOTH

1. INTRODUCTION

It is clear that the Human Rights Act 1998 (the HRA) is going to affect some areas of the common law rather more than others. The following practice areas are likely to be affected substantially and therefore form the subject of separate chapters:

- Medical Negligence
- Personal Injury Claims
- Environmental Health and Nuisance
- Mental Health
- Confidentiality: Privacy and Freedom of Expression
- Medical Law

This chapter aims merely to sketch out the potential impact of the HRA on other areas of the common law that are not dealt with in detail elsewhere in this book. It does not seek to be comprehensive; the idea is rather to flag up the possibilities of advancing Convention arguments in cases where its relevance seems less than obvious. I propose to consider very briefly the potential impact of the HRA upon the following disparate areas:

1. Landlord and Tenant
2. Contract
3. Trespass
4. Unlawful interference with goods
5. Economic Torts
6. Civil actions against the police

Article 8 reads:

1. *Everyone has the right to respect for his private and family life, his home and his correspondence.*
2. *There shall be no interference by a public authority with the exercise of this right except such as in accordance with the law and is necessary in a democratic society in the interests of national security, public safety or the economic well-being of the country, for the prevention of disorder or crime, for the protection of health or morals, or for the protection of the rights and freedoms of others.*

In *Kroon v Netherlands*[1] the Court stated that the "essential object" of Article 8 was:

"... to protect the individual against arbitrary action by the public authorities. There may in addition be positive obligations inherent in 'effective' respect for family life [and the other Article 8(1) values]".

2.1. How Far Does Respect for the Home Extend?

Perhaps surprisingly, there is no absolute right to a home.[2] But the concept of home includes the idea that the state will facilitate the right to live in one's home, rather than merely protecting it as a possession or property right.[3] See also the European Court of Justice's (ECJ's) discussion of enjoyment of private life and home in *Case 249/86 Commission v Germany*.[4] The European Court requires Member States of the European Union, when interpreting and implementing Community law, to act and to legislate in a way which respects the rights set out in the European Convention on Human Rights (ECHR). This case concerned an EC Regulation which guarantees migrant workers rights to have family members from their state of origin installed with them, subject to the availability of suitable housing. Germany rejected a worker's application under this provision on the basis that the housing he occupied was in a state of deterioration and was not therefore "suitable". This disclosed an interference in the worker's private home life contrary to Article 8 of the ECHR.

Home is generally defined as where one lives on a settled basis. Holiday homes and work hostels may fall outside the definition.[5] Home can include a place where one intends to live and is not confined to where one actually is

---

[1] (1994) 19 EHRR 263
[2] *X v FRG* (1956) 1 YB 202
[3] *Howard v UK* (1987) 52 DR 198
[4] [1989] ECR 1263
[5] *Kanthak v FRG* No 12474/86, 58 DR 94 (1988)

living.[6] In *Gillow* the States of Guernsey had refused to grant a new residence permit to a couple who had been absent from their self-built house on the island for eighteen years. The Commission accepted that the couple had always had an intention to return to the house in Guernsey. In these circumstances there was a right to (re)establish home life in the particular house. Further, given that the couple also maintained a house in England, it ought not to be ruled out that a person may have more than one home.

"Home" may cover some business premises, extending, for example, to a professional person's office.[7] It would appear to be an essential requirement that the professional's activities could be carried on as easily at home as at his office.

Once it is established that premises are "home", the first right protected is a right of access and occupation.[8] There is also a right not to be expelled or evicted from such premises.[9] This principle is vividly illustrated by the recent case of *Mentes v Turkey*[10] in which the applicants complained that state security forces had burned their homes, forcing them to evacuate their village in south-east Turkey. The Court found that the facts disclosed a particularly grave interference with the applicants' right to respect for private life, family life and home, and that the measure was devoid of justification. The Court also held that even though the first applicant probably did not own the house in question (her father-in-law did), she did live there for significant periods on an annual basis when she visited the village, and, therefore, her occupation of the house fell within the scope of the protection guaranteed by Article 8.

The property right in houses is protected, if at all, by Article 1 of the First Protocol ("Every . . . person is entitled to the peaceful enjoyment of his possessions. No one shall be deprived of his possessions except in the public interest and subject to the conditions provided for by law and by the general principles of international law".)[11] However, it may be open to question whether real property (as contrasted with personal property) is a possession. In *Howard v United Kingdom*,[12] the Commission decided that a compulsory purchase order for the house where the applicants lived interfered potentially with their rights under Article 8 as well as Article 1 of the First Protocol.

Importantly, the interests protected by "home" include the peaceful enjoyment of residence there. This principle has been established by the various aircraft noise cases.[13] This principle may be extended to both personal harassment (e.g., by a landlord or neighbour) and other forms of environmental interference with quiet enjoyment (e.g., failure to repair or maintain).

---

[6] *Gillow v UK* (1986) 11 EHRR 335
[7] *Niemietz v Germany* (1992) 16 EHRR 97; *Chappell v UK* A 152-A (1989)
[8] *Wiggins v UK* No 7456/76, 13 DR 40 (1978)
[9] *Cyprus v Turkey* Nos 6780/74 and 6950/75 (1976) 4 EHRR 482
[10] (1998) 26 EHRR 595
[11] *James v United Kingdom* (1986) 8 EHRR 123
[12] See N. 3 above
[13] For example, *Arrondelle v United Kingdom* 26 DR 5 (1982)

2.2. Likely Impact on Domestic Proceedings

Despite the laudable protection offered to occupiers of homes by Article 8, it is unlikely that its incorporation will have any major effect on domestic landlord and tenant actions. This is because the obligation on states is only to "respect" the interests set out in Article 8(1). Moreover, many landlords are not public authorities. Nevertheless, "respect" still imports a positive obligation on states. The Court has conceded a wide margin of appreciation to states to decide what respect requires in the circumstances of a particular application. (It is unclear quite how this margin of appreciation will be observed domestically, although the observations made by Lord Hope in *R v DPP ex parte Kebilene*[14] provide some early guidance in this area.) What the state has to do is to have regard:

> "to the fair balance that has to be struck between the general interest of the community and the interests of the individual, the search for which balance is inherent in the whole Convention".)[15]

Given that the above considerations apply to the establishment of the primary obligations under Article 8(1), and not even the justifications for derogating from them under Article 8(2), it is not going to be easy for tenants to establish a cause of action under Article 8. Moreover, the courts already ensure that any interference by public authorities with tenants' rights is in accordance with the law by means of the detailed notice provisions with which landlords have to comply.[16]

2.3. Other Articles

Section 27 of the Housing Act 1988 introduced a new tortious liability in damages against a landlord or a person acting on his behalf who *"unlawfully deprives the residential occupier of any premises of his occupation of the whole or part of the premises"*. Damages under Section 27 are assessed in accordance with Section 28. The provisions of Section 27 came into force on 15 January 1989 but are retrospective and apply to evictions and harassment occurring after 9 June 1988. For an attempt to argue that it was contrary to Article 7[17] to apply Sections 27 and 28 of the Housing Act 1988 retrospectively, see *Jones v Miah*.[18] In that case the plaintiffs, protected tenants of bedsitting rooms above a restaurant, were unlawfully evicted, having had their locks changed and their belong-

---

[14] [1999] 3 WLR 972. See chapter 2. The Convention and the Human Rights Act: A New Way of Thinking, for a discussion of the doctrine of margin of appreciation

[15] *Cossey v United Kingdom* (1991) 13 EHRR 622

[16] For example, Section 8, Housing Act 1988; Section 5, Protection from Eviction Act 1977

[17] *"(1) No one shall be held guilty of any criminal offence on account of any act or omission which did not constitute a criminal offence under national or international law at the time when it was committed . . ."*

[18] (1992) 24 HLR 578

ings packed up. At trial the judge found for the plaintiffs, awarding them £14,125 for the tort of unlawful eviction under Sections 27 and 28. The defendants appealed on the ground, inter alia, that it was contrary to EC law (of which Convention principles form a part) to give retrospective effect to the penal provisions contained in Sections 27 and 28. The Court of Appeal held that Sections 27 and 28 were not criminal legislation and did not grant any remedy enforceable by the criminal law. The sections merely granted a civil remedy in tort to the person injured. Accordingly, Article 7 could not have applied even if the ECHR had formed part of the domestic law of England and Wales.

Also, there have been three unreported cases in which attempts were made to raise the ECHR in the context of possession proceedings.[19] Unsurprisingly, each attempt failed. However, there may be some scope for tenants after 2 October 2000 to attempt to rely on Articles 8 and 14, and, possibly, Article 6.

Moreover, a glimpse of the future in relation to the rights of homosexuals to succeed to tenancies under the Rent Act 1977 may have been given by Ward LJ in his enlightened dissenting judgment in *Fitzpatrick v Sterling Housing Association*[20] – a dissent which has recently won the majority view in the House of Lords.[21] In that case, Mr Fitzpatrick had lived with the protected tenant of a flat of which the defendant was landlord, in a stable and permanent homosexual relationship since 1976. On the tenant's death in 1994, Mr Fitzpatrick applied to take over the tenancy but the defendant, although willing to provide smaller accommodation, refused. Mr Fitzpatrick's application to the county court for a determination that he was entitled to succeed to the tenancy was dismissed on the grounds that he had not lived with the original tenant "as his . . . wife or husband" within paragraph 2(2) of Schedule 1 to the Rent Act 1977 and that he was not "a member of the original tenant's family" within paragraph 3(1). His appeal to the Court of Appeal was also dismissed, although Ward LJ dissented forcefully, finding that Mr Fitzpatrick had lived with the deceased tenant as his husband or wife.

Finally, it is noteworthy that Ward LJ referred to comparative Commonwealth jurisprudence in this field. The Canadian material is excellent and voluminous,[22] and the New Zealand jurisprudence is also useful.[23] Such material may be difficult to bring in at first instance hearings, but will often be appreciated by appellate courts.

---

[19] *Mayor and Burgesses of LB Hounslow v Perera* (3 November 1982); *Metropolitan Property Realizations v Cosgrove* (27 January 1992); *Mayor and Commonality and Citizens of London v Prince* (6 June 1995) (all unreported)

[20] [1998] 2 WLR 225

[21] [1999] 3 WLR 1113

[22] See, in particular, *Constitutional Law of Canada, Vol 2 (Hogg)* and the *Canadian Charter of Rights Annotated*

[23] For example, *Re Dickinson* [1992] 2 NZLR 43 (rent review); *Armstrong v Attorney-General of NZ* [1995] 1 ERNZ 43

3. CONTRACT

At present, absent horizontal effect, it is difficult to see how the HRA is going to affect contract claims to any significant extent. There may, however, be scope for ingenious arguments. Would it be possible for a bona fide purchaser for value to argue that the operation of the *nemo dat* rule means that he has been deprived of his possessions in contravention of Article 1 of the First Protocol? The answer must be that this type of argument is extremely unlikely to succeed even if one disregards the general lack of involvement of public authorities in contract claims. If parties have contracted voluntarily, the HRA really has little role to play in the regulation of their conduct.

One exception may be contracts of employment – consider, for example, an action in breach of confidence between a public authority employer and an ex-employee who wishes to disclose something in the public interest.[24]

It is possible to foresee how Article 6 will affect arbitrations and adjudications in this field. Specifically, the system of adjudication provided for by Section 108 of the Housing Grants' Construction and Regeneration Act 1996 ("HGCRA 1996"); it would be open to claimants to argue that in certain circumstances such adjudication would involve a "determination" of their "civil rights" so as to draw in the protection of Article 6. Whether such an argument would succeed depends very much on whether the dispute in question has consequences for the claimant's livelihood.[25]

4. TRESPASS

The principle of the tort of trespass is that any direct invasion of a protected right by a positive act is wrongful and actionable, subject to justification. The current justifications exist for the purposes of promoting the most important interests – maintenance of public order, enforcement of the law, and preservation of life and property – and they frequently overlap. Moreover, an act cannot be unlawful if it is authorised by the legislature, a judge or a proper custom.

It is clear that the concept of protected rights will evolve in line with jurisprudence under the HRA. Direct invasion of those rights by positive acts will either result in the revival of the tort of trespass or will result in a new category of actions for breach of Convention rights. It is suggested that the latter outcome is more likely. Any attempt to shoe-horn the invasion of Convention rights within the English law of trespass is likely to be deeply unsatisfactory, especially given the existing interpretations of various derogations in the jurisprudence of the Court. Therefore, it is probable that trespass will remain a meandering

---

[24] cf. *Goodwin v UK* (1996) 22 EHRR 123

[25] See chapter 3 on Costs, Conditional Fees and Legal Aid for a discussion on the applicability of Article 6 in cases involving public benefits such as housing

backwater in the law of tort, relatively unaffected by the new flood of Convention jurisprudence.

5. UNLAWFUL INTERFERENCE WITH GOODS

Article 1 of the First Protocol reads:

> *"Every natural or legal person is entitled to the peaceful enjoyment of his possessions. No one shall be deprived of his possessions except in the public interest and subject to the conditions provided for by law and by the general principles of international law. The preceding provisions shall not, however, in any way impair the right of a State to enforce such laws as it deems necessary to control the use of property in accordance with the general interest or to secure the payment of taxes or other contributions or penalties".*

The observations made above about trespass may also prove true in relation to conversion and wrongful interference with goods under the Torts (Interference with Goods) Act 1977 ("the chattel torts").

Much of the Court's jurisprudence in relation to Article 1 of the First Protocol has concerned the expropriation of property by a public authority. An applicant generally has to show that the state's measures are "manifestly unjustified". The Court has traditionally allowed a wide margin of appreciation to states. In *James v United Kingdom*[26] it was recognised that states have a wide power to interfere with property rights in the general social and economic interest, even where the benefits fall to the advantage of particular individuals.

Inevitably, the question of compensation will always be a relevant factor when chattels are converted or wrongfully interfered with. Such case law as there is[27] suggests that positive obligations may arise in some circumstances when a state interferes with the enjoyment of possessions. Such obligations include obligations to provide compensation, expeditious processes and, where the interferences lead to the determination of a civil right, a process which fully satisfies Article 6(1).

If there were not already an established common law jurisprudence in relation to conversion and wrongful interference with goods, then Article 1 of the First Protocol would require the United Kingdom to regulate the "peaceful enjoyment" of possessions as between individuals. However, the common law is established (if confusing) in this field, and it is doubtful whether Article 1 of the First Protocol will change matters greatly.

The one area in which the Court's jurisprudence assists is in the definition of "possessions". The use of the word *"biens"* in the French text of the Convention indicates that a wide range of proprietorial interests were intended to be protected.[28] It embraces immoveable and moveable property, along with interests

---

[26] See N. 11 above
[27] *Hentrich v France* (1994) 18 EHRR 440
[28] See N. 8 above

such as shares[29] and patents.[30] The definition also encompasses contractual rights,[31] leases[32] and judgment debts.[33] The essential characteristic is the acquired economic value of the individual interest. The ascription and identification of property rights is for the national legal system, with few restrictions upon what a state may regard as capable of being owned. However, the mere fact that English law does not acknowledge as a legal right a particular interest, or does so in terms which do not result in it being recognised as a property right, does not conclusively determine that the interest is not a "possession" for the purposes of Article 1, First Protocol. The concept of "possession" is autonomous, evolving without reference to any other legal definitions, and the demonstration of an established economic interest by an applicant may be sufficient to establish a right protected by the Convention. In *Tre Traktorer Aktiebolag v Sweden*[34] the Court rejected the Government's argument that because a liquor licence conferred no rights in national law, it could not be a "possession" for the purposes of Article 1, First Protocol. It was essential to the successful conduct of the applicant's restaurant, and its withdrawal had adverse effects on the goodwill and value of the business.

For a brief recent discussion of the applicability of Article 1 of the First Protocol in the English courts, see the judgment of Lord Bingham LCJ in *R v Secretary of State for Health, ex parte Eastside Cheese Company*.[35] In that case, the minister had decided to make an Emergency Control Order under Section 13 of the Food Safety Act 1990 banning cheese, which resulted in its destruction without compensation. The applicants, specialist cheesemakers, submitted that the making of the Section 13 Order violated their fundamental rights guaranteed by Article 1 of the First Protocol. The Lord Chief Justice considered the cases of *Sporrong and Lonnroth v Sweden*[36] and *Holy Monasteries v Greece*[37] and reached the conclusion that the case was best regarded as one in which the state deemed it necessary to control the use of property in accordance with the general interest. He went on to hold as follows:

"Thus there must be proportionality between the means employed and the ends sought to be achieved, and a fair balancing of the interests of the public and those of private individuals. While the court must never abdicate its duty of review, it will accord a margin of appreciation to the decision-making authority. Particularly must this be true, in our view, where the decision-making authority is responding to what it reasonably regards as an imminent threat to the life or health of the public".[38]

[29] *Bramelid and Malmstrom v Sweden* 29 DR 64 (1982)
[30] *Smith Kline and French Laboratories v Netherlands* 66 DR 70 (1990)
[31] *Association of General Practitioners v Denmark* 62 DR 226 (1989)
[32] *Mellacher v Austria* (1989) 12 EHRR 391
[33] *Stran Greek Refineries and Stratis Andreadis v Greece* (1994) 19 EHRR 293
[34] (1984) 13 EHRR 309
[35] CA, July 1 1999, transcript pp 27–9 and [1999] C.O.D. 321
[36] (1982) 5 EHRR 35
[37] (1994) 20 EHRR 1
[38] Transcript, p 29

In conclusion, the Court of Appeal could see no room for an argument that the emergency action taken by the minister involved an unjustified violation of human rights on the part of the applicants.

6. ECONOMIC TORTS

The "economic torts" (deceit, malicious falsehood, passing-off, inducing breach of contract, intimidation, interference with contract, causing loss by wrongful means, conspiracy and abuse of power), as developed by the common law, apply to all cases where one person has deliberately caused financial loss to another. The impact of the HRA on this area of the law is unlikely to be extensive. Much may depend on whether specific examples of economic harm can be brought within the broad definition of "possessions" in the jurisprudence of the Court on Article 1, First Protocol (discussed above). Moreover, in order for a person to have been deprived of a possession, it is axiomatic that he must once have had an interest with an acquired economic value and not a mere expectation of the same.

There may also be scope for some conflict between the above torts and Article 10: see *Markt Intern v Germany*,[39] a case in which the attack focused on national laws which restricted the applicant's freedom of expression by making it unlawful to publish articles which caused loss to another private party.

Although the HRA is unlikely to make a huge difference to this field, there remains the Court's obligation under Section 3 to interpret the common law (and therefore to resolve disputes) in a way which is compatible with Convention rights.

7. CIVIL ACTIONS AGAINST THE POLICE

Police functions may give rise to potential breaches of Articles 2, 3, 5, 8 and 11. The rights protected under these Articles may only be restricted in such a manner as is "prescribed by law". Domestic laws which permit interference with these rights must be both clearly formulated and accessible.[40] The failure of the United Kingdom to incorporate Article 13 leaves open the interesting question of whether the existing class of common law civil actions against the police constitutes an "effective remedy" for the purposes of the Convention. It has previously been held that a police complaints procedure was an effective remedy in this context.[41]

Article 5 sets out the right to liberty and security of the person. A series of specific cases in which persons may lawfully be deprived of their liberty is set out in Article 5(1). Article 5(5) gives a right to compensation:

[39] (1989) 12 EHRR 161
[40] *Sunday Times v United Kingdom* (1979) 2 EHRR 245
[41] *X v Denmark* (1983) 5 EHRR 278

"Everyone who has been the victim of arrest or detention in contravention of the provisions of this Article shall have an enforceable right to compensation".

It is likely that Article 5 will provide a useful provision when considering liability for false imprisonment. However, the drafting of Article 5 has been criticised as confusing, a criticism borne out by the vast body of the Court's jurisprudence on the right to liberty and security of the person. Nevertheless, any faults with Article 5 do not necessarily make it less useful as an illustrative tool for advancing a false imprisonment claim.

The Court has considered the corollary of the requirement in Article 5(1) that detention be "lawful" to be that detention must not be arbitrary.[42] In fact, the limitations on police powers of arrest imposed by the Convention do not differ appreciably from those contained in English law.

Article 5(2) is similar to the common law principles concerning the statement of reasons for an arrest. Surprisingly, it gives no right to contact a lawyer.[43]

Article 5(3) requires a person to be "brought promptly" before a court. It seems unlikely that the detention provisions of the Police and Criminal Evidence Act 1984 (PACE) will be found to contravene the Convention.

As regards the use of force on arrest, John Alderson, former Chief Constable of Devon and Cornwall Police and champion of community policing, has suggested that the Convention only licences the minimum force necessary to achieve the desired objective.[44] Yet the use of lethal force has been permitted in certain circumstances.[45] It would seem that the restrictions imposed by English law on the use of force on arrest do not contravene the Convention. In any event, the Convention is likely to add little to common law claims based on use of excessive force on arrest.

Suspects' rights have been protected by the Court under Article 3, the prohibition of torture and inhuman or degrading treatment. With a few significant exceptions, the ECHR jurisprudence does not differ hugely from the common-sense, common law approach. Thus, mock executions, sensory deprivation and insulting language would provide a cause of action both under the common law and under the HRA. It would be open to a claimant to frame these claims separately. The ECHR claim could stand alone in its own right. However, solitary confinement is something of a grey area under the Convention jurisprudence – taken together with other degrading treatment, it can found a cause of action,[46] but taken alone, it may not be a breach.[47]

Police powers of search and seizure will breach the Convention if they do not accord with Article 8. In particular, the stopping of correspondence is an area

---

[42] *Engel v Netherlands* (1976) 1 EHRR 647; *Bozano v France* (1987) 9 EHRR 297
[43] See N. 36 above
[44] J Alderson, *Human Rights and the Police* (1984) Council of Europe, p 68
[45] *X v Belgium*, 12 Yearbook HR 174 (police officer who fired fatal shot during riot considered to be acting in lawful self-defence)
[46] *Ireland v United Kingdom* (1978) 2 EHRR 25
[47] Application 9907/82 (1984) 7 EHRR 533

fraught with difficulties.[48] A civil claim for damages for breach of Article 8 could certainly stand alone here. However, the damages are unlikely to be very sizeable.[49] Potential breaches of Article 1 of the First Protocol must also be considered here, although deprivation of property must apparently be permanent and not in accordance with the general interest in order to found a cause of action.[50] There is also the difficulty of ascribing an economic value to the letters.

7.1. Intimate Samples, Photographs and Fingerprints

The taking of intimate body samples may amount to a breach of Articles 3 and 8 as well as a battery at common law. However, taking and retaining photographs of a demonstration will not mean that the police are guilty of infringing the right to respect for private life.[51] Producing intimate photographs during a trial or keeping records such as fingerprints, photographs and documents relating to previous criminal cases have all been found to be necessary in a democratic society.[52]

7.2. Surveillance

Claims for breach of Article 8 will often be the only remedy available to those who have been subject to unreasonable surveillance by the police. Article 8 guarantees rights which receive little protection under English law. Any interference with the right to respect for private and family life by way of visual or aural[53] surveillance must be "in accordance with the law" and not merely a matter of administrative convenience or a short-cut.[54] Recently, the Third Chamber of the Court has ruled admissible a claim that the Crown Court's decision to allow a secretly taped conversation as evidence at the applicant's trial for drug dealing was unfair in breach of Article 6 and also violated Article 8, since it was not "in accordance with the law" (nothing in PACE authorised such surveillance).[55]

JUSTICE has recently been investigating the issue of legal remedies for privacy infringements in public space. Such infringement would include the use of CCTV and other forms of police surveillance. The argument for the utility and necessity of such surveillance in a democratic society may eventually prevail over the qualified rights set out in Article 8.

---

[48] *Schonenberger v Switzerland* (1989) 11 EHRR 202
[49] See chapter 5 on Remedies for a survey of the awards granted under Section 41 of the ECHR
[50] *Handyside v United Kingdom* (1976) 1 EHRR 737 (seizure of obscene books)
[51] *X v United Kingdom*, Coll. HR 90
[52] *X v Germany*, 5 Yearbook HR 230
[53] *Halford v United Kingdom* (1997) 24 EHRR 523
[54] *Klass v Germany* (1978) 2 EHRR 214
[55] *Khan vUnited Kingdom* Application No 35394/97, unreported

7.3. Immunity Regarding Investigative Work

The former police immunity in respect of acts and omissions in the course of police investigative operations[56] has been ruled contrary to the Convention in *Osman v United Kingdom*.[57] Public policy gave the police immunity from suit when negligence was alleged in relation to their failure to investigate and suppress crime. The Court repeated in *Osman* that the state (through the police) must take appropriate steps to safeguard the lives of those within its jurisdiction and then went on to set the parameters of this obligation:

> "For the court, and bearing in mind the difficulties involved in policing modern societies, the unpredictability of human conduct and *the operational choices which must be made in terms of priorities and resources, such an obligation must be interpreted in a way which does not impose an impossible or disproportionate burden on the authorities.* Accordingly, not every claimed risk to life can entail for the authorities a Convention requirement to take operational measures to prevent that risk from materialising . . .
>
> In the opinion of the court where there is an allegation that the authorities have violated their positive obligation to protect the right to life in the context of their above-mentioned duty to prevent and suppress offences against the person, it must be established to its satisfaction that the authorities knew or ought to have known at the time of a real and immediate risk to the life of an identified individual or individuals from the criminal acts of a third party and *that they failed to take measures within the scope of their powers which, judged reasonably, might have been expected to avoid that risk.*
>
> . . . *it is sufficient for an applicant to show that the authorities did not do all that could reasonably be expected of them to avoid a real and immediate risk to life of which they had or ought to have had knowledge*" (emphasis added).

The facts of *Osman* are shocking. Ahmet Osman, aged fourteen, became the object of a strong attachment on the part of one of his school teachers ("L"). Over the course of a year, L gave Ahmet a number of presents, stalked him, changed his name to "Ahmet Osman" and drove a van directly at Ahmet's school friend. Ahmet's home was vandalised and graffiti of a sexual nature about him was found near his school. The police were contacted on several occasions, both by the school and by Ahmet's family, and the decision was taken to arrest L on suspicion of criminal damage. However, instead of going to the school where L was teaching on the day in question, the police went to L's home and failed to arrest him. L disappeared on the following day. Three months later L broke into Ahmet's home and shot both Ahmet and his father, killing Ahmet's father. Ahmet and his mother commenced an action in negligence against the police which was struck out by the Court of Appeal in 1992 on the basis that the

---

[56] *Hill v Chief Constable of West Yorkshire* [1988] 2 All ER 238
[57] (1999) *Crim LR* 82; (1999) 5 BHRC 293

police enjoyed immunity from suit concerning alleged negligence in the investigation and suppression of crime.[58]

The judges of the Strasbourg Court were unanimous in finding a violation of Article 6(1) on the basis that the application of the blanket immunity rule in relation to police investigative work in this case amounted to an unjustifiable restriction on the applicants' right to have a determination of the merits of their claim. It seems that it will be very difficult for defendant police forces to have such claims struck out in future. The Court will have to examine each case on its merits.

Osman has since been applied by the Court of Session in Scotland in *Gibson v Chief Constable of Strathclyde Police*[59] in holding that it was fair, just and reasonable that a duty of care was owed by the police. However, the Strasbourg Court's judgment in *Osman* has also received some forceful criticism from Lord Browne-Wilkinson in *Barrett v Enfield LBC*.[60]

8. CONCLUSION

It is fair to say that an element of crystal ball gazing is involved in attempting to predict the likely effect of the Human Rights Act 1998 on the areas of the common law which I have included in this chapter. What is certain is that a raft of English human rights jurisprudence will be swiftly built on to the existing ECHR jurisprudence after 2 October 2000.

---

[58] *Osman v Ferguson* [1993] 4 All ER 344
[59] TLR 11 May 1999
[60] [1999] 3 WLR 79

7

Bringing and Defending a Convention Claim in Domestic Law: A Practical Exercise

PHILIPPA WHIPPLE

INTRODUCTION

Academic guidance abounds on the effects of incorporation of the European Convention on Human Rights. But to those of us who practise "on the front-line", the Human Rights Act 1998 is less about debates on paper and more about bringing and defending real claims on behalf of our clients. The purpose of this chapter is to provide a practical demonstration of the way Convention arguments can be deployed once the Act is in force.

This chapter comprises pleadings to reflect the particular facts of a case study based on the Mental Health Act 1983, which raises both common law and Convention arguments. The pleadings are footnoted to explain relevant matters of law or practice. The Mental Health Act 1983 will be one of the prime areas for Convention challenges. The case could be argued in domestic law as one of damages for false imprisonment or possibly battery, without the need to invoke the Human Rights Act 1998 Act at all. It is not a judicial review but a "writ action" (in the old language). The pleadings demonstrate how, in practice, Convention arguments can be used both to strengthen existing lines of argument, and to provide new areas of challenge outside the existing law. The 1998 Act is going to become part of our everyday lawyers' language, and we should become accustomed to using it alongside the sort of everyday arguments which we are already experienced in pleading and arguing.

The pleadings do not provide a blueprint for all Convention claims. But this form of pleading would meet current technical requirements under the Civil Procedure Rules 1998, and would state each side's case in a manner consistent with that generally adopted for the pleading of common law claims.

CASE STUDY

The facts are these:

1 January 2001:   (i.e. after the 1998 Act has come into force) A's general prac-
                    titioner Dr B is called out to see A by A's nearest relative, C.
                    Dr B advises attendance at the Hospital (for which D NHS
                    Trust is responsible) and arranges for C to take A there
                    together with a letter of referral. A complains about this and
                    states he does not want C to be his "spokesperson". On
                    arrival at the Hospital, A is angry and refusing to cooperate.
                    C applies for his admission A is assessed by Dr E, the duty
                    psychiatrist at the Hospital, who forms the view that A is
                    badly in need of psychiatric treatment and completes a
                    Section 3 medical recommendation.

                    Later on the same day, A is assessed by Dr F, who is inde-
                    pendent of the Hospital. Dr F also completes the Section 3
                    recommendation. A is then detained under Section 3 of the
                    MHA 1983 (compulsory admission for treatment for initial
                    period of up to six months).

1 July 2001:   A's Section 3 is renewed at expiry of the six month period. A
                    does not himself (or by his nearest relative) apply for review
                    within the relevant period of six months from date of Section
                    3 admission. Therefore the Hospital refers the case to the
                    MHRT at the expiry of the first six month period (pursuant
                    to Section 68(1) MHA 1983).

25 August 2001:   Hearing before MHRT. Dr G, independent consultant psy-
                    chiatrist reports on A's behalf to the MHRT

1 September 2001: A released from Hospital following hearing before MHRT.

1 August 2002:   A issues proceedings against D, the NHS Trust responsible
                    for the Hospital, alleging false imprisonment, battery and
                    breach of Convention rights.

IN THE HIGH COURT OF JUSTICE[1]   CLAIM NO
QUEEN'S BENCH DIVISION

B E T W E E N:

A[2]

Claimant

and

D NHS Trust

Defendant

PARTICULARS OF CLAIM[3]

---

1. At all material times D:

   a. Was the Authority responsible for the provision of psychiatric and nursing care at the District General Hospital (the "Hospital").

   b. Owed certain duties with respect to the reception, care and treatment of mentally disordered patients, the management of their property and other related matters as set out in the Mental Health Act 1983.

   c. In so far as it was engaged in carrying out its duties under the Mental Health Act 1983, was a public authority for the purposes of Section 6 of the Human Rights Act 1998 (the "1998 Act").[4]

---

[1] High Court or County Court? Although both have jurisdiction to deal with the HRA points, it is advisable to issue in the High Court if possible, not only because this is more likely to achieve a reasoned decision on difficult (and possibly novel) points under the Act; but also because only the High Court can make a declaration of incompatibility under Section 4 (if it comes to that), subject to the notice procedures of Section 5 being complied with

CPR Part 7, PD2.1 – 2.4 requires that the value of the claim must be more than £15,000 (if for personal injuries it must be for more than £50,000 but the damages sought here are not for personal injuries). The Claimant's claim in this case is worth at least that on common law principles alone. But if there was doubt as to the quantum of damages, it would be acceptable to commence an action such as this in the High Court by reason of "the complexity of the facts, legal issues, remedies or procedures involved" or "the importance of the outcome to the public in general"

[2] The Claimant in this case has been "directly affected" by the acts of the public authority which he challenges. Undoubtedly he is a victim: see Section 7(7) of the 1998 Act and Article 34 of the Convention

[3] The 1998 Act envisages a Claimant relying on the Act both in judicial review proceedings in direct challenge of the public authority; and in the course of other legal proceedings (Section 7(1)). Because on the facts of this case the Claimant potentially has a cause of action for false imprisonment/battery even in the absence of Convention arguments, it is sensible to issue ordinary proceedings for damages so as to combine all the allegations in a single action

[4] The 1998 Act is intended to distinguish between three types of bodies: (1) obvious public bodies; (2) hybrid public bodies; and (3) private bodies. The Act applies to *all* the acts of a body falling within (1), and to those acts of a hybrid body within (2) which can be classified as public in nature. There is good reason to argue that an NHS Trust is an obvious public body within (1): it is in many respects analogous to the police or prison authorities which have been cited as examples of obvious public bodies by the Lord Chancellor (*Hansard*, HL, 24 November 1997, col 811; and see House of Commons Committee debate, 17 June 1998, col 400 et seq). But even if not accepted as an obvious

2. On 1 January 2001 Dr B was called out to see the Claimant by the Claimant's nearest relative, C. Dr B was a general practitioner who had treated the Claimant on many previous occasions. Dr B advised C to take the Claimant to the Hospital as soon as possible and gave C a letter of referral to show to the Hospital staff.

3. C took the Claimant to the Hospital where C completed an application under Section 3 of the Mental Health Act 1983.

4. The Claimant repeatedly complained to the Defendant's staff that he did not want C to act for him as his "spokesperson" and that C was just trying to get the Claimant "out of the way". The Claimant was told by the Defendant's staff that as C was his nearest relative, C was the right person to act on behalf of the Claimant.

5. On or shortly after arrival at the Hospital, the Claimant was examined by Dr E, duty psychiatrist at the Hospital, who spent five minutes with the Claimant, and then noted that the Claimant was:
   a. extremely dishevelled;
   b. delusional; and
   c. had ideas of self-harm.

   Dr E concluded that the Claimant should be admitted to the Hospital for psychiatric treatment.

6. The Claimant was reluctant to cooperate and indicated that he was unwilling to be admitted to hospital.

7. Dr E then completed a recommendation in the prescribed form for admission for treatment of the Claimant, pursuant to Section 3 of the Mental Health Act 1983, on grounds that the Claimant was:
   a. Suffering from mental illness of a nature and degree which made it appropriate for the Claimant to receive medical treatment in a hospital; and
   b. It was necessary for the Claimant's own health and safety that he receive such treatment which could not be provided unless the Claimant was detained.

8. Dr E's recommendation for Section 3 detention was supported by a second recommendation in identical terms by Dr F, who had not personally seen, examined or assessed the Claimant.

public body it clearly would be a hybrid (the Lord Chancellor's own example of a hybrid being a body such as Railtrack) and is certainly exercising public functions in administering the MHA 1983, in which case it is caught by Section 6(3)(b) of HRA read with Section 6(5)

The distinction between categories (1) and (2) would only become material if the type of activity in issue was essentially private, such as employment of staff, in which event the hybrid body would not be subject to the 1998 Act although the obvious public body would be. The public / private activity distinction for hybrid bodies is likely to be the same as already exists in common law and is exemplified in cases such as *R v Derbyshire CC ex parte Noble* [1990] ICR 808

9. As a result of the recommendations of Doctors E and F, the Claimant was detained at the Hospital from 1 January 2001, where he underwent medical treatment to which he did not consent.

10. The Hospital referred the Claimant's case to the Mental Health Review Tribunal on 1 July 2001. In view of the forthcoming hearing, the Claimant arranged for a report to be obtained from Dr G, an independent consultant psychiatrist, who concluded that the Claimant did not then, and had not ever, satisfied the criteria of Section 3 of the Mental Health Act 1983.

11. The Mental Health Review Tribunal hearing took place on 25 August 2001. The Tribunal concluded:

   a. That the Claimant was not suffering from a mental illness of a nature or degree which made it appropriate for him to be detained in a hospital; and

   b. That it was not necessary for the health and safety of the Claimant that he should receive treatment which could only be provided if he was detained.

   Accordingly, the Tribunal directed the Claimant's discharge from the Hospital.

12. The Claimant was released from the Hospital on 1 September 2001.

13. The Defendant's treatment of the Claimant was negligent in the following ways:

PARTICULARS OF NEGLIGENCE

The Defendant, by its servants or agents:

   a. Concluded that the Claimant fulfilled the criteria of Section 3 of the Mental Health Act 1983. A competent assessment would have revealed that the Claimant was suffering a mental illness, but that:
      i. the illness did not require treatment in hospital; and/or
      ii. there was no risk of the Claimant harming himself or anyone else, and therefore that his detention was not required.

   b. Failed to examine the Claimant with sufficient care to arrive at a meaningful assessment of his condition. Dr E's examination lasted only five minutes; Dr F did not examine the Claimant at all.

   c. Recommended that the Claimant be detained under Section 3 of the 1983 Act.

   d. Failed thereafter to assess the Claimant adequately or at all, to determine whether he fulfilled the criteria of Section 3 of the Mental Health Act 1983. Such an assessment would (or should) have revealed that those criteria were not fulfilled.

14. By reason of the Defendant's negligence, the Claimant was deprived of his liberty and was falsely imprisoned.[5]

15. Throughout his period of detention at the Hospital, the Claimant was subjected to treatment to which he did not consent, in circumstances where the Claimant was competent to give or withhold valid consent. The Defendant thereby committed a battery upon the Claimant.[6]

16. Further, the Defendant has acted in a way which is incompatible with the Claimant's Convention rights, contrary to Section 6(1) of the 1998 Act, in the following ways:[7]

**PARTICULARS OF BREACH
OF CONVENTION RIGHTS**

Under Article 5(1) of the Convention[8]

a. Detained the Claimant when his mental disorder was not of a degree warranting compulsory confinement.

b. Failed to obtain sufficient objective medical expertise to establish that the Claimant was suffering from a mental disorder which was of a degree that compulsory confinement was warranted. In particular:

   i. Dr E had only spent five minutes with the Claimant; and

   ii. Dr F had not previously seen assessed or examined the Claimant, thus neither doctor's recommendation was a sufficient basis on which to detain the Claimant.[9]

c. Failed, by its servants or agents, Doctors E and F, to carry out an adequate assessment of the Claimant's mental state prior to applying for his

---

[5] There is authority for the proposition that negligence in the giving of a recommendation under the MHA 1983 is actionable and damages can be recovered for the detention which results from that negligence: see *Clerk and Lindsell on Torts* (London, Sweet & Maxwell, 1998) para 12–75

[6] The relevant principles relating to battery in medical cases have been set out by the House of Lords in *Re F (Mental Patient: Sterilisation)* [1990] 2 AC 1 which left the door open for such allegations where a patient had capacity to consent but did not give it (see Lord Goff at p73 B-D). However, the claim is unlikely to succeed at common law given Section 63 of the MHA 1983 (but see paragraph 16f. of the Particulars in relation to lack of consent founding a Convention claim)

[7] It is not, in an obvious case, necessary expressly to plead that the Claimant is a "victim" within Section 7(1). In this case the Claimant was directly affected by the action of the public body in question. But if there is likely to be any dispute about this it would be prudent to address the point in the Particulars

[8] Article 5(1) secures the right to liberty and security but is subject to certain qualifications including Article 5(1)(e) which allows the lawful detention of persons of unsound mind

[9] Allegations a. and b. are based on the standard set in *Winterwerp v Netherlands* (1979) 2 EHRR 387 which provides that three minimum conditions must be complied with in order for detention to be lawful: (1) the individual concerned must be reliably shown by independent medical expertise to be of unsound mind; (2) the individual's disorder must be of a nature and degree so as to justify detention; and (3) detention is only justified if and so long as the mental disorder persists. ECHR jurisprudence is applicable in the domestic courts by virtue of Section 2(1) of the HRA

detention (the Claimant repeats the Particulars of Negligence listed above).[10]

d. Failed to assess the Claimant after 1 January 2001 adequately or at all.[11]

Under Article 5(4)[12]

e. Failed to ensure that the lawfulness of the Claimant's detention was determined speedily. The Claimant contends that a period of almost eight months before the matter was brought before the MHRT was unduly long.[13]

Under Article 3[14]

f. Subjected the Claimant to treatment during the period 1 January 2001

[10] Dr E is clearly an employee or agent of the Hospital and the Defendant will be vicariously liable for his failures at common law or under the Convention. But Dr F, against whom the case is stronger, is not an employee. The argument could be mounted that Dr F was the agent of the Hospital in complying with Mental Health Act procedures (which require that at least one of the doctors is independent of the Hospital – Section 12(3) MHA 1983). But some commentators argue that NHS doctors are themselves – personally – acting as a "public authority" and so have personal duties to comply with the HRA (see *Blackstone's Guide to the HRA*, Wadham and Mountfield, p 37). The Lord Chancellor has stated that individual doctors fall into the "hybrid body" category (see N. 4 above) and are public authorities when carrying out their NHS obligations but not when carrying out private work (*Hansard*, HL, 24 November 1997, cols 811–12) Thus if the Defendant disputes liability for failures by Dr F, it would be proper to join Dr F in person as Second Defendant to face both the negligence and Convention allegations, although Dr F may have a defence to one or both types of allegation under section 139(1) of the MHA 1983, which bars proceedings in respect of acts done or purportedly done under the MHA, unless the act is done in bad faith or without reasonable care, and then subject to leave being given by the High Court (section 139(2)). But the essence of the claim against Dr F is lack of reasonable care, and so there are the makings of a case against him personally notwithstanding section 139(1). Section 139(1) and (2) could be challenged under the Convention (possibly article 13, or article 14 read with article 6; if they had the effect of preventing the Claimant from persuing his Convention rights in the domestic courts.

Both doctors here are acting within the NHS. There is uncertainty as to the extent to which private hospitals or practitioners will be caught by the 1998 Act. To the extent that private hospitals or doctors could be said to carry out certain functions of a public nature, they will come within Section 6(3)(b) (and see Section 6(5)). Close scrutiny of the particular activity which is alleged to constitute breach will be required to determine whether it comes within the public sphere

[11] This allegation is based on alleged breach of condition (3) of the *Winterwerp* conditions – see N. 9 above

[12] Article 5(4) gives the right to take proceedings by which the lawfulness of detention shall be decided speedily by a court

[13] The scheme of the Mental Health Act 1983 is to allow a Section 3 patient to bring his case before the MHRT at any time during the first six months' detention. If he does not do so, the Hospital must automatically refer his case to the MHRT: Section 68(1). There is no doubt that the Hospital here acted properly according to domestic law. But as a matter of Convention law it has been held that eight weeks may be too long for the initial determination of the legality of detention (*E v Norway* (1994) 17 EHRR 30); and that a period of four months may be too long for the periodic review of the lawfulness of the continued detention (*Koendjbihare v Netherlands* (1990) 13 EHRR 820). This is a challenge to the scheme of the domestic legislation

[14] Article 3 prohibits torture or inhuman or degrading treatment or punishment. In *Herczegfalvy v Austria* (1992) EHRR 437 the Commission was of the view that compulsory medical treatment, combined with artificial feeding and isolation, by an institute for mentally deranged offenders, amounted to a breach of Article 3. The Court disagreed, holding that it was justified by medical necessity. Relying on that authority, it is likely that the Claimant here will only succeed if he can show that his treatment was grossly in excess of what was reasonably justified

and 31 August 2001 without his consent. If the Defendant relies on Section 63 of the Mental Health Act 1983, the Claimant will contend that a patient's consent can only be dispensed with consistently with a Claimant's Convention rights in circumstances where the patient is incapable of giving valid consent, and that on the facts of this case the Claimant was not so incapable, as the Defendant knew or ought to have known.[15]

Under Article 8[16]

g. The Claimant repeats the allegations under f. above and contends that his treatment without consent also amounts to a breach of Article 8.

h. Failed to arrange for the Claimant to be represented by someone other than C as his nearest relative, in circumstances where the Defendant knew or ought to have known that the Claimant did not want C to act as his nearest relative. The Claimant contends that it is part of his right to respect for private life that he should be entitled to select which, if any, of his relatives should represent him.[17, 18]

17. The Claimant brings these proceedings within one year of his release from Hospital and thereby complies with the primary limitation period under Section 7(5)(a) of the 1998 Act. If and to the extent that any part of this claim falls outside the primary limitation period, the Claimant will seek an

---

[15] Section 63 MHA provides a blanket defence. Clearly doctors must be able lawfully to treat a non-consenting patient in cases of emergency or where the patient lacks capacity to consent, so Section 63 could not be said to be wholly incompatible with a patient's Convention rights. But what about cases where the patient in fact has capacity but is wrongly thought not to have capacity? In such circumstances it could be argued that the treatment given without consent was degrading or inhuman. The answer will in all likelihood depend on whether reasonable steps were taken to establish capacity – this would be consistent with the requirements for lawful detention on grounds of mental disorder as set out in *Winterwerp* (see N. 9 above). This is a further example of a Convention challenge to domestic law

[16] Article 8 gives the right to respect for family and private life. It has been held to extend to cover the physical integrity of the individual: *A v UK* [1998] 5 BHRC 137; [1998] FCR 597, and *X and Y v Netherlands* (1985) Series A 91 para 22. There is no reason why it should not be argued to extend also to such matters as treatment for psychiatric disorders and representation in medical matters. The ECHR has applied Article 8 in a broad and sometimes imaginative way. Its application as pleaded above would be novel, but in no way inconsistent with the tenor of Strasbourg jurisprudence on the Article

[17] Certain powers exist under Section 29 of the MHA to change the nearest relative or appoint someone other than the nearest relative in that role for prescribed reasons but the patient's preference is not one of those prescribed reasons. *X and Y v Netherlands* (see N. 17 above) may assist in establishing an Article 8 breach: criminal proceedings could not be brought against an adult abuser of a sixteen year old mentally handicapped girl due to a procedural gap in Dutch law, although civil proceedings could be brought by the girl. The Court held this was an infringement of Article 8 being a failure by the Dutch authorities to respect the girl's private life

[18] Finally, always consider whether an Article 14 breach (the non-discrimination Article) can be made out. Article 14 is not a free-standing article and depends on establishing some interference with rights under another article of the Convention. In this case, it might be possible to hinge a breach on Article 3, if (for example) the facts were that the Claimant was of African Caribbean ethnic origin and statistical evidence existed to demonstrate that more patients of that ethnic origin were detained under the Mental Health Act 1983 than of other ethnic origins

extension of that period pursuant to Section 7(5)(b) of the 1998 Act, on the grounds that:

a. The Claimant was unable to seek legal advice or assistance with the claim while he remained detained in Hospital (up to 1 September 2001).

b. He sought assistance in the bringing of this claim within a reasonable time thereafter.[19]

18. By reason of the matters stated above, the Claimant seeks damages for his unlawful detention between 1 January 2001 and 1 September 2001:

a. Pursuant to common law; and

b. Pursuant to Article 5(5) of the Convention.[20]

19. Further, the Claimant seeks interest on such amounts as he may recover in these proceedings pursuant to Section 35A of the Supreme Court Act 1981, for such period and at such rate as the Court shall think fit.

And the Plaintiff claims:

a. Damages in excess of £15,000.[21]

b. Interest thereon.

PHILIPPA WHIPPLE

Statement of Truth

I believe that the facts stated in these Particulars of Claim are true.

Signed:

SERVED etc.

---

[19] In keeping with the ordinary approach to pleading a Claimant's case on limitation, it is probably sensible for a Claimant to set out his case in the Particulars if limitation is obviously an issue which the Defendant will raise

[20] There is UK case law on the quantum of damages in false imprisonment cases – see, for example, *Thompson v Commissioner of Police of the Metropolis* [1997] 2 All ER 762; and *R v Governor of Brockhirst Prison ex p. Evans* [1997] 2 WLR 103. Niether case arose under the MHA 1983 but the principles applied to such a case would be similar. By Section 8 of the 1998 Act the domestic courts may grant such remedy or relief as they consider to be just and appropriate. The Strasbourg jurisprudence on quantum of damages must be taken into account (Section 2(1) of the 1998 Act; see Article 41 of the Convention which gives a Convention right to compensation). Awards in Strasbourg are generally speaking low by domestic standards. But against the trend of low awards was that in *Bozano v France* (1987) Series A No 124-F where an Applicant was awarded the equivalent of £11,000 for twelve hours' unlawful detention. The circumstances in that case were extreme and the size of award suggests that it included some element of punitive damages, although the ECHR has to date declined to award aggravated or exemplary damages in terms

If the Claimant makes out his case under both common law and under the 1998 Act, the Court will have to tussle with what is the appropriate measure of damages. Clearly the Claimant would not recover twice in so far as the Convention claims overlap with the common law claims

[21] £15,000 is the High Court threshold for bringing proceedings: CPR PD 7 para 2.1

IN THE HIGH COURT OF JUSTICE   CLAIM NO:
QUEEN'S BENCH DIVISION

B E T W E E N:

A

Claimant

and

D NHS Trust

Defendant

DEFENCE

---

1. References to paragraph numbers in this Defence are to paragraphs in the Particulars of Claim unless is otherwise stated. Paragraph 1 is admitted.[22]

2. As to paragraph 2:-

   a. It is admitted that by a letter dated 1 January 2001 the Claimant was referred to the Hospital by his General Practitioner, Dr B.

   b. The letter from the General Practitioner referred to the Claimant being psychotic, questioned whether he had been taking his prescribed medication, and stated:

      "Please see this young man urgently and admit, if appropriate"

   c. Paragraph 2 is accordingly admitted.

3. Paragraph 3 and 4 are admitted.

4. Paragraph 5 is admitted, save that it is denied that the examination by Dr E took only five minutes. It is averred that the examination, the result of which was recorded in the notes, took about twenty minutes.

5. Paragraphs 6 and 7 are admitted.

6. As to Dr F's assessment

   a. it is admitted and averred that Dr F saw and assessed the Claimant, spending at least twenty minutes with him. The Claimant did not appear to acknowledge, or be conscious of Doctor F's presence. The Claimant

---

[22] Consider in each case whether (i) the Defendant is a public authority; and if so, (ii) in relation to the activity giving rise to complaint, whether its nature is private. If it is private, there may be a defence on the basis that the body is a "hybrid" and not liable to Convention claims in respect of private law activities. In this case it seems clear that the NHS Trust is exercising a public function of administering the MHA 1983, so it is caught by the 1998 Act whether it is an "obvious public authority" or a "hybrid" Such questions may be more difficult, and more critical, in relation to private hospitals, or doctors treating patients privately (see N. 10 above)

refused to engage in conversation and simply rocked backwards and forwards without speaking.

    b. Paragraph 8 is denied to the extent that it conflicts with a. above, but is otherwise admitted.

7. Paragraph 9 is admitted. It is averred that the Claimant lacked capacity by reason of his mental illness to give or withhold valid consent.

8. Paragraphs 10 to 12 are admitted.

9. It is denied that the Defendant was negligent whether as alleged in paragraph 13 or at all. In particular and without prejudice to the generality of that denial:

    a. The Defendant complied with all of the statutory requirements for admission under Section 3 of the Mental Health Act 1983.

    b. The Claimant's condition warranted admission in that (i) he had been neglecting himself; (ii) he was delusional; and (iii) he was threatening to kill himself.

    c. He was reasonably found by Drs E and F to be suffering from mental illness of a nature and degree which warranted his admission for treatment and it was necessary for the Claimant's own health and safety that he receive such treatment, which could not have been provided unless he was detained.

    d. Doctors E and F assessed the Claimant with at least reasonable skill and care.

    e. If, which is denied, the assessment of Dr E and/or Dr F was in any respect inadequate, it is averred that following a full and adequate assessment detention would have been approved in any event.[23]

10. Further or alternatively, the Defendant denies that it is responsible for any negligent act or omission by Dr F who was not at the relevant time a servant or agent of the Defendant.[24]

11. It is admitted that the Claimant was deprived of his liberty, but denied that he was falsely imprisoned. The detention was pursuant to, and in accordance with the law. Paragraph 14 is therefore denied.

12. It is further denied that the Defendant has committed a battery upon the Claimant as alleged at paragraph 15 of the Particulars of Claim. The Defendant:

---

[23] Where the allegation is one of negligence leading to false imprisonment, it is questionable that causation arguments such as these – familiar though they are in the clinical negligence field generally will be entertained by the Courts (although they may well be relevant to the issue of quantum). The Courts are even less likely to entertain them in relation to claims under the 1998 Act.

[24] See N. 10 above. On receipt of this Defence, the Claimant will have to consider whether to join Dr F in person as the Second Defendant – but see section 139(1) which may provide Dr F with a defence; and section 139(2) by which the Claimant requires leave.

a. Relies upon Section 63 of the Mental Health Act 1983 to the effect that consent of the patient shall not be required for treatment such as in this case was given.

b. Contends that in any event the Claimant's mental disorder was such, or was reasonably believed by the Defendant's servants or agents to be such, that the Claimant lacked the capacity to give or withhold valid consent.

13. It is denied that the Defendant acted in breach of the Claimant's Convention rights as alleged at paragraph 16 of the Particulars of Claim or at all. Without prejudice to the generality of that denial the Claimant adopts the paragraph numbering in the Particulars of Claim and contends as follows:

Alleged breach under Article 5(1)

a.–c.

  i. The Defendant repeats paragraph 9 of this Defence. The Defendant relied on objective evidence from Doctors E and F to the effect that the Claimant was of unsound mind of a degree and nature which justified detention;

  ii. Further or alternatively, in so far as allegations are made concerning Dr F:

  A. the Defendant repeats paragraph 10 of this Defence and denies that it is responsible for any breach of the Claimant's Convention rights by Dr F who was not a servant or agent of the Defendant;[25]

  B. further or alternatively, it is denied that Dr F was a "public authority" for the purposes of Section 6 of the 1998 Act.

d. The Claimant was kept under constant review by the treating doctors who remained of the view that the Claimant's detention was justified.[26]

Alleged breach under Article 5(4)

e. It is admitted that formal review by the MHRT did not take place until 25 August 2001, but averred that such review:

---

[25] There is no point running this defence in relation to Doctor E who is a servant or agent of the Defendant for whom the Defendant would be vicariously liable in any event. See N. 10 above

[26] The outcome under this head of alleged breach of Article 5(1) will be dependent to a great extent on the same evidence and arguments as will be put forward in relation to the negligence claim. It is likely (but not certain) that if no negligence is established, then no breach of Article 5(1) will be established either

i. Took place pursuant to the statutory scheme contained within the Mental Health Act 1983 (Section 68) by which the Defendant was and is bound;[27]

ii. Took place with reasonable speed and expedition in the circumstances.

Alleged breach under Article 3

f. It is admitted that the Claimant did not consent to the treatment he was accorded while detained, but averred:

i. That the Claimant lacked the capacity to give or withhold valid consent by reason of his mental illness;

ii. In any event, his treatment, even if administered in the absence of consent, does not come within the ambit of Article 3;

iii. Further, the Defendant relies on Section 63 of the Mental Health Act 1983 which obviates the need for consent in circumstances such as applied in this case.

Alleged breach under Article 8[28]

g. The Defendant repeats paragraph 13 f. of this Defence and contends that the Claimant lacked capacity. If (which is denied) the Claimant did have capacity to withhold valid consent, the Defendant relies on Article 8(2) and contends that:

i. The detention was in accordance with domestic law; and

ii. That law is necessary to protect health and the rights and freedoms of others.

h. The Defendant contends that C was acting as nearest relative in accordance with the law at all times, which law was necessary, pursuant to Article 8(2).

14. It is further averred that the Defendant was under a positive obligation to detain the Claimant by virtue of Article 2 of the Convention, since at the time of admission on 1 January 2001:

---

[27] Article 5 gives rise to a right subject to defined limits – i.e. the right to liberty and security may be legitimately interfered with in certain prescribed circumstances (of which (e) is relevant here: the lawful detention of persons of unsound mind), *and* so long as the detention is in accordance with a procedure prescribed by law. The Defendant will want to argue that the Claimant's detention comes within the qualifications and thus that no breach has occurred

[28] The essence of the defence to both allegations under Article 8 is to rely on the derogation in Article 8(2)

a. The Claimant was threatening to harm himself and his detention was necessary to prevent self-harm.[29]

b. Alternatively, the Defendant reasonably believed the Claimant would harm himself and that his detention was necessary.[30]

15. Further or alternatively, if the Claimant establishes that his rights under Article 5(4) (speedy trial) and/or Article 8 (replacement of nearest relative) have been breached as alleged, the Defendant will contend:

   a. That it was acting pursuant to its duties under primary legislation, namely the Mental Health Act 1983, and it could not have acted differently in accordance with that legislation:

      i. The Defendant has no power in domestic law to refer cases to the MHRT save pursuant to Section 68 of the Mental Health Act 1983, which in this case required the Hospital to refer only after six months had expired because the Claimant had not himself appealed;

      ii. Section 29 of the Mental Health Act 1983 sets out an exhaustive list of circumstances for replacement of a nearest relative, none of which apply in this case. The Defendant thus had no power to secure replacement of C as nearest relative.

   b. In either case, the Claimant's sole remedy therefore is to seek a declaration of incompatibility of the relevant domestic legislation.[31]

16. The Claimant's claim under the Human Rights Act 1988 is barred by Section 7(5)(a) in that the proceedings were not brought within one year of the act complained of, namely the detention on 1 January 2001. It would not be equitable to grant a longer period, given:

   a. The Claimant had access to legal advice and assistance whilst detained in hospital; and

---

[29] The case could equally be made if the Claimant had threatened to harm others

[30] The 1998 Act is not always going to be a sword in the armoury of a Claimant; this is an example of the Convention being used as a shield to justify the Defendant's conduct. As a matter of common law a duty of care may require positive steps to be taken to protect a person from self harm (see *Kirkham v Chief Constable of Greater Manchester Police* [1990] 2 QB 283). Such an approach is mirrored under Convention law in cases such as *Osman v UK* [1999] 5 BHRC 293

[31] This is not what the Claimant wants to hear, as a declaration of incompatibility will not assist this particular Claimant in this case. But the possibility of a declaration being sought should be raised at an early stage to enable notice to be given to the Crown which will consider whether it wishes to be joined as a party (see Section 5 of 1998 Act)

The Claimant will want to dispute that a declaration of incompatibility is necessary at all. As to Section 68(1), the Claimant's best case will be that there is nothing in that Section, or the Mental Health Act 1983, which prevents a Hospital from referring a patient's case to the MHRT before six months have expired; the Section merely provides a "long-stop". (It may be advisable to put in a Reply to the Defence stating this, so that the Claimant's case is clear.) However, it is difficult to see a way around the Section 29 point: the Section appears to be exhaustive of the circumstances when application for replacement of nearest relative may be made, and a declaration of incompatibility may be the only available remedy

b. A further ten months has elapsed since his discharge from Hospital and the issue of these proceedings.[32]

17. The Claimant's claim to damages and interest under paragraphs 17 and 18 is accordingly denied.

PHILIPPA WHIPPLE

Statement of Truth

I believe that the facts stated in this Defence are true.

Signed:

Office:

SERVED etc.

[32] There is a one year time limit for bringing a claim under the Convention (Section 7(5)(a)) "beginning with the date on which the act complained of took place", but with a discretion analogous to that under Section 33 of the Limitation Act 1980 for the Court to extend the time limit under Section 7(5)(b)

8

The Impact of the Convention on Medical Law

PHILIP HAVERS QC AND NEIL SHELDON

1. INTRODUCTION

Inevitably, the potential impact of the Convention on medical law, by which we mean those areas of the law which impinge upon medicine other than medical negligence, is somewhat diverse. Indeed, it is an area which has been developed to only a limited extent under the Convention. Accordingly, this chapter addresses not so much the effect of the Convention on medical law hitherto as the potential effect of the Convention on medical law in the future, particularly if English lawyers and judges are prepared to use the Convention to inform and develop those areas of law which touch upon medicine.

2. PROLONGING LIFE

Over recent years there have been several cases in which declarations have been made by the Court to the effect that it is lawful for doctors to turn off life support systems for those reduced to a permanent vegetative state by some disaster (see, for example, *Airedale NHS Trust v Bland*).[1] The common law has been able to accommodate such a step on the basis that doctors are obliged always to act in the best interests of the patient and that circumstances may arise where it is in the best interests of the patient, who remains in a permanent vegetative state from which there is no hope of recovery, to turn off the life support system. The argument has also been advanced that such a step would, in some circumstances, be in the best interests of the community at large in view of the large resources of time, skill and money required in keeping such a patient alive. In the *Airedale* case Lord Mustill, in particular, gave detailed consideration to this argument but found that, although it was persuasive *"in social terms"*, it involved an assessment that the Court was not qualified to make.

The law in this area will have to be fully reconsidered in light of the provisions of Article 2 of the Convention. This Article, recognised as one of the most

[1] [1993] AC 789

fundamental contained in the Convention, protects the individual's right to life. Article 2(1) provides as follows:

> *"Everyone's right to life shall be protected by law. No one shall be deprived of his life intentionally save in the execution of a sentence of a court following his conviction of a crime for which this penalty is provided by law".*

As the wording of this provision makes clear, the state is under a positive obligation to ensure that an individual's life is properly protected by putting laws into place which provide for sanctions to be imposed on those who take life other than in accordance with the Convention. The question is whether this positive obligation may be extended to impose a duty on the state to provide the medical treatment necessary to preserve life.

This issue was raised in the case of *Association X v United Kingdom*.[2] The case concerned the provision of a vaccination programme by the UK Government during the course of which some of the children vaccinated suffered an adverse reaction and died. The Commission found on the facts that there was no evidence that the vaccine had been administered poorly or that the Government had in any way intended such adverse consequences to occur. However, the Commission made the following statement:[3]

> *"The concept that 'everyone's life shall be protected by law' enjoins the State not only to refrain from taking life intentionally but, further, to take appropriate steps to safeguard life".*

In the context of the *Association X* case, this statement may amount to no more than the requirement that a state is not negligent in its provision of health care services which is different from an obligation to provide an individual with a specific form of treatment. A negligence-style test was also adopted by the Court in the case of *Osman*.[4] In that case the Court was faced with the question of whether the police had taken sufficient steps to protect a family which had been repeatedly threatened by a teacher of one of the children. In holding that there had been no breach of Article 2, the Court found that there was no stage in the sequence of events culminating in the shooting of one of the family members at which the police knew or ought to have known that the family was at real risk.[5] A final example of the approach adopted by the Court in considering whether a state has fulfilled its obligations under Article 2 is provided by the case of *Guerra*.[6] In that case, the court held that the obligation of the state to inform its citizens of environmental circumstances which posed a potential threat to health extended only to *"circumstances which foreseeably and on substantial grounds present a real risk of danger"*.

---

[2] Application 7154/75 14 DR 31 (1978)
[3] At p 32
[4] (1999) 5 BHRC 293
[5] Paras 116 and 121
[6] (1998) 26 EHRR 357. See also chapter 10 on Environmental Rights

From this line of decisions, it would seem to be clear that a state will be considered to be in breach of Article 2 if it fails to do what is reasonable to protect the lives of its citizens. Therefore, despite the fact that the withdrawal of treatment from a patient on a life support machine would appear to be, prima facie, a breach of Article 2, it would be open to the health authority to argue that it would have been unreasonable to do otherwise. The two most obvious potential grounds for such an argument are the interests of the patient (the existing common law justification for such a step) and the interests of society at large (as considered by Lord Mustill in *Airedale*).

Moreover, the Commission has drawn a distinction between causing death by omission and causing death by a deliberate act. Thus, it has been held by the Commission that Article 2 does not require that passive euthanasia, by which a person is allowed to die by not being given treatment, be a crime.[7] A different answer would be likely in the case of active euthanasia, whereby death is accelerated by a positive act, although in a decision of the German *Verwaltungsgericht* of November 8 1959[8] a doctor was found not to have infringed Article 2 by the giving of overdoses of drugs to the terminally ill. It may be, therefore, that the turning off of a life support machine would be regarded not as a positive act but as part of an act of omission by which steps were not taken to keep a person alive.

A further point to note is that Article 3 requires that a person is not subjected to inhuman or degrading treatment. In the case of *D v United Kingdom*[9] the Court emphasised that amongst the rights protected by Article 3 is the right to die with dignity. There may well be circumstances in which it is considered that the continued provision of medical treatment to an individual in a permanent vegetative state constitutes a breach of his Article 3 rights in this way. Similar issues may be raised by the right to *"moral and physical integrity"* guaranteed by Article 8.

It is clear, therefore, that despite the unambiguous terms of Article 2, the matter is far from straightforward and the extent of the duties of the state in this area have yet to be defined. The common law has developed principally on the basis of what is best for the patient in light of expert medical opinion, and it is to be expected that there will be considerable judicial reluctance to impose treatment upon a patient where the evidence is that the treatment will not improve the patient's quality of life. In order to avoid the necessity of doing so, in cases in which Article 2 is invoked, the law will have to accommodate a limitation on the protection of the right to life, whether by adopting the arguments discussed above or otherwise.

---

[7] *Widmer v Switzerland* Application 20527/92 (1993), unreported
[8] NJW (1960) 400
[9] (1997) 24 EHRR 423

Secondly, there has been some recent litigation with regard to the carrying out of an enforced Caesarean section upon a mother who did not lack the capacity to consent.[10] In *ex parte S* the Court of Appeal rejected the contention of the health authority that the court had power to override a mother's refusal to agree to medical treatment to save the life of her unborn child if it was in the interests of the child so to do. The interesting question arises whether the child has a right to life under Article 2 of the Convention.

The question has arisen already in Strasbourg in the case of *Paton v UK*.[11] There the Commission ruled that the abortion of a ten week old fetus under British law to protect the physical or mental health of a pregnant woman was not in breach of Article 2. In doing so, the Commission stated that Article 2 does not recognise an absolute right to life of an unborn child but left open the question of whether Article 2 protects the unborn child at all or whether the fetus has a right to life under Article 2 subject to some limitations.

The point was given further consideration in the case of *Open Door Counselling and Dublin Well Woman v Ireland*.[12] Although not directly relevant to the case, which concerned the rights of the applicant to disseminate information about abortion rather than the right to abortion itself, the Commission did consider the submission made by the Irish Government that Article 2 also protected unborn life. Although it did not decide the point expressly, the Commission did state that the right to life protected under Article 2 could sometimes restrict the availability of an abortion. Unfortunately, the Court gave no guidance on the point in its judgment.

More recently, the Commission has considered the case of an unborn child whose life was threatened by the imminent deportation of its mother.[13] The claim under Article 2 was found to be inadmissible by virtue of the fact that the UK Government had deferred deportation at the request of the Commission and the child had been born alive, and so the point, once again, was not directly decided.

There is, therefore, no settled authority on the question which is, admittedly, an extremely difficult one given the diversity of opinion on the issue which exists between signatory states. In those circumstances it would seem likely that the Court, if called upon to deal directly with the scope of the applicability of Article 2 to the unborn child, would grant states a wide margin of appreciation. Although it stated in the *Open Door Counselling* case that the margin of appreciation offered to states in such matters was not unfettered or unreviewable, the Court did go on to find[14] that:

[10] See *R v Collins, ex parte S* [1998] 3 All ER 673. See also chapter 12 on Mental Health
[11] (1980) 3 EHRR 408
[12] (1992) 15 EHRR 244
[13] *Poku v United Kingdom*, No. 26985/85 (1996), unreported
[14] At para 68

"National authorities enjoy a wide margin of appreciation in matters of morals, particularly in an area such as the present which touches on matters of belief concerning the nature of human life".

There is, therefore, little encouragement in the Strasbourg jurisprudence to domestic courts to adopt a markedly different approach to the question of abortion and the rights of the unborn child than has hitherto been followed under the scheme of the 1967 Abortion Act. Just as the margin of appreciation doctrine appears to have restricted the Court in its dealings with this particularly sensitive moral question, so might domestic courts be persuaded that any development of the law in this area is a matter best left for Parliament.

However, in a recent Canadian case[15] which upheld the autonomy of the mother to refuse treatment in such circumstances, Major J, in a powerful dissenting judgment, expressed the view that someone must speak for those who cannot speak for themselves. It remains to be seen whether the English courts will do so. What would seem to be clear, however, is that any further liberalisation of the abortion legislation would have to be examined closely in light of the jurisprudence described above leaving open, as it does, the possibility that the fetus has some rights under Article 2(1).

In some situations, such rights as may be attributed to the unborn child under Article 2, may well come into conflict with the rights of the mother under Article 8 which protects her right to private life. It has long been recognised by the Court that the scope of this provision extends to cover the sexual relationships of an individual.[16] In *Bruggeman and Sheuten v FRG*[17] the Commission came to the view that the applicant's right to untroubled sexual relations as part of her private life extended to her right to an abortion in the event of an unwanted conception. The courts may be required in some cases to undertake a difficult balancing exercise between the conflicting Convention rights of the parties.

A further way in which the Convention may impact upon the question of enforced medical treatment is via the provisions of Article 12 and, in particular, the right to found a family. English law has long recognised the right of medical authorities to carry out sterilisations on incompetent adults or minors without their consent when the court considers that such treatment is in the best interests of the child concerned.[18] The Commission has, however, on at least one occasion regarded the right to found a family as an *"absolute right"* with which the state has no grounds for interfering.[19] This raises the possibility that the powers of medical authorities (and the courts) in this area may be severely curtailed.

---

[15] *Winnipeg Child and Family Services (North West Area) v G* [1997] 3 SCR 925
[16] See *Dudgeon v UK* (1981) 4 EHRR 149
[17] No. 6959 175 10 DR 100
[18] See, for example, the cases of *In Re F (Mental Patient: Sterilisation)* [1990] 2 AC 1 and *In Re B (a Minor) (Wardship: Sterilisation)* [1988] AC 199
[19] *X v UK* No. 6564/74 2 DR 105

4. FUNDING TREATMENT

Thirdly, there must now be some prospect of overturning the decision of the Court of Appeal in the recent case involving an application for judicial review of a decision by the Cambridgeshire Health Authority not to fund very expensive medical treatment for a young child which, on the evidence, would have been likely to prolong her life for only a few months (*R v Cambridgeshire Health Authority, ex parte B*).[20] Laws J quashed the decision of the health authority on the basis that the authority was under a positive duty to sustain life if there was a chance of survival, however small, but the Court of Appeal[21] held that the authority was entitled to refuse to do so on the basis that it was entitled, if not bound, to deploy its resources as best it could. Different considerations may now prevail once the Convention has been incorporated and the reliance of the Court of Appeal on the resource argument may not carry anything like as much weight. This question was examined by the Constitutional Court of South Africa in the case of *Soobramoney v Minister of Health*.[22] The appellant in that case was terminally ill with renal failure and was also suffering from heart disease. He was refused admission to hospital for ongoing dialysis treatment because of a shortage of resources which compelled the hospital to implement guidelines precluding chronic renal failure sufferers with heart disease from dialysis treatment. The applicant claimed that, in terms of the right not to be refused emergency treatment under Section 27(3) of the South African Constitution, construed with the right to life entrenched in Section 11, the state was obliged to provide the resources necessary for the ongoing treatment of his chronic illness for the purpose of prolonging his life. The Constitutional Court held that the respondent was not in breach of the requirement that "*No one may be refused emergency medical treatment*", because the absolute nature of that requirement had to be viewed in light of the further provision of the Constitution that "*Everyone has the right to have access to health care services*". When taken together, in the context of finite resources, the Court found that an unqualified obligation to meet health care needs, was impossible to fulfil. The fulfilment of one of the constitutional requirements would inevitably lead to a failure to fulfil the other. A balance had to be struck, and if that balance was arrived at in good faith and on the basis of rational decisions by the health authority, the court should be slow to interfere. In other words, the South African Court limited the scope of what appeared to be an absolute requirement by stipulating that it was enough for the state to act reasonably in the allocation of resources. The potential applicability of this approach to the question of the maintenance of treatment for those in a permanent vegetative state has been examined above. Whether it may be used post-incorporation to justify the with-

---

[20] [1995] 1 FLR 1055
[21] [1995] 1 WLR 898
[22] 4 BHRC 308

holding of treatment when such treatment offers the chance of survival or at least a positive effect on the patient's quality of life, remains to be seen.

However, even if it was found that the rational allocation of health care resources did not constitute a breach of Article 2, notwithstanding that it followed that an individual was deprived of potentially life-saving treatment, Article 14 of the Convention might come into play. Article 14 places an obligation on public authorities to secure Convention rights without discrimination on any ground. By definition, its operation does not presuppose a breach of any other Article and a measure which conforms in itself with a substantive provision of the Convention may contravene Article 14 because it is discriminatory in nature.[23]

Consequently, if potentially life-saving treatment was withheld from a patient because of, for example, his or her advanced age or even status as a sufferer of a terminal disease,[24] it might be argued that such action constituted a breach of Article 14 taken together with Article 2.

A further question may arise as to the applicability of Article 14 to the provision of private health care. One of the forms of discrimination expressly forbidden by the terms of Article 14 is discrimination on the basis of "property". The availability of private health care as an alternative to that provided by the state inevitably means that a person with the requisite financial resources could secure his Article 2 rights far more easily than someone reliant upon the state. Nor would he be subject to the type of resource allocation found to be unavoidable in *Soobramoney*.

Thus far the Court has shown itself to be reluctant to hold that Article 14 prohibits discrimination on the grounds of financial status. The point arose in the case of *Airey v Ireland*[25] but the Court declined to deal with it finding it unnecessary to do so in light of an established breach of another Article. On the face of it, however, there would seem to be some force in the argument that "property" in Article 14 should extend to cover an individual's financial status, and situations in which that individual's access to Convention rights is easier because of that financial status may be open to challenge in this way.

5. MEDICAL RECORDS

The collection of medical data and the maintenance of medical records may now be affected by Article 8 (the right to privacy) and Article 10 (freedom of speech). The application of Article 8 was considered in the case of *MS v Sweden*.[26] In that case, the applicant made a claim for compensation from the Social Insurance Office arising from a back injury caused by a fall at work. She

---

[23] See *Airey v Ireland* (1979) 2 EHRR 305
[24] See *Soobramoney*, N. 22 above
[25] (1979) 9 EHRR 203
[26] (1999) 28 EHRR 313, also discussed in some detail in chapter 11 on Confidentiality and Defamation

was a long term sufferer of spondylolithesis, a spine condition which can cause chronic back pain. The Office requested the applicant's medical records (without her consent) from the head of the clinic who had treated her for the back injury and, having found that the records suggested that an abortion had been performed due to previous back problems, making no reference to her alleged injury at work (the abortion having post-dated her back injury at work by some four years), rejected her claim finding that her sick leave had not been caused by the industrial injury. The Court held that although there had been an interference with her right to privacy under Article 8, the interference was justified since it served the legitimate aim of the protection of the economic well-being of the country as it was potentially decisive for the allocation of public funds. The Court did find, however, that in bringing the claim for compensation, the applicant had not waived the right to privacy protected by Article 8. This finding may have considerable impact upon the conventional approach of the English courts to this question, namely that a claimant who sues for medical negligence (or some other medically related complaint) automatically waives confidentiality in his or her medical records.

The importance attached by the Court to the preservation of the confidentiality of medical records was underlined in the case of *Z v Finland*.[27] At paragraph 95 of its judgment the Court stated:

> "The protection of personal data, not least medical data, is of fundamental importance to a person's enjoyment of his or her right to respect for private or family life as guaranteed by Article 8 of the Convention . . . without such protection, those in need of medical assistance may be deterred from revealing such information of a personal and intimate nature as may be necessary in order to receive appropriate treatment and even, from seeking such assistance, thereby endangering their own health and, in the case of transmissable diseases, that of the community".

The reasoning used by the Court in this case may suggest that the public interest, which was used to justify the Article 8 breaches in the *MS v Sweden* case, may not always be easy to identify.[28] Although it must certainly be regarded as appropriate that claims are properly investigated and that justice is as open as possible, the benefits to the public and the individual of encouraging frankness between patients and those treating them must be weighed in the balance. It may well be possible that a compromise position will develop in which the automatic right of a defendant to have sight of all the medical records of a claimant is qualified, perhaps in relation to the size of the claim or the ability of the defendant to demonstrate the likely impact of the records on the proceedings in question.

---

[27] (1998) 25 EHRR 371
[28] See the discussion of the confidentiality of medical records in the *Pinochet* case at p. 200

6. MEDICAL TRIBUNALS

An important part of the work of many who practise in medical law is representing (or prosecuting) those who appear at disciplinary tribunals of one sort or another. These may be hearings before the General Medical Council (GMC) or disciplinary tribunal hearings at a lower level. Article 6 may be of direct relevance to such tribunals.

Article 6 guarantees the right to a fair trial and is concerned principally with the issue of procedural fairness in the determination of both criminal charges and civil rights and obligations. Articles 6(2) and (3) set out the more detailed provisions concerning the rights of individuals involved in criminal proceedings.

The specific rights guaranteed by the Article include the right to a *"fair and public hearing"*, the right to an *"independent and impartial tribunal"* and the right to have one's case heard within a *"reasonable time"*. If the proceedings are deemed to be "criminal" in nature for the purposes of the Convention, then additional rights are specified, including the right of an individual to have legal representation provided free of charge if he is unable to afford it himself and the right to have adequate time and facilities provided to prepare his defence.

The first question that arises is whether Article 6 will apply to tribunals such as the GMC in the first place. In the recent case of *General Medical Council v British Broadcasting Corporation*,[29] the Court of Appeal found that the GMC was not a "Court" for the purposes of Section 19 of the Contempt of Court Act 1981 because, although it did follow procedural rules in the exercise of recognisably judicial functions, it was a self-regulating body rather than part of the *"judicial system of the State"*.

It is likely, however, that in determining whether Article 6 is applicable to such tribunals a different test will be applied. The test most consistently adopted by the Court is to ask whether the result of the proceedings in issue will be "decisive" in the determination of the individual's civil rights and obligations or of any criminal charge against him.[30] Applying that test to proceedings before a medical disciplinary tribunal which resulted in the suspension of the doctors concerned, the Court held that Article 6(1) was applicable on the basis that the decision of the tribunal was directly decisive of the applicants' right to practise medicine.[31] A similar conclusion was reached in the recent case of *Diennet v France*[32] in which it was held that the French Medical Disciplinary Council, which conducted disciplinary proceedings against doctors and others in France, fell within Article 6. In the case of *Stefan*[33] the GMC referred the Commission to the case of *Van Marle v Netherlands*[34] in support of the

---

[29] [1998] 1 WLR 1573
[30] See, for example, *Konig v Federal Republic of Germany* (1978) 2 EHRR 170, para 88
[31] *Le Compte v Belgium* (1981) 4 EHRR 1
[32] (1995) EHRR CD 491
[33] (1998) EHRR CD 130
[34] (1986) A–101

proposition that the evaluation of the fitness of an individual to practise on medical grounds did not constitute a determination of the individual's rights and obligations within the meaning of Article 6(1). The argument was rejected by the Commission, who noted that the proceedings were conclusive as to the applicant's ability to continue practising as a doctor.

The crucial question, therefore, would seem to be the extent of the powers of the tribunal concerned. If the tribunal had no power, whatever its decision, decisively to affect the private law rights of the individual before it, then it would be arguable that Article 6(1) did not apply to its proceedings. However, bodies which have the power, for example, to suspend an individual from practising medicine (such as the GMC) would fall within the ambit of Article 6.

The next question is whether such proceedings should be classified as "civil" or "criminal" for the purposes of Article 6. The Court applies three criteria in determining this issue:

(a) the classification of the proceedings in domestic law;
(b) the nature of the offence itself;
(c) the severity of the penalty that may be imposed.[35]

The classification of the procedure under domestic law is only one of the considerations. If domestic law classifies the proceedings as "criminal", that is decisive of the question, but if the proceedings are classified domestically as "civil" the Court goes on to conduct its own enquiry. In the two medical tribunal cases cited above the Court regarded the proceedings as civil, but it might nonetheless be arguable in the more serious GMC cases which result in the harshest sanctions, that the more rigorous protection afforded under Article 6 to those involved in criminal proceedings may apply.

The basic rights contained in Article 6(1) are almost certain to apply in any event. This could give rise to some interesting problems. For example, the requirement that the hearing be conducted by an independent and impartial tribunal might cause real difficulty where the tribunal cannot demonstrate that it is independent of either the doctor or, perhaps, the "prosecution". In this connection, it is essential to note that the Court has upheld a number of complaints under Article 6(1) on the basis, not that the tribunal in question in fact lacked independence or impartiality but that it may have given the appearance of doing so.[36]

It follows that there is very considerable scope under Article 6 for doctors and others to insist upon much higher standards of fairness and procedural safeguards in disciplinary hearings than may have applied hitherto.

[35] See *Engel v Netherlands* (1976) 1 EHRR 647
[36] This requirement has already led to a ruling by the High Court of Justiciary in Scotland that the system of appointing temporary sheriffs for a term of one year falls short of the requirements under Article 6 (incorporated by the Scotland Act 1998): *Starrs v Procurator Fiscal, Linithgow* 11 November 1999, *The Times*, 17 November 1999 (unreported). Such adjudicators lacked security of tenure, "one of the cornerstones of judicial independence". See also *Findlay v UK* (1997) 24 EHRR 221

One potential way in which the requirement of Article 6 may be overcome or, more accurately, ignored in relation to medical tribunals, is by the availability of an appeal from the decisions of such tribunals. Article 6(1) does not guarantee a right of appeal from such a decision but, where the decision is taken by an administrative or non-judicial body, any breach by that body of the requirements of Article 6(1) will be remedied if the state provides the individual with a right to challenge its decision before a court with full jurisdiction which does comply with the Article.[37] In order to give Article 6 proper effect it would seem to be necessary that the appellate body concerned is able to review the facts in full rather than be restricted to hearing appeals based only on points of law.

However, in the case of *Bryan v United Kingdom*,[38] the Court went as far as to say that in some specialised areas of law (planning in that case) it was sometimes necessary for a non-judicial administrative body to make findings of fact and make judgments based on policy considerations. In those circumstances, any breach of Article 6(1) committed by such a body could be remedied by means of a right of appeal to a judicial body based only on a point of law.[39]

7. INQUESTS

It has been asserted by at least one commentator on the Convention that Article 2 requires the proper investigation of all suspicious deaths. This would seem to be supported by the requirements of Article 13 which state that anyone who has his Convention rights violated must have an effective remedy before a national authority. Where an individual claims that one of his rights has been violated[40] and his claim is at least arguable,[41] there is an obligation on the state concerned to ensure that the claim is given proper consideration by an independent and impartial tribunal and that the individual is granted an effective remedy for any breach.

If this is correct the question may arise as to whether the present rather limited scope of enquiry undertaken at an inquest satisfies these requirements. The question may be especially pertinent where human rights are directly in play as in the *McCann* case. In that case, as explained in the first chapter, the Court (and the Commission) had investigated not only the circumstances immediately surrounding the killing of the three terrorists but also the prior planning and organisation of the operation as a whole. The current inquest procedure, limited as it is to discovering the means of death rather than the circumstances that surrounded it,[42] would not be able to undertake such an enquiry and might,

---

[37] See *Albert and Le Compte v Belgium* (1983) 5 EHRR 533
[38] (1995) 21 EHRR 342 (discussed in detail in chapter 10 on Environmental Rights)
[39] See also *Wickramsinghe v UK* (1998) EHRLR 338
[40] *Klass v FRG* (1978) 2 EHRR 214
[41] *Silver v UK* (1983) 5 EHRR 347
[42] *R v North Humberside Coroner ex parte Jamieson* [1994] 3 All ER 972

therefore, be regarded as too restricted to give proper effect to Article 2 taken together with Article 13.

This would be of considerable interest to the relatives of some deceased who may be contemplating civil proceedings arising out of the death but whose attempts at the subsequent inquest to widen the scope of the enquiry so as to examine the potential culpability of those who, for example, may have been treating the deceased are often ruled inadmissible by the coroner.

8. RIGHT TO FOUND A FAMILY

Following the interesting case of *Ex parte Blood*[43] it may now be arguable that a refusal by a public authority (for example, a health authority) to provide certain types of fertilisation treatment would be in breach of Article 12 which provides that *"men and women of marriageable age have a right to marry and found a family . . .".*

It is highly unlikely that the scope of this provision would extend to requiring a state to make a certain sort of treatment available. The considerable doubts that continue to surround the safety and efficacy of many treatments would mean that the Court would be very slow to interfere with the judgment of a Contracting State as to what was best for its citizens. However, as some treatments become more established and widespread it may be that states will have to show more to justify withholding them from their citizens.

More difficult questions arise where a given treatment is available and regarded by the state (subject to regulation) as safe but is only available to certain sections of the population. For example, some techniques, possibly including the only one likely to be effective for a particular couple, may only be available to those able to pay for them. The question of whether this might constitute discrimination on the grounds of "property" for the purposes of Article 14 has been raised above. There is also the case where the treating doctor withholds treatment from an individual woman based upon his assessment of her situation. The current domestic rules governing access to IVF treatment are far from coherent. Under Section 13(5) of the Human Fertilisation and Embryology Act 1990, a woman may not be provided with treatment *"unless account has been taken of the welfare of any child who may be born as a result of the treatment (including the need of that child for a father) and of any other child who may be affected by the birth".* This provision would appear to give the woman's treating doctor the power to refuse treatment on grounds other than her best interests. In doing so he may be compromising her Article 12 rights. The justification for doing so, namely the welfare of a child who has yet to be conceived or the economic or psychological effects of having another sibling on existing children, may not be regarded as sufficient for Convention purposes. There

---

[43] [1997] 2 All ER 687

might also be a breach of Article 12 if the treating doctor was to refuse treatment (as he is expressly authorised to do) on the basis that the patient was a single mother. The terms of Article 14 prohibit discrimination on the basis of membership of any social group. If single mothers were found to form such a group and were discriminated against in the provision of fertility treatment on that basis it would certainly be arguable that a breach was disclosed.

9. AIDS

The implications of the treatment by national authorities of individuals suffering from AIDS or infected with the HIV virus are wide ranging and have led to a large number of cases in Strasbourg. The majority of the case law appears to be concerned with the disclosure of an individual's HIV status (Article 8), the quality of treatment available to a sufferer were he to be expelled from a Contracting State (Article 3) and the speed at which states handle compensation claims by those negligently infected (Article 6).

9.1. Article 8

AIDS cases raise particularly difficult questions regarding the disclosure of a patient's condition and the apparent conflict between the duty of confidence owed by the doctor to the patient and the doctor's obligation to protect that individual's partner or those caring for him who might be at risk of infection.[44]

The guidance issued by the General Medical Council (Guidance from the GMC on Confidentiality, 7), advises that each patient should receive counselling explaining the need for disclosure and emphasising particularly the danger that non-disclosure poses for those caring for him. If after such counselling the patient refuses to consent to disclosure then his wishes should be respected. The one exception is where his sexual partner or those treating him would otherwise be at "serious risk" of infection.

The Court has shown itself willing to accept justifications for breaches of Article 8 in this area on similar grounds. For example, in the case of *TV v Finland*[45] the Commission found that prison staff should have access to information concerning an inmate's HIV status as long as access was restricted to only those staff who might realistically be at risk of infection. Similarly in *Z v Finland*,[46] the Court found that the prima facie breaches of Article 8, which arose when a woman's HIV status was revealed during the course of criminal proceeding against her husband (who was charged with deliberately attempting

---

[44] See chapter 11 on Confidentiality and Defamation
[45] 21780/93 76 DR 140 (1994)
[46] (1997) 25 EHRR 371

to infect others with the virus), were justified as being in pursuit of the prevention of crime.

9.2. Article 3

No issues have yet arisen regarding the standard of care provided by Contracting States to those suffering from AIDS. However, the inadequacy of care provided by a non-Contracting State did give rise to a successful claim for breach of Article 3 in *D v United Kingdom*.[47] That case concerned the decision of the UK Government to deport the applicant, a convicted drugs smuggler suffering from AIDS, to St Kitts. The applicant claimed that the treatment he would receive in St Kitts would be so poor as to amount to inhuman or degrading treatment. In light of the very advanced state of the applicant's illness the Court found that his expulsion would amount to a breach of Article 3.

Two questions arise from this decision. The first is whether it will now be open to any unsuccessful asylum seeker who is suffering from a serious medical condition to block his expulsion from a Contracting State if he can show that he would receive comparatively poor medical treatment back home. The second is whether the case will open the way for an influx of AIDS sufferers from the poorer countries of the world to those countries in Europe with superior health care systems.

As to the first of these questions, the Court made it clear in *D* that it had dealt with the case on the basis of its own exceptional facts from which it may be possible to infer that only exceptional cases of very serious illness might lead to the same result. As to the second, the Commission pointed out in *D* that the UK had not expelled the applicant immediately but had imprisoned him in the UK following his conviction on drugs charges. It was whilst he was in prison that he became dependent upon the medication he would not receive in St Kitts. Had the applicant not been treated in this way and expelled immediately a different conclusion may well have been reached. It may be, therefore, that the implications of *D v UK* are not as wide ranging as they appear at first sight.

9.3. Article 6

Most individuals infected in this way have simply proceeded against the state concerned for compensation. When such proceedings are brought the Court has emphasised that they must be dealt with quickly. In *X v France*,[48] the applicant, a haemophiliac, claimed compensation after receiving an infected blood transfusion. His appeal was still pending at the time of his death two years later. The Court held that although two years would not ordinarily constitute a serious

---

[47] (1997) 24 EHRR 423
[48] *Association X v United Kingdom*, discussed above

delay in resolving proceedings of this complexity, the special circumstances of the case meant that here it disclosed a breach of the right to a fair trial within a reasonable time under Article 6(1). A similar point was made in the cases of *Karakaya v France*[49] and *Vallee v France*.[50] There is no obvious reason why this principle should not be extended to any case involving terminal illness in which the claimant is likely to die within a short period, and domestic courts may have to review their timetables accordingly.

9.4. Article 2

No case has yet been brought under Article 2 against a state for failure to protect an individual's right to life on the basis of an HIV infection through a blood transfusion. On the face of it, there is no reason why such a claim should not be brought although the vaccination case[51] would suggest that the applicant, if he were to succeed, would have to show that the state had been in some way negligent in failing properly to regulate the blood supply.

[49] 9993/82 31 Dr 241 (1992)
[50] A 269-B
[51] A 289-C

9

Clinical Negligence and Personal Injury Litigation

ROBERT OWEN QC, SARAH LAMBERT and CAROLINE NEENAN

1. INTRODUCTION

The potential impact of the incorporation of the Convention on clinical negligence and personal injury work is much greater than a cursory glance at the provisions of the Convention would suggest. The Strasbourg Court and Commission have developed the Convention in an active, and often dynamic, manner so as to extend its reach far beyond what would appear at first sight to fall within its ambit. By virtue of Article 2 of the Human Rights Act 1998, a court or tribunal determining a question which has arisen in connection with a Convention right must take into account, inter alia, any relevant judgment of the Strasbourg Court and any relevant decision or opinion of the Commission, whenever made or given. It is therefore imperative to examine the case law which has developed under the relevant Articles in order to begin to appreciate the ways in which incorporation will influence clinical negligence and personal injuries work. The first part of this chapter will consider some of the ways in which the Convention may affect substantive issues in these fields. The second part considers how it may also affect procedural steps in litigation.

2. THE RELEVANT ARTICLES

The Articles which are likely to have an impact on these areas of law are Articles 2 (the right to life) and 3 (the prohibition on inhuman and degrading treatment). As explained in the introductory chapter, both Articles 2 and 3 confer absolute rights. No derogations are permitted from Article 2 (except in respect of deaths resulting from lawful acts of war)[1] or Article 3.

---

[1] Article 15(2)

2.1. Article 2

(1) Everyone's right to life shall be protected by law. No-one shall be deprived of his life intentionally save in the execution of a sentence of a Court following his conviction of a crime for which this penalty is provided by law.

(2) Deprivation of life shall not be regarded as inflicted in contravention of this Article when it results from the use of force which is no more than absolutely necessary

    (a) in defence of any person from unlawful violence;

    (b) in order to effect a lawful arrest or to prevent the escape of a person lawfully detained;

    (c) in action lawfully taken for the purpose of quelling a riot or insurrection".

The qualifications to the right to life which are listed in Article 2(2) are exhaustive and must be narrowly interpreted.[2]

The scope of Article 2 has been explored in earlier chapters for its potential impact on other areas of the common law.[3] We believe that Article 2 will have the greatest impact on clinical negligence and personal injury law. The Court has emphasised that Article 2 "ranks as one of the most fundamental provisions in the Convention" and that "together with Article 3, it enshrines one of the basic values of the democratic societies making up the Council of Europe".[4] Article 2 must be interpreted in light of the principle that the provisions of the Convention be applied so as to make its safeguards practical and effective.[5]

The fundamental nature of the right to life has also been acknowledged by the domestic courts: in *Bugdaycay v Secretary of State for the Home Department* Lord Bridge stated that the right to life is "the most fundamental of all human rights" and that when an administrative decision is taken which may put the applicant's life at risk, the basis of the decision calls for "the most anxious scrutiny".[6] Lord Goff observed in *Airedale NHS Trust v Bland*[7] that the principle of sanctity of human life, although fundamental, was not absolute and must sometimes give way to the principle of self-determination.

The right to life does, however, remain largely unexplored by the domestic courts. The judges are likely to be confronted with imaginative and progressive arguments as lawyers test the boundaries of the right to life.

The Strasbourg Court has noted on several occasions that the first sentence of Article 2(1) enjoins the state not only to refrain from the intentional[8] and unlaw-

---

[2] *Stewart v United Kingdom* (1984) 39 DR 162

[3] In particular, see chapter 10 on Environmental Rights

[4] *McCann v United Kingdom* (1995) 21 EHRR 97 at para 147

[5] *McCann*, see N. 4 above, at paras 146–7

[6] [1987] AC 514 at 531G, per Lord Bridge of Harwich

[7] [1993] AC 789 at 864B-C. See also Lord Browne-Wilkinson at 882 and Lord Mustill at 891. See further *St George's Healthcare NHS Trust v S* [1998] 3 WLR 936 (CA) 950E–951H

ful taking of life, but also to take appropriate steps to safeguard the lives of those within its jurisdiction.[9]

Section 6 of the Human Rights Act 1998 imposes a duty on public authorities to act compatibly with Convention rights, subject to specified exceptions.[10] "Public authority" includes a court or tribunal and any person certain of whose functions are functions of a public nature (Section 6(3)). According to the Home Secretary,[11] the effect of Section 6 is to create three categories, the first of which contains organisations which might be termed "obvious" public authorities, all of whose functions are public. The clearest examples are government departments, local authorities and the police. The second category contains organisations with a mix of public and private functions. The effect of Section 6(5)[12] is that those organisations, unlike the "obvious" public authorities, will not be liable in respect of their private acts. The third category is organisations with no public functions, which accordingly fall outside the scope of Section 6.

The Department of Health, health authorities and NHS Trusts should be classified as "obvious" public authorities. This has the consequence that these bodies are under a duty to act compatibly with the Convention in relation to both public law and private law matters. For example, in *Halford v United Kingdom*[13] the Court considered a complaint by the Assistant Chief Constable of Merseyside Police Authority that calls made from her home and office telephones were intercepted for the purposes of obtaining information to use against her in the sex discrimination proceedings which she brought against her employers. The Court upheld the complaint insofar as it related to calls made by the applicant from her office. The Court found that this interception constituted an "interference by a public authority", within the meaning of Article 8(2), with the exercise of the applicant's right to respect for her private life and correspondence.

The Lord Chancellor stated during the committee stage in the House of Lords that "public authority" will include doctors when caring for NHS patients, but not when they are treating private patients.[14] Therefore, doctors fall into the

---

[8] Article 2 is not confined to cases of intentional taking of life. See, for example, *Stewart v United Kingdom*, at N. 2 above, where the Commission rejected the Government's submission that Article 2 only concerns the intentional deprivation of life and does not apply to either accidental or negligent behaviour

[9] *LCB v United Kingdom* (1998) 27 EHRR 212 at para 36; *W v United Kingdom* (1983) 32 DR 190 at 200

[10] It is not unlawful for a public authority to act in a way which is incompatible with a Convention right if (a) as the result of one or more provisions of primary legislation, the authority could not have acted differently; or (b) in the case of one or more provisions of, or made under, primary legislation which cannot be read or given effect in a way which is compatible with the Convention rights, the authority was acting so as to give effect to or enforce those provisions (Section 6(2) of the Human Rights Act 1998)

[11] 314 HC Official Report (6th series) cols 409–10 (committee stage in the House of Commons)

[12] Section 6(5) provides in relation to a particular act, a person is not a public authority by virtue only of subsection (3)(b) if the nature of the act is private

[13] (1997) 24 EHRR 523

[14] See 583 HL Official Report (5th series) col 811 (24 November 1997)

second category and do not have a duty to act compatibly with the Convention in their private law relationships.[15]

The Commission stated in X v UK that the state must take "adequate and appropriate steps to protect life".[16] The Commission considered this duty to extend to the provision of adequate and appropriate medical care. A complaint was made that the vaccination of children was causing severe brain damage and, in some cases, death. The Commission considered the adequacy of the medical care but did not accept on the evidence before it that the scheme was poorly administered and that adequate and appropriate steps were not being taken to minimise the risks associated with vaccinations.

But it follows from the Commission's decision in X v United Kingdom that the domestic courts are likely to be faced with the argument that health authorities and NHS Trusts are obliged to make "adequate and appropriate " provision for medical care in all those cases where the right to life of a patient would otherwise be endangered. Furthermore, the protection afforded by the right to life extends beyond cases where loss of life has actually occurred to cases where injury has been sustained provided that there was a real and immediate risk to life: see Osman v United Kingdom.[17] In its report on the merits of the case, the Commission observed that:

> ". . . whilst as a general rule for a complaint to fall within the scope of Article 2 there must have been a loss of life, it was not excluded that acts or events of a life threatening character could properly be dealt with under the provision, in particular where the threat was real and immediate and the risk of death occurring was high".[18]

Thus Article 2 is likely to have far-reaching implications in the field of clinical negligence; and its application will give rise to a number of important and interesting issues.

First, the domestic courts are likely to be required to consider whether a lack of resources will provide a defence to a claim that adequate medical provision was not made: for example, if it could be shown that the patient would have avoided either death or injury if some new piece of equipment, albeit expensive, or further drug therapy had been made available, it may be no defence for the health authority or NHS Trust to say that it lacked the resources to purchase the equipment or drugs. Similarly Article 2 might also be invoked if it could be shown that death or injury would have been avoided if a more senior doctor (e.g. a consultant surgeon) had been available to carry out an operation.

---

[15] But see Murray Hunt, "The Horizontal Effect of the Human Rights Act" (1998) *PL* 423 for a discussion of the indirect effect of incorporation on pure private law actions

[16] (1978) 14 DR 31 at 33

[17] Application No. 26985/95, unreported, decision of the Court reported at (1999) 5 BHRC 293

[18] See also *Poku v United Kingdom* Application No. 26985/95, unreported: as there was no immediate or significant risk to health of either the applicant or her baby, the Commission found no basis on which the pending deportation could be found to disclose a violation of Article 2 of the Convention

As *R v Cambridge Health Authority, ex parte B* demonstrates, the domestic courts have hitherto shown a reluctance to interfere in the allocation of health authorities' limited resources.[19] But after the Human Rights Act comes into force, the domestic courts will have to reconsider their approach in the light of *Osman v United Kingdom*.[20] In *Osman* the Court repeated that the state must take appropriate steps to safeguard the lives of those within its jurisdiction and then set the parameters of this obligation. The complaint arose out of an allegation of negligence on the part of the police in the investigation and suppression of crime, and the lack of accountability in domestic law, public policy giving the police immunity from suit in such circumstances.[21] The Court stated:

> "For the court, and bearing in mind the difficulties involved in policing modern societies, the unpredictability of human conduct and *the operational choices which must be made in terms of priorities and resources, such an obligation must be interpreted in a way which does not impose an impossible or disproportionate burden on the authorities.* Accordingly, not every claimed risk to life can entail for the authorities a Convention requirement to take operational measures to prevent that risk from materialising".

In the opinion of the Court where there is an allegation that the authorities have violated their positive obligation to protect the right to life in the context of their above-mentioned duty to prevent and suppress offences against the person, it must be established to its satisfaction that the authorities knew or ought to have known at the time of a real and immediate risk to the life of an identified individual or individuals from the criminal acts of a third party and *that they failed to take measures within the scope of their powers which, judged reasonably, might have been expected to avoid that risk.*

> "*it is sufficient for an applicant to show that the authorities did not do all that could be reasonably expected of them to avoid a real and immediate risk to life of which they have or ought to have knowledge*".[22] (Emphasis added).

The weight of the burden which the Court has placed on the applicant remains to be explored. It is clear that the domestic court, should bear in mind the operational choices which must be made; but it appears that this may not always be

---

[19] [1995] 1 WLR 898 (CA), discussed in chapter 8 on Medical Law. See Generally R. James and D. Longley, "Judicial Review and Tragic Choices" (1995) *PL* 367 and D. O'Sullivan, "The allocation of scarece resources and the right to life under the ECHR" (1998) *PL* 389. *R v North & East Devon Health Authority, ex parte Loughlin* [1999] Lloyd's Rep Med 306 and *North West Lancs HA v A, D & G* [1999] Lloyd's Rep Med 399 at 408. For other resource based decisions, see *Re J (a minor) (child in care: medical treatment)* [1993] Fam 12 at 28 (CA), per Lord Donaldson MR: the court should not make orders of medical treatment with consequences for the use of health authority's resources since it was in no position to express a view as to how such resources should be deployed

[20] See N. 17 above

[21] The applicants also made complaints under Articles 6 and 8. The Article 6 aspects of the case are explored in more detail in chapter 2 The Convention and the Human Rights Act: a New Way of Thinking

[22] *Osman v United Kingdom*, see N. 17 above para 116

a complete answer. The question can only be answered in the light of all the circumstances of any particular case.

Although the domestic courts may exceptionally accept an argument challenging the allocation of resources in the circumstances of the individual case, an attack on the policies governing the organisation and administration of healthcare is even less likely to be successful. In *Taylor and Others v UK*,[23] the parents of children killed and injured by the attacks of the nurse Beverley Allitt, brought a complaint before the Commission which included an allegation that the systemic shortcomings of local health services (e.g. financial cutbacks, inadequate staffing levels) had resulted in a situation where an untrained and dangerous individual could be allowed to care for children without supervision. The Commission held that Article 2 did not extend to an examination of the organisation and funding of the NHS: "any doubts which may consequently arise as to the policies adopted in the field of public health are, in the Commission's opinion, matters for public and political debate which fall outside the scope of Article 2 and the other provisions of the Convention".

Secondly, the courts will no doubt have to explore the relationship between the duty imposed by Article 2 and the duty of care imposed by the domestic law of negligence. If a public authority is obliged to make adequate provision for medical care and fails to do so in circumstances where either death ensues or where injury is sustained in circumstances where there was a real and immediate risk to life, a breach of Article 2 will have been established; and the claimant should succeed without the necessity of establishing negligence.

Furthermore, it is unclear whether and to what degree standards of adequate and appropriate care will differ from the standard of care imposed upon a health authority or a NHS Trust or the medical practitioner for whom it is vicariously liable by the law of negligence. A medical practitioner owes a duty to exercise reasonable skill and care in the treatment of his patient. The test of negligence on the part of a medical practitioner was set out by McNair J in his direction to the jury in the well-known case of *Bolam v Friern Hospital Management Committee*.[24] Lord Scarman reformulated the test in the following terms in *Sidaway v Governors of Bethlem Royal Hospital*:[25]

> "a doctor is not negligent if he acts in accordance with a practice accepted at the time as proper by a responsible body of medical opinion even though other doctors adopt a different practice".

The *Bolam* test has survived a number of challenges in recent years;[26] but it will no doubt be argued that it is inconsistent with the duty imposed by Article 2. The concepts of "real and immediate risk" and "adequate care" have not as yet

---

[23] Application No. 23412/94, unreported

[24] [1957] 1 WLR 582 at 586

[25] [1985] AC 871 at 881F

[26] See *Whitehouse v Jordan* [1981] 1 WLR 246, *Maynard v West Midland Regional Health Authority* [1984] 1 WLR 634, *Sidaway v Governors of Bethlem Royal Hospital* (see N. 26), and *Bolitho v City & Hackney HA* [1998] AC 232

been extensively explored by the Court. It appears that it is not necessary to demonstrate gross negligence or wilful disregard of the duty to protect life.[27] It seems clear that if the care provided was negligent, then by definition it will not have been adequate; but the converse may not apply. If the care was not negligent, it would not necessarily follow that it was adequate.[28]

If the domestic courts find the obligation imposed by Article 2 to be more onerous than the common law duty of care, then the scope for liability on the part of health authorities and NHS Trusts could be significantly enlarged. Such a finding would of course have the inevitable and arguably highly unsatisfactory consequence that cases involving death, or the real and immediate risk to life, would be judged by a different standard from other cases of clinical negligence.

In personal injury practice, there will be scope for arguing that public authorities generally are obliged to make adequate provision for the health and safety of their employees whenever a failure to do so would endanger the life of the employee. The test of negligence (or breach of statutory duty) might again be superseded by the requirement to provide adequate protection. Likewise, lack of resources may provide no defence to a claim by an employee or his family where his life has been endangered or terminated. For example, if it could be shown that the employee would have avoided either death or injury if some new piece of safety equipment, albeit expensive, had been installed, it may be no defence for the public authority employer to say that he lacked the resources to purchase it .

It is interesting to consider whether the positive obligation to safeguard lives would require a member of the public to assist another in a case of medical emergency, and if an employer would thus be obliged to assist an employee suffering such an emergency at work. In *Hughes v United Kingdom*[29] the applicant alleged that her husband did not receive the prompt medical attention which may have increased his chances of resuscitation. In particular, she complained that English law fails to place a general obligation on persons to take prompt medical action in emergencies. The Commission held that, even assuming that Article 2 can be said to impose an obligation on states to protect individuals by such legal measures, in the circumstances of the present case, there was no appearance of a violation of Article 2. Thus the possibility of making such a complaint remains open.

Additionally, perhaps an employee with a known and serious condition, such as a serious asthmatic, could argue that she is entitled to work in a smoke-free environment.[30] In *Waltons & Morse v Dorrington*,[31] the Employment Appeals

---

[27] *Osman v United Kingdom*, see n. 17 above, at para 116

[28] In *Buckley v United Kingdom* (1997) 23 EHRR CD 129, the applicant complained of violations of the Convention arising from the treatment of and circumstances surrounding the death of her son. In deciding that the complaint under Article 2 was inadmissible, the Commission was influenced by the fact that the applicant's own medical and legal advisors were unable to conclude that there had been any negligence on the part of the hospital in relation to her son's death, and that in consequence no domestic proceedings had been commenced

[29] (1986) 48 DR 259

[30] See chapter 10 on Environmental Rights for the development of environmental rights against the state, based on Articles 2 and 8 of the Convention

[31] [1997] IRLR 488 (EAT)

Tribunal extended the employer's duty in relation to health and safety at work into the area of the working environment and the employee's welfare. A non-smoking employee succeeded in claiming constructive unfair dismissal after she left her employment following her move to an area which was close to heavy smokers.

In personal injury work it may be possible to frame actions against the Department of Health under Article 2 for failing[32] to provide adequate protection in circumstances where death or injury may otherwise result, for example in relation to the provision of information to the public[33] or banning certain drugs. A claim could arise out of the lack of information in relation to the dangers of BSE or GMOs, or a failure to ban a drug potentially harmful to a certain class, such as pregnant women. Again, it will be strongly arguable that the test in such a claim will not be negligence but the (possibly) higher standard of adequacy of protection and that the applicant should succeed if he can meet the *Osman* test, that is, show that the authorities did not do all that could be reasonably expected of them to avoid a real and immediate risk to life of which they have or ought to have knowledge.

The case of *L.C.B v United Kingdom*[34] demonstrates the Strasbourg approach to this type of claim. The applicant, who suffered from leukaemia, complained of a failure on the part of the state to monitor her father's exposure to radiation levels whilst he was stationed on Christmas Island during nuclear tests. She attributed her illness to that exposure and claimed that had the state provided her parents with information regarding the extent of her father's exposure to radiation and the risks which this engendered, and monitored her health from infancy, it would have been possible to diagnose her leukaemia earlier and to provide her with treatment which could have alleviated the risk to her life. She claimed breaches of Articles 2, 3, 8 and 13 (the unincorporated right to an effective remedy).

The Court observed that Article 2 required each state to take appropriate steps to safeguard the lives of those within its jurisdiction. In relation to the complaint that there had been a failure to monitor the father's exposure to radiation levels, the Court held that it did not have jurisdiction, as that complaint had not been raised before the Commission. Moreover, the complaint concerned events which took place before the United Kingdom's recognition of the competence of the Commission in 1966.

---

[32] By virtue of Section 6(6) of the Human Rights Act 1998, an act includes a failure to act

[33] Such actions would complement the common law position where a body making a negligent statement could owe a duty of care to a person who has suffered loss or damage through reliance on that statement, see, for example, *T v Surrey County Council* [1994] 4 All ER 577 where a local authority had negligently told a mother that there was no reason why her baby should not be placed in the care of a child-minder suspected of physical abuse by the authority. Scott Baker J held the authority liable for physical injury caused to the child by the child-minder

[34] (1998) 27 EHRR 212. See chapter 10 on Environmental Rights for a discussion of this decision's implications for the common law in the environmental context

The applicant also failed in relation to her second complaint, on the basis that records of contemporaneous measurements of radiation did not indicate that her father was in an area of dangerous levels of radiation, and further that in the late 1960s there could not be said to have been a causal link between exposure to radiation and leukaemia in a child subsequently conceived. Therefore, Article 2 had not been violated. However, the Court considered it to be arguable that, had there been reason to believe that she was in danger of contracting a life-threatening disease owing to her father's presence on Christmas Island, the state authorities would have been under a duty to have made this known to her parents whether or not they considered that the information would assist the applicant.

The Court concluded that in the light of the information available to the state at the relevant time concerning the likelihood of the applicant's father having been exposed to dangerous levels of radiation and of this having created a risk to her health, it could have been expected to act of its own motion to notify her parents of these matters or to take any other special action in relation to her.

It is also useful to consider the decision in *Guerra v Italy*[35] in this context. As David Hart explains in chapter 10 on Environmental Rights, the Court found a violation of Article 8 in respect of the failure of the authorities to provide the applicants with essential information relevant to their well-being, health and homes. It is worth repeating the facts of the case very briefly in order to explore their relevance to medical negligence and personal injury claims.

The applicants lived within a mile of a chemical factory classified as high risk in terms of hazards to the environment and to the local population. Indeed, workers from the factory had died of cancer. They complained that the authorities had not taken appropriate action to reduce the risk of pollution and to avoid accidents, contrary to Article 2, or to provide information about the risks to them, or details of how to proceed in the event of an accident, contrary to Article 10. The Court rejected their claim under Article 10 on the grounds that it was not applicable because Article 10 does not guarantee an unqualified right to receive information.[36] The applicants further relied upon Article 8, contending that the failure to provide them with relevant information had infringed their right to respect for their private and family life. The Court held unanimously that Article 8 had been violated. In the circumstances it was considered unnecessary to consider the case under Article 2. Although this was not a medical case (it was essentially environmental), one can see how this approach might be developed in the fields both of medical negligence and personal injury.

---

[35] (1998) 26 EHRR 357
[36] See chapter 11 on Confidentiality and Defamation for a discussion of the reach of Article 10 in this area

2.2. Article 3

"No one shall be subjected to torture or to inhuman or degrading treatment or punishment".

At first sight, this would seem to have no conceivable application to the law of medical negligence or personal injury; but this would be too simplistic a conclusion, at least as with regard to medical negligence. Although, in practice, Article 3 is often relied upon as a secondary basis of complaint to Article 2.

In *Tanko v Finland*,[37] the applicant, who suffered from glaucoma, complained that the enforcement of his expulsion would subject him to a risk of losing his eyesight in view of the inadequate facilities for treating him and possibly operating on him in Ghana. The Commission stated that it "does not exclude that a lack of proper care in a case where someone is suffering from a serious illness could in certain circumstances amount to treatment contrary to Article 3". However, the Commission did not find it established that the applicant could not obtain the requisite medication in Ghana or bring it with him when he returned there. The complaint was therefore manifestly ill-founded.

To advance such arguments would not necessarily involve proof of negligence as it would be for the Court to define what is meant by "proper care".

Chapter 8 on Medical Law makes reference to the case of *D v United Kingdom*,[38] where the Court considered the proposed expulsion of a convicted drug trafficker in the terminal stages of AIDS to a country where it was accepted that the absence of vital medical treatment would rapidly accelerate his death. The Court determined whether there was a real risk that the applicant's removal would be contrary to the standards of Article 3 in view of his present medical condition. The risk was assessed in the light of the most recent information on his state of health. The Court decided that in the "very exceptional circumstances" of the case and given the "compelling humanitarian considerations" at stake, that it must be concluded that the implementation of the decision to remove the applicant would be a violation of Article 3. The Court did not go as far as holding that the United Kingdom had an obligation not to withdraw medical treatment.

The Commission has held that medical treatment of an experimental character and without the consent of the person involved may under certain circumstances be regarded as prohibited by Article 3. In *X v Denmark*[39] the applicant was admitted to hospital to be sterilised. Prior to the surgical intervention, she was informed that the result would be almost irreversible and she signed a declaration that she consented. However, a few weeks later she found herself pregnant. Without informing the applicant, the surgeon changed the instrument to

---

[37] Application No. 23634/94, DR 77-A, p 133
[38] (1997) 24 EHRR 423
[39] (1983) 32 DR 282

one which was shown to be less effective according to a later survey. The Commission found that the operation was carried out in conformity with a generally acknowledged and dependable method and the introduction of the new instrument did not change the procedure of the operation as such, but was solely intended to prevent or minimise side-effects already known to the medical staff. The Commission also took into account that at the time of the operation there was no indication that the operation in question would be less effective and secure from a medical point of view. In the circumstances, the Commission found it obvious that the operation itself could not be considered to be a medical experiment and could not, therefore, constitute a violation of Article 3.

"Treatment of an experimental character" may mean no more than treatment which has not yet become properly established; in which case it could be of wide application. Moreover, it may be possible to demonstrate absence of consent where the doctors have failed to notify the patient in advance that the treatment proposed is of an experimental nature.

In addition, it is already well-established that there is an obligation under Article 3 to provide adequate medical treatment for persons in detention[40] (for example, in a mental hospital). In *Hurtado v Switzerland*[41] the Commission found that Article 3 had been violated, when a person who had been forcibly arrested was not given an x-ray, which revealed a fractured rib, until six days after he had requested it.

3. PRACTICE AND PROCEDURE IN MEDICAL NEGLIGENCE AND PERSONAL INJURY LITIGATION

3.1. Article 6: Right of Access

Article 6 provides procedural safeguards in the determination of a litigant's civil rights, when a dispute exists in relation to such a right or rights. The outcome of the dispute must be determinative of the litigant's civil rights. Being procedural rather than substantive, Article 6 applies both to personal injury litigation between private individuals and between a private individual and the state, and to clinical negligence claims against NHS Trusts, claims in contract against private health providers, and in claims against GPs. It is, accordingly, not limited to circumstances where an individual pursues the state or an emanation of it. The state bodies regulated by Article 6 are the courts themselves.[42]

Article 6 guarantees a number of rights: the right to a fair hearing, a public hearing (save in certain circumstances),[43] with judgment publicly pronounced;

---

[40] *Kotälla v The Netherlands* (1978) 14 DR 238: Article 3 is not violated when a prisoner serving a life sentence gets the medical attention which his bad state of health demands but is not freed
[41] (1994) Series A 280-A
[42] See Section 6(3) of the Act
[43] Article 6 (1) provides that judgment shall be pronounced publicly but the press and public may be excluded from all or part of the trial in the interest of morals, public order or national security in

a hearing within a reasonable time by an independent and impartial tribunal. The rights provided by Article 6 have been interpreted so as to give rise to a right of access to a court in the first place.[44]

The right of access is not absolute and may be subject to limitations in that Contracting States enjoy a margin of appreciation. The right however must be effective in practice, and whilst limitations on access may be permissible they will not be so if they restrict the right such that the very essence of it is impaired.[45] Furthermore, the restriction will not be compatible with Article 6 unless it pursues a legitimate aim and there is a reasonable relationship of proportionality between the means employed and the aim sought to be achieved.

Being procedural, Article 6 does not provide substantive rights, rather it is concerned with the procedure applicable to the determination of whatever rights the substantive law of the state provides. A total procedural bar could however have the effect of abrogating the existing substantive right, and in those circumstances Article 6 could have effect. Thus, whilst the Convention enforcement bodies may not create by way of interpretation of Article 6 a substantive civil right which has no legal basis in the state concerned, they can intervene were the state to remove from the jurisdiction of the courts, for example by way of introducing immunity, an existing substantive right. The intervention is one of restraint or control rather than prohibition.[46]

In *Osman*[47] the Court found that the blanket immunity from suit enjoyed by the police is just such a breach of Article 6(1). The applicants alleged that the dismissal by the Court of Appeal of their negligence action against the police on grounds of public policy contravened Article 6(1) and the Commission agreed. The United Kingdom Government maintained that the applicants could not rely on any substantive right in domestic law, in that an essential element required for the establishment of a duty of care owed was a finding that it was fair, just and reasonable for such a duty to be imposed, and public policy considerations meant that it was not. Thus, ran the respondent state's argument, the Court could not assist as it would be creating a substantive right. The Court however found that the applicants must be taken to have had a right, derived from the law of negligence, to seek an adjudication on the admissibility and merits of an arguable claim that they were in a relationship of proximity to the police, that the harm caused was foreseeable, and that in the circumstances it was fair, just and reasonable not to apply the exclusionary rule outlined in *Hill v Chief Constable of South Yorkshire Police*.[48]

a democratic society, where the interests of juveniles or the protection of the private life of the parties so require, to the extent strictly necessary in the opinion of the court and special circumstances where publicity would prejudice the interests of justice

[44] *Golder v United Kingdom* (1975) EHRR 524, *Airey v Ireland* (1979) 2 EHRR 305
[45] *Ashingdane v United Kingdom* (1985) 7 EHRR 528
[46] *Fayed v UK* (1994) 18 EHRR 393
[47] *Mulkiye Osman and Ahmed Osman v UK* (1999) 5 BHRC 293; see also discussion of this issue in chapter 5 on Remedies
[48] [1990] 1 WLR 946

The effect of Article 6(1) is that an immunity or special defence should not prevent an action arising out of an existing substantive right from taking place at all. This has recently been recognised at the highest domestic level in the context of personal injury litigation in *Barrett v Enfield London Borough Council*.[49] Great care would appear to be needed in striking out, at an interlocutory stage, claims based on a developing area of law.

3.2. Article 6: Representation and Equality of Arms

The right to a fair trial and of access to justice can include the right to representation,[50] if such representation is considered necessary in order to ensure that a litigant's right of access is effective.

Litigation in this country is adversarial in nature, and a litigant is entitled not to be at a significant disadvantage compared to the other party,[51] a concept sometimes referred to as equality of arms or a level playing field. Whether in a particular case this leads to a right to representation, and the nature of such representation, depends on a number of factors including the litigant's ability to put the case himself, the relative importance of the issues raised, the existence of other opportunities for determination of the issues, demonstration of at least reasonable prospects of success, and the extent to which legal representation is compulsory (which in clinical negligence and personal injury litigation it is not). The Civil Procedure Rules (CPR) Part 1 in fact explicitly recognises that dealing with a case justly involves ensuring so far as is practicable that the parties are on a equal footing, enshrining this as part of the overriding objective.[52]

Equality of arms requires that each party be afforded a reasonable opportunity to present his case, including his evidence, under conditions that do not place him at a substantial disadvantage vis à vis his opponent.[53] This may well be an argument which could be used to assist a party whose expert fails to comply with CPR Part 35.1.2 and whose expert a court declines to allow to give evidence, see for example *Edwin John Stevens v R J Gullis*.[54] The refusal of a court to order a report as requested by a party has been held to be capable of rendering a trial unfair.[55] This might assist a litigant such as the appellant defendant in *David John Baron v Brian Lovell*,[56] where the Court refused to admit his expert opinion out of time. The Court has already found a breach of Article 6(1) where a court-appointed expert prepared a medical report in administrative

---

[49] [1999] 3 WLR 79 HL
[50] *Airey v Ireland* (1979) 2 EHRR 305; see also *Perks v United Kingdom* (October 12 1999)
[51] *Lithgow v UK* (1986) 8 EHRR 329, *Neumeister v Austria* (1968) 1 EHRR 91
[52] CPR Part 1.1(2)(a) and (c)
[53] *Kaufman v Belgium* (1986) 50 DR 98 at 115
[54] 27 July 1999, CA
[55] *H v France* (1989) 12 EHRR 74
[56] TLR 14 September 1999, CA

proceedings, the applicant successfully contending that this was contrary to the adversarial principle.[57]

In small claims there has been an apparent move to discourage representation at trial. On 26 April 1999 the small claims limit increased from £3,000 to £5,000. This probably has discouraged litigants from seeking legal advice and representation in relation to claims worth £5,000 or less given that only fixed costs are recoverable even if a party is successful at trial.[58] Likewise legal aid is generally not available as any damages would be likely to be consumed by the statutory charge. However, this jurisdiction only applies to personal injury claims worth £5,000 or less where the claim for damages for personal injuries is not more than £1,000,[59] and accordingly only very minor personal injury and few clinical negligence claims are likely to fall within this jurisdiction.

Conversely, within the other tracks the availability of costs recovery following the instruction of counsel has become easier by reason of there no longer being any need to obtain a certificate for counsel. On the contrary, the court need only, should it feel it necessary, certify that a particular attendance (for example of leading and junior counsel on an interlocutory application) was not appropriate.

The high cost of civil proceedings could be said to infringe the right of access.[60] In *Maltez v Lewis* [61] the claimant, relying on CPR Part 1.2, applied for an order preventing the defendant from using leading counsel at trial, in circumstances where she would be relying on junior counsel. The Court refused her application, recognising that it is an important ingredient of a free society that every citizen has a fundamental right to choose counsel as they wish, and the powers conferred by the CPR should not be interpreted so as to restrict or remove that right. Interestingly it was said that a court would, however, be prepared to ensure that one party was not subjected to excessive costs because the other party had instructed expensive advisers, and if the parties could each afford a different type of legal assistance, the court could make orders to ensure the level playing field was achieved, for example, by allowing a smaller firm of solicitors more time than a large and experienced one, or by ordering the latter to prepare the court bundles.

In relation to the costs of a solicitor, the Court of Appeal in *Sullivan v Co-operative Insurance Society*[62] has recently held that it was not reasonable to expect one party to pay the other party's costs of having used London solicitors in connection with litigation conducted in Manchester. Thus, whilst the choice of representation is a subjective one, the question of reasonableness in deter-

---

[57] *Mantovelli v France* (1997) 24 EHRR 370
[58] CPR Part 27.14
[59] CPR Part 27.1(2)
[60] *X and Y v Netherlands* 1 DR 66. See also chapter 3 on Costs for a full discussion of this issue
[61] 4 May 1999 TLR
[62] 19 May 1999 TLR, CA

mining whether the other party should pay the costs of the chosen representation is an objective one.

In relation to non-legal representation, by a McKenzie friend, the Court of Appeal has recently given guidance *in R v Bow County Court ex parte Michael John Pelling*[63]. The applicant for judicial review was a McKenzie friend who frequently acted for reward in family proceedings. He applied for review of a decision of a county court judge who refused to hear him in an ex parte application to the judge in chambers (private). In dismissing his application on the basis that he had no standing, because the litigant in person himself should have applied (rather than the McKenzie friend), the court said that:

> "by definition chambers proceedings are not open to the public. A member of the public has no right to be present in chambers proceedings for the very reason that they are private".

The court was unable to accept that there was a right of a McKenzie friend to be present in chambers, and found no inconsistency or ambiguity in the common law and Article 6, upon which the applicant had relied. The applicant was a member of the public, nothing more, and therefore could be excluded where the interests of juveniles or protection of the private lives of the parties so required, and therefore was consistent with both Articles 6 and 8. The right to assistance was the right of the litigant who could ask the court for such assistance to be given. The conclusion is that where a hearing is in open court there is a right to a McKenzie friend, a right solely vested in the litigant. Where the hearing is in chambers (in other words, private) there is a discretion in the judge as to whether to permit the presence of a McKenzie friend.

> "There is no obligation on the judge to give reasons for the exercise of his discretion in relation to who may be present at chambers proceedings. His duty is to consider the litigant's application on its merits and in the context of the case before him, i.e. on a case by case basis . . . he will consider the nature, sensitivity and complexity of the case".

Pelling has now been ruled admissible by the Third Chamber of the Strasbourg Court on the issue of whether the refusal of the national court to grant him a public hearing and a public judgment breached his rights under Article 6(1) and deprived him of a remedy under Article 13.[64]

3.3. Article 6 and Limitation

Access to the Court is circumscribed by the rules on limitation. Within personal injury litigation there would be appear to be discrepancies between limitation periods depending upon how an injury was sustained. In cases of injury arising

---

[63] TLR 18 August 1999
[64] *Pelling v United Kingdom*, Application No. 0035974/97, September 14 1999, unreported

from deliberate assault or trespass the primary limitation period is six years.[65] This period is not subject to a claimant's date of knowledge and nor is the court invested with any discretion to dis-apply the period. The current rules can cause confusion, for example, in the case of a claimant whose claim in clinical negligence includes an allegation of lack of consent. In respect of the claim in negligence the limitation period is three years, but the claim is subject to a six-year period. Whilst he could seek a discretionary extension pursuant to Section 33 in respect of allegations in negligence, at six years in trespass his claim in trespass would be absolutely barred. If his claim were solely based on intentional trespass, he is obviously disadvantaged as against a claimant who claims in negligence, for no immediately apparent reason.

The Strasbroug Court considered this issue in *Stubbings v United Kingdom*.[66] In *Stubbings* the applicants all suffered child sex abuse, which left them with psychological or psychiatric problems. They all applied to the Court on the basis that the rules on limitation denied them access in violation of Article 6(1) as none of them knew of the injury, or causation of the injury, until they were counselled in adulthood, after their twenty-fourth birthdays. They also complained of a breach of Article 8 in that failure to provide a remedy for childhood sexual abuse was a failure of the state's positive obligation to protect their right to respect for their private lives; and for breach of Article 14, on the basis of the different limitation periods allowed to those who suffered intentional or unintentional injury. The case failed on all grounds, the Court holding that the victims of intentionally and unintentionally inflicted harm could not be said to be analogous and that different considerations applied, for example, that it may be more obvious to the victim of intentional wrongdoing that they have a cause of action. Further, even if a comparison could properly be drawn between the two groups it was reasonable and fell within the margin of appreciation afforded to Contracting States to create separate regimes for deliberately and non-deliberately inflicted harm. The decision is perhaps surprising, although the Court has recently confirmed this stance in *Stuart v United Kingdom*.[67] Here the applicant complained that the limitation on claims to the Criminal Injuries Compensation Board, in respect of offences committed before 1979 against victims by assailants who were living as family members, breached her rights under Articles 3 and 8, together with Articles 13 and 14. The Court ruled the complaint inadmissable, since neither Articles 3 nor 8 imposed a positive obligation on states to provide unlimited compensation to victims of sexual assault, and therefore Articles 13 and 14 could not apply.

What might be still open to challenge? It is worth considering whether a long stop provision, such as is provided by Section 11A of the Limitation Act 1980, in respect of claims alleging breach of the Consumer Protection Act 1987, pro-

---

[65] Section 2 Limitation Act 1980
[66] (1996) 23 EHRR 213
[67] Application No. 41903/98, unreported

hibiting any claim to be brought after the expiry of ten years, falls foul of Article 6(1). In the light of *Stubbings* however this seems unlikely.

Section 6 of the Human Rights Act creates a direct cause of action against a public authority which breaches a Convention right. This provides a claimant who pursues, for example, a clinical negligence claim with a separate cause of action, say for breach of Articles 2 and/or 3. For this, yet a different limitation period applies, of one year, beginning with when the act complained of took place, subject to extension when the court considers this equitable. The Human Rights Bill as originally drafted did not lay down this limitation period in relation to Section 6 cases and the relevant Section, 7(5), was introduced during parliamentary debates. The one-year period is subject to any shorter domestic limitation period (such as for judicial review), but what about where the domestic limitation period is longer than one year, as in personal injury claims? The one-year period has caused some consternation and it has been suggested that it is itself a potential breach of Article 6(1). For example, a litigant relying on breach of Article 2 within a claim for clinical negligence has one year in which to bring the Convention claim but three years for the negligence allegations. However, as we have seen from *Stubbings*, the Strasbourg Court is prepared to accord a fair amount of flexibility to Contracting States in setting limitation periods for different types of actions.

The human rights organisation *Justice* has broached this issue in correspondence with the Home Secretary, Jack Straw. The written response has been that clause 7(1) (a) had to be aligned with something, and whilst in many ways judicial review was considered to be the nearest sort of proceeding, the one-year was chosen as being more generous. This one-year period it is said relates only to proceedings brought under clause 7(1)(a). If a claimant proceeds under clause 7(1)(b), that is if he brings proceedings under an existing cause of action and relies upon his Convention rights as an additional argument in support of his case, the limitation period will be the one which applies in the normal way to the existing cause of action. This is the government's stated view. How it will apply in practice remains to be seen.

3.4. Article 6: Hearings in Public

Article 6 promotes open justice. Not only is a litigant entitled to a public hearing, he is also entitled to have the judgment publicly pronounced and made available publicly.[68] The right to a public hearing is however qualified, as has been seen, and can be waived.[69] Unlike the right to a public hearing, the right to public pronouncement of the judgment is not subject to restrictions within the text of the Article itself.

---

[68] *Preto v Italy* (1983) 6 EHRR 182
[69] *Hakansson v Sweden* (1990) 13 EHRR 1

The restrictions provided within the body of Article 6 allow the Court a margin of appreciation but reliance on them to create a restriction needs to be proportionate. It should be noted that human rights case law indicates that the right to a public hearing applies with full effect only to first instance decisions and is restricted in application to appeal proceedings. In domestic litigation this may have little impact given that the Court of Appeal sits in public in the ordinary course of events.

Unless one of the exceptions applies, a litigant should be entitled to challenge the holding of proceedings in private, or an order for secrecy in relation to the Court's findings. This appears to have been anticipated in personal injury cases by the Court of Appeal in *Hodgson and Others v Imperial Tobacco*.[70] The judge in chambers had made an order that the parties and their legal advisers should not make any comment to the media about the litigation without the leave of the court. The claimants appealed on the basis firstly that there was no jurisdiction to make an order in those terms in the absence of a finding of contempt of court or other unlawful act and, more interestingly, on the basis that the order breached Article 10 of the Convention. The appeal was successful, and in giving judgment Lord Woolf considered the nature of hearings in chambers and held that the use of the word "secret" in the notes to Section 67 of the Supreme Court Act 1981 does not accurately reflect the significance of a hearing being in chambers rather than in open court; rather the position was more accurately stated by Jacob J in *Forbes v Smith*:[71] a chambers hearing was in private in the sense that members of the public were not given admission as of right, as a matter of administrative convenience. Proceedings in chambers were not confidential and disclosure of what had occurred in the proceedings could, and a judgment or order should, be made available to the public except in exceptional circumstances. As a general rule there should be public access to hearings in chambers and information available as to what occurred at such hearings. Whilst considered as a breach of Article 10, the case is a direct indication of the impact of Convention rights within court procedure.

The Civil Procedure Rules have been drafted with a view to ensuring compliance with the requirement for a public hearing. The general rule, provided for by Part 39.2 (1), is that a hearing is to be in public. CPR Part 39.2(3) does allow for a hearing to be in private if that is necessary to protect the interests of a child or patient, for example, the hearing of approval of a compromise or settlement on behalf of a minor, or application for payment of money out of court to such a party (PD 39 1.6). The courts are beginning to put these changes into effect in that generally now interlocutory hearings are in public, and in relation to small claims hearings, formerly held in chambers and usually in private, the public are admitted. Hearings are listed "in public as in chambers", meaning apparently that counsel need not robe but the public can attend. Locked doors and keypad

---

[70] [1998] 1 WLR 1056
[71] [1998] 1 All ER 973

access to the district judge's rooms are being removed in some county courts, and thus there is unlikely to be any failure to provide the right to a public hearing under the CPR.[72] Where the judge exercises his discretion under the Practice Direction to order a hearing in private, the judgment itself may be pronounced in public. In *Beatham v Carlisle Hospitals NHS Trust*[73] Mr Justice Buckley stated that whilst some applications would be listed in private this was only for the period of counsel's submissions, as such submissions might include reference to negotiations. However, his Lordship recognised a public interest in the basic facts and disposal of such cases and thus ruled that the actual giving of approval would be in public. As a general rule counsel's opinion should now be provided to enable the Court to take a view in advance on the merits. There is said to be no general reason why the press should not have access to the pleadings, but the Court will consider any special features of the case making this undesirable, for example, the inclusion of a medical report. Of course it is usually the claimant rather than the defendant who seeks publicity and such a claimant may not in any event object to disclosure of his medical details to the press.

A judgment need not actually be given orally, it is sufficient that it is publicly available.[74]

3.5. Article 6: "Within a Reasonable Time"

Article 6 refers to a hearing within a reasonable time. Time usually runs in civil proceedings from commencement until enforcement and costs proceedings are included if they are a continuation of the substantive proceedings.[75] What is a reasonable time depends on the circumstances,[76] and a seriously ill party is entitled to exceptional diligence.[77]

Defendants facing claims from grievously injured claimants under permanent disability will be familiar with *Turner v W H Malcolm Ltd*[78] which provides that a claim by such a claimant should not be dismissed for want of prosecution. The CPR allow a court to take any step for the purpose of managing the case and furthering the overriding objective.[79] The rules also allow for the striking out of a statement of case if it appears that there has been a failure to comply with a rule, practice direction or order.[80] Recently Lord Woolf MR, in

---

[72] Although a colleague reports being told in a south coast county court that whilst instructions had been received that the public were to be admitted to hearings in the district judges' chambers, the court, with a view to discouraging this, had ensured that there were no seats available, thus a member of the public would have to stand and would hopefully choose not to stay!

[73] TLR 20 May 1999

[74] *Preto v Italy* (1983) 6 EHRR 182

[75] *Robins v UK* , September 1993, 1997, RJD 1997-V No 49

[76] *Darnell v UK* (1993) 18 EHRR 205

[77] *X v France* (1992) 14 EHRR 483

[78] (1992) 136 *Sol Jo*

[79] CPR Part 3, 3.1(m)

[80] CPR Part 3, 3.4(c)

considering an appeal arising out of a strike out order[81] has stated that past authorities (including presumably those relating to want of prosecution and abuse of process) are of no application now that the CPR are in force, the CPR being a new and self contained code. In reliance on Article 6 a defendant could perhaps argue that the court should not have blanket rules against striking out certain types of claim and should rather leave it to the claimant to incur the costs of the subsisting claim and of re-issue, even if under a permanent disability.

Whilst the parties, and in particular the claimant, are responsible for the progress of proceedings, the CPR do impose duties on the courts to manage litigation. The courts must also ensure compliance with Article 6 concerning the reasonable time requirement. In cases of delay caused not by the system or any common law rule, but by the sloth of a private individual litigant, arguably the complainant Could ask the court (via Section 6 HRA) to interpret the rules so as to accord with Article 6. There is also a duty on the Court under Section 3 HRA to interpret subordinate legislation (including the CPR) in compliance with Convention rights. These routes may well assist a party applying for a strike out, in particular as the overriding objective includes ensuring that the case is dealt with expeditiously and fairly[82] and the court's management powers include the giving of directions to ensure that the trial proceeds quickly and effectively.[83] It has been suggested that the sanction of striking out infringes a claimant's right of access to the Court, but the right of access as we have seen is capable of being subject to restrictions and must sit with the other guarantees of trial within a reasonable period and dealing even handedly with the parties. This is of course to differentiate between striking out at an early stage on the basis that there are no reasonable grounds for bringing or defending the claim (as to which see Right of access above) and striking out for breach of a procedural rule, as a punitive sanction.

3.6. Article 8: The Right to Privacy

The rights protected by Article 8 are wide-ranging and ever developing. The rights protected are substantive, and accordingly at first glance a distinction would appear to arise between personal injury litigation between private individuals and clinical negligence claims against private practitioners and GPs on the one hand, and clinical negligence claims against the NHS and personal injury claims against state bodies on the other. The Court's interpretation of Article 8 would suggest however that whilst this may be true when considering a claim against the alleged infringer of the right, nonetheless the state may itself owe obligations to a party where a private individual has infringed his Article 8 right, and this in the longer term may lead to domestic intervention to prevent

---

[81] *Biguzzi v Rank Leisure PLC* [1999] 1 WLR 1926
[82] CPR Part 1, 1.1(d)
[83] CPR Part 1, 1.4(1)

infringement by a private individual. To elaborate, Article 8(1) provides that everyone has the right to respect for his private life etc, and this may include an obligation on the state to ensure that private individuals do not prevent other private individuals from enjoying their protected rights, in other words, it may be up to the state to ensure the respect.[84] Not every interference with an Article 8 right gives rise to redress, the right is qualified, and thus interference will be acceptable if it is in accordance with the law and is necessary in a democratic society in a number of specified respects.[85] In the realm of litigation it might be anticipated that interference will be said to be in the interests of the economic well-being of the country, see for example *MS v Sweden*, below.

3.7. Article 8: Physical Integrity

Privacy under Article 8 extends the right of privacy to a right of physical integrity.[86] This could pose difficulties for a defendant who requires a claimant to see a particular doctor or undergo a particular test. Under domestic law if a claimant has a reasonable objection based on the intrusive, painful or repetitive nature of the test requested, or a legitimate objection to the doctor proposed this will be accommodated, but it now appears that a claimant has a further right to object based on Article 8. Reference to the Convention has already been made in a county court case[87] concerning an application by a defendant in a personal injury action for an order from the judge to allow the defendant's solicitors to inspect the claimant's scarring. The Court upheld the claimant's objections, observing that it "would constitute an invasion of [the claimant's] own personal privacy to expect scarring of that nature to be examined by a solicitor and not a medical practitioner".

3.8. Article 8: Video Surveillance

As we have seen,[88] Article 8 rights extend to ensuring respect for a person's private space. A recent growth area in personal injury and medical negligence litigation is video surveillance. The type of video made on behalf of a claimant, the "a day in the life of" record of usually a catastrophically injured claimant, is of course made with consent. However, more usually, video evidence is obtained by engaging enquiry agents to carry out covert surveillance in an attempt to produce evidence of the claimant taking part in some form of activity incompatible with his damages claim. At present a claimant is liable to be followed on an hour

---

[84] *X and Y v The Netherlands* (1986) 8 EHRR 235
[85] Article 8(2)
[86] *X and Y v The Netherlands* , N. 41 above
[87] *Francome v Williams* 30 October 1998, unreported
[88] See chapter 10 on Environmental Rights and chapter 6 on General Common Law Claims

by hour basis without regard for his privacy. Some enquiry agents even obtain entry to a claimant's home under false pretences in order to assess their home lifestyle and lead the claimant into conversation. It must be obvious that a claimant may be undertaking personal activities during the surveillance, and indeed such surveillance is usually done as a fishing expedition. It is a growth industry.[89]

Surveillance involving intrusive videoing, in particular in a person's home or garage would possibly fall within the definition of intrusion into that person's private space. Much video surveillance however takes place outside, on the way to the shops, the park, and so on. It must be a greater extension of the concept of private space to say that following and videoing a litigant whilst he undertakes activities of a private day to day nature is an actionable invasion. Being photographed in public would appear not to be an infringement of any right, as the activities of the tabloid press demonstrate. Evidence obtained from CCTV is routinely used in criminal prosecutions.

Objections are difficult in domestic law, as there is no property in a person's image. It is possible that such conduct could be complained of as harassment under the Harassment Act 1997, if repeated and blatant, but it is surely only a matter of time before this practice is challenged as a breach of Article 8.[90]

3.9. Article 8: Medical Records

A person's medical history and medical records have been held to be part of that person's private life.[91] Since this subject and the relevant case law, particularly *MS v Sweden*, has been discussed in some detail in chapter 8 on Medical Law, it will not be repeated here; suffice it to say that in that case the Court did not consider that the applicant's right to insist on non-disclosure of her medical records was not waived by her having a compensation claim. Whilst it is right that the position in domestic proceedings is that a claimant's medical records are confidential and cannot be disclosed without the claimant's written authority (usually provided to the defendant by the claimant's solicitors), in practice a claimant is obliged to disclose the entirety of his medical records as these are considered to be relevant documents. A claimant can object to disclosure, but will then lose the right to proceed as the claim will be stayed.[92]

Part of the reason the applicant was unsuccessful in *MS* was that Swedish law had appropriate safeguards in place. In reliance on Article 8 would it now be open to a claimant to argue that the rule in *Hipwood*[93] represents an unjustified

---

[89] See the discussion of the High Court decision in *R v BSC ex parte BBC*, 9 July 1999 in chapter 11 on Confidentiality and Defamation

[90] See chapter 11 on Confidentiality and Defamation for a full discussion of the scope of Article 8

[91] (1999) 28 EHRR 313; see also chapter 11 on Confidentiality and Defamation

[92] *Hipwood v Gloucester Health Authority and Others* [1995] PIQR 447

[93] See n. 92 above

interference with his or her private life? Defendants are presently used to being able to call for all medical records, following Lord Justice McCowan's decisions in that case, on an appeal based on Section 53 of the County Courts Act 1984, that there was no need to turn for assistance to Article 8(1) and that where liability, causation and damages are all in issue all the medical records are almost certain to be relevant. Whilst a defendant health authority could raise the same argument of the legitimate aim of safeguarding public funds, there are no limits on disclosure that the defendant can rely on to argue that the interference was proportionate. Theoretically all relevant entries in the records could be disclosed, but nothing more, so that defendants would be precluded from trawling through them. Who however would then be left to determine relevance? It is hard to imagine that this should be left to the claimant. Perhaps all records would need to be placed before the master or district judge to determine relevance, presumably without the assistance of representation. Just this course of action was however rejected in *Hipwood* on the basis that it would put a very heavy burden on district judges and masters. From a defendant's perspective possibly his best argument if faced with a reluctant claimant is to rely on his right to equality of arms under Article 6.

4. CONCLUSION

The extent of the impact of incorporation on the fields of clinical negligence and personal injury will depend predominantly upon two factors: first, the readiness of domestic lawyers to embrace the philosophy which underpins the Convention and to apply that philosophy so as dynamically to extend its reach; and, secondly, the willingness of the judges to follow where the lawyers lead. We have few doubts on the first score. English lawyers are likely to show themselves to be at least as imaginative in applying the law of the Convention as their more cautious Continental counterparts. As to the judges, only time will tell. We hope that the challenge will be met.

10

Environmental Rights

DAVID HART

1. INTRODUCTION

At first sight, a convention on human rights sounds unpromising territory in which to detect environmental ones. However, once one has made the mental adjustment to regard all matters environmental as potentially affecting man, it does not take long to discover plenty of material which will enable future human rights claimants to litigate environmental issues. This chapter analyses the material arising out of the European Convention on Human Rights, and seeks to predict which will provide the more fertile areas of dispute. It will be apparent just how many of the cases referred to have been decided by the Strasbourg Court in the last five years. Given the open-textured nature of the rights in issue, one can be tolerably sure that the next five years will give rise to a similar crop of case law.

The incorporation of the European Convention on Human Rights (ECHR) into domestic law will lead to claimants saying that they have environmental rights which have been infringed by public bodies, either directly or by failing to enforce environmental laws or standards against private polluters. As we shall see, the rights of importance are the substantive Articles 2 (life), 8 (home, private and family life) and Article 1, First Protocol (peaceful enjoyment of possessions) of the Convention, and the procedural guarantees of Article 6(1) (fair trial), 13 (remedies) and 14 (no discrimination). Finally, rights arise in environmental protest cases under Articles 10 (freedom of expression) and 11 (freedom of association).

One should also note a parallel development, namely the United Nations Economic Commission for Europe's (UNECE's) Convention on Access to Information, Public Participation in Decision-Making and Access to Justice in Environmental Matters agreed at Aarhus in June 1998. The United Kingdom has already signed this Convention and via its Freedom of Information Bill intends to implement parts of the same into domestic law.[1] The rest is likely in time to become incorporated into domestic law as a result of proposed changes to European Union law.[2]

---

[1] Home Office, Freedom of Information: Consultation on Draft Legislation Cm 4355

[2] Margaret Wallstrom, Environmental Commissioner, to the European Parliament, 2 February 1999, noted in ENDS, No. 296, p 41

1.1. No Express Right

In the ECHR, there is no express environmental right, either collectively or personally. See, stating the obvious, the Commission in *X & Y v Germany*[3] ("no right to nature preservation") and *Powell & Rayner v United Kingdom*.[4] In this, it is unlike a number of human rights instruments, including, by way of example, the South African Final Constitution of 1996, Section 24, where such an express right is articulated in these terms:

> "Everyone has the right –
> to an environment that is not harmful to their health or well-being; and to have the environment protected, for the benefit of present and future generations, through reasonable legislative and other measures. . . ."

The Supreme Court of Appeal of South Africa recently explained what it saw to be the benefits of such an express rights thus:[5]

> "Our Constitution, by including environmental rights as fundamental, justiciable human rights, by necessary implication requires that environmental considerations be accorded appropriate recognition and respect in the administrative processes in our country".

In the typical case of environmental harm caused or threatened to an individual or their property, the omission of an express right is of little significance because of Articles 2 and 8 and their protection of life, private life or home. However, a right to claim in respect of general environmental harm would assist claimants who do not have such an individual connection, but who wish to litigate matters of wider environmental importance, such as, say, impact upon biodiversity or upon the oceans.[6] As we shall see, the circumstances in which they can do so under the Convention are severely limited by the restrictive basis upon which such applicants can claim standing to sue.

1.2. Sources of Law

In the last ten years or so, a number of substantive environmental complaints have been considered in the Strasbourg case law. One should note not only the important decisions of the full Court in Strasbourg but also admissibility rulings by the Commission and the various Chambers of the Court which replace it, which, if less authoritative than those of the full Court, are still illustrative of the

---

[3] (1976) 5 DR 161

[4] (1986) 4 DR 5

[5] *Director Mineral Development v Save the Vaal Environment* 12 March 1999 (unreported).

[6] For a review of the international law, see Boyle and Anderson (eds) *Human Rights Approaches to Environmental Protection* (Oxford, Clarendon Press, 1996) 43–69. For a short and excellent summary of the pros and cons of an enforceable environmental right, see chapter 16 by P.Z. Eleftheriadis in Alston (ed) *The EU and Human Rights* (Oxford: Clarendon Press, 1999)

way in which the Strasbourg judges go about deciding rights cases. In addition to the Strasbourg case law, and the domestic cases which have arisen and will arise in greater numbers, it is also necessary to bear in mind interpretations of similar provisions by other constitutional courts and human rights institutions such as the United Nations Human Rights Committee. Finally, one should not forget the decisions of the European Court of Justice (ECJ) in Luxembourg upon points of Community law. Respect for human rights forms an integral part of the general principles of Community law, and Convention rights and Strasbourg decisions are often relied upon before the ECJ.[7]

2. THE VICTIM REQUIREMENT

Strasbourg case law has defined "victim of a violation" under Article 34 (giving the right of individual application to the Court) as limited to persons "directly affected" by the act or omission of the Member State. The Human Rights Act 1998 (HRA) has deliberately limited a claim against a public authority for an unlawful act or omission under Section 7(1) to those who are victims of the unlawful act or omission, and makes express reference to the Article 34 test under Section 7(7).

Similarly, under Section 7(3) HRA, an applicant in judicial review proceedings is to have "sufficient interest" to commence those proceedings relying upon a breach of human rights only if he or she is a victim of, and thus directly affected by, the unlawful act. The effect of this is expressly to limit the class of claimants, particularly as compared with the more open "sufficient interest" test which has latterly allowed non-governmental organisations concerned by the policy implications of a decision to challenge it in judicial review proceedings.[8]

This "victim" test will be of great significance in much environmental human rights litigation. Two environmental cases demonstrate this. In *Tauiria v France*,[9] the Commission rejected as manifestly ill-founded an application by residents of Tahiti that planned French nuclear tests violated Articles 2, 3, 8 and 14 of the Convention. As the Commission said:

> "It is only in highly exceptional circumstances that an applicant may nevertheless claim to be a victim of a violation of the Convention owing to the risk of a future violation . . . he must produce reasonable and convincing evidence of the likelihood that

[7] See, generally, *The EU and Human Rights*, chapters 23 and 27

[8] See *R v Secretary of State of the Environment ex parte Greenpeace* [1994] Env LR 76 in which Otton J allowed Greenpeace to challenge a decision that BNFL could increase activities at Sellafield. Contrast Greenpeace's lack of success in standing before the ECHR Commission in another nuclear power plant challenge, *Greenpeace Schweiz v Switzerland* (1997) 23 EHRR CD 116 and in the *Asselbourg* case, considered below. Greenpeace has fared equally badly when seeking standing to challenge the European Community Regional Development Fund: and the EU Commission: see *Stiching Greenpeace v European Commission* [1998] All ER (EC) 620, in which Advocate-General Cosmas gives a penetrating analysis of standing issues in the environmental context

[9] (1995) D & R 83-A 113

a violation affecting him personally will occur; mere suspicion or conjecture is insufficient in this respect".

It held that the applicants were not victims, because they lived over 1000km from the test site and had not produced convincing evidence that any future tests would affect them personally.

One should note, however, that part of the Commission's reasoning for being so restrictive in respect of threatened violations under Article 34 was the obligation upon an applicant to exhaust local remedies under Article 35 of the Convention before going to Strasbourg. The Article 35 obligation does not apply to a domestic complainant. Despite that, domestic courts are directed by Section 7(7) HRA to apply the Strasbourg "victim" test and hence its caselaw.

The second example is *Asselbourg & Greenpeace Luxembourg v Luxembourg*.[10] The applicants complained that the state granted a licence for a new steel works with insufficiently onerous environmental conditions, and that their complaint to the Conseil d'Etat had been rejected without consideration of the merits. They sought to bring claims under Articles 6(1) (right to a fair hearing) and 8 (right to private life). The Court decided that their claims were inadmissible because they had not shown that they were victims under Article 34. It was incumbent upon a claimant to show, in a detailed and defensible way, that because of inadequate steps taken by the authorities, the degree of probability of the occurrence of harm to them was such that it could constitute a violation.

It is inevitable that the "victim" requirement will present a significant obstacle to many applicants whose environmental concerns about a proposed development are genuinely based upon the precautionary principle but are insufficiently detailed in the eyes of the courts. I foresee many challenges to environmental decisions being rejected on this ground.

3. SUBSTANTIVE RIGHTS

3.1. Right to Life (Article 2)

"Everyone's right to life shall be protected by law . . ."

So far the Strasbourg Court has considered that this applies only to a right to physical life, as opposed to the right to a full enjoyment of life free from environmental impairment. Contrast the far more proactive approach of the Constitutional Court of India, which has found that the right to life "includes the right of enjoyment of pollution-free water and air for full enjoyment of life".[11]

---

[10] 29 June 1999 unreported admissibility decision by Second Section of the Court.

[11] *Kumar v State of Bihar* AIR 1991 420. For a discussion of the Indian cases, see *Human Rights Approaches to Environmental Protection*, N. 6 above, at pp 217ff

The state's environmental obligations under Article 2 have been considered in a number of recent cases. In *Guerra v Italy*[12] (facts below) whilst the majority did not consider Article 2, two concurring members of the Court thought that there would have been a violation of Article 2. Judge Jambrek put it thus:

> "If information is withheld by a government about circumstances which foreseeably and on substantial grounds present a real risk of danger to health and physical integrity, then such a situation may also be protected by Article 2 of the Convention".[13]

The important thing to note is that the "circumstances" do not have to have been created by the government or public authority involved; it is that they had the power to stop or avert the problem and did not do so. The second case is *L.C.B v United Kingdom*.[14] The applicant's father served on Christmas Island during atmospheric testing between 1957 and 1966. The applicant was diagnosed as suffering from leukaemia in 1970. Her complaint about failure to monitor her father's condition failed. However, the Court held that, had there been information available to the authorities which should have given them cause to fear that the applicant's father had been exposed to radiation and/or that his exposure might give rise to a risk to the applicant, then the authorities would have been under a duty to provide such information to the applicant's family or to the applicant. In that event, that would have been within the scope of the state's obligations to safeguard the lives of those within its jurisdiction.

Article 2 might therefore apply to an environmental enforcement body, including a local authority, which identifies some significant hazard whilst exercising its responsibilities, and does not do enough either to make those likely to be affected by the hazard aware of the dangers or to exercise its powers to stop the hazard. The result of proving a breach of Article 2 (as with Article 8) may seem startling, especially for domestic tort lawyers. In a potential damages claim, such a breach gives a cause of action under Sections 6 and 7 of the Human Rights Act 1998. It thus does away with any issue of whether there is a duty of care at common law owed by public authorities to private citizens, and the difficulties presented by the law of negligence in such cases as *X v Bedfordshire CC*[15] and *Stovin v Wise*[16] which currently make such a common law claim very difficult to bring. In addition, a breach gives an applicant grounds for judicial review on the basis that any breach of his human rights amounts to unlawfulness under Section 6 HRA.

Thus, in certain cases, claimants will be able to sue or seek judicial review where they had no recourse before. But just as important will be the likely shift in the attitudes of local authorities and central government consequent upon the threat of such claims. Those involved with the commencement and maintenance

---

[12]   (1998) 26 EHRR 357
[13]   Ibid. at 387
[14]   (1998) 27 EHRR 212
[15]   [1995] 2 AC 633
[16]   [1996] AC 923

of controversial processes may find themselves under great pressure from their regulators to produce continuing environmental data responsive to the concerns of objectors, over and above the environmental statement needed at the introduction of the new process. They may have to stiffen the resolve of local authorities taxed with allegations that the authority is in breach of its Article 2 obligations in not enforcing the need for, say, further groundwater or methane investigations near a landfill site or air and soil sampling near an allegedly dioxin-producing incinerator.

However, the very wide terms of the *L.C.B.* judgment have to be tempered by the recent case of *Osman v United Kingdom*.[17] In the context of an Article 2 claim, the Court sounded a note of caution for those eager to rely upon it:

> "For the court, and bearing in mind the difficulties in policing modern societies, the unpredictability of human conduct and the operational choices which must be made in terms of priorities and resources, such an obligation must be interpreted in a way which does not impose an impossible or disproportionate burden on the authorities. Accordingly, not every claimed risk to life can entail for the authorities a convention requirement to take operational measures to prevent that risk from materialising".

Such a dictum is readily transposable from the policing context in which it was made to the general environmental regulatory context. It will be cited often in attempts to ward off Article 2 claims against environmental regulators.

3.2. Degrading Treatment (Article 3)

"No one shall be subjected to torture or to inhuman or degrading treatment or punishment".

This is unlikely to assist an environmental complainant. In *Lopez Ostra v Spain*[18] the operation of a waste treatment works twelve metres away from the complainant's home caused such a serious impact on her life that she moved away. Despite that, the use of the works did not violate Article 3. The complaint was however declared admissible on this ground by the Commission.

3.3. Right to Privacy and Home Life (Article 8)

"Article 8(1) Everyone has the right to respect for his private and family life, his home and his correspondence.

Article 8(2) There shall be no interference by a public authority with the exercise of this right except such as is in accordance with the law and is necessary in a democratic society in the interests of national security, public safety or

---

[17] (1998) 5 BHRC 293 at 321, para 116 (Full Chamber), (2000) 29 EHRR 245 at 305
[18] (1994) 20 EHRR 277

the economic well-being of the country, for the prevention of disorder or crime, for the protection of health or morals, or for the protection of the rights and freedoms of others".

This Article is the first port of call for an environmental claimant under the Convention. Once the claimant has demonstrated an interference with his or her right, then it is for the public authority to justify that interference under Article 8(2).

Importantly, Article 8 has been construed as imposing both a "positive obligation" on states to take reasonable and appropriate measures to secure applicants' rights against incursions by other parties, whether private or public, and a "negative obligation" not to interfere with applicants' rights, save insofar as the state can justify such interference by showing that it comes within Article 8(2).

The first significant Strasbourg environmental case, *Powell & Rayner v United Kingdom,*[19] is a good example of the two-stage process involved in Article 8 claims. The applicants complained of noise from Heathrow Airport. The Court held that Article 8 was material, because the quality of the applicants' private lives and the scope for enjoying the amenities of their homes had been adversely affected by the noise. However, the policy approach adopted and the noise abatement measures put in place by the United Kingdom could not be said to have exceeded its margin of appreciation under Article 8(2), the importance of Heathrow to the British economy being a relevant consideration.[20]

A similar approach to *Powell* was taken by the Commission in *S v France.*[21] The existence of a nuclear power station less than three hundred metres from an eighteenth century chateau on the banks of the Loire, creating noise, glaring lights at night and a disturbance to the microclimate, and halving the value of the property, did amount to interference with an Article 8(1) right. However, the interference was justifiable and proportionate under Article 8(2) given the benefits of the energy thus provided and the fact that the applicant had already recovered 250,000 French francs from the Conseil d'Etat for the interference.

Lopez Ostra v Spain[22] was the first successful substantive environmental claim decided by the Strasbourg Court. Several tanneries built a waste treatment plant, with state subsidy, twelve metres from the applicant's home. The regulators then did little if nothing to mitigate the environmental effects of the plant. Disruption to living conditions and serious health problems were (not surprisingly) alleged, and disputed.

The Court found a violation of Article 8(1), notwithstanding the absence of any specific finding as to the likely cause of the health problems, in these terms:

[19] (1990) 12 EHRR 345
[20] Other airport noise cases from the United Kingdom were the subject of friendly settlements after being declared admissible, i.e *Arrondelle* 19 D & R (1980) 186 (settled for £7,500) and *Baggs* 44 D & R 13 (1985) and 52 DR 59 (settled for £24,000)
[21] 65 D & R (1990) 250
[22] (1994) 20 EHRR 277

"Naturally, severe environmental pollution may affect individuals' well-being and prevent them from enjoying their homes in such a way as to affect their private and family life adversely, without, however seriously endangering their health".[23]

The violation of Article 8(1) could not be saved by Article 8(2):

"the State did not succeed in striking a fair balance between the interests of the town's economic well-being – that of having a waste treatment plant – and the applicant's effective enjoyment of her right to respect for her home and her private and family life".[24]

The Strasbourg Court (unanimously) awarded compensation of four million pesetas (worth about £16,000 today), assessed "on an equitable basis", to cover both pecuniary and non-pecuniary damages. No detailed breakdown of the sum awarded is to be found in the judgment. It (like many of the Strasbourg Court judgments on compensation) will be of little assistance when a domestic court is faced with the task of taking into account the principles applied by the Strasbourg Court: see Section 8(4) HRA and Article 41 of the Convention.[25]

A less extreme example of environmental pollution than *Lopez* is presented by the case of *Timmer v Netherlands*.[26] *Timmer*, via his company, complained of a pig farm a short distance away (fifty metres, rather than the recommended sixty three metres), and of his inability to persuade the domestic administrative court to order the pigowner to take remedial action. The Commission, not deciding the issue of whether the company could sue for the personal rights in issue under Article 8, concluded that the administrative courts were entitled to come down in favour of the pigfarmer, and thus the claim was manifestly ill-founded. The Commission appears to have attached weight to a number of factors set out by the domestic court, that the licence to keep pigs was issued two years before *Timmer* acquired the land,[27] that *Timmer's* house was in an agricultural area, and that the costs of the suggested remedial works were significant, whereas the chances of success of those works were questionable.

The *Timmer* case raised an interesting and important argument concerning the abilities of companies, as opposed to individuals, to complain of breaches of Article 8. Domestically, there has been a recent decision that companies are not entitled to a right of privacy under Article 8 by Forbes J in *R v Broadcasting Standards Commission ex parte BBC*.[28] Similarly, in the *Allenbourg* case (supra), a *Greenpeace* association with a registered office near the steel works complained of was held not to be able to complain of breaches of Article 8 because nuisance and disturbance can only be experienced by natural persons. This topic is however controversial and I see no reason in principle why companies should not be able to complain about infringements of Article 8. I do not

[23] Para 51 of the judgment
[24] Para 58
[25] See chapter 5 on Remedies
[26] Commission 22 October 1997, unreported
[27] Unlike the domestic "no defence that the plaintiff came to the nuisance" rule
[28] 9 July 1999, unreported

expect that Forbes J's decision in the *BBC* case will be the last word on this point.

The decision in *Guerra v Italy*,[29] already referred to in the context of Article 2, contains perhaps the most important recent pronouncement of the Court on environmental rights under the Convention. The population of an Italian village successfully complained about the local government's maladministration in respect of a nearby dangerous chemical works. It was held by the Strasbourg Court that the local government's failure to give the local people

> "essential information that would have entitled them to assess the risks they and their families might run if they continued to live at Manfredonia, a town particularly exposed in the event of an accident at the factory".[30]

amounted to a breach of Article 8.

The factual background to this conclusion was a history of incidents at the works, including one explosion in 1976 where 150 people had to be hospitalised with acute arsenic poisoning. The complaint was against the local authority for failing to act. The applicants could not show that they had been directly injured by that failure. They claimed an order against the state to decontaminate the area and to carry out an epidemiological study to identify the health effects of the past emissions. The delegate of the Commission thought that a full report of past events and their impact was warranted.[31] Apart from awarding each applicant ten million lire (about £3,000), the Court left it up to the state to decide how to redress the violation.

As already observed in the Article 2 context, the notable feature about the judgment of the Court in *Guerra* is the emphasis upon a positive obligation to inform local people about health matters. That potentially extends beyond a duty to provide existing environmental documents (as is provided for domestically in the Environmental Information Regulations 1992 and 1998) but also to carry out and publish a review of the health risks if circumstances warrant it.

Just how far the decision goes is highly controversial. Claimants will say that Article 8 per *Guerra* goes much further than existing provisions, requiring a full review of hazards by a regulator to be provided to those likely to be affected. Regulators may argue that performance within their existing statutory obligations is sufficient compliance with their positive obligations under Article 8. They will say that the ruling should not be taken out of the context of a specific case of maladministration in which the local government had failed over many years to comply with a specific statutory duty to provide such emergency information to local people. They will finally contend that any given decision not to inform the local population can be defended on Article 8(2) grounds.

---

[29] (1998) 26 EHRR 357

[30] Para 60, at 76f

[31] The Commission allowed the claim under Article 10, not Article 8. The Article 10 claim was dismissed by the Court, whereas the Article 8 claim was sucessful

A similar conclusion was reached in *McGinley & Egan v United Kingdom*.[32] This concerned Christmas Island nuclear testing. The Court held that where a government engages in hazardous activities, which might have hidden adverse consequences on the health of those involved in such activities, respect for private and family life under Article 8 requires that an effective and accessible procedure be established which enables such persons to seek all relevant and appropriate information.

I have already referred to the Aarhus Convention on Access to Information, Public Participation in Decision-Making and Access to Justice in Environmental Matters. The Government intends to make amendments to the existing Environmental Information Regulations via the Freedom of Information Bill, and regulations thereunder so as to harmonise the domestic conditions for access to environmental information with those agreed under the Aarhus Convention.[32a] Draft regulations have not yet been published by the Home Office, and we must await them before assessing the significance of this commitment. In addition, the Commission of the European Union proposes to implement the rest of this Convention, via a combination of its proposed Directive on Environmental Liability and by amendment to the existing Environmental Information Directive.[33]

One should note that one of the general obligations assumed by the signatory states to the Convention (Article 5(1)) is that they

"shall ensure that:
  (a) Public authorities possess and update environmental information which is relevant to their functions;
  (b) Mandatory systems are established so that there is an adequate flow of information to public authorities about proposed and existing activities which may significantly affect the environment;
  (c) In the event of an imminent threat to human health or the environment, whether caused by human activities or due to natural causes, all information which could enable the public to take measures to prevent or mitigate harm arising from the threat and is held by a public authority is disseminated immediately and without delay to members of the public who may be affected".

There is a striking similarity between this wide obligation and the 1998 developments of the Court's Article 2 case law in *Guerra* and *L.C.B*, and, as we shall see, in *McGinley* under Article 8. In my view, this general obligation, albeit not yet implemented into domestic law, is likely to give further support to a wide reading of the dicta in *Guerra* and *McGinley*.

What about the more intangible aspects of family life which might provide assistance to environmental litigants? There are some cases of interest in this

[32] (1998) 27 EHRR 1
[32a] s. 73 of the Bill
[33] See N. 2 above

context, and perhaps some room for development. So, the right of minorities to respect for their cultural values has been considered under this head.[34] In *G & E* Lapp shepherds, fishermen and hunters claimed that the proposed flooding of a 2.8 square kilometre area of their ancestral hunting grounds by a hydro-electric project would be in breach of Article 8. The Commission found this capable of falling under Article 8(1), but decided that because the interference was justifiable under Article 8(2), the complaint was manifestly ill-founded and hence inadmissible. *G & E* was approved by the Commission in *Buckley v United Kingdom*,[35] a gypsy case. A similar principle was successfully invoked before the UN Human Rights Committee when considering the right to "family" in Article 17 of the International Covenant on Civil and Political Rights in the case of *Hopu v France*.[36] The disturbance of an ancestral burial site by a hotel development on land leased by France was capable of amounting to arbitrary interference with the privacy and family life of ethnic Polynesians.

The importance of an Article 8 claim to environmental litigants is that it enables them to raise directly against a government or public authority issues which would often have failed at common law because, for example, a court would find no duty of care to exist. The common law difficulties are well illustrated by the decision of the Court of Appeal in *Lam v Brennan & Torbay Council*[37] where a claim against the council for granting planning permission and failing to serve abatement and enforcement notices upon the creator of a statutory nuisance was struck out as disclosing no cause of action. An Article 8 claim might lie in such circumstances if the Council (as in *Guerra*) had signally failed to protect the interests of local inhabitants.

But it should be noted that, just as a Convention right may entitle a claimant to escape some restrictive rule of the common law, so the derogations, in this case under Article 8(2), entitle the respondent public authority to defend on a front much broader than that allowed by domestic law. This double effect is well illustrated by the *Docklands* litigation, domestically known as *Hunter v Canary Wharf*,[38] and in particular the claims concerning nuisance by dust to tenants and their families, which (under the name of *Khatun v United Kingdom*), when it reached Strasbourg was held by the Commission to be manifestly ill-founded and hence unarguable.[39]

It was thought by Lord Cooke of Thorndon, dissenting in *Hunter*, that those whose claims in nuisance were struck out because they were not tenants may have a potential claim under Article 8. The Commission agreed with him, to the

---

[34] *G & E v Norway* (1983) 35 D.R.30. See also two cases concerning the MV Estonia, *Bendreus v Sweden* 8 September 1997 and *Berglund v Sweden* 16 April 1998 (both unreported) in which the Commission discussing but not deciding whether the applicants had an Article 8 right in respect of Sweden's plans to concrete over the wreck in which their relatives had died

[35] (1996) 23 EHRR 101

[36] (1997) 3 BHRC 597

[37] [1997] PIQR P488

[38] [1997] AC 655

[39] 26 EHRR CD 212

extent that the claimants came within the provisions of Article 8(1) and further that there was a breach of the terms of Article 8(1).

However, before the Commission, the Government ran the public benefit argument under Article 8(2) which had failed domestically in the guise of a statutory authority defence to the claim in nuisance. That Article 8(2) defence succeeded. In classic Convention language, the regeneration of Docklands pursued "a legitimate aim", and the interference with rights corresponded to a "pressing social need" and was "proportionate to the aim or aims pursued". The Commission, taking into account that there were no allegations of personal injury from the dust, said that it could not "find that a fair balance has not been achieved" between the interference on the one hand and the justification on the other.[40] The Commission also recognised the margin of appreciation allowed to Contracting States, who are in a better position to make an initial assessment of the necessity of a given interference. Hence, said the Commission, the case was unarguable.

All of the above justifications can be advanced by a public authority in a domestic Human Rights Act claim, with the possible exception of the principle of margin of appreciation[41] given to Member States. There may remain a debate about the applicability of that principle at a domestic level. Sir John Laws[42] considers that that is a concept applicable only to an international tribunal, and not to the domestic courts whose job it will become to adjudicate on Convention disputes. Lester & Pannick[43] agree but consider that an analogous doctrine will be recognised, namely that there are some circumstances in which the legislature and the executive are better placed to make difficult choices between competing considerations. This latter passage has been approved by Lord Hope in *R. v DPP ex parte Kebeline*,[44] in a passage which explicitly recognises that there will be areas of judgement within which the judges will defer on democratic grounds to the considered opinion of the elected body whose acts or omissions are in issue.

Finally, a breach of one's Article 8 rights by a decision of a public authority provides grounds for judicial review on the basis that the decision is unlawful under Section 6 HRA. As with the claims for damages, it is of course open to the public authority to justify its decision under Article 8(2). But one should not simply assume that such a decision can be justified on traditional irrationality grounds, as the Strasbourg Court's decision in *Smith & Grady v United Kingdom*[45] demonstrates. The Ministry of Defence successfully justified its

---

[40] Claimants from leading domestic environmental cases have not fared well in Strasbourg. In *Stockton v United Kingdom* (unreported, 15 January 1998, cf. *A.B v South West Water* [1993] QB 507) claimants in respect of the Camelford incident in 1988 in which aluminium sulphate was tipped into their water supply had no success under Articles 8, 6(1) and 13. One complaint was that there should have been a public enquiry into the episode

[41] This doctrine is discussed in chapter 2 The Convention and the Human Rights Act: A New Way of Thinking

[42] (1998) *PL* 258

[43] *Human Rights Law & Practice* (Butterworths, London, 1999)

[44] [1999] 3 WLR 972

[45] 27 September 1999, unreported

blanket ban on homosexuals, and hence an interference with their Article 8 rights, before domestic courts, on the basis that the ban was not irrational.[46] That succeeded because of the high threshold required. The Strasbourg Court, on the other hand, said that the irrationality test effectively excluded consideration of issues such as whether the ban answered a pressing need or was proportionate, and that therefore the United Kingdom was in breach of Article 8 when taken with the right to an effective remedy under Article 13.[47] Therefore a more intrusive analysis may be required from the courts when human rights issues are raised upon judicial review.

3.4. Right to Property (Article 1 of the First Protocol)

"Article 1(1)1 every natural or legal person is entitled to the peaceful enjoyment of his possessions

1(1)2 No one shall be deprived of his possessions except in the public interest and subject to the conditions provided for by law and by the general principles of international law.

1/2 The preceding provisions shall not, however, in any way impair the right of a state to enforce such laws as it deems necessary to control the use of property in accordance with the general interest or to secure the payment of taxes or other contributions or penalties".

This tends to be unprofitable ground for a claimant, because of the width of the qualifying provision, which enables public authorities to justify their actions. As can be imagined, a number of attempts have been made to bring claims in respect of planning decisions which significantly affect the use and value of the owner's land, with little success. After a short description of some of the underlying principles, there follows a brief summary of these attempts.

"Possessions" in the opening words of the Article is defined widely, and includes things of economic value such as licenses (for liquor), rights (to fish) and most interests in goods and land (see, for instance, *Chassagnou v France*[48] concerning the right not to have neighbours hunting on one's land). They also include legal claims if sufficiently established: *National Provincial BS v United Kingdom*[49] where retrospective repeal of an existing set of proceedings concerning the overpayment of tax was said by the Court to be justifiable. Any steps taken by a regulator to interfere with those "possessions" must strike a fair balance between the demands of the general community and the requirements of the protection of the individuals' fundamental rights. There must be a reasonable relationship of proportionality between the means employed and the aims

---

[46] [1996] QB 517
[47] See the section on Article 13 below, and chapter 5 on Remedies
[48] 29 April 1999, unreported
[49] (1997) EHRR 127

pursued. Put another way, in the balancing of the interests to the community versus the interests of the individual, has the claimant suffered an excessive burden?

In reaching that decision, it is of importance to see whether compensation is available. If there is *deprivation* of the claimant's property under Article 1(1)2, then there is normally an inherent right to some compensation reasonably related to the value of the property. If, however, there is *control* of use of property (within Article 1(2)), then that does not as a rule import any right to compensation.

The distinction between "possession" and "control" is an important one. If the Court holds that the applicant has been "deprived" of his property, the level of compensation awarded will be a material factor in deciding whether there has been a reasonable relationship of proportionality between the means employed and the aim sought to be realised. The amount of compensation should normally be related to the value of the property. "Control" of use does not carry with it an implicit right to compensation: *Baner v Sweden*.[50]

Now to some examples of this Article, from which it will appear that it will only assist in the most extreme cases. A strong case which still did not lead to a successful claim under Article 1 Protocol 1 without the help of an additional claim under the Convention was *Pine Valley Developments v Ireland*.[51] In 1977 outline planning consent was given for a site. In 1982, that consent, with a number of others, was declared a nullity by the Supreme Court, but not before the claimants had expended significant sums on the site. An Act was then passed giving compensation in respect of all the other consents affected by the ruling, but not the claimants' consent. A claim under Article 1 Protocol 1 on its own failed. However, the claimants did succeed on a different ground. They said that there was no objective justification in the difference in treatment between them and the other affected individuals, and therefore succeeded under a combination of Article 1 Protocol 1, and Article 14 which, as we shall see, forbids discrimination.

Another illustration is provided by *Fredin v Sweden*.[52] The applicants had a permit to exploit a gravel pit, which was revoked pursuant to a law on nature conservation. The applicants complained of violation of property rights. The Court held that the revocation was a "control on the use" of the property, but that:

(i) it had a legitimate aim in view of the fact that "in today's society the protection of the environment is an increasingly important consideration", and that
(ii) the margin of appreciation had not been exceeded, in view of the fact that the applicants had no legitimate expectation that the permit would not be revoked.

---

[50]   (1989) 60 DR 128
[51]   (1991) 14 EHRR 319
[52]   (1991) A 192

This decision shows that the revocation of licenses is generally considered to be a "control" of use of property rather than a "deprivation" of the property, the control being directed not to the license itself but to the underlying business interests.

R v N Lincolnshire Council ex parte Horticultural Sales (Humberside) Ltd,[53] a decision of Lightman J, is a domestic illustration of how Article 1, Protocol 1 may be of little practical assistance. The applicant had planning permission for peat extraction since 1951. Planning control moved due to boundary changes, from Doncaster MBC to Humberside MBC and then to N Lincs Humberside MBC erroneously omitted the applicant's planning permission from its First List, and N Lincs inherited that List. Because the applicant and others thought that the applicant's sites were included on Doncaster MBC's First List, the applicant did not seek rectification of the N Lincs First List within three months, with the result that, under Schedule 13 of Environment Act 1995, the applicant's planning permission was extinguished. N Lincs said it had no power to extend the three month period. The applicant argued that N Lincs did have discretionary implied power, relying upon Article 1 of the First Protocol. Lightman J said "No", pointing out that there was a wide margin of appreciation on the regulator and no individual or excessive burden on the applicant arising out of what had happened.

In this review of cases in which rights to property have not availed claimants, it is worth noting *Reg v Secretary of State for the Environment ex parte Standley*,[54] a recent environmental case decided by the European Court of Justice in Luxembourg. Farmers complained that the Nitrates Directive[55] offended against their right of property because it limited the amount of nitrogen compounds they could use on their land, and hence it reduced income and land values. They relied upon the fact that the nitrate concentrations in the water which had triggered those restrictions had been in part caused by non-agricultural sources. The ECJ, recognising that the right to property was part of the general principles of European Community law,[56] confirmed that the exercise of the right to property was not absolute, and could be restricted:

> "provided that those restrictions in fact correspond to objectives of general interest pursued by the Community and do not constitute a disproportionate and intolerable inteference, impairing the very substance of the rights guaranteed".[57]

Not surprisingly, the restrictions in question were found not to impair the "very substance of the rights guaranteed".[58]

---

[53] [1998] Env. LR 295

[54] [1999] 3 WLR 744

[55] Council Directive 91/676/EEC

[56] Based upon cases such as *Hauer v Land Rheinland-Pfalz* [1979] ECR 3727

[57] Ibid., para 54 at p 767

[58] See, for two further domestic illustrations of how Article 1, Protocol 1 disputes are decided in practice, *R. v Secretary of State for Health ex parte Eastside Cheese* (CA, [1999] EuLR 968) in which cheese stocks were impounded, and *Booker Aquaculture* [1999] Eur.LR, in which fish stocks were ordered to be destroyed. *Eastside* lost, whereas *Booker* won. Both relied upon Article 1, Protocol 1

3.4.1. Compulsory Purchase and Blight

It is unlikely that the present domestic regime of compulsory purchase law would offend against the provisions of Article 1, Protocol 1 even though a number of criticisms can be levelled at it. For instance, land may be under threat of compulsory purchase for a period of some years without the owner necessarily having any remedy. The difficulty about such a claim is that in the ECHR case law, only extreme cases of blighted land attract any compensation, and more modest periods of delay are unlikely to offend because of the interest in the acquiring authority retaining a reasonable degree of flexibility.

Sporrong & Lonnroth v Sweden [59] is the best example of such an extreme case. The Swedish equivalent of a compulsory purchase order affected two areas of land in question for twenty three years and eight years respectively, and an accompanying ban on any construction works lasted for twenty five years and twelve years respectively, in all cases before being revoked. It was, not surprisingly, held by the Court that there was an interference "affecting the very substance of ownership" which the Member State could not justify.

In contrast, a recent attempt to complain of more temporary blight failed at the admissibility stage. In *Moore v United Kingdom*[60] the value of the applicant's property was affected by amendments to a structure plan which proposed a major housing development, together with a business and science park. The applicant complained of an inability to sell the land in the light of those amendments. The Third Section of the Court confirmed that the right to possessions does not guarantee the right to enjoy the possessions in a pleasant unchanged environment, and that, in contrast to the *Sporrong* case, where the effects had been to render "virtually non-existent" the applicants' power of sale, it held that the changes to the structure plan did not amount to a disproportionate restriction on the applicant's power to dispose of his property.

Additionally, complaints about the precise level of compensation awarded on acquisition have not found favour with the Strasbourg Court to date, and are unlikely to assist domestic applicants. In two leading cases, it has been stressed that, where acquisition of assets serves some legitimate social economic or other public policies, considerable latitude in the level of compensation is allowed to the Member State: see *Lithgow v United Kingdom*[61] on the nationalisation of the aircraft and shipbuilding industries, and *James v United Kingdom*[62] on the impact of the Leasehold Reform Act 1967 upon the Duke of Westminster's holdings in Belgravia.

On the other hand, in *Immobiliare Saffi v Italy*,[63] a recent ruling upholding the applicant's claim under Article 1 Protocol 1, the Court made an award to a

---

[59] (1982) 5 EHRR 35
[60] 15 June 1999, unreported
[61] (1986) 8 EHRR 329
[62] (1987) 8 EHRR 123
[63] 28 July 1999, unreported

company for uncompensated "control" of an apartment block it had acquired. The "control" was simply the failure by the state to provide police assistance in the execution of a possession order, which the applicant had obtained when one of the sitting tenants' leases had expired. The Strasbourg Court acknowledged that the policy of not executing possession orders was a measure in the interests of resolving Italy's acute housing shortage; nevertheless, it considered that the applicant company had suffered an "excessive burden" in this respect, and it upheld the applicants claim for the rent it would have collected between the date of the possession order and the date of the judgment.

4. PROCEDURAL RIGHTS

4.1. Fair Trial (Article 6(1))

"In the determination of his civil rights and obligations or of any criminal charge against him, everyone is entitled to a fair and public hearing within a reasonable time by an independent and impartial tribunal established by law . . ."

This Article may be of considerable significance for environmental litigation. It enables a complainant to argue, whether in judicial review proceedings or in a civil claim for damages against a public authority, that he or she has not been given a fair hearing of his or her civil rights. Those "civil rights", according to Strasbourg Court learning, may include rather more than the conventional tortious or contractual claim for damages or an injunction, and the phrase is not to be interpreted by reference to domestic definitions but to an "autonomous" Strasbourg Court case law about what is or is not "civil".[64]

4.1.1. Civil Rights

So, a general substantive right to peaceful enjoyment of property (a right protected by Article 1 of the First Protocol and by Article 8) will need to be given Article 6(1) procedural protection. Such protection will also cover applications by a company to a regulator for an environmental licence: see *Benthem v Netherlands*.[65] In that case the necessity for the licence was closely connected with the applicant's right to use possessions in accordance with the law and had thus a proprietary character.

Article 6(1) protection will also extend to circumstances where the complainant's right is claimed in the context of dealings between other parties, say, a neighbour claiming that his property rights are affected by someone else's application for an environmental licence, as long as the decision by the state in respect of that licence is directly decisive of the complainant's rights. As we have

---

[64] See chapter 3 on Costs, Conditional Fees and Legal Aid for further discussion of Article 6
[65] (1986) 8 EHRR 1

already seen, the neighbour must show that he is a "victim" and hence directly affected by the decision under Article 34. As we shall see, he must also show that the link between the decision and his rights was sufficiently close to bring Article 6(1) into play. This in practice imposes a very similar test.

The following Strasbourg cases are examples of some of these principles applied in the environmental context:

(i) in *Fredin v Sweden*,[66] the absence of any form of judicial review of the decision by the Government to revoke a gravel company's exploitation permit violated the gravel company' s rights under Article 6(1). A small amount of compensation was paid.

(ii) in *Zander v Sweden*,[67] a licensing board renewed a company permit to tip industrial waste. In doing so, it dismissed the demands of neighbouring property-owners that there should be a condition in the permit that the company should be obliged, as a precautionary measure, to supply free drinking water in case of the owners' well being polluted by cyanide. The Court held that the property-owner's rights were at stake (in view of the possible impact of the permit on the value of their property) and that since they had an arguable entitlement in Swedish law to protection against their water being polluted, which was their "civil right", it was a violation of Article 6(1) to refuse them the possibility of judicial review of the board's decision. The Court took account of the fact that the owner had standing under Swedish law to ask the regulator to require the company to take precautionary measures as conditions of the permit, and could appeal the regulator's decision. Thus, notwithstanding that there were substantial public law elements to the dispute, the Court considered that the owner's civil rights were at stake.

The most recent decision by the full Court is *Balmer-Schafroth v Switzerland*.[68] This case raises more questions than it answers, not least because it fits ill with the earlier decision in *Zander*. Swiss nationals living within five kilometres of a nuclear power station opposed the extension and the 10 per cent expansion of the station's production licence on safety grounds. The Federal Council (in other words, the Government) dismissed these objections. There was no available domestic appeal or judicial review. The Commission, by sixteen votes to twelve, was of the opinion that there was a breach of Article 6(1).

The Court, by twelve votes to eight, disagreed. It considered that the applicants had failed to show that the operation of the power station exposed them to a danger that was not only serious but specific, and above all, imminent.[69]

---

[66] (1991) 13 EHRR 784. The Fredins made a second successful visit to Strasbourg in 1993, to complain of Sweden's failure to give them an oral hearing before the Supreme Administrative Court: (1994) A 373-A

[67] (1993) 18 EHRR 175

[68] (1998) 25 EHRR 598

[69] Compare the admissibility decision in *Greenpeace Schweiz v Switzerland* (April 1997) 23 EHRR CD 116 in which the Commission (shortly before the decision in *Balmer-Schafroth*)

These conclusions were drawn from the findings of the Federal Council, which was of course the decision which the applicants wished to review. So, said the Court, the connection between the decision of the Federal Council and the right invoked by the applicants was too tenuous and remote; it was therefore not a "civil right". The Court appear only to have concluded that the applicants could satisfy the "victim" test because the Federal Council had allowed some objectors, including the applicants, to participate in the proceedings before it.

A spirited minority of eight objected that the conclusion that there was no "civil right" at issue was in effect question-begging; as it put it "Does the local population have to be irradiated before being able to exercise a remedy?" The minority considered that an applicant needs show that there was a genuine and serious dispute and there is a likelihood of risk and damage; it may suffice that there is proof of a link and of a potential danger. It expressly referred to the importance of reinforcing the "precautionary principle" within international environmental law, and of "full judicial remedies to protect the rights of individuals against the imprudence of authorities".

In *P.N. v Switzerland*,[70] a variant of the argument used by the majority in *Balmer-Schafroth* led the Commission to conclude that an air noise claim was inadmissible. It was held that, because the applicant lived twelve kilometres from the offending airport and the aircraft overflying his house would be at a height of more than 1,000 metres, the applicant had not substantiated that the noise nuisance had reached a level which would raise an issue under Swiss law and therefore would amount to a genuine and serious dispute in respect of his property rights under Article 6(1).

As one can see, in adjudicating Article 6(1) claims, the Strasbourg Court has often formed a view on the merits of the underlying civil claims, and relied upon that view as an important factor in determining whether there is or is not a genuine civil dispute.

4.1.2. Fair and Public Hearing by an Independent and Impartial Tribunal

The commonest form of decision-making in environmental matters is of course administrative. So, the Environment Agency decides on applications for a discharge consent under the Water Resources Act 1991, and for a waste management licence, or an Integrated Pollution Control authorisation under the Environmental Protection Act 1990. A local planning authority is charged with granting or refusing planning permission. The Secretary of State for the Environment, Transport and Regions may determine an appeal against conditions imposed on a discharge consent.

As we have seen, any of these decisions may be determinative of an individual's civil rights. Article 6(1) requires, not that the original decision has to be

concluded, on very similar facts concerning another nuclear power station, that those closest to the station had an Article 6(1) claim, whereas those further away did not

[70] 11 September 1997, unreported

taken by a court, but that there is a right to challenge that decision in a court. In most cases, there is the possibility of challenging such decisions by way of judicial review. The issue therefore arises whether that challenge, which can only be on issues of law, is sufficient compliance with the requirements of Article 6(1).

The leading case is *Bryan v United Kingdom*.[71] The applicant had constructed brick buildings on his land, claiming that they were agricultural barns and therefore no permission was needed for them. The council served an enforcement notice on the basis that they were houses. Bryan appealed to a planning inspector, and lost. He then pursued a statutory appeal to the High Court, for which a point of law was required. He lost, and leave to appeal to the Court of Appeal was refused. He then complained to the Strasbourg Court that he had not had a fair hearing.

The Court decided that he had had a fair hearing. However, this was only because of the cumulative effect of the proceedings before the planning inspector (which did not on their own offer sufficient guarantees of independence and thus did not by itself comply with Article 6(1))[72] and the possibility of a statutory appeal to the High Court on a point of law (which did). It recognised that in a specialised field it was entirely appropriate for an administrative body to make findings of fact and policy decisions, with a review on a point of law thereafter. The Court was however careful to confine its ruling to the specific circumstances of the case where it held that there was no essential dispute on the primary facts, as opposed to the inferences to be drawn from those facts.

The *Bryan* decision concerned the rights of the recipient of an enforcement notice, though identical considerations will apply in a typical case in which the inspector rules against an application for planning permission. Additionally, the grounds upon which one can pursue a statutory appeal to the High Court and a judicial review are identical. Generally speaking, therefore, a developer, when faced with a refusal to grant planning permission, will have little chance of persuading a domestic court that the current system offends against Article 6(1).

Less straightforward will be cases where the applicant has not had an oral hearing at the administrative stage or stages, and where his only access to court is by way of the limited challenge afforded by judicial review. A good example is the objector to the grant of planning permission who is of course in a very different position from the developer. He has a right to information under the Local Government Act 1972, but in practice there is only a limited timescale in which to read and digest this. He may be able to respond to the developer's case, though if the application involves issues of any complexity of which he has not yet had notice, that response may be limited. His contribution, if any, at the meeting of the authority itself is likely to be limited by practical problems such as lack of time in a busy agenda before the planning committee. The view of the planning officer reporting to the committee may say no more than that the offi-

---

[71] (1996) 21 EHRR 342

[72] To similar effect see *Smith v Secretary for Trade and Industry The Times*, 11 October 1999, where employment tribunals were said potentially to fall foul of the same objection

cer has considered the objection, and thus the committee itself may absorb little of what the objector wishes to say. When it decides to grant permission, the committee gives no reasons. The objector has no right of appeal from such a grant of planning permission by the local planning authority. His only chance is then to challenge the grant by way of judicial review. Unless there has been some obvious procedural unfairness,[73] it can be very difficult to challenge the grant in the absence of reasons.

The question therefore arises whether in such circumstances the objector has had a "fair hearing" before the planning authority. If he has not, then, from the coming into force of the HRA, he will be able to make direct complaint to the planning committee (if he gets the opportunity) that he is not receiving a fair hearing, and then can seek to make the same case by way of judicial review of the grant of permission.

I consider that, in the starkest of cases, the answer may well be that the objector has not had a fair hearing. In a planning application where there is a direct clash of oral evidence between objector and developer about, say, existing noise, a court may find that the objector, facing all the practical difficulties set out above, did not have a fair hearing before the local planning authority. An Article 6(1) claim will significantly assist a claimant to argue that the decision was procedurally unfair and should therefore be quashed.

The *Bryan* case was considered domestically in *R v Secretary of State for Wales ex parte Emery*,[74] where such a challenge failed. This involved judicial review by an applicant who wanted public access to a riverbank footpath. The decision under challenge was that of the Secretary of State not to direct the local authority to modify the definitive map of its area to show the footpath as a public path. There was a direct clash of written evidence between the owner and witnesses who had used the path over the years. The court answered an attack on the procedures involved (i.e. no oral hearing either before the authority or before the Secretary of State) by acknowledging the conformity of judicial review with Article 6(1), following *Bryan*. Two features of the case should be noted; the point ultimately proceeded by way of concession, and the judge commented that, absent a claim of irrationality successful on other grounds, "the adequacy of judicial review may not be so apparent to the applicant in this case".

4.1.3. Is Article 6(1) Just a Procedural Safeguard?

Article 6(1) is primarily a procedural right, not a substantive right. The conventional illustration of this is the *Powell & Rayner* case,[75] concerning air noise at Heathrow. The applicants advanced an Article 6(1) claim on the basis that their right of access to court had been removed by the immunities against civilian air

---

[73] As, for example, in *R v Rochdale MBC ex parte Brown* [1997] Env LR 100
[74] [1996] 4 All ER 1
[75] (1990) 12 EHRR 345

noise claims in Section 76(1) of the Civil Aviation Act 1982; what remedy remained was theoretical and illusory. The ECHR did not accept this claim. The applicants did not have a substantive right in respect of claims caught by the immunity, and so no question of Article 6(1) procedural protection arose. *Glass v United Kingdom*,[76] an attempt by a resident of Richmond to complain that he could not bring a statutory nuisance complaint in respect of Heathrow noise because of a provision in Section 79(6) of the Environmental Protection Act 1990, also failed before the Commission.

Contrast the recent case of *Osman v United Kingdom*.[77] A public policy immunity (against liability for policing errors) may not be enough to nullify a civil right in national law, with the result that what, in domestic law, may be regarded as a substantive defence, may in Strasbourg, be an infringement of one's right to a fair hearing under Article 6(1). That raises the possibility of challenging a common law immunity, such as, for example, the royal prerogative being used to defend a nuisance claim against the armed forces, on Article 6(1) grounds. One should however note that *Osman* has elicited a controversial response domestically, not least from Lord Browne-Wilkinson in *Barrett v London Borough of Enfield*[78] who found the Strasbourg Court's account of domestic tort law "difficult to understand" and subjected the critical passage of the Court's judgment to a penetrating analysis. I anticipate that in the very near future this difficult area will be clarified either by Strasbourg or domestically.

The upshot for a United Kingdom applicant seeking to mount an Article 6(1) claim where he wishes to object to an environmental licence on precautionary grounds, is that he must establish the following:

(i)   that he is a victim under Article 34;
(ii) that the precautions identified are to guard against risks which are not too remote and not tenuous;
(iii) that judicial review, given its very limited scope, does not in the circumstances of the case amount to effective review of the administrative decision.

4.2. Right to an Effective Remedy (Article 13)

"Everyone whose rights and freedoms as set forth in this Convention are violated shall have an effective remedy before a national authority notwithstanding that the violation has been committed by persons acting in an official capacity".

This Article, as has been noted in chapter 5 on Remedies, has not been included in the Schedule to the Human Rights Act 1998, on the basis that no

---

[76] Unreported, 3 January 1997
[77] (1998) 5 BHRC 293, (2000) 29 EHRR 245
[78] [1999] 3 WLR 79

such incorporation is necessary because of the remedies provided by Section 8. If circumstances were to arise where there was a freestanding Article 13 claim, the remedy would have to be obtained from the Strasbourg Court. It, and the case law upon it, is however likely to be considered via Section 2 of the Act, directing domestic courts to take into account any Strasbourg learning. As the Lord Chancellor put it in Committee:

> ". . . the courts may have regard to Article 13. In particular, they may wish to do so when considering the very ample provisions of [s.8(1) HRA]".[79]

In *Powell and Rayner v United Kingdom*,[80] reversing the opinion of the Commission, the European Court ruled that Article 13 was not violated because there was no arguable claim that Article 8 had been violated by the noise abatement regime in place (which consisted of measures such as regulation of aircraft movements, insulation grants, and schemes for purchase of certain noise-blighted properties). Therefore, the statutory exclusion of a remedy in nuisance for noise conforming with the Rules of the Air did not matter; and in relation to noise caused by aircraft exceeding those levels, the common law remedy of nuisance remained.

4.3. Freedom from Discrimination in respect of Protected Rights (Article 14)

"The enjoyment of the rights and freedoms set forth in this convention shall be secured without discrimination on any grounds such as sex, race, colour, religion, political or other opinion, national or social origin, association with a national minority, property, birth or other status".

It is not necessary to establish a breach of another Article of the Convention for Article 14 to apply, but it is necessary to make a prima facie case out under another Article. We have seen its effect most clearly in the *Pine Valley* case, in which the Article 1 Protocol 1 claim succeeded, but only in conjunction with the Article 14 claim that the legislation had singled out the applicants as the only ones not to be compensated.

Reliance was also placed upon Article 14 in *Fredin v Sweden*.[81] The Commission decided that a complaint that a gravel company whose permit had (uniquely) been revoked had been "singled out for special treatment" was admissible. The complaint was not however substantiated.

There is however possible scope for development of a claim under Article 14 in environmental cases. In a recent decision in a landlord and tenant dispute,[82]

---

[79] *Hansard* HL, 18 November 1997, col 475
[80] (1990) 12 EHRR 355
[81] (1991) 13 EHRR 784
[82] *Larkos v Cyprus* (unreported, 18 February 1999). See *Chassagnou v France* (unreported, 29 April 1999) for another example: no objective justification for a law which compelled the transfer of hunting rights to the local community from landowners owning less than 20 hectares, but which left unaffected those owning more than 20 hectares

the Court ruled that the applicant, a state sector tenant, had been discriminated against (in breach of Article 14) when the Finance Ministry as landlord had denied him his right to enjoyment of his home (Article 8). This was because rent control legislation, which continued to be enjoyed by private tenants, had been disapplied to public sector tenants.

It is not difficult to conceive of other issues in which an applicant points to an Article 8 right coupled with a complaint under Article 14. One case in which a variant of this argument was attempted was *Khatun*,[83] the Docklands case. The applicants said that the rule in *Hunter v Canary Wharf*, which limited damages to the impact of the nuisance upon the letting value of the property, had two discriminatory effects. The first was to lead to very distinct levels of damages for the same dust nuisance depending on whether the claimant lived in a house worth £25,000 or £2 million. The second was a consequence of the first, namely that the Canary Wharf claimants had little prospect of recovering any sums, given the cost-ineffectiveness of pursuing small claims. The Commission dismissed this shortly, saying that the applicants had failed to show that there were others in a similar situation who had been treated differently. However, one can imagine circumstances where applicants could identify specific individuals whose houses, at ten times the value, gave an entitlement to ten times the damages.

There is a similar argument, arising out of the common law rule that "what is a nuisance in Belgravia may not be one in Bermondsey". Why should those living in poorer areas face a higher threshold before they can establish a cause of action? I would have thought there are good grounds for the common law of nuisance to develop, under the influence of Articles 8 and 14, so as to seek to erode any difference in thresholds. Certainly, in the case of whether the tort is constituted, I can see no objective ground justifying this discrimination. If so, this may be an area where the Convention has significant effect on litigation between private citizens.[84]

4.4. Freedom of Expression and Association

Article 10, guaranteeing freedom of speech, and Article 11, on freedom of association, provide important backing for those wishing peacefully to protest about environmental issues. The use of Article 10, and the caveats to which it is subject, is well illustrated by *Steel v United Kingdom*.[85] Various environmental protestors who had been imprisoned for their refusal to be bound over claimed violation of their various rights under the Convention, including Article 10. However, the Court agreed with the state's arguments that the arrests and

---

[83] See under Article 8
[84] See Jonathan Cooper on horizontal effect in chapter 4
[85] (1998) 5 BHRC 339

detention were permissible infringements of the applicants' freedom of expression in preventing disorder and in protecting the rights of others under Article 10(2), and the detention following the applicants' refusal to be bound over was an infringement of this freedom justified by the need to maintain the authority of the judiciary. Since it had reached this decision under Article 10(2), it did not consider the equivalent exception in Article 11(2). This decision indicates that challenges to the binding over jurisdiction of magistrates under the Convention are unlikely to succeed before national courts.

The protection of Article 11, namely the right to freedom of association, played a part in the recent decision of the House of Lords in *DPP v Jones*,[86] in which a right to use the highway for peaceful and non-obstructive protest was upheld.

5. CONCLUSIONS AND PREDICTIONS

The Convention's major impact on substantive environmental rights will be via Article 8 claims which bypass the various restrictions imposed by the torts of negligence and nuisance, and will thus involve public authorities having to meet and justify under Article 8(2) any decisions which significantly affect the home life of citizens. It will also enable judicial review of decisions taken in disregard of an applicant's Article 8 rights. In the more serious cases, Article 2 will operate in a similar way, with public authorities having to justify why they did not take further steps to avoid some risk to life.

In particular, claims will lie against regulators concerning their failure to intervene and enforce against hazards created by industrial concerns likely to affect health or enjoyment of neighbouring properties.

A *Guerra*-type claim, enabling local people to argue an entitlement to environmental information on hazards in their area, irrespective of whether such information currently exists, may also be of considerable significance in future dealings with regulators.

Rights under Article 6(1) may assist third party objectors wishing to intervene in the various administrative procedures under which most environmental licences are granted, with a view to obtaining a "fair hearing". I consider that there will be a number of instances where the current system, as it operates in practice, will be found not to afford that protection.

That said, the Strasbourg case law to date is not a series of victories for environmental claimants. As for the future, the "victim" requirement, coupled with the *Balmer-Schafroth* threshold under Article 6(1), will significantly limit the number of public interest claims able successfully to raise Convention points. In addition, in a number of cases, applicants have succeeded in showing prima facie breaches of a substantive Article, only to fail because the public authority

[86] [1999] 2 WLR 625

can show justification for its actions. The breadth of the policy issues brought into play, particularly in such substantive cases, and the evidence needed to advance or combat such contentions, is likely to change the structure of much environmental litigation.

11

Confidentiality and Defamation

ROSALIND ENGLISH

These areas of common law practice are arguably the most likely to respond to pressure to change under the Convention, the first because it represents an inchoate privacy right, the second because it invariably elicits arguments based on free speech. To complicate matters, the key Convention rights are not at all in opposition; on the contrary, they are on two sides of the same coin. One side is Article 8, which guarantees protection for an individual's private life. The flip side of the coin is Article 10 which guarantees freedom of expression and the freedom to receive information; this freedom must on occasion give way to the reputation or rights of others or the interests of confidentiality. Thus the common law actions for breach of confidence and defamation will normally involve consideration of both rights. The first part of this chapter looks at the extent to which the incorporation of Articles 8 and 10 will affect confidentiality. The second part considers their impact on defamation.

1. CONFIDENTIALITY AND THE PROTECTION OF PRIVACY

Until incorporation of the Convention there has been no general protection for privacy in English law. Instead, a patchwork of actions has been relied upon, with varying rates of success, to protect privacy. Breach of confidence is the most useful tort, defamation is the most celebrated. In addition, depending on the circumstances, the following are relevant:

- Malicious falsehood
- Trespass
- Nuisance (limited to property owners)
- Protection from Harassment Act 1996
- Data Protection Act 1984, restricting access to data held on computer files
- Data Protection Act 1998, restricting access to certain categories of manual files
- Codes of Practice for media monitored by the Press Complaints Commission and the Broadcasting Complaints Commission.

The gaps between these causes of action are self-evident. Trespass, for instance, is limited to property owners and does not cover incursions on privacy that do not interfere with the land, such as aerial photographs[1] or the placing of windows in neighbouring property.[2] Only those with a right to the land affected may take an action in nuisance.[3] Whilst the scope of the new statutory tort of harassment has not yet been fully explored, there is an important exemption for activities, which might otherwise be caught under Section 1 of the Act, which are considered "reasonable" in the "particular circumstances". This exemption was no doubt drafted with the activities of journalists and private investigators in mind. As for the Broadcasting Complaints Commission, it cannot entertain anticipatory complaints about breaches of privacy under the code of practice where the programme has not yet been broadcast (Section 143 of the Broadcasting Act 1990).[4]

So the only tort that is sufficiently flexible to cover these gaps is breach of confidence. Will it expand under the pressure of Article 8? To answer this question, it is necessary to sketch out the development of this cause of action, a background which to an extent explains its limitations.

Confidence has attracted judicial intervention over the years on a number of different bases, ranging from property, contract, bailment, trust, fiduciary duty, unjust enrichment to a broad notion of good faith, particularly in the employer/employee relationship. In the nineteenth century confidence was extended to cover non-commercial information: in *Prince Albert v Strange*[5] the Court intervened to prevent the misuse of private information despite the fact that there was no financial detriment to the confider. But it took a full century for the developing law of confidence to cover the revelation of intimate information.[6] *Spycatcher*[7] confirmed that confidence does not depend on the commercial worth of the information. Lord Keith stated that "The right to personal privacy is clearly one which the law should in this field seek to protect".[8] The fact that it took so long for the glimmerings of a privacy-protecting tort to emerge demonstrates that the law of confidence is, like so many common law torts, an instrument of public policy rather than a right that was conceived to be for the benefit of the individual.

The tort of breach of confidence is made up of three elements.[9] The information must have the "necessary quality of confidence about it"; this information must "have been imparted in circumstances importing an obligation of confidence" and there must have been an "unauthorised use of that information to the detriment of the party communicating it". Once it is established that

---

[1] *Bernstein v Skyways & General* [1978] 3 WLR 136
[2] *Tapling v Jones* (1815) 4 Camp. 219
[3] *Hunter v Canary Wharf* [1997] AC 655
[4] Prompting Sedley J to observe that "it follws that in this field and to this extent, as elsewhere in English law, the individual is without an effective remedy before a national authority if the right to respect for his or her private and family life is violated", *R v BCC ex parte Barclay*, 2 October 1996
[5] (1849) 1 Mac & G.25
[6] *Duchess of Argyll v Duke of Argyll* [1967] 1 Ch 302
[7] *Attorney-General v Guardian Newspapers Ltd (No.2)* [1990] 1 AC 109
[8] *Ibid.* at 255
[9] *Coco v A.N.Clark Engineers Ltd* [1969] R.P.C. 41 at 47

confidential information has been used as a "springboard" to the obtaining of other information (in other words further information has been sought to verify the original confidential information) such use would constitute "unauthorised use".[10]

It can be seen immediately that the class of confidentiality claimants is not the same as the potential class of privacy claimaints. The range of interests which qualify for the protection of confidence is limited by the *Coco* criteria. Because of mutuality of interests, confidence can protect relationships arising out of contract,[11] domestic relationships[12] and other confidential relationships, based on a reasonable expectation of privacy, such as doctor/patient, lawyer/client, priest/penitent, bank/customer, etc.

Confidence will fall away once the information is aired in public. This is the important limiting principle of "public domain",[13] which does not take into account the damage that the public airing may have done to the claimant. This is an important limiting factor in the domestic approach to privacy that is likely to change under the incorporated right to privacy. Indeed, the public domain factor did not prevent Morland J from granting the Prime Minister's family an injunction against the further publication of the memoirs by their former nanny, Rosalind Mark. The confidentiality agreement in her employment contract was upheld even after one and a half million copies of the offending newspaper had reached the British public, and the Blair family doings had been published on the Internet.

Where domestic courts will feel more familiar in the great confidentiality/ privacy debate is in the consideration of the "public interest", which the Convention allows in certain circumstances to justify interference with individuals' privacy. For decades, confidentiality has in certain circumstances been negated by the public interest. Thus, for example, there is "no confidence in iniquity".[14] This is a much more broadly articulated exception to privacy rights than the Convention would allow, although as we shall see from the Strasbourg cases below, the airing of iniquitous practices has generally attracted the protection of Article 10, freedom of speech and the press.

In domestic law, public interest may also prevail against the withholding of certain types of confidential information where there is a real need for disclosure for reasons of health and for the protection of the rights of others (to put it in Article 8 terms). In *W v Egdell*[15] the Court of Appeal held that the confidence in

---

[10] *Seager v Copydex Ltd* [1967] 1 WLR 923
[11] *BSC v Granada Television Ltd* [1981] 1 All ER 417
[12] *Argyll v Argyll* [1967] Ch 302: the normal "confidence and trust" that is judicially assumed to exist in marriage. Duty of confidence includes homosexual and extra-marital relationships: *Stephens v Avery* [1988] 2 All ER 477
[13] This principle received ample judicial attention in *Attorney-General v Guardian Newspapers Ltd (No 2)* [1990] 1 AC 109 and *Attorney General v Blake, Jonathan Cape Limited* [1998] 2 WLR 805
[14] *Gartside v Outram* (1856) 26 LJCh 113: here Wood VC refused an injunction to employers to prevent ex-employees disclosing their fraudulent dealings
[15] [1990] 1 Ch 359

a pyschiatric report on a paranoid schizophrenic patient could be limited in the public interest, since people were arguably being exposed to death or serious harm.[16] More recently, the law on confidentiality has had to take account of the proper functioning of regulatory agencies. Information obtained in the course of police interviews, where the prosecution is discontinued, may normally not be disclosed to a third party. However, the public interest in the efficient regulation of professions may in certain circumstances dictate that regulatory agencies should be able to see that information: see *Woolgar v Chief Constable of Sussex Police and UKCC*.[17]

The common law of confidence has received its most recent drubbing in the High Court in its decision concerning the physical and mental fitness of Senator Pinochet to be extradited to Spain to stand trial for interntional crimes of torture and kidnapping. In *R v Secretary of State for the Home Department ex parte Amnesty International and others*[18] it was decided that fairness as a principle of good administration should prevail over Pinochet's right to prevent the disclosure of his confidential medical reports. Fairness to the states requesting extradition and human rights groups required that they should have sight of these medical reports. This conclusion was much influenced by what can be conveniently called the "Pinochet effect"; the judgment is replete with vague references to this "unique case" with "extraordinary features"; the "enormity of the alleged crimes"; the "monumental importance" of the decision that the Secretary of State had been poised to make; "the integrity of the international criminal justice system" and Pinochet himself as an "alleged 'enemy of humanity' ". The Court also considered arguments under Article 8, and its conclusions will be explored below; suffice it to point out here that where intense media interest is present, the protection afforded by confidentiality appears to be flimsy indeed.

Another separate area of confidentiality in English law relates to legal professional privilege and litigation privilege. The first arises out of the lawyer/client relationship referred to above; the second stems from the procedural right to a fair trial. The law of privilege is itself a presumption of confidentiality; however, documents subject to discovery in legal proceedings may not be protected by confidence, nor is the duty of confidence to another a ground for refusal by a witness to answer questions or to produce documents if ordered to do so by a court.[19] As we will see from some of the Strasbourg cases discussed below, this has become something of a catalyst for claims under both Article 6 (the right to a fair trial) and the right to privacy under Article 8.

---

[16] The public interest does not always prevail against confidentiality even where health is at stake, particularly in AIDS cases. In *X v Y* [1988] 2 All ER 648 a health authority obtained an injunction preventing the publication of a story leaked by health authority employees to the press about two doctors who had AIDS: the public interest in protecting confidentiality of patients generally and AIDS patients in particular (because they otherwise might not identify themselves) outweighed the public interest in disclosure

[17] [1999] Lloyd's Rep Med, 335

[18] 15 February 2000

[19] Although the court will only enforce discovery or require disclosure from a witness if disclosure is necessary for the attainment of justice in a particular case: *D v NSPCC* [1978] AC 17

As far as remedies are concerned, again, the right to privacy is likely to make significant inroads into the present judicial approach to breach of confidence. At the moment, if a claimant succeeds in establishing breach of confidence, the availability of remedies depends wholly on the circumstances of the disclosure of information rather than the extent of the injury suffered by the claimant. An injunction will only be awarded if the information has not already reached the public domain.[20] In addition to these, the Court may order, in appropriate cases, delivery up of confidential documents, an account of profits,[21] a grant of a constructive trust over the assets acquired by the defendant in breach of confidence, or an order for discovery to disclose the source of the breach of confidentiality. Rarely, if ever, are damages granted for the breach of confidence itself.

From this very brief survey it is possible to identify a number of limitations to the tort of confidence which suggest that it falls some way short of the protection afforded by Article 8. The law of confidence is based, not on the injury to the confider, but on the importance of confidential relationships. This means that there will be no remedy where the claimant's sole complaint is that personal information has been published without his consent – for example, by a newspaper which has obtained information without any trespass or breach of any pre-existing agreement with the injured party. This was demonstrated by the case of *Kaye v Robertson*.[22] Here the claimant was unable to take an action in confidence for unauthorised publication of photographs that were taken while he was lying unconscious in a hospital bed recovering from serious head injuries. The circumstances in which the journalists acted disclosed no trespass, no pre-existing relationship with the claimant, therefore no relationship of confidence.

That is the main difficulty in claiming the protection of confidence. There are other limitations. Because there is no right to confidentiality of private information as such, the common law defences, such as the principle of public domain and the public interest in certain types of disclosure tend to defeat confidentiality from the word go, rather than being weighed in the balance against an accepted interference with privacy in the course of the litigation.

2. CONFIDENTIALITY AND PRIVACY UNDER ARTICLE 8

Under Article 8 the purpose of the law is to protect individuals against invasions of privacy, whereas an action for breach of confidence is not to prevent harm to

---

[20] *Spycatcher*, loc.cit., Lord Keith at 262
[21] Which is available even if the information is already in the public domain: *Attorney General v Jonathan Cape Limited (Third Party)* [1998] 2 WLR 805
[22] [1991] FSR 62

the confider so much as to ensure that information communicated in confidence will in general be protected. A good example of this is the recent ruling in *Swinney and Another v Chief Constable of Northumbria Police (No 2)*.[23] Here the High Court held, despite the general rule of immunity of the police for actions in negligence,[24] that the police owed informants a duty to take reasonable care to avoid unnecessary disclosure to the general public of the information that might reveal their identity. If this case had been decided under Article 8, the grounds for the judgment would have been based on the reasonable expectation enjoyed by the informant that his right to a private life would not be infringed. The domestic court applied a different test, balancing the public policy of police immunity against the public interest in enforcing the general duty of confidentiality in these circumstances. In this sense, the severity of the injury suffered by the claimant was immaterial. Given the difference in focus, will the absorption of Strasbourg principles here have a significant impact on the existing common law protection for private and personal information?

Article 8 of the European Convention on Human Rights (ECHR) provides that:

1. *Everyone has the right to respect for his private and family life, his home and correspondence.*
2. *There shall be no interference by a public authority with the exercise of this right except such as is in accordance with the law and is necessary in a democratic society in the interests of national security, public safety or the economic well-being of the country, for the prevention of disorder or crime, for the protection of health or morals, or for the protection of the rights and freedoms of others.*

Neither the Commission nor the Court have attempted any comprehensive definition of these rights. Indeed the case law suggests that Article 8 might cover a growing number of issues, and change character over time.[25] It has already developed from a merely "negative" obligation, which only requires states not to interfere with privacy rights, to one imposing a "positive" duty on states to prevent private parties from interfering with other people's privacy. In *X and Y v the Netherlands* [26] the Court said:

"[Article 8] does not merely compel the state to abstain from . . . interference: in addition to this primarily negative undertaking, there may be positive obligations inherent in an effective respect for private and family life . . . These obligations may involve the adoption of measures designed to secure respect for private life *even in the sphere of relations between individuals themselves*".

There are four protected interests under Article 8: private life, home and family life, and correspondence. Confidentiality is generally protected by the first category, which is therefore the focus of the following discussion.

---

[23] *The Times*, May 25 1999

[24] *Hill v Chief Constable of West Yorkshire Police* [1989] AC 53

[25] See the discussion on the ECHR as a "living instrument" in chapter 2, The Convention and the Human Rights Act: A New Way of Thinking

[26] (1986) 8 EHRR 235

2.1. Private Life

The Court has indicated that this is not simply a right to be left alone. In *Niemitz v Germany*[27] it observed that:

> ". . . it would be too restrictive to limit the notion [of private life] to an 'inner circle' in which the individual may live his own personal life as he chooses and to exclude therefrom entirely the outside world not encompassed within that circle. Respect for private life must also compromise to a certain degree the right to establish and develop relationships with other human beings".[28]

The right to a private life protects two types of confidential information: business communications and private information whose disclosure in some way causes injury to the individual. Conversely, Article 8 has been relied upon to afford access to certain types of confidential information, if that information relates to the private life of the individual seeking access.

2.1.1. Business Confidentiality

In *Niemitz v Germany* a warrant had been issued to search N's premises for evidence relating to the author of an insult to a judge and an attempt to bring pressure on him. This warrant was framed in broad terms, authorising the search and seizure of "documents" without confining itself to those documents which revealed the identity of the author of the offensive letter. The search impinged on professional secrecy to an extent which was held by the Court to be disproportionate. Affirming the application of Article 8 to business confidentiality, the Court stated that:

> "There appears furthermore to be no reason of principle why this understanding of the notion of 'private life' should be taken to exclude activities of a professional or business nature since it is, after all, in the course of their working lives that the majority of people have a significant, if not the greatest, opportunity of developing relationships with the outside world".

It was significant that Niemitz owned his office premises personally; so far there has been no definitive ruling from the European Court of Human Rights on whether the right to privacy extends beyond human or natural persons to corporations and companies and the High Court in this country has recently ruled that it does not.[29]

Nevertheless, the extension of Article 8 to cover offices is a significant step, and this interpretation has been confirmed by the ruling in *Halford v United*

---

[27] (1993) 16 EHRR 97

[28] See the Third Chamber's confirmation of this approach in *Carter v United Kingdom*, Application No. 3541/97, 29 June 1999

[29] *R v Broadcasting Standards Commission ex parte BBC*, July 7 1999; the relevant "right to privacy" in this pre-incorporation decision is enshrined in the governing statute of the BSC, Part V of the Broadcasting Act 1996, Section 110(1)(b)

Kingdom.[30] The applicant, an assistant chief constable who had brought discrimination proceedings against her employers, was successful in her claim that the interception of her private telephone conversations on an internal network at Merseyside Police HQ interfered with her right to private life.[31] There are now proposals afoot to implement the *Halford* judgment by regulating the interception of all telephonic communications, whether public or private (in other words, covering in-house networking systems).[32]

In *Kopp v Switzerland*[33] a lawyer complained that his right to a private life under Article 8 had been breached when the Federal authorities tapped his office telephone calls for three weeks in the course of investigating suspected offical secrets offences by his wife. The order stated that conversations relating to his work as a lawyer should be disregarded, and Swiss law accords legal professional privilege to information directly flowing from the lawyer-client relationship. To this extent, the Swiss Government argued that business confidentiality under Article 8 received adequate recognition under Swiss law. However, there was an exclusion in the relevant national provisions in respect of information that is not specifically connected with a lawyer's work on instructions from a party to proceedings. The Court held that the distinction in Swiss law between matters arising specifically out of the lawyer-client relationship and a lawyer's other activities was insufficiently clear. Without the necessary precision for individuals to predict their legal liability, a rule of national law cannot be said to be "in accordance with the law", one of the conditions for the exceptions permitted under Article 8.

2.1.2. Disclosure of Private Information

Article 8 covers the collection of information of the state about an individual; this will amount to an interference with an individual's private life if conducted without his consent and unjustified by any of the legitimate aims under Article 8(2).[34] Recently this head of claim has been extended to situations where private information is disclosed to third parties. The decisions in this area from Strasbourg (discussed below) relate to state action only, but because of the "positive" nature of the state's obligations under Article 8, this claim could arguably be raised in the context of breach of confidence by private parties, since the failure of the state to regulate such activities could disclose a violation. At the moment the Strasbourg Court accords a wide margin of appreciation to

---

[30] (1997) 24 EHRR 523

[31] The reasonable expectation of privacy that employees should enjoy should receive some protection under the Data Protection Act 1998 which will provide a code of practice to protect employees from interception of telephone calls and electronic mail in the workplace

[32] See the Government consultation paper *Interception of Communications in the United Kingdom* Cm Paper 4368, June 1999

[33] 25 March 1998

[34] *X v United Kingdom* No. 9702/82 30 DR 239 (1982)

Contracting States in this area[35] but there is no reason in principle why this aspect of Article 8 should not be taken into account by a domestic court in a case where the injury to the confider constitutes a significant invasion of their rights and it is argued that confidants in this situation should be under a legally enforceable obligation to observe confidentiality.

In *Z v Finland*[36] the applicant complained that her rights under Article 8 had been breached when, in the trial of her husband for rape and attempted manslaughter, her doctors were compelled to testify as to her HIV status. The Court held that the proceedings had been adopted in pursuit of two legitimate aims under Article 8, the prevention of disorder or crime and protection of health and morals. These were not held to be disproportionate because Finnish law stipulated sufficiently limited circumstances in which medical evidence could be disclosed without the patients' consent and provided appropriate protections for the individual. The Court did uphold the applicant's claim in respect of part of the Court's judgment containing references to confidential medical data. These were not supported by "cogent reasons"; the national court had a discretion under Finnish law not to publish its full reasoning but to put out an abridged version of the judgment which omitted the witnessses' full names. Given that it had failed to exercise this discretion, the publication of the judgment amounted to a violation for which the applicant was awarded non-pecuniary damages of 100,000 Finnish marks (approximately £11,000).

A similar issue arose, this time under Article 6, in *Vernon v United Kingdom*.[37] The applicant in this case had claimed damages in personal injury proceedings for post-traumatic stress disorder he had suffered as a result of witnessing the deaths of his two young children in an accident caused by the defendant. In separate proceedings claiming custody of his remaining children, he had produced other psychiatric reports which appeared to contradict the medical evidence of his mental condition in the personal injury action. The Court of Appeal required the applicant to produce these reports in the personal injury proceedings. The applicant complained that he had thus been required to act against his own interests and therefore was denied a fair trial contrary to Article 6. The Chamber of the Strasbourg Court rejected this claim as manifestly ill-founded, finding,

> "no basis for objecting on grounds of fairness to the approach adopted by the appeal court judges who found that the rules governing disclosure should not be interpreted in such a way as to facilitate the running of contradictory claims in simultaneous proceedings".

A similar ruling was made in *L v United Kingdom*.[38] Here the applicant complained that the imposition of a disclosure condition on a report prepared for care

---

[35] *Winer v United Kingdom No. 10871/84* 48 DR 154
[36] (1998) 25 EHRR 371
[37] Application No. 38753/97 7 September 1999
[38] Application No. 34222/96

proceedings under the Children Act 1989 and an order directing disclosure of the report to the police breached her rights under Articles 6 and 8. The Chamber of the Court found the complaint under Article 6 manifestly ill-founded and inadmissible, because the disclosure condition did not render the care proceedings generally unfair, and that the privilege against self-incrimination under that Article related chiefly to criminal proceedings. In relation to the complaint under Article 8, the Chamber found that any interference with her rights presented by the disclosure condition was compatible with Article 8(2), in particular "the protection of health and morals" and the protection of the "rights and freedoms" of her child.

The Strasbourg Court, in other words, allows Contracting States considerable flexibility in matters concerning the admission of evidence, including issues relating to legal professional privilege and litigation privilege.[39]

In HIV disclosure cases the Strasboug authorities often find that there are public interest justifications for infringing an individual's right not to have personal information divulged without their consent. In *TV v Finland*[40] the Commission held that the disclosure to prison staff of a prisoner's HIV status was justified as being necessary for the protection of their health and other rights. It was significant in this context that the prison staff in question were directly involved in his custody and they were themselves subject to duties of confidentiality.

Another legitimate aim, which has been successfully relied upon in Strasbourg, is the economic well-being of the country. In *MS v Sweden*[41] the applicant had made a claim for compensation for a work-related back injury. In the course of their investigations the Social Insurance Office ascertained that this back problem was not connected with her occupation at all, and refused her claim. She then claimed under the Convention that the submission of her medical records by a hospital to the Social Insurance Office breached her rights to privacy under Article 8. The Court held that the disclosure had involved an interference with that right because of the highly sensitive and personal data contained in the medical records in question. However, the interference served the legitimate aim of the protection of the economic well-being of the country, as it was potentially decisive for the allocation of public funds. The ruling in this case may provide an argument for future challenges, under Article 8, to covert video surveillance of personal injury claimants. In *J.S. v United Kingdom*[42] the Commission rejected a complaint that the applicant had suffered a violation of her Article 8 rights where she claimed to have been subject to covert surveillance by an insurance company. The fact that this claim was rejected because the

---

[39] See also *L v United Kingdom* Application No. 34222/96

[40] No. 21780/93 76A DR 140

[41] (1999) 28 EHRR 313. Other aspects of this judgment are explored in the chapter 8 on Medical Law. See also *K and T v Finland*: disclosure of private information to child welfare officer in care proceedings justified in the interests of health and rights of the children (Admissibility Decision of the Fourth Chamber Application No. 25702/94, unreported (8 June 1999)

[42] Application No. 21120/93

insurance company's activities did not engage the responsbility of the state means that this admissibility decision is not the last word on this subject, as far as national courts' approach to this problem is concerned.

The application of Article 8 to the disclosure of information to third parties has also been endorsed by the European Court of Justice. In *X v Commission of the European Communities*[43] an applicant for a job with the Commission who had refused an AIDS test was required to undergo a general blood test which indirectly revealed the fact that he was HIV positive. He was refused employment. He claimed that his Article 8 rights had been violated by the Commission and the Court upheld his claim, stating that the right to a private life as enshrined in the Convention is a fundamental right protected by the legal order of the Community.

> "The Court of Justice has held that the right to respect for private life, embodied in Article 8 of the ECHR and deriving from the common constitutional positions of the member states, is one of the fundamental rights protected by the legal order of the community . . . It includes in particular a person's right to keep his state of health secret".

2.1.3. Access to Personal Information

Where certain types of personal information are essential for an individual's knowledge about his own past, denial of access to this material may amount to a breach of Article 8: *Gaskin v United Kingdom*.[44] The applicant wanted to take proceedings against a local authority for personal injuries he claimed he had suffered when he was in their care as a child. Access to some of his files was denied on the basis of confidentiality. The Court took the view that this information constituted the only coherent record of the applicant's early childhood and formative years and that the refusal of the local authority to grant the applicant access, without any kind of independent scrutiny to determine the genuineness of the confidentiality claim, amounted to an infringement of the right to a private life in Article 8.

The position adopted by the Strasbourg Court in *Gaskin* does not mean that Article 8 will provide grounds for access to information in all circumstances. The Court's scrutiny of the justification depends upon the nature of the information which is secretly compiled. In *Leander v Sweden*[45] the Court held that the use of information in a secret police register for the purposes of assessing a person's suitability for employment on a post of importance for national security, coupled with a refusal to allow the applicant access to this information, amounted to a breach of Article 8(1) but was justified by the legitimate aim under 8(2) of protecting national security.

---

[43] C–404/92P [1995] IRLR 320
[44] (1989) 12 EHRR 36
[45] (1987) 9 EHRR 433

2.2. Confidentiality and Freedom of Expression under Article 10

Article 10 provides as follows:

1. *Everyone has the right to freedom of expression. This right shall include freedom to hold opinions and to receive and impart information and ideas without interference by public authority and regardless of frontiers. This Article shall not prevent States from requiring the licensing of broadcasting, television or cinema enterprises.*
2. *The exercise of these freedoms, since it carries with it duties and responsibilities, may be subject to such formalities, conditions, restrictions or penalties as are prescribed by law and are necessary in a democratic society, in the interests of national security, territorial integrity or public safety, for the prevention of disorder or crime, for the protection of health or morals, for the protection of the reputation or rights of others, for preventing the disclosure of information received in confidence, or for maintaining the authority and impartiality of the judiciary.*

Although on the face of it Article 10 imparts a duty to ensure the free flow of information, it is worth noting that the right to information is subject to a number of limitations. Firstly, Article 10 does not guarantee access to information which is not already available.[46] The right to seek out information is thus contingent on the consent of the producer of that information. In *Z v Austria*[47] the Commission stated that the applicant, a social security lawyer, could not challenge under Article 10 national legislation establishing a computer database of social security case law on the basis that access to this data was too restricted. The claim was distinguished from *Gaskin* in the sense that Z was not claiming information concerning his own personal data but the right of access to general information. And, unlike Article 8, this element of Article 10 does not impose a positive obligation on Member States. This has implications for the role of Article 10 in confidentiality litigation between private parties, since there are no Strasbourg authorities to support the proposition that the state's authority is engaged when one private party prevents another from obtaining information.

In addition to the above limitations, Article 10(2) sets out a number of specific justifications for withholding confidential information, which can be grouped under the following headings:

(1) Impartiality of the Judiciary
(2) National Security
(3) Information Received in Confidence and the Rights and Reputations of Others.

2.2.1. Impartiality of the Judiciary

Although the Strasbourg Court has in the past deferred to arguments that certain types of information must be withheld from the public gaze to ensure a fair

---

[46] (1987) 9 EHRR 433
[47] No. 10392/83, 56 DR 13 (1988)

trial, the "Thalidomide" litigation demonstrated early on that governments must be wary of limiting press freedom in the interests of an impartial judiciary. The prevention of a publication because it might have put pressure on the parties to the litigation, or prejudge the issues, was held to go further than was necessary in a democratic society for maintaining the authority of the judiciary.[48] Equally, the Strasbourg Court is unsympathetic to appeals by respondent states to justifications under Article 10(2) where the information, once confidential, has reached the public domain. In the "Spycatcher" litigation[49] the Government argued that the injunction was a legitimate measure in the interests both of national security and of maintaining confidence in the judiciary. The Strasbourg Court accepted that these were legitimate aims under Article 10(2). However, it considered that the imposition of injunctions from the date that the extracts from the book entered the public domain when they were published in the United States, represented a disproportionate interference into press freedom. It has taken a similar line in relation to the imposition of convictions for breach of official confidence under the French penal code.[50]

Most contempt of court measures usually fall within this permitted justification, particularly when they are found to be consonant with the fair trial requirements of Article 6. In *Worm v Austria* [51] the applicant, a journalist, was convicted for influencing the course of a criminal trial after writing an excoriating article about the prosecution of a former minister of finance for tax evasion. The Court held that even public figures such as the defendant minister are entitled to the enjoyment of the guarantees of a fair trial set out in Article 6, which in criminal proceedings include the right to an impartial tribunal, on the same basis as every other person.

2.2.2. National Security

The Court has frequently observed that the enjoyment of rights enshrined in the Convention does not stop at the army gates. Most defence issues that come before the Strasbourg authorities concern the compatibility of military tribunals with the fair trial rights guaranteed by Article 6 but there is a line of case law dealing with official secrets and duties of confidence imposed on military personnel. In *Hadjianastassiou v Greece*[52] the applicant, a serving officer, was convicted and sentenced for having disclosed military information of minor importance, relating to a secret arms project. The information was classified as a military secret. The study in question was intended for communication to a private arms manufacturer for a fee. The Court held that the aim of the restriction – national security – was legitimate and taking into account the "special

---

[48] *Sunday Times v United Kingdom* (1979–80) 2 EHRR 245
[49] *Sunday Times v United Kingdom* (1992) 2 EHRR 245
[50] *Fressoz and Roire v France* (1999) 5 BHRC 692
[51] (1998) 25 EHRR 454
[52] (1992) 16 EHRR 219

conditions" attaching to military life, and the obligation of discretion imposed on its personnel, the Greek military courts could not be said to have overstepped the limits of their margin of appreciation.

However, measures to prevent publication or distribution on the basis of the confidential nature of the subject matter generally cease to be justifiable or proportionate once the material has been made public. In *Vereniging Weekblad "Bluf" v Netherlands*[53] it was held that the seizure of a weekly periodical publishing classified material from the Dutch security service was disproportionate since 2,500 copies had already been sold at night and the continued ban no longer served any purpose, notwithstanding the Court's acknowledgement that the security services could claim a high level of protection.

2.2.3. The Rights of Others and Information Received in Confidence

In *X v Morgan-Grampian*[54] an injunction had been granted to prevent the publication of leaked confidential information. The claimants sought disclosure of the source. The Court of Appeal ruled that the protection of journalists' sources under Section 10 of the Contempt of Court Act 1981 could be outweighed by the "interests of justice" to the employer of the source of the leaked document, particularly since the source had stolen the document. When the journalist failed to observe the court order he was fined £5,000 for contempt. The Strasbourg Court[55] held that this amounted to an unjustifiable breach of his rights under Article 10. Whilst the "interests of justice" amounted to a legitimate aim ("rights of others" under Article 10(2)), the injunction had already provided sufficient protection to the company to satisfy those interests and the consequent contempt order had been disproportionate.

The application of Article 10 to editorial confidentiality demonstrates that freedom of speech may itself be dependent on certain types of information being withheld from disclosure. Indeed in a German case a dispute between a journalist wishing to publish "inside" information about a newspaper and that newspaper's wish to preserve editorial confidentiality was determined by the Constitutional Court under the Basic Law's right to free speech; both claims, in other words, were articulated in terms of free speech.[56]

Sanctions are sometimes found to be justified where journalists deliberately breach confidentiality. In Application 10343/83[57] a journalist who had published a confidential parliamentary document was punished and fined. The Commission found the measure could be justified for preventing disclosure of the material received in confidence and was not disproportionate since the

---

[53] (1994) 20 EHRR 189
[54] [1991] 1 AC 1
[55] *Goodwin v United Kingdom* (1996) 22 EHRR 123
[56] BverGE 66,116 (1984). See the discussion of this case in Markesinis, "Privacy, Freedom of Expression and the Human Rights Bill: Lessons from Germany" 115 *LQR* 47
[57] 6 October 1983 35 DR 224

applicant was an accredited journalist who had known the document was confidential, and use of penalties was aimed at maintaining the credibility of the system.

2.3. The Impact of the Convention on Confidentiality

As the survey of cases above demonstrates, the rights to privacy and freedom of expression do not necessarily stand in a relationship of tension with each other, since Strasbourg case law generally gives considerable weight to press freedom, not only under the dedicated guarantees of Article 10 but also under the exception listed in 8(2) for measures taken in the interests of the "rights and freedoms of others". Conversely, Article 10 is sometimes limited by considerations of confidentiality and the privacy interests of others, whether categorised as "rights" or "reputation".

It is unlikely that the incorporation of Article 8 into domestic law will bring about a revolution in the determination of privacy claims where the press is involved. There has been manifest reluctance by the Strasbourg authorities to accept that Article 8 rights should provide a platform for press regulation. In *Earl Spencer and Countess Spencer v the United Kingdom*[58] the applicants claimed that the the absence in English law of a legal remedy for intrusions by the popular press into their private lives amounted to a breach of the state's positive obligations under Article 8. The Government argued that they had not exhausted their local remedies since they could, in principle, have pursued an action in confidence. All the *Coco* elements had been present; the defendants had published a report based on information that had the necessary quality of confidence (the second applicant's admission to a medical clinic); the publishers could reasonably have inferred that this information was confidential (a friend of the applicants had passed it on), and the use of this information was clearly unauthorised.

The applicants argued that an action in confidence would not have been available to them in respect of information already published (the "public domain" limitation); they also claimed that it would have been impossible in practice to prove that the circumstances imported a duty of confidence. The Commission rejected all these arguments, concluding that the state of uncertainty in the law of confidence which prevailed before 1990 had been largely resolved by *Spycatcher*. The application was thus declared inadmissible for non-exhaustion of local remedies as required by Article 26 (now 34) of the Convention. The fact that the Commission considered that there were adequate remedies to be exhausted, even in the absence of any privacy law, suggests that a high level of protection will not be accorded to Article 8 when press freedom is at stake. Another illustration of the Strasbourg authorities' position on this issue is

[58] (1998) 25 EHRR CD113

provided by a recent admissibility decision in *Barclay v United Kingdom*.[59] The applicant alleged that the absence of adequate protection of their privacy against the public broadcast of a BBC television programme filmed without their consent on their private island denied them the protection required under the Convention Articles 8 and 13. The applicants sought to distinguish their situation from that of the Spencers, saying that they could not have sought an injunction because the relevant "wrong" in English law was trespass (for which no injunction would have been available) not breach of confidence. The Third Section of the Strasboug Court rejected their claims on the facts, refusing to accept that the island, on which the applicants had not been present at the time of filming, constituted their "private and family life, or their home".

This approach is likely to be followed when national courts come to consider privacy versus freedom of expression under the Human Rights Act. This is because Section 12, a late amendment to the Bill to calm press fears of rearguard privacy legislation, requires judges to have "particular regard" to Article 10 when freedom of expression is at stake. This will arguably have the effect of creating a formal hierarchy of ECHR rights where none exists in the original Convention. Such an approach has already been presaged in *R v Broadcasting Standards Commission ex parte British Broadcasting Corporation*.[60] Here the Court accepted the defendant's argument that a corporate body could not claim that its privacy had been infringed by covert filming of its over the counter transactions. However, the judgment went further in narrowing that right by suggesting that the activity thus filmed did not have "the necessary quality of *seclusion* so as to engage the concept of privacy". If this added ingredient is required each time a claim to Article 8 privacy is made, the likelihood is that Article 10 will trump on nearly every occasion. There will be no scope for complaint by a personal injury claimant, for example, when his activities on a football field are covertly filmed by the insurers' enquiry agent; such material does not have the necessary quality of "seclusion".

Even where press freedom is not directly in point, the present approach of domestic courts to Article 8 suggests that public interest may well prevail over privacy and confidentiality in controversial cases. Mention was made earlier[61] of the High Court decision in the Pinochet medical confidentiality case. Addressing the respondents' argument that disclosure of Pinochet's medical reports would violate his Article 8 rights, the court said that such disclosure would be justified by the legitimate aim of the prevention of crime (which includes the prosecution of crime). It took the view that an order for further disclosure would be "in accordance with the law"; that it would have, in other words, the necessary qualities of legitimacy and foreseeability which any measure needs to possess in order to pass muster under the Convention. This is a

---

[59] Application No. 35712/97, 18 May 1999, unreported
[60] see N. 26 above ·
[61] At p. 188

worrying conclusion. Quite why the proposed disclosure would be "pre-dictable", as the court suggested, and "required by the common law" is not entirely clear – disregarding, as one should, the intense media interest in the Pinochet affair, it is surely the case that the respondent's predictions had been entirely different; that in the light of the express assurance given to him by the Secretary of State, and the common law of confidentiality, his medical records would not be disclosed.

By way of a postscript to this section, a word needs to be said about legal pro-fessional privilege. This area of confidentiality may not be as inviolate as it once was; the new Civil Procedure Rules[62] make a radical inroad here. They provide that when the Court is considering whether to make a wasted costs order,

"For the purpose of this rule, the Court may direct that privileged documents are to be disclosed to the court and, if the court so directs, to the other party to the application for an Order".

This aspect of the rules may well disclose a violation of Article 8, possibly in conjunction with Article 6.[63] Indeed, even without the aid of Article 8, it has recently been held by Toulson J[64] that this particular rule (48.7(3)) is *ultra vires* the Civil Procedure Act 1997, since Parliament could not have intended by non-specific statutory words to have created a power to cut down the substantive right to legal confidentiality.

3. DEFAMATION AND FREEDOM OF EXPRESSION

Defamation laws are generally considered under Article 10(2), which permits measures aimed to protect the reputation and rights of others. The right to a pri-vate life under Article 8 is also relevant to defamation actions. Most Strasbourg jurisprudence in this area relates to criminal sanctions for defamation; the United Kingdom is unique amongst the Contracting States in concentrating defamation actions in the civil courts. However, some of the rulings by the Strasbourg Court have been relevant to the common law of defamation if only in the sense that the "chilling effect" of jury awards in this country sometimes presents no less a threat to criminal sanctions elsewhere. In the following para-graphs only the common law features of defamation will be discussed; thus the legislative cap on damages;[65] the recent lifting of immunity for statements made in Parliament, and the proposed abolition of juries in some defamation

---

[62] Part 48.7 (3)

[63] See chapter 3 on Costs and Conditional Fees for further discussion of costs orders and their compatibility with Article 6

[64] In *General Mediterranean Holdings v Patel* [1993] 3 All ER 673. Toulson J went on to find a breach of Article 6 as well

[65] Passed in consequence of the adverse ruling in *Tolstoy Miloslavsky v United Kingdom* (1995) 20 EHRR 442

proceedings under the rules brought in pursuant to the Defamation Act 1996[66] will not form part of the analysis.

The English law on defamation has been described by one academic as "the oddest" of the torts:[67]

> "he (the plaintiff) can get damages (swingeing damages!) for a statement made to others without showing that the statement was untrue, without showing that the statement did him the slightest harm, and without showing that the defendant was in any way wrong to make it (much less that the defendant owed him any duty of any kind)".

Notwithstanding this and other strong criticisms levelled at defamation over the years, there has been no case in Strasbourg where the onus of proof in English libel law has been considered as a whole to be in breach of Article 10. In fact, the most litigated feature of the English law of defamation is the lack of legal aid. The Strasbourg authorities have categorically stated that it is not unreasonable to exclude certain categories of proceedings from assistance, given the limited financial resources of most civil legal aid schemes, and the exclusion of defamation has not been considered to be arbitrary.[68] The argument advanced in *Munro v United Kingdom*,[69] that legal aid is indispensible in defamation proceedings due to the complexity of the substantive law in the High Court, has been ruled inadmissible by the Commission. This principle applies whether Article 6 is being used as a sword (a means to institute defamation proceedings) or as a shield (lack of legal aid to defend a libel action did not disclose a breach of Article 6: *H.S. and D.M v United Kingdom*).[70]

Defamation in English law is not a privacy tort. It does not cover disclosure of accurate information, however personal. Nor is a statement defamatory if it does not have a "sting"; however damaging in other terms, if it does not lower the claimant in the estimation of right-thinking people generally, it will not provide grounds for an action in defamation. The significance of this in Convention terms is that these limitations on the tort of defamation may not be made the subject of a complaint under Article 6, since none of them constitutes a "civil right" known to English law, and Article 6 is not a vehicle for the creation of new rights.[71]

The features of defamation most likely to come under Convention attack are the range of common law defences. If the Court is satisfied that the statement is one of fact, the onus is on the defendant to justify it, in other words prove the

---

[66] Effective as from 28 February 2000

[67] Weir, *A Casebook on Tort*, 8th ed. (London: Sweet & Maxwell, 1996) p 525

[68] *W v United Kingdom* Application No. 10871/84

[69] Application No. 10594/83, 52 DR 158 (1987). It must be noted that defamation lawyers may now take on both defence and claimants' cases on a conditional fee basis

[70] Application No. 21325/93

[71] *Fayed v United Kingdom* (1994) 18 EHRR 393. The Strasbourg Court has not taken this approach to all Article 6 claims in relation to national rules of immunity; in *Osman v United Kingdom* (1999) 5 BHRC 293 the Court rejected the United Kingdom's argument that the applicants had no substantive right for the purposes of the applicability of Article 6(1) to the rule of police immunity

truth of the allegation. If the report was a fair and accurate coverage of court or parliamentary proceedings, it is covered by absolute privilege and is immune from attack. If the Court accepts that the statement is of an opinion only, the defence of "fair comment" may be available, provided the defendant is able to establish that the views could honestly have been held by a fair-minded person on facts known at the time. In order to benefit from the defence of fair comment, the statement has to be a statement of opinion as opposed to a statement of fact. The difficulty of identifying most statements as either "fact" or "opinion" has been exacerbated by the House of Lords' ruling in *Telnikoff v Matusevitch*[72] that the statement should be considered in isolation, so that a writer who has made a "comment" on an article may find himself liable for defamation if his statement appears to be one of "fact" out of context. Even if the statement does qualify as "fair comment" the claimant may defeat this defence if he can prove "malice", in other words that the defendent published an opinion not genuinely held, or based his comments on information he knew to be false.

The defendant may also argue that the statement is covered by "qualified privilege", which only applies where the publisher has a specific duty in communicating the words to another party who has a specific interest in receiving them, such as the communication of a public grievance to the proper authorities. At the moment, the availability of this defence is considered on a case by case basis. In *Reynolds v Times Newspapers*,[73] the respondent newspaper argued that there should be a generic qualified privilege extending to publication by a newspaper to the public at large of information, including assertions of fact concerning government and political matters, which affect the people of the United Kingdom. The Lords rejected this argument, preferring to maintain the status quo, under which qualified privilege does not extend automatically to press reports of matters in the public interest, unless in the particular circumstances of the case there is clearly a "duty" on the newspaper to make the disclosure and there is a corresponding "interest" in the public to receive it. The circumstances of the publication are relevant in establishing the "duty" and "interest" elements (questions of law for the judge) and not, as the Court of Appeal had suggested below,[74] a separate test of fact (for the jury) in determining whether privilege should apply. The reasonableness of the defendant's conduct will thus be scrutinised before the defence of qualified privilege will be allowed, the onus being on the defendant to prove that he acted reasonably.

This outline of defences shows that the English law of defamation, like the action for breach of confidence, has a different focus to the corresponding interests in the ECHR. Article 10 focuses on freedom of expression, to be balanced against the rights to reputation of others. Defences to defamation action on the other hand are articulated on the basis of the protection of reputation; they are not, in other words, designed to advance the interests of free speech. Likewise,

---

[72] [1991] 4 All ER 817 HL
[73] [1999] 3 WLR 1010
[74] *Reynolds v Times Newspapers and others* [1998] 3 WLR 862

the protection of reputation is articulated as a public interest, rather than as an individual right, enforceable through an action in defamation:

> "Reputation is an integral and important part of the dignity of the individual. It also forms the basis of many decisions in a democratic society which are fundamental to its well-being: whom to employ or work for, whom to promote, whom to do business with or to vote for. Once besmirched by an unfounded allegation in a national newspaper, a reputation can be damaged for ever, especially if there is no opportunity to vindicate one's reputation. *When this happens, society as well as the individual is the loser. For it should not be supposed that protection of reputation is a matter of importance only to the affected individual and his family. Protection of reputation is conducive to the public good. It is in the public interest that the reputation of public figures should not be debased falsely*".[75]

The following examination of the relevant Strasbourg case law in this area illustrates this point.

3.1. Defamation and the Right to a Fair Trial

It was mentioned above that the *Reynolds* case concerned the ECHR compatibility of the present defence of qualified privilege. The House of Lords has concluded that the common law obligation on the defendant to set out the circumstances of the publications in order to establish the reasonableness of its behaviour, is compatible with Article 10; and the majority rejected the argument that political information should be developed as a new subject matter category of qualified privilege, whereby the publication of all such information would attract qualified privilege, whatever the circumstances. There was no logical or practical reason, in their view, for carving out political information as a special category of speech deserving particular defences.

The *Reynolds* case also involves a conflict between freedom of expression and an important countervailing right, the right of the claimant to a fair trial in defamation proceedings. If there were a blanket defence of qualified privilege for political speech, this would impose an effective bar to defamation actions taken by all political claimants. This would present an impermissible restriction on those individuals' rights of access to court guaranteed by Article 6 of the Convention. The newspaper argued that the generic privilege it was seeking for political matters in the public interest could only be defeated by the plaintiff proving unreasonable conduct or lack of reasonable care on the part of the defendant, whereas the present position requires the defendant to establish reasonableness.

As we have seen, this argument failed to win the majority in the Lords. But even the status quo presents potential Article 6 problems, foreshadowed by the

---

[75] Lord Nicholls, *Reynolds v Times Newspapers and others*, N. 70 above

Court of Appeal in *Saif al Islam Gaddafi v Telegraph Group Limited*.[76] This was a ruling on leave to amend a defence which was decided before the Lords rejected the three-part test for qualified privilege set out by the Court of Appeal in *Reynolds*; nevertheless, it illustrates some of the potential difficulties when Article 10 interests collide with Article 6 interests in defamation proceedings. In the particular circumstances of the case, the defendants' publication certainly satisfied the interest and duty tests for qualified privilege. What it was not prepared to do was to provide evidence of the reasonableness of its behaviour in collating the evidence for the allegations in the article, and relied instead on the protection of sources under the newspaper rule and Section 10 of the Contempt of Court Act 1981.[77] Gaddafi argued that if no details were forthcoming about the sources of the information, the circumstantial test was not satisfied and the defence of qualified privilege should not be allowed. The Court of Appeal rejected this argument, holding that the defendant could rely on its statutory and common law immunities whilst at the same time maintaining its qualified privilege defence. Whilst this judgment is clearly in accord with the principle of press freedom under Article 10, it would be open to claimants in similar defamation proceedings to argue that this breached their rights to "equality of arms" under Article 6.[78] Indeed, Lord Steyn observed in *Reynolds* that,

> "Given the procedural restrictions in England (to discovery by the press) I regard the recognition of a generic qualified privilege of political speech as likely to make it unacceptably difficult for a victim of defamatory and false allegations of fact to prove reckless disregard of the truth".

3.2. Defamation and Freedom of Speech

Article 10 actions represent the mirror image of claims made under Article 6 in respect of defamation. Here the question is to what extent defamation laws are permitted to infringe the right to freedom of expression under the Convention. Although Article 10 protects expression against "interferences by a public authority", there is no question that Article 10 will be considered in defamation proceedings involving private parties.[79] Article 10 covers all forms of expression, and the protection it guarantees is not limited to verifiable forms of expression. It

---

[76] 28 October 1998

[77] It is worth noting that in the USA the more extensive privilege granted to the press in communicating matters of political issues, under the rule in *New York Times v Sullivan* 401 US 265 (1964), is counterbalanced by the requirement of full disclosure by way of extensive and onerous pretrial discovery

[78] While the Strasbourg Court has repeatedly emphasised that rules of evidence are a matter for national courts alone, it does not allow those rules to prejudice proceedings (*Dombo Beheer v Netherlands* (1994) 18 EHRR 213; *Schuler-Zgraggen v Switzerland* A 263 (1993) and *X v Austria* No. 5362/72 42 CD 145)

[79] See Jonathan Cooper's discussion on Horizontality in chapter 4. For a prescient analysis of the potential application of free speech and privacy rights in private law, see Markesinis, "Privacy, Freedom of Expression and the Human Rights Bill" 115 *LQR* 47

is often said that the Court affords the highest protection to political speech, and although political figures are not explicitly excluded from the protections afforded by 10(2) ("the reputation or rights of others") in most of its judgments concerning defamation proceedings against journalists who have written articles criticising politicians, the Court has upheld press freedom. The leading case is *Lingens v Austria*.[80] Here the applicant was convicted of criminal defamation (punishable by imprisonment) for accusing the Austrian Chancellor of minimising Nazi atrocities in the Second World War, and the only way he could escape criminal liability was by proving the truth of this statement. The Strasbourg Court ruled that the relevant Article in the Austrian criminal code, which was no doubt legitimate within Article 10(2) since it sought to protect the reputation of others, was not a necessary measure in a democratic society for achieving that purpose. The Court was of the view that it is unacceptable to impose criminal proceedings for value judgements, the truth of which cannot be proved without a great deal of difficulty. The Court has also stated repeatedly that regard must be had to the pre-eminent role of the press in imparting information and ideas on matters of public interest.

As has been noted, most of the Court's judgments under Article 10 concern criminal sanctions for defamation. However, some of this jurisprudence is directly relevant to the scope of civil defamation in terms of its compatibility with Article 10. *Thorgeirson v Iceland*[81] is a case in point. The applicant journalist was convicted of defaming the police by publishing several articles critical of the conduct and discipline of the Reykjavik police force, referring to them, amongst other things, as "beasts in uniform". The articles contained references to stories of police brutality. In English defamation law such hearsay would be regarded as statements of fact by the writer himself, although he probably would have escaped liability on the basis that his allegations were directed at unidentifiable members of the force. The Court found that he was expressing opinions and not facts, so the obligation to prove their truth was an unjustified interference with his rights under Article 10. This approach may have an impact on the distinction between fact and opinion for the purposes of the defence of fair comment in defamation proceedings, since it appears that on matters of general, political interest, the Court is more inclined to regard comments as involving the statement of the author's opinion rather than a statement of fact, and, if fact, not to allow the state to demand the truth of each allegation.

More recent examples of the Strasbourg Court's contextual approach may be found in *Oberschlick v Austria (No 2)*[82] and *De Haes and Gijsels v Belgium*.[83] In *Oberschlick* the publication by the applicant of an article about a politician bearing the title "*Trottel*" (idiot) was held to be a statement of opinion, the truth of which did not need to be established in order to mount a defence to a charge

---

[80]   (1986) 8 EHRR 103
[81]   (1992) 14 EHRR 843
[82]   (1998) 25 EHRR 357
[83]   (1998) 25 EHRR

of criminal defamation. In reaching this conclusion, the Court stated that the comment should be considered in the light of the speech by the politician to which the applicant's article formed a response. In *De Haes* the journalist applicants had published articles accusing four Belgian judges of bias in their handling of a controversial custody case. They said the judges had found for the notaire father because they shared the same extreme right-wing views, an allegation unsupported by evidence. Nevertheless, the Strasbourg Court held that the convictions for defamation were as a whole disproportionate since it had not been established that the allegations had no basis in fact.

Given these precedents, the markedly different method of identifying statements of opinion adopted by the House of Lords in *Matusevich* may have to be reconsidered.

The onus on defendants in English defamation law to justify statements of fact may come under ECHR attack, particularly where the alleged defamatory statement is based on an official report which may itself be privileged. In *Bladet Tromso and Stensaas v Norway*[84] the Strasbourg Court considered a complaint by a newspaper editor and journalist that convictions for defamation breached their rights under Article 10. The newspaper had published articles based on an interview with a seal hunt inspector who had written an official report, alleging breaches of hunting regulations and acts of cruelty by the seal hunters. The official report had been withheld from public disclosure pending further investigation, and on the strength of this the national court had convicted the applicants of defamation, observing that they should have made their own inquiries as to the truth of the allegations before publishing. The Strasbourg Court upheld the applicants' complaint under Article 10. "The press should normally be entitled", the Court observed, "when contributing to public debate on matters of legitimate concern, to rely on the contents of official reports without having to undertake independent research".

3.3. The Impact of the Convention on Defamation

As the very brief discussion above demonstrates, there are a number of common law features in defamation that will come under Convention challenge. Whether such challenges will be successful will depend upon the attention paid by national courts to arguments based, not only on the Strasbourg case law on states' defamation systems, but on analogies drawn from the much more fluid and arguably more useful jurisprudence under Article 6. As it has been pointed out above, the right to a fair trial extends into all areas of litigation, whether or not the state is involved. At the moment, defamation litigation in Strasbourg tends to be largely confined to Article 10 because that Court only has to deal with state respondents seeking to rely on the permitted limitations to free speech

---

[84] (2000) 29 EHRR 125

rights set out in Article 10(2). Opponents in private defamation proceedings will not be so restricted, and future libel claimants will be able to produce the full panoply of guarantees under Article 6 the minute their alleged defamers attempt to rely on Article 10 and any common law or legislative provision which allows them to avoid their normal duties of disclosure in legal proceedings. And even if the national courts refuse to allow fair trial rights to override the free speech rights of libel defendants, there is one more weapon left in the claimants' arsenal: recourse to Strasbourg under Article 13, on the basis that the United Kingdom, despite incorporation of the Convention, has failed to afford them an effective remedy before the national authorities.

12

Mental Health

JEREMY HYAM

1. INTRODUCTION

This chapter deals with the impact of the incorporation of the European Convention on Human Rights on mental health litigation. It has been written at a time when the Mental Health Act 1983 (MHA) is under full scale review by an Expert Committee on behalf of the Government. Some of their draft proposals are incorporated in this chapter. As will be seen, one of the aims of the draft proposals it to have an exhaustive statutory scheme for dealing with mental patients, thus excluding the residual common law doctrines which have served to fill such gaps as were left by the Mental Health Act 1983. The proposals and the urgency for reform have been caused not just by the enactment of the Human Rights Act (HRA), but also by recent decisions of the House of Lords with regard to the compulsory treatment of mental health patients and the unlawfulness of detention without treatment. A recurring and problematic topic raised in the cases and by the draft proposals is that of incapacity. It is tentatively submitted that a proper understanding of the applicability of the rights enshrined in the Convention to mental health patients can only be gained by understanding to what extent and why those patients are incapacitated, and then seeing to what extent it is possible to accord them Convention rights in a non-discriminatory way. This chapter attempts to give an overview of the likely effect of incorporation of the Act on mental health law while highlighting particular problem areas which are the subject of ongoing consultation.

1.1. Terminology: Negative and Positive Rights and Obligations

In the interpretation of the Articles of the Convention and the particular rights contained in them, the text of the Convention document has been interpreted as conferring both positive and negative obligations on states. The words "negative obligations" reflect the classical English political philosophy which underlies much rights based argument. The negative obligation is not to interfere with the individual's fundamental rights, e.g. to refrain from torture and from placing impermissible restrictions upon the freedom of expression.

Positive obligations by contrast are those where the state must take action to secure human rights. In the decisions of the Commission and the Court the terminology of "securing rights" derives from Article 13.[1]

"Positive obligations" are usually associated with economic, social and cultural rights that have financial implications for the state that must secure them, for example the requirement to provide adequate healthcare resources, but they are not always so limited. The text of Article 2(1) protects the right to life by law; to provide conditions that are not inhuman (Article 3) and to provide courts, legal aid and translators in connection with the right to a fair trial (Article 6.1). Other positive obligations have been read into the Convention. In *Marcx v Belgium*[2] it was held that Article 8 does not merely compel the state to abstain from interference but:

> "In addition to this primary negative undertaking, there may be positive obligations inherent in an 'effective respect' for family life".

In that particular case, Belgian family law did not give effective respect for family life because it failed to recognise an illegitimate child as a member of the mother's family.

1.2. Positive Obligations and the Proposals for a New Mental Health Act

At the time of writing the final proposals on a new Mental Health Act are not yet published. The draft proposals currently available include the addition of "positive rights" (in the sense used above) to the Mental Health Act. It has been recommended that patients under compulsion would gain certain positive rights which might include:

(a) right to independent legal and medical advice;
(b) right to information about their treatment and care;
(c) right to an authorised representative;
(d) right of access to medical records;
(e) right to adequate level of service, including on-going care after compulsion.

In the right described at (e) is said to be implied a principle[3] which is central to the draft proposals, namely, reciprocity. The inclusion of this principle in primary legislation is, to say the least, controversial. The principle is defined in the draft proposals as follows:

---

[1] This, as has been pointed out in previous chapters, is an article conspicuously absent from the articles given "further effect" by the HRA. The Lord Chancellor has however assured Parliament that the same protection, and thus the same positive rights are secured by clause 8(1) of the Act. For good measure he has said that where relevant Article 13 and its case law would be relevant to domestic judicial decision-making. See Francesca Klug , "Pepper and Hart and All That" (1999) *PL* Summer 246

[2] (1979) 2 EHRR 330

[3] The Committee has proposed that the principles underlying the provisions of a new Mental Health Act should be included in the Act itself as an aid to its interpretation. There is a precedent for such an approach in both the Family Law Act 1996 and the Children Act 1989

"*Reciprocity*: where society imposes an obligation on an individual to comply with a programme of treatment and care it should impose a parallel obligation on the health and social care authorities to provide appropriate services including on-going care following discharge from compulsion".

It is immediately apparent that the financial burden on the state of such a principle is potentially very substantial.[4]

The draft proposals make some of the following suggestions:

(a) A redefinition of "mental disorder". The expert committee responsible for the draft proposals favours a broad definition of mental disorder, namely: "Any disability or disorder of mind or brain whether *permanent or temporary* which results in an impairment or disturbance of mental functioning".

(b) That there should be a public law duty on local authorities to assess those in contact with services and whose condition is deteriorating.

(c) Mental Health Review Tribunals ("MHRTs") to be replaced with a special tribunal.

(d) No involuntary treatment save in an emergency. Admission to assessment made by at least two professionals of whom one must be medical. During the period of the assessment the multi-disciplinary team should complete an assessment of the patient's capacity, and assessment of risk, a diagnosis of mental disorder and agree a care and treatment plan.

(e) A framework for all compulsory treatment, including the preparation of a treatment plan and a new definition of "best interests".

This change of approach brought about by the HRA will have a significant impact upon mental health litigation in two separate ways. First, on the detention of mental patients at common law, namely those informally admitted and treated under the common law doctrine of necessity. As the House of Lords in the recent case of *R v Bournewood Community Mental Health Trust, ex parte L*[5] has confirmed, Section 131(1) of the MHA 1983 preserves the common law power of hospitals to detain and treat mental patients without recourse to the procedures under the Act where those patients either:

(a) have the capacity to consent and do voluntarily consent to admission and treatment ("voluntary patients"); or

(b) do not have the capacity to consent but do not manifest any objection to treatment: "informal patients".

Secondly, there will be a significant impact on the detention of patients under the MHA. This impact has already borne fruit in the form of the draft proposals. The exercise of statutory powers will come under close scrutiny to ensure that such detention is in compliance with the Articles of the Convention. It cannot be assumed that because detention is lawful under the current MHA, that it is

[4] The Final Proposals, published 15th November 1999, revealed that principles, such as reciprocity, are not incorporated into the new Act itself, but are contained in notes for guidance
[5] [1998] 3 WLR 106

"*according to law*" and thus automatically in compliance with the Convention. The Act was drafted with relatively little regard to the provisions of the ECHR or the jurisprudence of the Commission and the Court. There are likely to be many cases where the procedure and conditions of detention under the MHA fail to recognise the rights enshrined in the Convention. In the light of the impending implementation of the Human Rights Act, the MHA is at present under review, the final proposals to be published in late 1999.

As was explained in chapter 9 under Section 6 of the HRA, it is unlawful for a public authority to act in a way which is incompatible with a Convention right. "Public authority" includes (a) a court or tribunal; and (b) any person certain of whose functions are functions of a public nature. In the mental health sphere this is of significance in that:

(a)   the phrase "court" or "tribunal" means that the Convention will have to be applied at first instance by the Mental Health Review Tribunal. It will be possible to put forward Convention arguments before the MHRT; and

(b)   those who perform duties under the MHA will be likely to fall within the category of persons certain of whose functions are of a public nature. Thus healthcare providers' failure to act in accordance with Convention rights will be challengeable.

The question of which bodies or persons fall into the definition under Article 6 has caused more controversy than any other in the passage of the Act through Parliament. In the course of debate[6] the Home Secretary stated the important distinction he had made based on a desire to provide a modern and wide protection against the abuse of human rights:

"As we are dealing with public functions and with an evolving situation, we believe that the test must relate to the substance and nature of the act, not to form and legal personality".

The particular effect that such a definition has in relation to mental health is that those persons who make decisions of a public nature in relation to the treatment and detention of mentally disordered patients, may be exposed to challenge under the Convention. The protection will not be limited by a specific list of decision-makers, whether that be the MHRT or, under the draft proposals, a widened pool of authorised mental health professionals who have power to impose compulsory assessment.

2. THE DETENTION OF PATIENTS

2.1. At Common Law: The Doctrine of Necessity

This doctrine was only recognised fully by the House of Lords in *Re F (Mental Patient) (Sterilisation)*.[7] F was a thirty six year old mentally handicapped

---

[6] HC 17 June 1988
[7] [1990] 2 AC 1

patient. She was profoundly disabled and suffered an arrested or incomplete development of the mind. She had the verbal capacity of a two year old and the general mental capacity of a four or five year old. She was unable verbally to express her views but could indicate her likes and dislikes – for example people, food, clothes and routine. She is described in the report as a "voluntary" patient but would have been properly categorised as an "informal" patient because she did not have the capacity to appreciate her need to be in hospital and receive treatment or the capacity to fully understand what consent to that treatment was. Because she had been informally admitted, she was not subject to compulsory detention under the MHA. During the time at the hospital she had formed a relationship with a male patient. The hospital staff considered that she would be unable to cope with the effects of pregnancy and giving birth and that, since all other forms of contraception were unsuitable, it would be in her best interests to be sterilised. The House of Lords held that there was no jurisdiction in the High Court to approve or disapprove the giving of medical treatment to persons who lacked the capacity to consent. The lawfulness of the decision to sterilise depended upon whether the treatment was in the best interests of the patient. In coming to this decision their Lordships relied on an important comparison made by Lord Donaldson in the Court of Appeal:

"There is a clear and logical connection between the position of an adult who through an accident is temporarily deprived of the power of consent, the emergency treatment case where consent being unobtainable is not required, and the case of an adult who through permanent disability is equally unable to consent. The difference is largely, although not entirely, one of time scale".

Lord Goff used this comparison to distil the principle underlying the common law justification for intervention. He said:

"In truth, the relevance of an emergency is that it may give rise to a necessity to act in the interests of the assisted person, without first obtaining his consent. Emergency is however, not the criterion or even a prerequisite; it is simply a frequent origin of the necessity which impels intervention. The principle is one of necessity, not of emergency".

Therefore once the treatment was justified by the doctrine of necessity, it could only be criticised if it fell outside the ambit of what treatment would be authorised by a responsible body of medical opinion (see *Bolam v Friern Hospital Management Committee*).[8]

Unfortunately, the doctrine of necessity gives rise to difficult questions in relation to informal patients which have yet to be fully worked out. Treatment is lawful so long as the patient is incapable of giving consent, and does not manifest objection to treatment (i.e is compliant). But who is to decide if the incapacitated patient is truly incapacitated, and who is to judge whether a patient is being truly compliant? If in both cases it is the treating doctor, there is no

[8] [1957] 1 WLR 582

procedural mechanism to check the correctness of the decision and thus the lawfulness of the detention and treatment. If there is a lack of procedural safeguards then, it is likely that the incapacitated person's rights may be infringed. Of course no one doubts that mental health professionals owe a duty of care to patients and that they will almost invariably act in what they consider to be the best interests of the patient. But as Lord Steyn observed in *Bournewood*:

"... neither habeas corpus nor judicial review are sufficient safeguards against misjudgments and professional lapses in the case of compliant incapacitated patients. Given that such patients are diagnostically indistinguishable from compulsory patients, there is no reason to withhold the specific and effective protections of the Act of 1983 from a large class of vulnerably mentally incapacitated individuals. Their moral right to be treated with dignity requires nothing less".

Although an informal patient does have a "right of access" to a court by means of habeas corpus or judicial review to determine the lawfulness of his detention and treatment, what use is that right if it cannot be effectively utilised by him because of his incapacity? The Court of Appeal in *St George's Healthcare National Health Service Trust v S*,[9] aware of the problems which face a Health Trust when it is difficult to ascertain whether a patient has the capacity to consent, has issued the following guidelines:

"In many cases the patient's general practitioner or other responsible doctor might be sufficiently qualified to make the necessary assessment, but in serious or complex cases involving difficult issues about the future health and well being or even life of the patient, the issue of capacity should be examined by an independent psychiatrist, ideally one approved under Section 12(2) of the Mental Health Act 1983".[10]

These guidelines however fall short of being the "positive obligations" owed to this type of informal patient under the ECHR. Recognising this legislative gap the Expert Committee is currently considering including the following within its recommendations:

(a) the creation of an appropriate structure for substitute decision making;
(b) the provision of advocacy;
(c) the extension of the remit of the successor body to the MHAC;
(d) the introduction of the same safeguards with regard to the approval of treatment for mental disorder as would apply to those under compulsion under the new Mental Health Act.

It seems unlikely that the present common law doctrine of necessity, as preserved by Section 131 of the MHA, would survive challenge under the Convention. In particular, the doctrine fails to take into account the question of proportionality. Under the Convention, the onus is on the public authority to establish that the particular circumstances of the case justify the measure pro-

---

[9] [1998] 3 All ER 673
[10] Per Judge LJ at 703h

posed. This would appear to conflict with the *Bolam* test, which allows even disproportionate intervention provided that the treatment is in accordance with what would have been authorised by a responsible body of medical opinion. Furthermore, for the purpose of Articles 8 to 12, derogation from the right is only permissible where it is "prescribed by law". This means that the state must be able to show that its conduct must have some basis in domestic law, whether statute or common law.[11]

It is at best doubtful whether the doctrine of necessity is sufficiently precise to meet that requirement. The law will need to change. The moral rights to which Lord Steyn referred will, after incorporation, become legal rights providing a cause of action in themselves. Parties will be able to seek damages under Section 8 of the Act for infringement of those rights. Whether the necessary changes are made by judicial development of the common law doctrine of necessity; by amendment of existing legislation; or by radical reinterpretation of those statutory provisions, this area of mental health law is fertile ground for rights-based argument.

The House of Lords in *R v Bournewood Community Health Trust, ex parte L* (see above) confirmed that a mentally ill patient who does not have the capacity to consent (an informal patient) may be deprived of his liberty at common law without recourse to the Act and be treated under the principle of the common law doctrine of necessity.

The evidential problem is, of course, that Lord Goff held that L was not in fact "detained". But as we shall, see the Convention approach to deprivation of liberty is to look at the substance of the deprivation of liberty and not to quibble about the technical meaning of words. In *Bournewood*, Lord Goff treated the question of whether or not L was detained as the same question as whether or not L was falsely imprisoned under common law principles. He did so precisely because he did not want to be distracted by the meaning of the word "detention", a word which was defined by the Court of Appeal as follows:

"A person is detained if those who have control over the premises in which he is have the intention that he shall not be permitted to leave those premises and have the ability to prevent him from leaving".

There was a noticeable difference between the requirements for detention given by the Court of Appeal and the requirements laid down by the common law for the tort of false imprisonment to be committed, in particular the requirement for a "complete" deprivation of liberty. This was the point on which both Lords Steyn and Nolan dissented. For them it was a matter of fact and degree, not one of absolutes. Thus Lord Steyn held that L was in fact detained but that such detention was justified in the circumstances by the common law doctrine of necessity.

---

[11] *Silver v UK* (1983) 5 EHRR 347 and *Malone v UK* (1984) 7 EHRR 14 at 40

It is at least arguable that incorporation of the ECHR would require a different result on the same facts. The test of deprivation of liberty involves considering

> "the concrete situation of the individual concerned and account must be taken of a whole range of criteria such as the type, duration, effect and manner of implementation of the measure in question".[12]

This is broader than the test applied by Lord Goff; in other words whether the tort of false imprisonment (a traditional common law concept) had been committed. When taken together with the question of whether the doctrine of necessity can survive incorporation, it is clear that there will be ample basis for challenging decisions made under the common law.

It is worth noting that the draft proposals for the new MHA include proposals to ensure that the new Act is so far as possible exhaustive and will thereby exclude the necessity for common law detention. Whether the proposals are effective in this aim remains to be seen.

3. THE DETENTION OF PATIENTS UNDER THE MHA

3.1. The Convention and its Jurisprudence

Under Section 2 of the Act, a Court or Tribunal in determining a question under the Act must have regard to the relevant decisions of the Court and Commission. To understand how the separate provisions of the Convention will apply to Mental Health Act cases, it is necessary first to look at the rights to be protected and then to see what principles have been applied by the Court and the Commission in enforcing or protecting those rights.

Article 2

Article 2 protects the right to life. This encompasses not only a duty on behalf of a State to refrain from the intentional and unlawful taking of life, but also a duty to take appropriate steps to safeguard the lives of those within its jurisdiction (*Osman v UK*).[13] Mr Osman had brought an action in the United Kingdom against the police in respect of their failure to protect him from a "stalker" who ultimately injured him seriously and killed his father. The action was struck out in the national courts. The Strasbourg Court held that there was,

> "a positive obligation on the authorities to take preventive operational measures to protect an individual whose life is at risk from the criminal acts of another individual".

---

[12] *Ashingdane v United Kingdom* (1985) 7 EHRR 528
[13] (1999) 5 BHRC 293

But as was noted in the following paragraph, "positive" obligations must not be interpreted in such a way as to impose an impossible or disproportionate burden on public authorities. In *Osman* the police could not rely on the immunity granted to them by the common law in respect of operational decisions. The decision affects mental health law in two ways:

(a) First, it is arguable that healthcare providers performing statutory functions under the MHA come under a Convention duty to protect mental patients whose lives are at risk. This might mean that an action would lie for failure to take operational measures to prevent, for example, suicide. Analogies may be drawn with suicides of prisoners in custody: in *Kirkham v Chief Constable of Manchester*[14] the Court of Appeal ruled that the police should be liable for the suicide of a prisoner whom they should have known was suffering from clinical depression. The House of Lords has recently ruled on this issue, saying that where a prisoner of sound mind commits suicide by taking advantage of a breach of duty by the authorities the police, though liable, would not have to pay full damages.[15]

(b) Secondly, it is also arguable that healthcare providers come under a further Convention duty to take measures to prevent mental patients who are known to be dangerous from threatening the lives of others. This difficult problem for healthcare providers has been the subject of further government proposals and emergency legislation in Scotland and is considered below.

4. DETENTION WITHOUT TREATMENT

Lawful detention under the Mental Health Act requires the detainee to suffer a condition capable of treatment.[16] Most recently in *Reid v Secretary of State for Scotland*.[17] the Lords had to grapple with the difficult issue of whether a patient suffering from psychopathic disorder was entitled to be discharged if his condition was not able to be alleviated by treatment. Overruling *R v Canons Park Mental Health Review Tribunal, ex parte A*[18] it was held that both the order for detainment and the review for discharge must take the patient's treatability into account. If the patient was not treatable then he or she should be released, although a conditional discharge was both lawful and in accordance with the Convention.[19] Lord Hope confirmed that regardless of how "medical treatment" was defined (and it was given a wide definition in *Reid*), some form of treatment is required to make the detention lawful.

[14] [1989] 2 KB 283
[15] *Reeves v Commissioner of Police for the Metropolis* [[1999] 3 WLR 363
[16] See *Hutchison Reid v Secretary of State for Scotland and Another* (1999) 1 ALL ER 481; *R v Canons Park Mental Health Review Tribunal ex parte A* (1995) QB 60 (CA)
[17] [1999] 1 All ER 481
[18] [1994] 2 ALL ER 659
[19] See *Stanley Johnson v UK* (1997) EHRLR 105–8; *Luberti v Italy* (1984) 6 EHRR 440

On 19 July 1999 new Government proposals: *Managing Dangerous People with Severe Personality Disorder (DSPDs) – Proposals for Policy Development* were published. The stated purpose of these proposals is to ensure that the public is better protected from those people who present a "high risk to society" by reason of their severe personality disorder. Often such people will have been convicted and imprisoned for a criminal offence, and their continued detention, or recall will be justified by reference to evidence of their past offending. The proposals however also encompass those who are detained not by virtue of any criminal offence, but by virtue of their mental disorder alone.

The proposals state that the new framework for managing DSPDs must be in accordance with the ECHR; but there is a risk that the proposals may flout Article 5(1)(e) insofar as they seek to introduce new powers to detain indefinitely on the basis that the detainee might otherwise commit an offence.

In support of the new proposals the Government relies on the fact that the Strasbourg Court has held in *Van Droogenbruck*[20] and *Weeks v UK*[21] that it is not an infringement of an individual's right to liberty to recall someone who has been released from prison following their conviction for an imprisonable offence. But it would seem likely that the Government's proposals do not properly address the question of the legality of recall of a patient whose original detainment was justified only on the basis that he was a patient suffering from a disorder or unsoundness of mind. The issue is illustrated by the cases of both *Johnson v UK* and *Luberti v Italy*,[22] although both were cases where the person detained had committed an imprisonable offence. *Johnson* is authority for the proposition that once it has been found that a patient is no longer suffering from a mental disorder, an unconditional immediate release is not mandatory, but the conditions of such release insofar as they require intervention by third parties, must be capable of being met within a reasonable time.[23] In *Luberti v Italy*, in the light of the detained person's history of serious disorderly behaviour and criminal offending, the Court considered that the responsible authority could properly "proceed with caution" in effecting his release. The difficult question remains for the situation where a person is detained but has not committed an imprisonable offence, and yet it is said that the general interest of public safety justifies continued detention of a person no longer treatable.

This difficulty is emphasised by Article 18 of the Convention which provides as follows:

"The restrictions permitted under this convention to the said rights and freedoms shall not be applied for any purpose other than those for which they have been prescribed".

When this passage is read in conjunction with Article 5(1)(e) namely, the power to detain for "the prevention of the spreading of infectious diseases, of persons

---

[20] (1981) 4 EHRR 443
[21] (1987) 10 EHRR 293
[22] See N. 17 above
[23] *R v MHR Tex parte Hall*, *The Times*, 5 October 1999

of unsound mind, alcoholics or drug addicts or vagrants", it would seem that the detention for the protection of the public by reason of the risk to society presented by the patient would not be within the scope of lawful detention under Art. 5(1)(e).

Article 3

"No one shall be subjected to torture or to inhuman or degrading treatment or punishment".

When patients are detained under the MHA, treatment is allowed which is by medical opinion in the patient's best interests. Where such treatment is sanctioned by professional medical opinion, as it must be, it is hard to think that such treatment would be inhuman or degrading. There may however be cases where the treatment authorised is well in excess of that justified for achieving the desired end, or alternatively that the treatment is such that no reasonable body of professional medical opinion would support it. In such cases there may be the possibility of Article 3 infringement. A useful case which gives guidance on the principles that govern such a challenge and what sort of treatment amounts to "inhuman or degrading" is the case of *Herczegfalvy v Austria*.[24]

The applicant was a Hungarian refugee. He was by trade a TV repairer who had committed various criminal offences, including acts of violence against his wife and acts of physical aggression against his business clients. He was detained in an institute for "mentally deranged offenders" between May 1978 and November 1984. He was in a physically weakened state (he had been on hunger strike and suffered from pneumonia). He complained, inter alia, that between 15 January and 14 February 1980 he had been handcuffed to a bed with a belt placed around his ankles. The justification for such restraint was said to be "the danger of aggression and the death threats he was making". The applicant said that other belts had been put around his thighs and stomach and that the restraints had only been untied for the first time on 2 February; in order for him to obtain his files and writing materials with which to write down his complaints!

The Commission held unanimously that the applicant's compulsory medical treatment and the way in which it was administered, combined with his artificial feeding and isolation, amounted to inhuman and degrading treatment. The Court unanimously held that it did not, stating:

"The Court considers that the position of inferiority and powerlessness which is typical of patients confined in psychiatric hospitals calls for increased vigilance in reviewing whether the Convention has been complied with. While it is for the medical authorities to decide, on the basis of the recognised rules of medical science, on the therapeutic methods to be used, if necessary by force, to preserve the physical and mental health of patients who are entirely incapable of deciding for themselves and for

---

[24] (1992) 15 EHRR 437

whom they are therefore responsible, such patients nevertheless remain under the protection of Article 3, the requirements of which permit of no derogation . . . however, the evidence before the Court is not sufficient to disprove the Government's argument that, according to the psychiatric principles generally accepted at the time, medical necessity justified the treatment in issue".

What is interesting about this decision (apart from the complete disagreement between the Commission and the Court as to what amounted to inhuman and degrading treatment) is the means by which the Court held such treatment to be justified. Whilst holding that Article 3 permits of no derogation, it seems that detention and treatment which is authorised by a responsible body of medical opinion may not be in breach of Article 3.

This decision would appear to downgrade a positive right of the individual into a duty on behalf of the treating doctors to act reasonably when coming to their decision as to what is in a patient's "best interests".[25]

Another example of the use of Article 3 in the mental health context is *Aerts v Belgium*.[26] In that case A was detained in the psychiatric wing of a prison because he was adjudged too mentally ill to be criminally responsible and there was nowhere else to put him. Inter alia he complained that the treatment he received in the psychiatric wing of the hospital was inhuman and degrading. It was recognised by the Court that ill-treatment must have attained a minimum level of severity if it was to constitute "inhuman and degrading treatment" for the purposes of Article 3. Notwithstanding that the degree of severity had to be considered in the light of the understanding and vulnerability of the patient, and in that sense it was always a matter of fact and degree in every case. On the facts in *Aerts*, no violation was found.

Article 5

Article 5(1):-

> "Everyone has the right to liberty and security of person. No one shall be deprived of his liberty save in the following cases and in accordance with a procedure prescribed by law;
> (a) the lawful detention of a person after conviction by a competent court;
> (b) the lawful arrest or detention of a person for non-compliance with the lawful order of a court or in order to secure the fulfilment of any obligation prescribed by law;
> . . .
> (e) the lawful detention . . . of persons of unsound mind, alcoholics or drug addicts or, vagrants".

---

[25] Cf. *St George's Healthcare NHS Trust v S* : a procedure that was clearly in the best interests of a mother and her unborn child should *not* have been performed in the absence of consent, where a mother was capable of giving consent.
[26] (1999) 5 BHRC 582

Article 5(4)

"Everyone who is deprived of his liberty by . . . detention shall be entitled to take proceedings by which the lawfulness of his detention shall be decided speedily by a court and his release ordered if his detention is not lawful".

Article 5(1)(e) is the only provision of the Convention which explicitly refers to mentally disordered patients: "Persons of unsound mind".

Under the MHA Section 1 "mental disorder" means: a mental illness, arrested or incomplete development of mind, psychopathic disorder and any other disorder or disability of mind. "Psychopathic disorder" is defined as: "a persistent disorder or disability of mind (whether or not including significant impairment of intelligence) which results in abnormally aggressive or seriously irresponsible conduct on the part of the person concerned".

It is worth noting a significant change to the definition of mental disorder considered in the draft proposals.[27] The committee has favoured a broad definition of the basic diagnostic criterion for mental illness and has been attracted by the Law Commission's definition.[28] The Law Commission was making recommendations with regard to incapacity and was keen to establish a definition which was not restricted to psychiatric disorder. They selected as a term for mental disability "any disability or disorder of mind or brain, whether permanent or temporary, which results in an impairment or disturbance of mental functioning". This new definition will be important in the determination of such disabled persons' Convention rights, and may widen the scope of protection of both the Act, and thereby the effect of the Convention itself.

Although the wording of Article 5 refers to "detention and arrest" (words which have acquired a technical meaning in English common law and statute, e.g. P.A.C.E 1984) the Strasbourg Court has stated that the right which is at stake is the right not to be arbitrarily deprived of one's liberty. A substantial body of case law has developed as to what amounts to deprivation of liberty (see, inter alia, *Guzzardi v Italy*[29] where the applicant was required by a judicial compulsory residence order to live for sixteen months on a remote island off the coast of Sardinia on suspicion of illegal mafia activities) but the guiding principles are conveniently summarised in *Ashingdane v United Kingdom*.[30]

A had been detained in a secure special hospital. His condition improved and a transfer to a local psychiatric hospital was authorised by the Home Secretary. A dispute arose between the hospital staff at the local hospital. The dispute meant that he was not accepted into the local hospital. He therefore remained detained in the secure special hospital. He complained that his continued detainment in the secure special hospital was unlawful, and that his inability to

---

[27] Draft proposals of the Mental Health Act Review Expert Committee (set up October 1998)
[28] LC 231 para 3.8 –3.13
[29] 3 EHRR 333, paras 91–3
[30] (1985) 7 EHRR 529 at 541

challenge the lawfulness of the refusal to transfer him was a breach of Article 5(4). His complaint was not upheld. Article 5(4) enabled an individual to challenge the lawfulness of his detention, it was not the appropriate means to challenge the conditions of that detention. The following guidance was given on the meaning of deprivation of liberty.

> "According to the established case law of the Court, Article 5(1)(e) is not concerned with mere restrictions of liberty of movement which are governed by Article 2 of Protocol No. 4. In order to determine whether circumstances involved deprivation of liberty, the starting point must be the concrete situation of the individual concerned and account must be taken of a whole range of criteria such as the type, duration, effect and manner of implementation of the measure in question. The distinction between deprivation of and restriction upon liberty is merely one of degree or intensity, and not one of nature or substance".

It is significant to note that in *Ashingdane*, A was held in an open, i.e "unlocked" ward but was still detained. Two Swedish cases serve to illustrate that the question of whether a person is detained is dependent upon an examination of the precise conditions of the detention. In *W v Sweden*[31] the applicant, who had been detained under the relevant Swedish mental health legislation, secured her provisional discharge before the local discharge council. She was provisionally released, but with an order that she should take a particular medication, and that she should present herself for medical control at the hospital once every fortnight. The Commission considered that the restrictions on her liberty incorporated in this order were not so severe that the applicant's situation after her provisional release could be characterised as a deprivation of liberty.

A similar result on similar facts was reached in *L v Sweden*[32] where it was noted by the Commission that:

> "Although the applicant had been physically released from the hospital as a result of her provisional discharge, it does not automatically follow that she was no longer 'deprived of her liberty'. For instance, a person detained in a psychiatric hospital would clearly still be regarded as 'deprived of his liberty' even if he was occasionally allowed to leave the hospital premises".

The Commission took a similar view in *Nielsen v Denmark*,[33] a case decided on special facts. Although the Commission decision in *Nielsen* was subsequently overturned by the Court by majority of 9:7, the reasoning is still valid. The applicant was a minor who was held in a mental hospital not as a result of the state's exercise of its powers of detention under the relevant Mental Health Acts, but as a result of an exercise of parental authority. The Court found on the facts that the conditions of his detention were not significantly different from those which obtained when a child was held in hospital for some physical impairment: i.e. the ward door was locked, but the children were often allowed out to playgrounds

---

[31] Application No. 12778/87
[32] Application No. 10801/84
[33] See *Nielsen v Denmark*, Comm. Report 12 March 1987; (1988) 11 EHRR 175

and museums etc. accompanied by staff. It was observed by the Court that family life, and especially the rights of parents to exercise parental authority over their children, having due regard to their parental responsibilities, were rights recognised and protected by Article 8. This was a crucial factor in the decision which affected the appraisal of the conditions of N's detention, and deprived him of the protection of Article 5. It is proper to observe that this decision is probably less an indication of how rights are played off against each other than evidence that the Court is generally reluctant to intervene in the parent/child sphere.

Lawful Detention and "Persons of Unsound Mind"

Deprivation of liberty by detention in a mental institution will not be "lawful" if either the detention fails to comply with the procedure of the domestic law, or if it is not in conformity with the purpose of the restrictions permitted by Article 5(1)(e) and is not warranted on the facts of the case. The landmark case is *Winterwerp v Netherlands*[34] where the Court set out the guiding principles governing what is "lawful" detention and a "person of unsound mind".

The applicant, W, had been compulsorily detained under the relevant Netherlands legislation. He had been detained by Court Orders which had been reviewed periodically, but had not been notified that such proceedings had been in progress, nor was he allowed to appear or be represented. Furthermore, some of his requests for release had not been forwarded to the Court by the Public Prosecutor (it was apparently lawful for the Public Prosecutor to refuse to do so).

In the judgment of the Court three minimum conditions which must be complied with for a detention to be lawful are set out:

(a) Valid detention depends upon the individual concerned being reliably shown by objective medical expertise to be of unsound mind.
(b) The individual's mental disorder must be of a nature and degree as to justify detention.
(c) Detention is only justified if and so long as the mental disorder persists.

The Court also dealt with the procedural safeguards which are necessary to ensure compliance with Article 5(4) at paragraph 60:

"It is essential that the person concerned should have access to the Court and the opportunity to be heard either in person or, where necessary, through some form of representation, failing which he will not have been afforded the fundamental guarantees or procedure applied in matters of deprivation of liberty".

"Mental illness may entail restricting or modifying the manner of exercise of such a right but it cannot justify impairing the very essence of the right. Indeed, special procedural safeguards may prove called for in order to protect the interests of persons who, on account of their mental disabilities, are not fully capable of acting for themselves".

These last comments are particularly relevant to the detention of informal patients at common law who by virtue of their incapacity are unable to utilise

[34] (1979) 2 EHRR 38

their right of access to a court. If the Court's judgment is that the fact of in-capacity must not diminish the essence of the right of speedy access to a court, then the burden is surely on the state to provide the procedural safeguards to ensure that the positive right of access to a court can be exercised by the patient notwithstanding his incapacity. If the incapacitated patient cannot look after his "best interests" himself, the court or a responsible third party must do so for him.

The right to a speedy decision has the further implication that review pro-ceedings must be carried out with due expedition. Otherwise continued deten-tion will be in breach of Article 5 since the length of continued detention would be arbitrary. In *Musial v Poland*[35] there was a five month delay while medical records were forwarded to psychiatrists undertaking an independent assessment of the applicant. It was held that the delay had led to a breach of the principle underlying Article 5, namely the protection of individuals against arbitrariness as regards any measure depriving them of their liberty.

5. EMERGENCY CONFINEMENT AND TREATMENT

An exception to the first of the *Winterwerp* criteria noted above is where the detention is necessary because it is an emergency. In such a case the requirement that there is a prior independent medical examination is temporarily abrogated by reason of the emergency. *X v UK*[36] is illustrative of this exception.

X had been convicted of an offence of wounding with intent to cause grievous bodily harm. He was sent to a secure mental hospital. In 1971 the Home Secretary authorised his conditional discharge. In 1974 pursuant to his powers under Section 66 of the Mental Health Act 1959, and acting upon information he had received, the Home Secretary issued a warrant for his recall. X com-plained that his recall was unlawful and in breach of Article 5(1), and that in breach of Article 5(4) he had had no opportunity to have the lawfulness of his detention after recall speedily decided by a court. In argument the Government referred to the "usual procedure" which then applied in relation to recall, namely that the person was simply informed that he was being recalled to Broadmoor by the Home Secretary.

The Strasbourg Court held unanimously that there had been a breach of Article 5(1) because X had not been given prompt and sufficient reasons for his arrest and recall. Nevertheless, it was also held that:

> "It cannot be inferred from Winterwerp that the 'objective' medical expertise therein referred to *must* be obtained before rather than after confinement on the grounds of unsoundness of mind".

But while the emergency circumstances justified X's recall as an emergency mea-sure for a short duration, X's further detention, after the time when he could

---

[35] 25 March 1999, unreported
[36] (1981) 4 EHRR 188

reasonably have been independently examined, was indefensible and in breach of Article 5(1).

The Expert Committee's draft proposals note the practical difficulties often faced by those seeking to implement an urgent MHA Assessment. In particular, securing the attendance of both authorised support workers and Section 12 doctors. The Committee have suggested one emergency containment power which could be initiated in relation to any patient by a duly trained and authorised social worker, nurse or medical practitioner. If the emergency arose outside hospital, the involvement of both an approved mental health worker and a medical practitioner would be required. It would be available only in cases of urgent necessity and would authorise containment in hospital for a maximum of twenty four hours. During the period of containment only emergency treatment under the equivalent of Section 62 MHA would be permitted. If a formal assessment was not imposed by the end of that period then the authority to detain would automatically collapse.

5.1. The Meaning of "access to a Court"

X v UK is also an important authority on the right of access to a court. In *X* the Court revisited the *Winterwerp* criteria set out above and enlarged upon them. It was held that the lawfulness of detention must be able to be tested by a judicial body that is independent of the executive and possesses court-like attributes; and that the procedure for such review must conform with traditional principles of natural justice.

The Court held that the Article 5(4) right was not secured by informal methods such as intervention by a Member of Parliament, requests by the detainee; and the intervention of a responsible medical officer (RMO), because none of those methods constituted an "independent" review procedure. Although there was a Mental Health Tribunal available to the applicant, its function was advisory only, and therefore did not possess the necessary court-like attributes which Article 5(4) required.

As a consequence of this decision the Mental Health Act 1983 was amended to allow restricted patients the right of access to tribunals which had power to order their discharge, a power which previously had vested only in the Home Secretary.

6. LIKELY AREAS OF CHALLENGE

Having set out the above guiding principles on which the courts will act in determining Article 5 claims as they arise in the municipal courts, it is helpful to highlight some areas of potential challenge.[37]

---

[37] For an extremely helpful and extensive review of the possible areas of challenge see O. Thorold, "The implications of the ECHR for United Kingdom Mental Health Legislation" (1996) *EHRLR* 619

6.1. Failure to Obtain a Prior Medical Report

Under Section 42(3) of the MHA 1993, the Home Secretary may recall a patient conditionally discharged by him or by a tribunal. He or she can do so without requesting a medical recommendation. In the absence of such prior medical recommendation, such a recall is likely to be in violation of Article 5. It is worth noting that in an emergency situation where it is impracticable to comply with the *Winterwerp* criteria then there is unlikely to be a violation. Where however such emergency procedures are used simply to bypass the formal procedures, or where such emergency procedures are not justified on the facts, there may be potential violations.

In *K v UK*[38] K had been convicted of manslaughter with diminished responsibility in 1971 and had been detained under a hospital order without limit of time. In March 1985 he was conditionally discharged by a MHRT but subsequently committed two assaults on young women. In April 1986 he was sentenced for three years to run concurrently in respect of the two assaults. Just prior to his release from prison the Home Secretary issued a warrant of recall stating that as soon as he was released he was to be taken to Broadmoor. The Home Secretary gave as his reasons the commission of the assaults but did not obtain up to date evidence in support of the continued deprivation of liberty. It was held by the Strasbourg Court that there had been a breach of Article 5(1). Certain minimum conditions of lawfulness were not respected, in particular there was no up to date objective medical expertise showing that K was continuing to suffer from a true mental disorder, or that his previous psychiatric disorder persisted.

6.2. Delayed Release

A brief analysis of the *Winterwerp* criteria (above) might lead one to think that once it is established that the pre-conditions justifying detention no longer exist, a patient should be immediately and unconditionally released. In *Stanley Johnson v United Kingdom*,[39] the Strasbroug Court fell short of mandating such immediate release. The facts of that case are instructive.

J was a restricted patient at Rampton Hospital. He was found to be no longer suffering from mental disorder. He was conditionally discharged. It was a condition of his discharge that he lived in a hostel and was supervised by a psychiatrist and a social worker and that his release should be deferred until a suitable placement was found. No hostel accommodation could be found for him. He therefore had to remain at Rampton. Between June 1989 and January 1993 there were three tribunal hearings. In May 1990 and April 1991 the tribunal could not

---

[38]   40 BMLR 20
[39]   (1999) 27 EHRR 296

find him appropriate hostel accommodation and throughout that period he had to remain at Rampton. It was only at the third hearing that he obtained an absolute discharge and was released.

Although the Court did not hold that immediate release was required by the provisions of Article 5 once it was shown that the preconditions justifying detention had ceased to exist, it was stressed that appropriate safeguards should be in place so as to ensure that any deferment of discharge was not unreasonably delayed. In the case of *Johnson* it most certainly had. It is worth noting that under the Expert Committee's draft proposals, the principle of recipriocity would seem to require that there is a positive obligation to provide adequate resources properly to manage treatment after discharge.

In another recent case[40] the Strasbourg Court made it clear that delay in release cannot be remedied by retrospective validation of detention. The applicant, who was suffering from mental derangement, was eligible for early release following a conviction for manslaughter. The Public Prosecutor applied for an extension of the detention, but ten weeks after the original period had ended, the Court held that the detention between the end of the original period and the grant of the extension was in breach of Article 5. Where there are procedural rules for the extension of detention, therefore, they must be complied with strictly.

The cause of delay in many cases will be delay in access to a tribunal or a court. It has been held[41] that eight weeks may be too long a delay for the initial determination of the legality of detention Further, it has been held[42] that a period of four months' delay may be too long for the periodic review of the lawfulness of continued detention. There remain good grounds for arguing by reference to the standards set in the cases referred to above that an annual review is too long and is in breach of Article 5(4).

6.3. Legal Aid and Access to the Courts

The availability for Legal Aid for human rights challenges has been exhaustively dealt with by Guy Mansfield QC in his chapter on Costs, Conditional Fees and Legal Aid. The current position in relation to MHRTs is that ABWOR (assistance by way of representation) is granted in all cases before MHRTs unless it appears that approval for assistance should not be given. This covers the costs of a solicitor preparing a client's case and representation at a hearing. Furthermore, permission for an independent psychiatric report will usually be granted if the RMPO's report contains (or it is known that it will contain) recommendations which are not acceptable to the client.

---

[40] *Erkalo v Netherlands* (1999) 28 EHRR 509
[41] In *E v Norway* (1994) 17 EHRR 30
[42] In *Koendjbihare v Netherlands* (1990) 13 EHRR 820

As was noted in the case of *Winterwerp*, and *X v UK*, the review of detention must be carried out by a tribunal or court with "court like" attributes. Furthermore, the proceedings must conform with the principles of natural justice. Whether the principles of natural justice require representation with the benefit of legal aid is an interesting point. The case of *Megyeri v Germany*[43] would seem to suggest that the state has a positive duty to ensure representation of mental patients who require it. Those who may need representation most are those who are incapacitated and cannot consent to treatment.

6.4. Burden of Proof

At present under the MHA to justify detention the state must prove that there is a mental disorder. Once detained a patient must prove that the disorder no longer subsists. Article 5(4) implies that no individual should be deprived of his liberty unless justified. It must be for the state to justify continued detention and not for the patient to have to justify his grounds of release. There are good grounds for arguing that the Convention requires the burden of proof (which lies on the applicant to justify his grounds of release) to be reversed.

6.5. Article 6(1)

"In the determination of his civil rights and obligations or of any criminal charge against him, everyone is entitled to a fair and public hearing within a reasonable time by an independent and impartial tribunal established by law".

It can be seen that there is a certain amount of duplication between the Article 5(4) right of access to a court and the Article 6(1) right. Article 5(4) does not properly cover the situation where what is required is not a review of detention, but rather a fair hearing on affairs consequential on or related to that detention. When a person is detained under the MHA he is not automatically deprived of his right to administer property. However, an application may be made by a third party to the Court of Protection to assume jurisdiction over the detained person's affairs. A possible infringement of Article 6 may arise because the Court of Protection Rules do not grant or prescribe an opportunity for the detained person to be heard, either in person or by an authorised representative.

Article 6 would also be applicable in the context of decisions of professional bodies concerning registration and regulation, since this would have an impact upon the civil rights and obligations of healthcare providers themselves. This would have the greatest impact in the sphere of professional disciplinary proceedings.[44]

[43] (1992) 50 EHRR
[44] See by comparison *Diennet v France* (1995) HRCD 491 and *Stephan v UK* (1998) 25 EHRR CD 130

In *Stephan v United Kingdom* the applicant was a doctor who despite repeated applications for full registration was only given a limited registration which then became subject to conditions after complaint by a patient in 1992. She appealed from the registration body (the GMC) to the Privy Council, who found no question of law raised by the appeal and accordingly dismissed it. The applicant complained, inter alia, that she had been denied a fair hearing in accordance with Article 6.

It was held by the Commission that the guarantees of independence that did exist, namely a limitation on the individual members sitting where they had had previous contact with the case did not suffice to ensure the requisite appearance of independence. However, following *Bryan v UK*,[45] even where an adjudicatory body determining disputes over *"civil rights and obligations"* does not comply with Article 6(1), no violation can be found if the proceedings before that body are subject to subsequent judicial control

Notwithstanding that the Privy Council could only review the legal and procedural aspect of the decisions, and there was no re-determination of the facts decisive of the Health Committee's decision, it was held that the Privy Council review was sufficient to comply with the provisions of Article 6(1).[46]

Finally, it has been argued that the availability of judicial review is sufficient to ensure compliance with Article 6. However, the limited scope of judicial review, dependent upon the illegality, irrationality or procedural impropriety of the tribunal, suggests that some extra safeguards may have to be introduced to such proceedings.

Although Article 5(4) does not guarantee a right to judicial review of such breadth as to empower the court on all aspects of the case, including questions of pure expediency, to substitute its own discretion for that of the decision-making authority, the review should however be wide enough to bear on those conditions which are essential for the "lawful" detention of a person according to Article 5(1).[47]

6.6. Article 8

An example of an Article 8 challenge can be seen from the case of *Herczegfalvy v Austria* (above), where the violation alleged was that the mental hospital had prevented the applicant from corresponding. In that case the power by which the municipal authority acted was so broadly drafted as to make no distinctions between types of mail and correspondence. There is unlikely to be a similar

---

[45] (1996) 21 EHRR 342

[46] For further cases on this subject see *Gautrin v France* Nos 21257/93 to 21260/93 where the Court found a violation of Article 6 and *Diennet v* France (supra) where the Court did not. See also *Chahal v United Kingdom* (1997) 23 EHRR 413 for a similar issue in relation to asylum, where the national security elements of his case meant that he had not effective remedy by judicial review for his Convention claims

[47] See *E v Norway* (1994) 17 EHRR 30 para 49

challenge to the provisions in the MHA 1983 which are precisely drafted and provide that interference can only be justified where it is demonstrated that it is in the patient's interests. In *Y v UK*[48] a patient detained at Broadmoor complained that his Article 8 right had been infringed because he had been prevented from sending a telegram to his mother in relation to his appeal. While the Commission agreed that the Article 8 right to respect for private and family life extended to correspondence, there had been no infringement because the applicant had not been prevented from sending a letter and delivering the message in person to his mother two days later.

It is worth noting that in the proposals for a new Mental Health Act the Expert Committee suggest guidance for information sharing between healthcare professionals. While these proposals have not yet reached concrete form in the shape of statutory provision, there is a likely Article 8 challenge on the basis that the width of such information sharing breaches the right of confidentiality to which the mentally disordered patient is entitled.

Article 8 also becomes relevant when other family members are involved. In *J.T. v UK*,[49] the applicant claimed there had been a breach of Article 8 because she had been unable to apply to change her "nearest relative" under the 1983 Act. Her nearest relative until that time had been her mother, with whom she had had an unhappy and difficult relationship, and whom she now wanted to prevent receiving personal information relating to reviews before the Mental Health Tribunals. The appellant argued that she could not make a Section 29 application herself, and could not compel others to do so on her behalf. The Commission unanimously held the complaint admissible. It was found that the infringement on the applicant's right to respect for her private life was found "not to be necessary in a democratic society" because it was disproportionate to the aim pursued. The single most important factor in the decision was the fact that the list of grounds for changing the nearest relative set out in the Mental Health Act 1983 was exhaustive and precluded the applicant from properly raising her complaint.

Nielsen v Denmark (see above) is also an example of the possibility of conflict between Article 5 and Article 8 rights where the disordered patient is a minor.

6.7. Article 10

An Article 10 claim will often overlap with an Article 8 claim, particularly in a case relating to the right to correspond. Correspondence sent by or to patients may currently be stopped under the provisions of Section 134 of the MHA 1983. The exercise of such power is likely to be in accordance with paragraph 2 of Article 10 which delineates the "right to receive and impart information and ideas". The derogation: "where necessary in the interest of the safety of the

[48] (1977) 10 DR 37
[49] Application No. 2694/95

patient or for the protection of other persons" would therefore it seems be perfectly in accordance with Article 10. Save for this observation, one cannot predict the circumstances in which an Article 10 claim might arise; suffice it to say that the relevant authorities may have to establish the proportionality of these measures when challenged. It will not be enough, in other words, to point to a legitimate justification in Article 10(2) and leave it at that.

6.8. Article 12

Article 12 gives men and women of marriageable age the right to found a family. While restrictions on this right may be properly made for the prevention of disorder or crime, the same reasoning may not apply to those detained under the MHA. It could therefore be argued that a deprivation of the facilities necessary to enjoy conjugal rights may amount to a breach of Article 12. In *X and Y v Switzerland*[50] two fellow prisoners complained of the lack of their right to exercise the right to found a family. The complaint was rejected on the basis that in order to prevent disorder or crime (although what crime was not precisely indicated) such conjugal rights could properly be denied.

It has been persuasively argued by Thorold[51] that a request by a psychiatric patient to enjoy conjugal visits ought to engage a different set of considerations from those raised by prisoners because mental health detention lacks any penal element which, in a prison context, could justify the restriction.

The right to marry and found a family is also of relevance in cases where the authorities seek to sterilise a mental patient, as in, for example, *Re F* (above, N. 5), although in such cases it will almost always be the case that the patient does not have the capacity to enter into a contract of marriage, and consequently there is no corresponding right which requires protection.

6.9. Article 14

"The enjoyment of rights and freedoms set forth in the Convention shall be secured without discrimination on any ground".

If in practice a provision of the MHA noticeably discriminates against a person on any ground then there is again the possibility of challenge. The Expert Committee in its draft proposals regards the principle of non-discrimination as central to the proper treatment and care of those suffering from mental disorder, particularly when that provision is under compulsion. It has however provisionally concluded against recommending that it be included as an express principle within the Act itself. As the Committee reports there is:

---

[50] (1981) 4 EHRR 139
[51] Implications of the Convention for UK Mental Health Legislation (1996) EHRLR 634

"Immense difficulty in incorporating a principle of non-discrimination on grounds of mental disorder at the start of an Act which then proceeds to empower the relevant authorities to compel individuals essentially on grounds of mental disorder. Instead the Committee would recommend:

"(i) that the principle be given considerable emphasis within the Code of Practice;

(ii) that government be invited to address the issue of non-discrimination in relation to such areas as employment, travel, insurance, housing and education".

It seems likely that the relevance of any future Article 14 challenge will probably relate to these specific areas of service provision rather than the mental health treatment itself.

7. CAPACITY AND CONSENT

In *St George's Healthcare NHS Trust v S*,[52] the Court of Appeal considered the case of a mother who refused to consent to an induced birth which was in the best interests of both herself and her child. In considering the status of the viable fetus the crucial question was said to be:

"If human life is sacred why is a mother entitled to refuse to undergo treatment if this would preserve the life of the foetus without damaging her own?" [per Judge LJ at 688c]

The tension between the mother's right to self-determination and the interests of the fetus had been considered in the earlier case of *Re MB (an adult: medical treatment)*.[53] On that occasion the Court held that, had the mother been competent for the purposes of refusing consent, medical intervention would not have been lawful for the protection of the interests of the unborn child, even at the point of birth.

In *Re MB* the mother had not been competent to give consent, but in *S* the mother was able to give articulate oral and written instructions explaining the grounds upon which she refused treatment and demonstrating that she understood the medical advice that she had been given. The inference drawn by those treating her was that a woman refusing treatment in such circumstances must be suffering from a mental disorder. The Court felt it possible that she had. However, this was clearly not the reason for her admission and the question of whether any such disorder justified her detention had not been considered. It was held that the right of a pregnant woman to autonomy and self-determination was not diminished merely because she acted in a way that appeared to be morally repugnant. Whilst pregnancy increases a woman's personal responsibilities, it does not diminish the right to decide whether or not to undergo medical treatment.

[52] [1997] 2 ECR 541
[53] Ibid

It is worthwhile to consider what would have been the impact of incorporation on these decisions. Undoubtedly Article 8 of the Convention incorporates the right of self-determination. That right has been stated by Lord Justice Butler-Sloss in *Re MB* in the following terms:

> "A competent woman who has the capacity to decide may for religious reasons, other reasons, or no reasons at all, choose not to have medical intervention even though the consequences may be death or severe handicap to the child she bears or her own death".

There is however the possibility of a conflict with the unborn child's possible Article 2 right to life. The Strasbourg authorities have not yet had to decide the question of whether Article 2 protects the unborn child at all, although they have indicated that in certain circumstances the fetus has an interest worthy of protection under the Convention. Unfortunately they have not yet specified those circumstances.

In *Paton v UK*,[54] the applicant was a husband who, having failed to obtain an injunction to prevent the termination of his wife's pregnancy, argued that the Abortion Act 1967 which authorised the termination of his wife's pregnancy violated Article 2. It was declared by the Commission that the right to life of the fetus was not absolute and that since abortion at ten weeks was authorised by the Abortion Act 1967 and was in accordance with the wishes of the mother to avoid injury, termination did not contravene Article 2(1).

The issue was considered again in the unreported case of *H v Norway*.[55] Here the question again was whether termination was lawful under the relevant Abortion Act (the fetus was fourteen weeks old). It was held that each had a wide discretion as to what age a fetus could be lawfully aborted, and that termination at fourteen weeks was within that discretion. However, the Commission did state that it could not exclude the possibility of protection for the unborn child under Article 2(1).

There are grounds for arguing that since a thirty six week old fetus is sufficiently developed both physically and mentally to be able to survive and have a worthwhile life independently of its mother, then such a fetus has a right to life which ought to be protected under Article 2. Such a right should outweigh unreasonable or irrational refusal by a mother exercising her Article 8 right of self-determination.

In *MB* Lord Justice Butler-Sloss noted the contradictory state of the law in this area:

> "Although it might seem illogical that a child capable of being born alive is protected by the criminal law from intentional destruction and by the Abortion Act from termination otherwise than as permitted by the Act but it is not protected from the (irrational) decision of a competent mother not to allow medical intervention to avert the risk of death, this appears to be the present state of the law".

[54] [1980] 3 EHRR 408
[55] (1990) (No. 17004/90)

There is also much force in an observation made by Major J in his dissenting judgment in *Winnipeg Child and Family Services (Northwest Area) v G*:[56]

"Where the harm is so great and the temporary remedy so slight, the law is compelled to act . . . someone must speak for those who cannot speak for themselves".

Logic would seem to require that the rights which are accorded to a fetus, or a child notwithstanding his lack of capacity, should also be accorded to the mentally incapacitated adult.

The definition of incapacity, and in particular some of the practical fears raised by the *Bournewood* case referred to earlier in this chapter, is a subject to which the Expert Committee on Mental Health Act reform have given considerable thought. As the Committee states:

"Exactly what constitutes incapacity varies. Different levels of capacity apply to different tasks, writing a will, for example, or giving consent to hazardous treatments, and different legal interpretations apply in different contexts, the concept of criminal capacity, for example. Capacity will also vary according to how much information a person is given and how much support is made available. Finally capacity will vary in any one individual, both over the years and according to the severity of his or her disorder at the time".

The Law Commission has stated that it favours a presumption against lack of capacity, and this presumption is endorsed by the Expert Committee. A presumption against lack of capacity gives priority to an individual's autonomy. However, when one is dealing with mental patients who suffer a degree of incapacity and may be heavily sedated by medication, it is often the case that compliance or lack of complaint is taken for consent. Thus in *Bournewood*, the "informal" patient was incapacitated but compliant to the treatment he received. In a less severe case it could be said that a presumption in favour of a patient having capacity might lead to continued detention which was arguably in breach of his right not to be deprived of his liberty (i.e. had a substitute decision-maker been appointed to intervene and oppose continued detention on the ground that the patient lacked capacity to consent, but that continued treatment was not in his best interests).

Under the Law Commission's definition a person lacks capacity in essentially two situations:

(1) when unable to understand or retain the information relevant to taking the decision;
(2) when able to understand the relevant information but prevented by his or her mental disability from using that information to arrive at a choice.

This definition is consonant with the decision of the Court of Appeal in *Re MB*. However, the Expert Committee have suggested a broader definition which includes those who do *not* lack intellectual capacity but nonetheless reach deci-

---

[56] (1997) 3 BHRC 611

sions they would not have reached had they been suffering from the disorder. Such a broad definition would seem not to clarify what is a difficult category analysis but only to encourage argument.

Yet the way in which incapacity is defined is obviously of crucial importance because it determines the ambit of treatment without consent which would otherwise be a trespass. When a patient is treated without consent he or she is treated, on the approval of psychiatric and medical opinion under a compulsory order which should respect his or her best interests. The best interests decision is therefore a decision made in substitution for the incapacitated patient's. That decision should recognise such human rights as the patient would have but for the incapacity from which he or she suffers (the principle of non-discrimination), but must also reflect the fact that the patient is under compulsion precisely because he or she suffers from incapacity.

The Law Commission who have done much work in this area has produced proposals on best interests treatment which emphasise the need to take into account:

(a) the ascertainable past and present wishes of the person concerned and the factors that person would consider if able to do so;

(b) the need to permit the person to participate as far as possible or to improve his or her ability to participate;

(c) the views of other people whom it is appropriate and practicable to consult about the person's wishes and felling and what would be in the person's best interests;

(d) whether the proposed treatment is the least invasive and restrictive alternative.

It is to be hoped that a new Mental Health Act will incorporate these proposals.

8. CONCLUSIONS

The above examples demonstrate a number of ways in which a challenge may be made to detention under the Mental Health Act 1983 or at common law, and the principles relevant for determining whether or not a violation of the European Convention on Human Rights has occurred. It must at the very least be arguable that incorporation would necessitate a different result in the case of *Bournewood* on exactly the same facts, firstly because, if L was "detained" in the wider sense of being deprived of his liberty, then he was entitled to the minimum basic procedural safeguards of speedy access to a court to ensure the validity of his continued detention. Secondly, as Lord Irvine has recently stressed, the courts will no longer have to find an ambiguity in order to depart from the canons of statutory construction and uphold Convention rights:

"On the contrary the Courts will be required to interpret the legislation so as to uphold the Convention rights unless legislation itself is so clearly incompatible with the Convention that it is impossible to do so".[57]

In that case the radical reinterpretation of Section 131(1) of the Mental Health Act 1983 to distinguish between informal and voluntary patients, for which the appellant in *Bournewood* contended, may well become permissible.

As can be seen from the particular problems highlighted above, much work needs to be done to ensure a new Mental Health Act is Convention compliant. The peculiarly vulnerable state of mental patients, and the need to give them proper protection of their human rights, notwithstanding that in many cases they lack the capacity necessary for true autonomy, make this developing area of law fertile ground for rights based argument.

---

[57] "The Development of Human Rights in Britain under an Incorporated Convention on Human Rights" [1998] *PL* 121

13

Bibliography and Guide to Sources

OWAIN THOMAS

1. GENERAL TEXTBOOKS AND REFERENCE BOOKS

P. Alston, M. Bustelo and J. Heenan, *The EU and Human Rights* (Oxford, OUP, 1999)

C. Baker, *Human Rights Act 1998: A Practitioner's Guide* (London, Sweet & Maxwell, 1998)

E. Barendt, *Freedom of Speech* (Oxford, Clarendon Press, 1987)

P. Birkinshaw, *Freedom of Information* (London, Butterworths, 1996)

C. Boyle and M. Anderson, *Human Rights Approaches to Environmental Protection* (Oxford, Clarendon Press, 1996)

A. Clapham, *Human Rights in the Private Sphere* (Oxford, Clarendon Press, 1996)

L. Clements, *European Human Rights: Taking a Case Under the Convention* (2nd Edition) (London, Sweet & Maxwell, 1999).

J. Coppel, *The Human Rights Act 1998: Enforcing the European Convention in the Domestic Courts* (London, Wiley, 1999)

B. Dickson, *Human Rights and the European Convention* (London, Sweet & Maxwell, 1997)

E. Ellis, *The Principle of Proportionality in the Laws of Europe* (Oxford, Hart Publishing, 1999)

D. Feldman, *Civil Liberties and Human Rights in England and Wales* (Oxford, Clarendon Press, 1993)

D.J. Harris, M. O'Boyle and C. Warbrick, *Law of the European Convention on Human Rights* (London, Butterworths, 1995)

D.J. Harris and S. Joseph, *The International Covenant on Civil and Political Rights and United Kingdom Law* (Oxford, OUP, 1995)

M. Hunt, *Using Human Rights Law in English Courts* (Oxford, Hart Publishing, 1997)

M. Hunt and Rabinder Singh (eds), *A Practitioner's Guide to the Impact of the Human Rights Act* (Oxford, Hart Publishing, 1998)

F. Jacobs and R. White, *The European Convention of Human Rights* (Oxford, OUP, 1996)

M. Janis, R.Kaye and A. Bradley, *European Human Rights Law* (Oxford, OUP, 1996

P. Kempees, *A Systematic Guide to the Case – Law of the European Court of Human Rights*, 1960–1996 (three volumes) (Martinus Nijhoff, 1998)

A. Le Sueur, J. Herberg and R. English, *Principles of Public Law* (London, Cavendish, 1999)

Lord Lester and D. Pannick, *Human Rights Law and Practice* (London, Butterworths, 1999)

Liberty, *Liberating Cyberspace* (London, Pluto Press, 1999)

B. Markesinis, *Protecting Privacy* (Oxford, Clarendon Press, 1999)

J.G. Merrills, *The Development of International Law by the European Court of Human Rights* (Manchester University Press, 1993)

K. Reid, *A Practitioner's Guide to the European Convention of Human Rights* (London, Sweet & Maxwell, 1998)

R. Singh, *The Future of Human Rights in the United Kingdom* (Oxford, Hart Publishing, 1997)

K. Starmer and S. Sedley, *European Human Rights Law* (London, Legal Action Group, 1999)

R. Toulson, *Confidentiality*, Toulson and Phipps eds., (London, Sweet & Maxwell, 1996)

P. Van Dijk, *Theory and Practice of the European Convention on Human Rights* (3rd Edition) (Kluwer Law International, 1998)

J. Wadham and H. Mountfield, *The Human Rights Act 1998: Blackstone's Guide* (London, 1998)

C.G. Weeramantry, *Justice Without Frontiers: Protecting Human Rights in the Age of Technology* (Two Volumes) (Kluwer Law International, 1998)

P. Wetterstein, *Harm to the Environment: the Right to Compensation and the Assessment of Damages* (Oxford, Clarendon Press, 1997)

2. COURT REPORTS

The official series of court judgments is published by the German publishers, Carl Heymanns Verlag in series A up to and including 1995 (Nos.1–338) and since 1996 in yearly volumes of reports published as *Reports of Judgments and Decisions*.

European Human Rights Reports are published by Sweet and Maxwell and begin in 1979. The first volume contains nearly all the judgments of the court prior to this date and this series is therefore very comprehensive.

Judgments since October 1996 and up to date information, including pending cases, can be found on the Internet at – www.dhcour.cor.fr.

3. COMMISSION REPORTS

Commission cases are published in numerical volumes from 1955 to 1974 as *Collection of Decisions* and since 1974 as *Decisions and Reports*. These contain selected admissibility decisions of the Commission, reports of Friendly Settlements and merits reports of the Commission in cases decided by the Committee's ministers. It should be noted that the volumes of *Collection of Decisions* i.e. cases pre-1975, are likely to be of historical significance only today.

Since 1981 the *European Human Rights Reports* have contained certain important Commission decisions which appear at the end of each volume of these reports.

Commission cases are found on the Internet at – www.dhcommhr.coe.fr.

4. OTHER REPORTS

The Digest of Strasbourg Case Law relating to the European Convention on Human Rights from 1984 onwards is a joint project run by the Council of Europe and the University of Utrecht. It contains a digest of case law by reference to the Convention Articles. It is also published by Carl Heymanns Verlag.

The *Yearbook of the European Convention on Human Rights* contains some Commission decisions on admissibility as well as institutional information.

Butterworths Human Rights Cases includes cases heard by the European Court of Human Rights as well as many other international courts such as the US Supreme Court, the South African Constitutional Court and the Inter American Commission on Human Rights.

5. OTHER NATIONAL AND INTERNATIONAL JURISDICTIONS

Given that by virtue of Section 2(1) of the Human Rights Act 1998 the domestic courts will be required to *"take into account"* Strasbourg jurisprudence, and in turn Strasbourg jurisprudence is informed by the state of the law in other Contracting States, it will become necessary to use the law of those other Contracting States when relevant when pursuing a human rights case. Other materials likely to be relevant include:

International Human Rights Reports. This is an international series covering decisions from major human rights treaty areas.

Council of Europe materials (including parliamentary assembly, Committee of Ministers, Committee for the Prevention of Torture)

Case law of the European Court of Justice

European Parliament recommendations

Other European and International Treaty Provisions

6. TRAVAUX PREPARATOIRES

These are published by the Council of Europe but in practice are unlikely to provide significant assistance given that they do not in general give guidance on points of construction which are likely to arise today. Perhaps more importantly the principle of interpretation whereby the Convention is interpreted as a living instrument means that the original intention is by now much less significant.

7. JOURNALS

European Human Rights Law Review (Sweet and Maxwell Ed. Emmerson)
A number of the traditional domestic law journals contain articles of relevance such as the Modern Law Review, the Law Quarterly Review and the Oxford Journal of Legal Studies. See for example "Local Authorities, the Duty of Care and the ECHR" (1998) OJLS 1; "Human Rights in the New Millenium" (1998) Med Leg J Vol 67 Pt 1 pp 35–9; "Privacy, Freedom of Expression and the Human Rights Bill: Lessons from Germany" (1999) Markesinis, LQR Vol 115 p 47; "Rights Brought Home for Children" (1999) MLR Vol 63 p 350 (Family Life, Immigration, The Right to Life and Education); "Human Dignity, Human Rights and Human Genetics", Beyleveld and Brownsword (1998) MLR Vol 61 p 661; "Public Authorities under the Human Rights Act 1998", Bamforth (1999) CLJ.

8. CITATIONS

The following is a guide on citation of the more common reports.

A	Series A, publications of the European Court of Human Rights, cases are reported by reference to volume and more specifically by paragraph number.
CD	Collection of decisions of the European Commission of Human Rights, 1959 to 1974, volumes 1 to 46.
DR	Decisions and reports of the European Commission on Human Rights 1975–
EHRR	The European Human Rights reports
EHRR CD	Commission supplement containing summaries and extracts from commission decisions.
Digest	Digest of Strasbourg case law 1984–
YB	The year book of the European Convention on Human Rights.
BHRC	Butterworths Human Rights cases, cited by volume number.
IHRR	International Human Rights reports 1994–

9. PRECEDENT

As has already been discussed there is no formal doctrine of precedent which binds either the Court or the Commission. It is important to bear in mind when preparing a case which is similar to others previously decided by the Court or Commission that the Convention is interpreted as social and cultural conditions evolve. The Court does have the power to depart from a line of authority, but the public interest in legal certainty and consistency militates against doing so.

In terms of the varying weight to be attached to particular decisions, Court judgments are of more importance than decisions of the Commission or the Committee of Ministers. The most authoritative decisions are those of the plenary Court and those decisions which are unanimous or are supported by a large majority are the most persuasive. In relation to decisions on admissibility, these rarely set out the Commission's view on the merits and it should be borne in mind that where the Commission has found a case inadmissible for being manifestly ill-founded, this does not necessarily mean that the point taken is unarguable.

Since November 1998 the Committee of Ministers has not made decisions on the merits and the Commission has ceased to exist. The new system of a Grand Chamber and smaller Chambers means that the Grand Chamber exercising an appellate function will command greater authority than decisions of the smaller Chambers. It also leaves open the possibility that differently constituted smaller Chambers will take different views on similar issues.

Index

Abortion, 122, 123
  horizontal application of human rights
    standards, 68
  information, 68, 122
  Ireland, 68
  margin of appreciation, 122, 123
  mental patients, 232–4
  sexual relationships, right to untroubled, 123
Absolute rights, 19–20
  discrimination, freedom from, 19
  family, right to found, 19
  inhuman or degrading treatment or
    punishment, freedom from, 19
  life, right to, 19
  marry, right to, 19
  retroactive criminal offences and punish-
    ment, freedom from, 19
  slavery, servitude or forced or compulsory
    labour, freedom from, 19
  torture, freedom from, 19
Abuse of power, economic tort of, 97
Access to court,
  absence of national remedy, 37
  construction of right, 37
  costs, *see* Costs
  damages claims, 45–7
  defamation, 40–1
  dispute, requirement for, 35, 37
  economic and social rights, protection of, 36–7
  effective, 37
  essence of right impaired, where, 37
  fact, right in, 37
  high cost of proceedings, 47
  immunity, common law, 15
  judicial separation, 40, 41
  justification for restriction, 37
  lawyer/client confidentiality, 50
  legal aid, *see* Legal aid
  legal professional privilege, 50
  limitation, 149–51
  margin of appreciation, 30–1
  medical negligence, 145–7
  mental patients, 214, 224–5, 227–8
  personal injury cases, 46–7, 145–7
  proportionality of restrictions, 30, 37
  public policy and, 15
  qualified rights, 29, 36, 146
  removal of whole class of claims, 37
  restrictions imposed by State, 37
  security for costs, 49

source of right, 29
  see also Conditional fee agreements; Costs;
    Fair hearing, right to; Fair trial
    guarantees; Legal aid
Access to personal information, 194–5
Adjudication,
  contract, 94
Adoption,
  damages, Strasbourg, 83
  natural father, not consulting, 83
Aerial photographs, 186
AIDS,
  asylum seekers with, 132
  blood transfusions, damages where resulting
    from, 80, 132
  deportation of sufferer, 13, 131, 132
  disclosure of HIV status, 131, 192, 193, 194
  doctors with, confidentiality of, 187n
  fair and public hearing, right to, 132–3
  generally, 131
  immigration controls, 13
  inhuman or degrading treatment, 132
  negligent infection with virus, 80, 131
  private life, interference with, 131–2, 192
  quality of treatment, 131
  right to life, 132
Aircraft noise, 91, 165–6, 179–80, 181
Anton Pillar orders, 19
Appeals,
  equality of arms, 39
  fair trial guarantees, 16, 29
Arbitration,
  contract, 94
Armed forces,
  homosexuality, 74
  occupation of property, 83–4, 91
Arrest,
  force, use of, 98
  liberty and security of the person, right to
    98, *see also* Police
  statement of reasons for, 98
Artificial feeding,
  inhuman or degrading treatment or
    punishment, 109n, 219
  mental patients, 109n, 219
Assault,
  inhuman or degrading treatment or
    punishment, 13
  torture, 13
  see also Battery

Assembly, freedom of, *see* Freedom of assembly
Association, freedom of, *see* Freedom of association
Asylum,
  AIDS sufferers, 132
  family life, right to private, 83
  risk of ill-treatment on return, 19–20, 132

Bailment,
  confidentiality, 186
Bankruptcy proceedings,
  civil proceedings, 35–6
Battery,
  intimate samples, 99
  medical cases, 108n
  mental patients, 105n, 108n
  principles, 108n
  sterilization of mental patients, 108n
  see also Assault
Bill of Rights,
  Hong Kong, 64
  New Zealand, 58, 66–7
  United States, 65
Blood transfusions, AIDS resulting from, 80, 132
Bosnia,
  Serbs in, 13
Breach of confidence,
  confidentiality, 186–9
Breach of contract, inducing, 97
Breach of privilege to legislature,
  criminal proceedings, 33
Breach of trust,
  confidentiality, 186
Bringing claim, *see* Claim, bringing and defending Convention
Broadcasting Complaints Commission Code of Practice, 185, 186
Business premises,
  home, respect for, 17, 91

Caesarean section, enforced, 122
Canada,
  horizontal application of human rights standards, 64
Capacity,
  mental patients, 110n, 209, 213–16, 232–5
Care proceedings,
  confidentiality, 193
  damages, Strasbourg, 83
    denial of participation in proceedings, 80
  denial of participation in, damages for, 80
  family life, right to private, 83
Cause of action,
  incompatible acts, *see* Incompatible acts
CCTV, use of, 99, 156
Certiorari, 8
CFA, *see* Conditional fee agreement

Chemical hazards, 143, 163, 167
Child abuse,
  damages, 85
  inhuman or degrading treatment or punishment, 62
Child minders, 142
Civil Procedure Rules 1998,
  claim, bringing and defending Convention, 103
  jurisdiction, 105n
  litigant in person, 52
  overriding objective, 47
  public hearing, 152–3
  threshold for bringing proceedings in High Court, 111
  value of claim, 105n
Civil proceedings,
  access to court,
    proper participation before tribunal, 42–3
  bankruptcy proceedings, 35–6
  basis of right, 35
  classification as, 33, 34–6
  criminal proceedings distinguished, 33
  defamation, 41
  detention in context of, 50–1
  "directly decisive" proceedings, 35, 36
  disciplinary proceedings, 35
  examples, 34–6
  judicial separation, 40, 41
  justifiable issues, 36
  legal aid, 39–44
    arbitrary refusal, 42
    damages claims, 45–7
    defamation, 41
    detention in context of, 50–1
    excluded categories, 40–2
    financial criteria, 41
    frivolous cases, 42
    institute proceedings, right to, 39–40
    limited resources, 42
    margin of appreciation, 46
    merits of claim, 41
    opponent in receipt of legal aid, 43
    police accountability, 41
    pre-trial applications, 40
    proper participation before tribunal, 42–3
    proportionality, 45
    prospect of success, no reasonable, 42
    qualified right, 45
    relevant criteria, 40
    repeated applications, ban on, 43
    restrictions on right, 42–3
    riskiness of case, 41
    separation proceedings, 40
    stakes involved, 40
    status of opposing party, 43
    unfair dismissal application, 41
    vexatious applications, 42

nature of dispute, 35
private persons, rights and obligations
    between, 35
proper participation before tribunal, 42–3
public rights distinguished, 33–6
purpose of proceedings, 35
remoteness in effect, 34
social insurance cases, 34, 36
unfair dismissal application, 41
see also Access to court; Civil Procedure
    Rules 1998; Conditional fee agreements;
    Costs; Fair hearing, right to; Fair trial
    guarantees; Legal aid
Civil rights and obligations,
civil servants' employment, 34
health insurance benefits, 34
meaning, 14, 34–5
social insurance, 34, 36
see also Civil proceedings; Fair trial
    guarantees; Hearing, right to fair
Civil service employment,
civil rights and obligations, 34
public rights, 36
right of access to, 18
Claim, bringing and defending Convention
claim in domestic proceedings, 103–17
Civil Procedure Rules 1998, 103
compensation, 111
Convention claim rights, particulars of
    breach of, 108–11
damages, 111
generally, 103
inhuman or degrading treatment, 109–10
judicial review, 103, 105n
jurisdiction, 105n
leave to bring proceedings, 111
liberty and security of person,
    defence, 114
particulars of claim, 108–9
limitation, 111, 116
mental health case study, 103–17
    Convention claim rights, particulars of
        breach of, 108–11
    defence, 112–17
    facts of case, 104
    limitation, 111, 116
    negligence, particulars of, 107–8
    particulars of claim, 105–12
    Statement of Truth, 112, 117
negligence, particulars of, 107–8
particulars of claim, 105–12
private life, respect for,
    defence, 115
    particulars of claim, 110–11
Statement of Truth, 112, 117
value of claim, 105n
vicarious liability, 109n
victims, 108n

Codes of Practice,
Broadcasting Complaints Commission, 185,
    186
confidentiality, 185
Press Complaints Commission, 185
Committee for the Elimination of Racial
Discrimination (CERD), 64
Committee of Ministers,
decisions of, 6
Common law,
development, 59–60
Human Rights Act, application of 59,
    89–101, *see also under individual*
    headings e.g., Medical negligence;
    Trespass
safeguarding rights through, 1, 3
Companies,
confidentiality claims against, 191
damages, 78
environmental rights complained of by, 166
inspector's reports, 14
shares as property rights, 18
Comparative law,
Canada, 65
Germany, 67
Hong Kong, 64
Ireland, 67–8
Netherlands, 67
New Zealand, 66–7
South Africa, 66
United States, 65–6
Compensation, *see* Damages
Compulsory labour, 13
Compulsory purchase, 174–5
Conditional fee agreements, 44–7
cases not running on, 44
draft funding code, 44–5
high cost cases, 44, 45
Legal Services Commission (LSC), 44
public interest cases, 45
Thai Trading agreement, 46
see also Legal aid
Confidentiality,
access to personal information, 194–5
aerial photographs, 186
bailment, 186
breach of confidence, 186–9
breach of trust, 186
Broadcasting Complaints Commission Code
    of Practice, 185, 186
business confidentiality, 190–2
care proceedings, 193
class of claimants, 187
Codes of Practice, 185
companies, claims against, 191
contract, 186
data protection, 185
disclosure of private information, 192–4

Confidentiality (*cont.*):
  fiduciary duty, 186
  freedom of expression, 17, 195–8
    confidence, information received in, 197–8
    generally, 195–6
    impartiality of judiciary, 196–7
    journalistic sources, 197–8
    limitations on right, 195–6
    national security, 197
    rights of others, 197–8
  good faith, 186
  HIV status, 131, 192, 193, 194
  impact of Convention, 198–200
  interception of telephone calls, 191
  journalistic sources, 197–8
  legal professional privilege, 188
  litigation privilege, 188
  malicious falsehood, 185
  medical records, 25–6
  mutuality of interests, 187
  national security, 197
  nineteenth century, in, 186
  nuisance, 185, 186
  police interviews, information obtained
      during, 188–9
  privacy under common law, 185–9
    bailment, 186
    breach of confidence, 186–9
    breach of trust, 186
    class of claimants, 187
    Codes of Practice, 185
    contract, 186
    data protection, 185
    fiduciary duty, 186
    good faith, 186
    legal professional privilege, 188
    litigation privilege, 188
    malicious falsehood, 185
    mutuality of interests, 187
    nineteenth century, in, 186
    nuisance, 185, 186
    police interviews, information obtained
        during, 188–9
    public domain, information in, 187, 199
    public interest, 187–8
    relationship of confidence, 188–9
    tort, 186
    trespass, 185
    unjust enrichment, 186
  private life under Article 8, interference
      with, 189–95
    access to personal information, 194–5
    business confidentiality, 190–2
    care proceedings, 193
    companies, claims against, 191
    disclosure of private information, 192–4
    generally, 189–90
    HIV status, 192, 193, 194

    impact of Convention, 198–200
    interception of telephone calls, 191
    legitimate aims, 193–4
    nature of obligation, 190
    police immunity, 189
    positive obligation, 190
    private life, 190
    psychiatric reports, 193
    purpose of law, 189
  psychiatric reports, 193
  public domain, information in, 187, 199
  public interest, 187–8
  relationship of confidence, 188–9
  tort, 186
  trespass, 185
  unjust enrichment, 186
  windows in neighbouring property, placing,
      186
  see also Defamation
Conspiracy, 97
Constitutional tort, emergence of, 55
Contempt of court, 14
  criminal proceedings, 33
  freedom of expression, 58
Contract,
  adjudication, 94
  arbitration, 94
  confidentiality, 186
  effect of HRA on claims involving, 94
  interference with, 97
  property rights, 94
Convention rights,
  absolute rights, *see* Absolute rights
  definition, 5
  duty to protect, 60–1
  impact, 9
  interpretation, *see* Interpretation of
      Convention rights
  particulars of claim, 108–11
  positive obligations, 60–1
  qualified rights, *see* Qualified rights
  rationale, 29
  unqualified rights, 19, *see also* Absolute
      rights
Conversion,
  unlawful interference with goods, 95
Corporal punishment,
  horizontal application of human rights
      standards, 62
  inhuman or degrading treatment or
      punishment, 13, 62
  torture, 13
Correspondence, respect for,
  damages, 99
  economic value, 99
  freedom of expression, 17
  interference, 17, 98–9
  mental patients, 229–30

nature of right, 17
police, 98–9
qualification to rights, 17
qualified rights, 20
telephone tapping, 21–2
Costs,
  access to court, 47–50
    high costs, 47
    security for costs, 49
    wasted costs orders, 49–50
  Convention cases, 48
  general rules, 47–8
  generally, 29
  high cost of proceedings, 47
  security for, 49
  wasted costs orders, 49–50
  see also Conditional fee agreements; Legal
    aid
Courts,
  incompatible acts, 7
  provision of, 32
  public authority, 7, 16, 57–8
Courts martial, 33
Criminal offences,
  remand in custody for accused, 14
  retroactive, 16, 19
Criminal proceedings,
  breach of privilege to legislature, 33
  civil proceedings distinguished, 33
  classification as, 33
  contempt of court, 33
  courts martial, 33
  disciplinary proceedings not, 33
  Engel criteria, 33
  equality of arms, 39
  hearing, right to fair, 33
  legal aid, 45
  liberty and security of the person, right to,
    13
  meaning, 33
  orderly conduct, sanctions to ensure, 33
  penalty, 33
Cross-examination,
  denial of, damages for, 80
  equality of arms, 38
  see also Access to court; Conditional fee
    agreements; Costs; Fair hearing, right
    to; Fair trial guarantees; Legal aid

Damages,
  adoption, 83
  AIDS resulting from blood transfusions, 80
  care proceedings, 80, 83
  claims,
    access to court, 45–7
    bringing and defending Convention in
      domestic proceedings, 111
    legal aid, 45–7

constitutional rights and, 85–6
correspondence, respect for, 99
cross-examination, denial of, 80
deportation, 79
discretion to grant, 71
due process, denial of, 80–2
duty of care, common law, 85
European Court of Human Rights, *see*
  Strasbourg awards *below*
extradition, 79
fair trial guarantees, 78, 80–2
family life, right to private, 83
feelings, injury to, 81–2
hearing, right to fair, 85
Human Rights Act 1998, 84–7
  absence of duty, 84–5
  child abuse, 85
  common law duty of care, 85
  duty of care, 85
  no existing tort, 84
  present position, 84–5
  privacy, 84
inhuman and degrading treatment, 79
legal representation lacking, 81
liberty and security of the person, right to,
  79
loss of earnings, 78
New Zealand, 86
opportunity, loss of, 81
pecuniary damage,
  Strasbourg awards, 77–8
private life, interference with,
  Human Rights Act 1998, 84
  Strasbourg awards, 82
public hearing, lack of, 81
quantum, assessment of, 8
race discrimination, 2–3
rape, 79
refuse, refusal of grant to dump, 81
right to life, 78
SAS Gibraltar shootings, 78
self-incrimination privilege, denial of, 77
sexual abuse, 82
Strasbourg awards, 76–84
  adoption, 83
  AIDS resulting from blood transfusions,
    80
  building interests, 77
  care proceedings, 80, 83
  companies, 78
  cross-examination, denial of, 80
  deportation, 79
  domestic proceedings, influence on,
    81–2
  due process, denial of, 80–2
  extradition, 79
  fair trial guarantees, 78, 80–2
  fair trial rights, 78

Damages (*cont.*):
  family life, right to private, 83
  feelings, injury to, 81–2
  generally, 71–2, 76
  home, respect for, 83
  inhuman and degrading treatment, 79
  legal representation lacking, 81
  liberty and security of the person, right to,
    79
  loss of earnings, 78
  no real damage suffered, 84
  non-pecuniary damage, 78–84
  opportunity, loss of, 81
  pecuniary damage, 77–8
  planning cases, 77
  police custody, assault whilst in, 79
  private life, interference with, 82
  property rights, interference with, 83–4
  public hearing, lack of, 81
  rape, 79
  refuse, refusal of grant to dump, 81
  rejection of claim, reasons for, 84
  right to life, 78
  SAS Gibraltar shootings, 78
  self-incrimination privilege, denial of, 77
  sexual abuse, 82
  speculative cases, 81
Data protection,
  confidentiality, 185
  interception of communications, 191
  see also Confidentiality
Debts, ownership of,
  property rights, 18
Deceit, 97
Declaration of incompatibility,
  application, 75
  availability, 6, 8
  controversial legislation, 75
  continuing operation of offending provision,
    75
  effect, 8, 75
  enforcement of offending provision, 75
  fast track amendment procedure, 8, 75
  horizontal application of human rights
    standards, 59
  interpretative obligation, 75
  joinder of Crown, 75
  political effect, 8
  power to make, 8, 59
  prevention of terrorism, 75–76
  procedure, 75
  rationale, 74–5
  Remedial Order, 8, 75
  satellite legislation to primary legislation, 76
  White Paper *Rights Brought Home*, 74
Declarations (judicial review), 8, 71
Defamation,
  access to court, 40–1

accurate information disclosed, 201
  civil right, 201
  common law, 201
    defences, 201–3
  damage, 201
  defences, 201–3
  development of law, 57
  fair and accurate coverage, 201–2
  fair comment defence, 202
  fair trial, right to, 203–4
  freedom of expression, 17, 200–3, 204–6
    common law defences, 201–3
    relevant articles, 200
  impact of Convention, 206–7
  legal aid, 40–1, 201
  malice, 202
  privilege, 202
  qualified privilege, 202, 203, 204
  relevant articles, 200
  United States, 65
  see also Confidentiality
Defending claim, *see* Claim, bringing and
  defending Convention
Delay,
  hearing, right to fair, 32
  release of mental patients, 226–7
Deportation,
  AIDS sufferer, 13, 131, 132
  asylum, entitlement to, 19–20
  damages, 79
  fair trial guarantees, 14
  family life, right to private, 14, 83
  inhuman or degrading treatment or
    punishment, 87, 132
  interim order, 79
  liberty and security of the person, right to,
    13, 14, 87
  unborn child threatened by mother's, 122
Deprivation of liberty, *see* Liberty and security
  of the person, right to
Deprivation of property, *see* Peaceful
  enjoyment of possessions
Detention,
  arbitrary, 98
  criminals detained in psychiatric wings, 220
  false imprisonment, 14, 98, 215
  lawful, 51, 108n
  liberty and security of the person, right to,
    13, 14, 51, 108–9, 114, 215–16, 220–224,
    226–7, 228
  meaning, 221–2
  medical treatment, 145
  mental patients, 107n, 108n, 109n
    access to court, 214, 224–5, 227–8
    Bolam test, 140, 213, 215
    capable of treatment, condition, 217–18
    capacity, 109–10, 213–16, 232–4
    challenge, likely areas of, 225–32

common law, 212–16
compliant patients, 213–14
conditions of lawful detention, 108n
consent, 109–10, 115, 213–16, 232–4
criminals detained in psychiatric wings,
    220
emergency, 224–5
failure to obtain prior medical report, 226
false imprisonment, 215
lawful detention, 223–4
legal aid, 46, 51
liberty and security of the person, right to,
    13, 14, 51, 108–9, 114, 215–16, 220–4,
    226–7, 228
meaning of detention, 221–3
medical treatment, 145
MHA, under, 216–17
necessity, doctrine of, 212–16
proportionality, 214–15
public, protection of, 217, 218–19
reform proposals, 211, 214
restraints, 219–20
sterilization, 212–13
time take to determine legality, 109, 114,
    116
unsound mind, lawful detention of
    persons of, 108n, 223–4
without treatment, 217–24
PACE 1984, 98
police, 97–8
seclusion, in,
    inhuman or degrading treatment or
    punishment, 13
solitary confinement, 98
see also Liberty and security of the person,
    right to
Dicey, 9
Disciplinary proceedings,
    civil proceedings, 35
    courts martial, 33
    criminal proceedings, not, 33
    fair hearing, right to, 33, 127–9
    legal aid, 44
    public authority, 7
Disclosure of journalistic sources,
    freedom of expression, 197–8
    "newspaper rule", 15
Discrimination,
    absolute right to freedom from, 19
    Committee for the Elimination of Racial
        Discrimination (CERD), 64
    common law protection, 18
    environmental rights, 172, 181–2
    family, right to found, 130
    freedom from, 18, 19
    health care provision, 125
    horizontal application of human rights
        standards, 60

International Convention on the Elimination
    of all forms of Racial Discrimination,
    63
landlord and tenant, 93
mental patients, 110n, 231–2
possession proceedings, 93
private parties, by, 63–4
race, *see* Race discrimination
statutory protection, 18
UN Human Rights Committee, 63
Duty of care, common law,
    damages, 85

Economic torts, 97
Education, right to, 19
Effective remedy, right to, 72–4
    access to court, 37
    environmental rights, 180–1
    inquests, 129
    police, against, 97
Elections, right to free, 19
Emergency control orders, food safety, 96
Emergency terrorist measures,
    Ireland, 23
    margin of appreciation, 23
Environmental rights,
    aircraft noise, 91, 165, 179–80, 181
    arsenic poisoning, 167
    chemical hazards, notification of, 143, 163,
        167–8
    companies, claims by, 166
    compulsory purchase, 174–5
    discrimination, 172, 181–2
    effective remedy, right to, 180–1
    enforcement notices, 177–9
    fair and public hearing, 175–80
        administrative decisions, 177–8
        civil rights, 175–7
        directly decisive decisions, 175–6
        enforcement notices, 177–9
        generally, 175
        independent and impartial tribunal, 177–9
        operation of provisions, 175
        procedural safeguards, 179–80
    family life, right to private, 160, 168–70
    freedom of association, 182–3
    freedom of expression, 182–3
    generally, 159
    gypsies, 169
    home, respect for, 160, 164–71
    information, right to receive, 143, 162–3,
        167, 168
    inhuman or degrading treatment or
        punishment, 164
    judicial review, 170
    legitimate aims, 170
    margin of appreciation, 170
    minorities and cultural rights, 169

Environmental rights (*cont.*):
  nitrate concentrations, 173
  no express right under Convention, 160
  nuclear testing, 34, 168
  peaceful enjoyment of possessions, 171–5
    availability of compensation, 172
    combination of Articles, claims under a,
      172–3
    control and possession distinguished, 172
    nitrate concentrations, 173
    planning decisions, 171
    "possessions", 171–2
    qualified right, 171
  pig farms, 166
  planning, 77, 171–3
  planning blight, 174–5
  pollution, 165–7
  predictions, 183–4
  pressing social needs, 170, 171
  private life, interference with, 160, 164–71
  procedural rights, 175–83
    discrimination, 181–2
    effective remedy, right to, 180–1
    fair trial, 175–80
  property rights, see peaceful enjoyment of
      possessions *above*
  proportionality, 170, 171
  right to life, 162–4
  sources of law, 160–1
  South Africa, 160
  substantive rights, 162–75
    inhuman or degrading treatment or
      punishment, 164
    peaceful enjoyment of possessions, 171–5
    private life, interference with, 160, 164–71
    right to life, 162–4
  victim requirement, 161–2
  waste management licences, 177
  waste treatment plants, 165–6
Equality of arms,
  access to facilities, 38
  appeal, 39
  circumstances of, 38
  civil proceedings, 38
  criminal proceedings, 39
  cross-examination, 38
  disadvantage, placing at a, 804
  examples of violation, 38–9
  knowledge of evidence, 38–9
  legal aid, 39, 43
  meaning, 15–16
  medical negligence, 147–9
  "newspaper rule", 15
  participation in process, 38
  personal injury cases, 147–9
  principles, 39
  reasonable opportunity to present case, 39
  requirement, 33, 38–9

  right to, 33, 38–9
  scope, 38
European Commission of Human Rights,
  approach, 61–4
  case law, 60, 61–4
  decisions of, 6
European Convention on Human Rights, 11
  construction of Articles, 10
  drafting, 3
  incorporation, see Incorporation of
    Convention
  "living instrument", as, 7, 10–11
  protected rights 11–19, *see also under
    individual headings*
  ratification, 5
  scope of rights protected by, 10
  see also Convention rights *and under
    individual headings e.g. Freedom of
    expression*
European Court of Human Rights, 11
  approach, 61–4
  case law, 60, 61–4
  decisions of, 6
  interpretative approach, 11, 60
  jurisprudence, 11–19
  obligation of English courts to follow, 11
  practicable and effective safeguards, 11
  right to life, 10, 11–12
Euthanasia, 121
Eviction, 92–3
  home, respect for, 17
Executions, 120
Experimental medical treatment, 144–5
Experimental treatment,
  medical negligence, 13
Expression, freedom of, *see* Confidentiality;
    Defamation; Freedom of expression
Extradition,
  damages, 79
  death penalty, to face,
    inhuman or degrading treatment or
      punishment, 13
    liberty and security of the person, right to,
      13, 14

Fair and public hearing,
  absence of national remedy, 37
  AIDS sufferers, 132–3
  civil proceedings, 32
  civil rights, 33–6
    civil/criminal divide, 33
    courts martial, 33
    courts, provision of, 32
    criminal proceedings, 33
      damages, 85
  Strasbourg, 77–8, 80–82
  defamation, 203–4
  delay, 32

disciplinary proceedings, 33, 127–9
diversity in national practice, 31
entitlement, 16, 32
environmental rights, 175–80
    administrative decisions, 177–8
    civil rights, 175–7
    directly decisive decisions, 175–6
    enforcement notices, 177–9
    generally, 175
    independent and impartial tribunal, 177–9
    operation of provisions, 175
    procedural safeguards, 179–80
equality of arms, *see* Equality of arms
generally, 32, 52
horizontal effect of HRA, 57
interpretation, 32
investigations, police, 101
legal aid, provision of, 32
margin of appreciation, 31, 152
mental health, 210, 228–9
oral hearing, 33, 38, 151
planning applications, 36
possession proceedings, 93
private hearings, 152
pronouncement of judgment in public, 151
public rights, 36
test of, 38
translators, 32
tribunals, 127–9
See also Conditional fee agreements; Costs;
    Fair trial guarantees; Legal aid
Fair trial guarantees, 14–16
absence of national remedy, 37
access to court, *see* Access to court; Costs;
    Legal aid
appeals, 16, 29
civil rights and obligations, 14
    meaning, 14
costs, *see* Costs
creation of civil rights not recognised, 14
criminal offences, 14
damages, Strasbourg, 80–2
deportation, 14
development of law, 14
equality of arms, *see* Equality of arms
first instance, breach of Art. at, 16
hearing, *see* Hearing, right to fair
immigration controls, 14
immunity from action, 14–15, 100–1, 180
    company inspector's reports, 14–15
    police, 15, 100–1, 180
institute proceedings, right to, 39–40
international level of cases, 14
legal aid, *see* Legal aid
margin of appreciation, 30
mental health, 210
privilege, 14–15
procedural fairness, 29

proportionality, 30
public hearing, entitlement to, 16, 151–3
public law, 14
qualified rights, 29, 151
reasonable time, right to trial within, 16,
    153–4
reasons for decisions, 16
requirements, 29
tribunal established by law, right to
    independent and impartial, 16
False imprisonment,
detention, 14, 98, 215
liberty and security of the person, right to,
    14, 98
mental patients, 103, 105n, 215
Family life, right to private, 16–17
    asylum, 83
care proceedings, 83
CCTV use, 99
damages, Strasbourg, 83
deportation, 14, 83
environmental rights, 160, 168–70
establishment and development of
    relationships with other human beings,
    16
four interests, 16
"home", 17
horizontal application of human rights
    standards, 62
illegitimate children, 210
offices, 17
police, 97, 98, 99
positive obligation to protect, 16, 210
qualified rights, 17, 20
scope of family life, 16–17
sexual relationships, 16, 123
surveillance, 99
see also Correspondence, respect for; Home,
    respect for
Family, right to found,
absolute rights, 19
discrimination, 130
generally, 18
IVF treatment, 130–1
marry, right to, 131
medical law, 123, 130–1
mental patients, 231
prisoners, 231
refusal of fertilisation treatment, 130
reproductive technology, 18, 130–1
sexual relationships, 16, 123
sterilisations, 123
Fast track amendment procedure,
declaration of incompatibility, 8, 75
Feelings, injury to,
damages,
    Strasbourg awards, 81–2
    United Kingdom awards, 81–2

Fetus, right to life of, 122, 123, 232–4
Fiduciary duty,
  confidentiality, 186
Fingerprints,
  police taking, 99
  private life, interference with, 99
Food safety,
  emergency control orders, 96
Force used on arrest, 98
Forced labour, 13
Free elections, right to free, 19
Freedom of assembly,
  common law restrictions, 17–18
  highway, legal use of, 18
  qualified rights, 20
Freedom of association,
  environmental rights, 182–3
  qualified rights, 20
  trade union membership, 17
Freedom of expression,
  confidence, information received in, 197–8
  confidentiality, 17, 195–8
    confidence, information received in, 197–8
    generally, 195–6
    impartiality of judiciary, 196–7
    journalistic sources, 197–8
    limitations on right, 195–6
    national security, 197
    rights of others, 197–8
  contempt of court, 58
  correspondence, respect for, 17
  defamation, 17, 200–3, 204–6
    common law defences, 201
    relevant articles, 200
  democracy, foundation of, 17
  disclosure of journalistic sources, 197–8
  economic torts, 97
  environmental rights, 182–3
  impartiality of judiciary, 196–7
  importance of right, 17
  information, right to receive, 143, 162–3
  journalistic sources, 197–8
  litigation on-going, where, 58
  medical records, 125–6
  mental patients, 230–1
  national security, 197
  qualified rights, 20, 195–6
  relevance to common law, 17
  right to life and, 143
Freedom from discrimination,
  generally, 18
  public authorities, 18
Freedom of religion,
  horizontal application of human rights
    standards, 60
  importance of provisions, 17
  qualified rights, 20
Freedom of speech, *see* Freedom of expression

Freedom of thought,
  horizontal application of human rights
    standards, 60
Freehold, acquisition of,
  property rights, 37
Freezing order,
  property rights, 19

Germany,
  Drittwirkung, 67
  horizontal application of human rights
    standards, 67
Gibraltar,
  IRA members, shooting of, 12
Good faith,
  confidentiality, 186
Goods, unlawful interference with, *see*
    Unlawful interference with goods
Goodwill,
  property rights, 18
Gypsies,
  environmental rights, 169
  home, respect for, 169

Harassment,
  landlord and tenant, 91, 92
  surveillance, 156
Health insurance benefits,
  civil rights and obligations, 34
Health and safety,
  medical negligence, 141–2
  smoking, 141–2
Highway, legal use of,
  freedom of assembly, 18
HIV, *see* AIDS
Home, respect for,
  access, 17
  access, right of, 91
  aircraft noise, 91, 165, 179–80, 181
  armed forces, occupation by, 91
  business premises, 17, 91
  damages, Strasbourg, 83
  environmental rights, 160, 164–71
  eviction, 17, 92–3
  expulsion, 17
  gypsies, 169
  harassment by landlord, 91, 92
  "home", 17, 90–1
  homosexuals, 93
  impact of HRA on domestic proceedings, 92
  intention to live at place, 90–1
  live in home, right to, 90
  migrant workers, 90
  no absolute right to home, 90
  occupation, 17, 91
  offices, 17, 91
  peaceful enjoyment, 91
  police, 97

possession proceedings, 93
professional person's office, 17
property rights, 91
provision, 90
qualification to rights, 17
qualified rights, 20
"respect", 92
settled basis, 90
unlawful eviction, 92–3
Homosexuality,
  armed forces, 74
  home, respect for, 93
  possession proceedings, 93
  remedies, 74
Hong Kong,
  Bill of Rights, 64
  horizontal application of human rights
    standards, 64
Horizontal application of human rights
standards, 53–69
  abortion, 68
  approach of courts to duty, 58–60
  Canada, 64
  common law, application to, 59
  comparative law,
    Canada, 65
    generally, 64
    Germany, 67
    Hong Kong, 64
    Ireland, 67
    Netherlands, 67
    New Zealand, 66–7
    South Africa, 66
    United States, 65
  conclusions, 68–9
  constitutional tort, emergence of, 55
  corporal punishment, 62
  declaration of incompatibility, 59
  definition, 55
  discrimination, 60
  extension of scope of HRA, 57–61
  fair trial, right to, 57
  family life, right to private, 62
  freedom of religion, 60
  freedom of thought, 60
  generally, 53
  Germany, 67
  Hong Kong, 64
  International Convention on the Elimination
    of all forms of Racial Discrimination,
    63
  interpretative obligation, 58–60
  Ireland, 67
  meaning, 54–5
  Netherlands, 67
  New Zealand, 66–7
  non-State actors, 55
  positive obligations, 60–1

privacy law, 59
public international law, 61
sexual abuse, 62
South Africa, 66
Strasbourg, approach of, 60, 61–4
trade union membership, 62
United States, 65
Hospitals,
  private, 109n, 137
  public authority, 105n, 137
Housing, *see* Landlord and tenant
Human rights,
  accountability, 54
  philosophical questions, 54
  standards, 54
Human Rights Act 1998,
  bring and defending claim, *see* Claim,
    bringing and defending Convention
    claim in domestic proceedings
  commencement, 5, 26
  damages, *see under* Damages
  horizontal effect, *see* Horizontal
    application of human rights
    standards
  impact, 26
  implied repeal, doctrine of, 59
  importance, 26–7
  leave to bring proceedings, 111
  legal aid for cases under, 43
  limitation period, 151
  parliamentary sovereignty, 5, 53, 56
  purpose, 3, 5, 55
  shield, use as, 115n
  subordinate legislation, 58, 59
  vertical effect, *see* Vertical effect of human
    rights standards
  watershed, as, 53
Hybrid public authorities, 105n, 112n, 137
  example, 106n, 137
  incompatible acts, 7
  liability, 7

Illegitimate children, 210
Immigration controls,
  AIDS sufferers, 13
  fair trial guarantees, 14
  inhuman or degrading treatment or
    punishment, 13
  liberty and security of the person, right to,
    14
Immunity from action,
  fair trial guarantees, 14–15, 100–1, 180
  police, 15, 100–101, 180
Impartiality of judiciary,
  freedom of expression, 196–7
Implied repeal, doctrine of,
  Human Rights Act 1998, 59
  statutory construction, 6

Incompatible acts, 7–8
  cause of action, new, 7
  courts, 7
  hybrid public authorities, 7
  limitation period, 8
  professional disciplinary bodies, 7
  public authorities, 7–8
  right to sue, 7
  tribunals, 7
  victim of act, 7
  see also Public authority
Incorporation of Convention, 5–8
  "back door" , by, 9
  cause of action, new, 7–8
  impact, 9–26
    ambiguities in common law, 9
    common law, 11–19
    consideration of Convention pre-
      incorporation, 9–10
    English law, on, 9
    enjoyment of rights under Convention, 9
    generally, 9
    interpretation of domestic law pre-
      incorporation, 9–10
    "living instrument", Convention as, 10–11
    rights under Convention, 9
    testing of actions of public authorities, 9
    undecided domestic law, 9
    Wade, 9
  interpretation, technique of 6, *see also*
    Statutory construction
  "living instrument", Convention as, 10–11
  political pressure on Government, 8
  rationale, 1
  revolutionary approach, 9
  routes, 5–6
  statutory construction 6–7, *see also*
    Statutory construction
  techniques used, 5–6
India,
  right to life, 10
Inducing breach of contract, 97
Industrial diseases,
  legal aid, 44
Industrial injuries,
  confidentiality of medical reports, 26
  medical negligence, 26
Inhuman or degrading treatment or punish-
    ment,
  absolute rights, 12–13, 19
  AIDS, 132
    deportation of person with, 13
  artificial feeding, 109n, 219
  assault, 13
  child abuse, 62
  claim, bringing and defending Convention in
    domestic proceedings, 109–10
  corporal punishment, 13, 62

  damages, Strasbourg, 79
  definition, 13
  deportation, 87, 132
  detention in seclusion, 13
  dying with dignity, 121
  environmental rights, 164
  euthanasia and, 121
  experimental medical treatment, 144
  extradition to face death penalty, 13
  freedom from, 12–13
  immigration controls, 13
  insulting language, 98
  medical law, 121
  medical negligence, 13, 135, 144–5
  mental health, 109, 210, 219–20
  mental patients, 109, 210, 219–20
  mock executions, 98
  parental punishment, 62
  particulars of claim, 109
  personal injury cases, 135, 144–5
  police, 97, 98
  political asylum, 13
  public emergencies, 12–13
  sensory deprivation, 98
  solitary confinement, 98
  terrorism, 13
  third party carrying out/threatening, 13
  wars, 12
  see also Torture
Injunctions, 71
  availability, 8
  person with right to bring proceedings for, 7
Innocence, presumption of, 75
  terrorism, reverse onus provisions and, 8
Inquests, 129–30
  effective remedy, right to, 129
  right to life, 129
Insulting language,
  inhuman or degrading treatment or
    punishment, 98
  police use, 98
Interception of communications,
  data protection, 191
  police, by, 137
  private life, interference with, 191–2
Interference with contract, 97
Interference with family life, *see* Family life,
    respect for
Interference with private life, *see* Private life,
    interference with
Interference with property rights, *see* Property
    rights
International Convention on the Elimination
    of all forms of Racial Discrimination,
  private parties, 63
International Covenant on Civil and Political
    Rights,
  New Zealand, 66

private parties, 63
Interpretation of Convention rights, 6–7
  Committee of Ministers, decisions of, 6
  Contracting States, decisions of other courts
    of, 7
  European Commission of Human Rights,
    decisions of, 6
  European Court of Human Rights, decision
    of, 6
  horizontal application of human rights
    standards, 58–60
  persuasive decision of other courts, 7
  statutory construction, *see* Statutory
    construction
  "take into account", decisions required to, 6
Intimate samples,
  battery, 99
  liberty and security of the person, right to,
    99
  police taking, 99
  private life, interference with, 99
Intimidation, tort of, 97
Invasion of the home, *see* Home, respect for
Investigative work by police, negligent, 100–1,
    120, 139
Ireland,
  abortion, 68
  emergency terrorist measures, 23
  horizontal application of human rights
    standards, 67
  solitary confinement, 98
IVF treatment, 130–1

Joinder of Crown,
  declaration of incompatibility, 75
  proceedings under HRA 1998, 116
Judges,
  immunity from action, 86–7
Judgment debts,
  peaceful enjoyment of possessions, 96
Judicial review,
  acts of public authorities before commence-
    ment of 1998 Act, 8
  claim, bringing and defending Convention,
    103, 105n
  environmental rights, 170
  mental patients, 214
Judicial separation,
  access to court, 40, 41
  legal aid, 40, 41

Kurdish minorities in Turkey,
  right to life, 12
Kosovo, Serbs in, 13

Labour,
  compulsory, 13
  forced, 13

Landlord and tenant,
  aircraft noise, 91
  discrimination, 93
  eviction, 92–3
  harassment, 91, 92
  home, extent of, 90–1
  homosexuals, tenancies for, 93
  impact of HRA on domestic proceedings, 92
  maintenance, 91
  noise, 91
  possession proceedings, 93
  private landlords, 92
  quiet enjoyment, interference with, 91
  repairs, 91
  retroactive criminal offences and punish-
    ment, freedom from, 92–3
  unlawful eviction, 92–3
  see also Home, respect for
Lawyer, access to,
  liberty and security of the person, right to,
    98
Lawyer/client confidentiality,
  access to court, 50
Leases,
  peaceful enjoyment of possessions, 96
Leave to bring proceedings,
  Human Rights Act 1998, 111
  mental patients, 111
Legal aid,
  access to court, 39–44
    arbitrary refusal, 42
    damages claims, 45–7
    defamation, 40–1, 201
    excluded categories, 40–2, 51
    financial criteria, 41
    frivolous cases, 42
    institute proceedings, right to, 39–40
    limited resources, 42
    merits of claim, 41
    opponent in receipt of legal aid, 43
    personal injury cases, 46–7
    police accountability, 41
    pre-trial applications, 40
    prospect of success, no reasonable, 42
    relevant criteria, 40
    repeated applications, ban on, 43
    restrictions on right, 42–3
    riskiness of case, 41
    separation proceedings, 40
    stakes involved, 40
    status of opposing party, 43
    unfair dismissal application, 41
    vexatious applications, 42
  arbitrary refusal, 42
  budget, 45
  civil proceedings, 39–44
    arbitrary refusal, 42
    damages claims, 45–7

Legal aid (*cont.*):
  civil proceedings (*cont.*):
    defamation, 41, 201
    detention in context of, 50–1
    excluded categories, 40–2, 51
    financial criteria, 41
    frivolous cases, 42
    institute proceedings, right to, 39–40
    limited resources, 42
    margin of appreciation, 46
    mental patients, detention of, 51
    merits of claim, 41
    opponent in receipt of legal aid, 43
    police accountability, 41
    pre-trial applications, 40
    proper participation before tribunal, 42–3
    proportionality, 45
    prospect of success, no reasonable, 42
    qualified right, 45
    relevant criteria, 40
    repeated applications, ban on, 43
    restrictions on right, 42–3
    riskiness of case, 41
    separation proceedings, 40
    stakes involved, 40
    status of opposing party, 43
    unfair dismissal application, 41
    vexatious applications, 42
  criminal proceedings, 45
  damages claims, 45–7
  defamation, 40–1, 201
  disciplinary proceedings, 44
  draft funding code, 44–5, 73
  equality of arms, 39, 43
  excluded categories, 40–2, 51
  frivolous cases, 42
  generally, 29
  high cost cases, 45
    investigative costs, 44, 45
  Human Rights Act cases, 43
  industrial diseases, 44
  ineffectual lawyers, 32n
  institute proceedings, right to, 39–40
  investigative costs, 45
  judicial separation, 40, 41
  Legal Aid Board (LAB), replacement of, 44
  Legal Services Commission (LSC), 44–5, 51
  liberty, right to, 50
  liberty and security of the person, right to, 50–1
  limited resources, 42
  margin of appreciation, 46
  mental health, 46, 51, 210
  Mental Health Review Tribunal, 227
  mental patients, 46, 51, 210, 227
  merits of claim, 41
  minors, 46
  negligence, 44

  opponent in receipt of legal aid, 43
  personal injury cases, 45, 46
  police accountability, 41
  pre-trial applications, 40
  private civil right, whether, 29, 34–6
  proportionality, 45
  prospect of success, no reasonable, 42
  public interest cases, 45, 73
  remedies, 73
  repeated applications, ban on, 43
  requirement to provide, 32
  restrictions on right, 42–3
  status of opposing party, 43
  tribunal hearings, 44
  unfair dismissal application, 41
  vexatious applications, 42
Legal Aid Board,
  replacement, 44
Legal professional privilege, 188, 193
  access to court, 50
  substantive right, 50
Legal representation,
  conditional fees, *see* Conditional fee
    agreements
  costs, *see* Costs
  generally, 29
  legal aid, *see* Legal aid
  medical negligence, 147–9
  mental patients, 227–8
  personal injury cases, 147–9
  see also Access to court; Equality of arms,
    Fair trial guarantees
Legal Services Commission (LSC), 44, 51
Libel, *see* Defamation
Liberty and security of the person, right to, 13–14
  arbitrary detention, 98
  arrest, 98
    force used on, 98
    lethal force, 98
    statement of reasons for, 98
  authorisation, 14
  categories in which authorised, 14
  claim, bringing and defending Convention in
    domestic proceedings,
    defence, 114
    particulars of claim, 108–9
  compensation, 97–8
  contempt of court, 14
  criminal offences,
    remand in custody for accused, 14
  criminal procedure, 13
  damages, Strasbourg, 79
  defence, 114
  deportation, 13, 14, 87
  detention, *see* Detention
  extradition, 13, 14
  false imprisonment, 14, 98

immigration, 14
intimate samples, 99
lawful detention, 51, 97–8
lawyer, access to, 98
legal aid, 50–51
lethal force used on arrest, 98
malicious prosecution, 14
medical treatment, 145
mental patients, 13, 14, 51, 108–9, 114,
   215–16, 220–4
mock executions, 98
particulars of claim, 108–9
police, *see* Police
procedural rights, 14
promptly brought before court, person must
   be, 98
qualified right, 50, 97–8, 115n
searches, police, 98
seizure by police, 98
statement of reasons for arrest, 98
suspect's rights, 98
see also Detention
Licences,
   peaceful enjoyment of possessions, 96
Life, right to, *see* Right to life
Life support systems, 119–20, 121
Limitation period,
   access to court, 149–51
   HRA claims, 151
   incompatible acts, 8
   long stop provisions, 150–1
   personal injury cases, 8, 149–51
   proceedings under 1998 Act, 8, 111, 116
   sexual abuse, 150
Litigant in person,
   Civil Procedure Rules, 52
Litigation privilege, 188, 193
LSC, 44

Malicious falsehood, 97, 185
Malicious prosecution,
   liberty and security of the person, right to,
      14
Mandamus, 8
Mareva injunctions, 19
Margin of appreciation,
   abortion, 122, 123
   access to court, 30–1
   basis, 25
   emergency terrorist measures, 23
   environmental rights, 170
   fair and public hearing, 31, 152
   fair trial guarantees, 30
   importance of doctrine, 17
   legal aid, 46
      local factors, 30
   meaning of doctrine, 22–3, 30
   medical law, 122–3

national courts, approach of, 23–4
   post-incorporation position, 23
   public law, 24
   public morals, protection of, 30
   qualified rights, 22–3
   role of principle, 23–4
   scope, 30–1
   unborn children, 122
Marry, right to,
   absolute rights, 19
   family, right to found, 131
   generally, 18
   mental patients, 231
   see also Reproductive technology, 18
Medical law, 119–33
   abortion, 122, 123
   AIDS, *see* AIDS
   allocation of medical resources, 124–5,
      138–41
   Caesarean section, enforced, 122
   chronic illness, treatment of, 124
   discrimination in health care provision, 125
   enforced medical treatment, 122–3
   euthanasia, 121
   fetus, right to life of, 122, 123, 232–4
   funding treatment, 124–5
   generally, 119
   inhuman or degrading treatment, 121
   inquests, 129–130
   life support systems, 119–20, 121
   margin of appreciation, 122–3
   medical records, 125–6, 156–7
   medical tribunals, 127–9
   negligence, *see* Medical negligence
   personal injury litigation, *see* Medical
      negligence; Personal injury cases
   prolonging life 119–21, *see also* Right to life
   provision of medical treatment, 120–1,
      124–5
   reproductive technology, *see* Reproductive
      technology
   resources, lack of, 124–5, 138–41
   terminally ill patients, 121
   tribunals, medical, 127–129
   vaccinations, 120, 132
   see also Right to life
Medical negligence,
   access to court, 145–147
   AIDS through blood transfusions, 86, 132–3
   banning drugs, 142
   Bolam test, 140, 213, 215
   chemical hazards, 143
   detention, persons in, 145
   domestic law, 140–1
   equality of arms, 147–9
   experimental medical treatment, 13, 144–5
   freedom of expression and, 143
   generally, 135

Medical negligence (*cont.*):
  health and safety, 141–2
  industrial injuries, 26
  information provision by health authority,
      142
  inhuman or degrading treatment or
      punishment, 13, 135, 144–5
  medical records, 126, 156–7
  physical integrity, 155
  public hearings, 151–3
  radiation exposure, monitoring of, 142–3
  relevant articles, 135–45
  representation, 147–9
  right to life, *see under* Right to life
  smoking, 141–2
  vaccinations, 138
  vicarious liability, 140–1
  video surveillance, 155–6
Medical records, confidentiality of,
  proportionality, 26
Medical tribunals, 127–9
Mental health,
  access to court, 225
  capacity, 110n, 209, 213–16, 232–5
    reform proposals, 211, 234
  case study, 103–17
  conclusions, 235–6
  detention, 212–26
    "according to law", 211
    challenge, likely areas of, 225–32
    common law, 212–16
    criminals detained in psychiatric wings,
        220
    emergency, 224–5
    inhuman or degrading treatment, 219–20
    liberty and security of the person, right to,
        220–4
    MHA, under, 216–17
    necessity, doctrine of, 212–16
    persons of unsound mind, 223–4
    reform proposals, 211, 214
    right to life, 216–17
    without treatment, 217–24
    see also under Mental patients
  fair and public hearing, 210, 228–9
  fair trial guarantees, 210
  generally, 209
  inhuman or degrading treatment or
      punishment, 109, 210
  legal aid, 46, 51, 210, 227
  *Managing Dangerous People with Severe
      Personality Disorder (DSPDs) –
      Proposals for Policy Development*, 218
  mental disorder, 211, 221
  Mental Health Act 1983,
    burden of proof, 228
    detention under, 216–17
    drafting, 212

  mental disorder, 221
  psychopathic disorder, 221
  review 209, *see also* reform proposals
      above
  treatment under, 219
  Mental Health Review Tribunal,
    legal aid, 227
    reform proposals, 211
  negative rights and obligations, 209–10
  positive rights and obligations, 209–10
  psychopathic disorder, 221
  public authority, 212
  reform proposals, 210–12
    access to medical records, 210
    assessments, 211
    authorised representative, right to, 210
    capacity, 211, 234
    care and treatment plan, 211
    compulsory treatment, 211
    detention, 211, 214
    emergency treatment, 211
    financial implications, 211
    generally, 209
    impact, 211
    independent advice, 210
    informal patients, 211
    information rights, 210
    involuntary treatment, 211
    level of service, 210–11
    mental disorder, definition of, 211, 221
    patients' rights, 210–12
    positive rights, 210
    reciprocity, 210–11
    tribunals, 211
    voluntary patients, 211
  review of law, 209
  right to life, 210, 216–17
  "securing rights", 210
  sterilization of patients, 108n, 123, 212–13
  translators, 210
  see also Mental patients
Mental Health Review Tribunal,
  legal aid, 227
  reform proposals, 211
  see also Mental health; Mental patients
Mental patients,
  abortion by, 232–234
  access to court, 214, 224–5, 227–8
  artificial feeding, 109n, 219
  battery, 105n
  bringing domestic claim, 103–17
  capable of treatment, condition, 217–18
  capacity, 110n, 209, 213–16, 232–5
  case study, 103–17
  challenge, likely areas of, 225–32
    access to courts, 227–8
    burden of proof, 228
    correspondence, respect for, 229–30

delayed release, 226–7
discrimination, 231–2
failure to obtain prior medical report, 226
fair and public hearing, 228–9
family, right to found, 231
freedom of expression, 230–1
generally, 225–6
legal aid, 227
liberty, deprivation of, 226–7, 228
marry, right to, 231
private life, respect for, 229–30
representation, 227–8
right to life of unborn fetus, 232–4
consent to detention, 109–10, 115, 213–16, 232–4
correspondence, respect for, 229–30
criminals detained in psychiatric wings, 220
defending domestic claim, 103–17
delayed release, 226–7
detention,
    access to court, 214, 224–5, 227–8
    Bolam test, 140, 215
    capable of treatment, condition, 217–18
    capacity, 109–10, 213–16, 232–4
    challenge, likely areas of, *see* Challenge,
        likely areas of *above*
    common law, 212–16
    compliant patients, 213–14
    conditions of lawful detention, 108n
    consent, 109–10, 115, 213–16, 232–4
    domestic proceedings, 107n, 108n, 109n
    duty of care owed by professionals, 214
    emergency, 224–5
    failure to obtain prior medical report, 226
    false imprisonment, 215
    informal patient, 214
    inhuman or degrading treatment, 219–20
    lawful, 223–4
    legal aid, 46, 51
    liberty and security of the person, right to,
        13, 14, 51, 108–9, 114, 215–16, 220–224,
        226–7, 228
    meaning of detention, 221–3
    medical treatment, 145
    MHA, under, 216–17
    necessity, doctrine of, 212–16
    proportionality, 214–15
    psychopathic disorders, patients with, 217
    public, protection of, 217, 218–19
    reform proposals, 211, 214
    restraints, 219–20
    right to life, 216–17
    severe personality disorders, 218–19
    sterilization, 212–13
    time take to determine legality, 109, 114,
        116
    unsound mind, lawful detention of
        persons of, 108n, 223–4

without treatment, 217–4
discrimination, 110n, 231–2
domestic proceedings, 107n, 108n, 109n
emergency confinement, 110n, 224–5
failure to obtain prior medical report before
    detention, 226
fair and public hearing, 210, 228–9
false imprisonment, 103, 105n, 215
family, right to found, 231
fetus, right to life of, 122, 123, 232–4
freedom of expression, 230–1
inhuman or degrading treatment or
    punishment, 109, 210, 219–20
judicial review, 214
leave to bring proceedings, 111
legal aid, 46, 51, 210, 227
liberty and security of the person, right to,
    13, 14, 51, 108–9, 114, 215–16, 220–224,
    226–7, 228
*Managing Dangerous People with Severe
    Personality Disorder (DSPDs) –
    Proposals for Policy Development*, 218
marry, right to, 231
nearest relative, 110, 116
necessity, doctrine of, 212–16
private life, interference with, 110–11, 115
private life, respect for, 229–30
proportionality, 214–15
psychopathic disorders, patients with, 217
public, protection of, 217–19
representation, 227–8
restraints, 219–20
review of law dealing with, 209
right to life, 216–17
    unborn fetus, 232–4
severe personality disorders, 218–19
sterilization, 108n, 212–13
threatening lives of others, 217
translators for, 210
treatability, 217–18
unsound mind, lawful detention of persons
    of, 108n, 223–4
without treatment, detention, 216–24
see also Mental health
Mentally handicapped persons,
    sexual abuse claims by, 62, 110n
Migrant workers,
    home, respect for, 90
Minors,
    legal aid, 46
    sterilization, 123
Mock executions,
    inhuman or degrading treatment or
        punishment, 98
Morals, protection of, 30

National security,
    confidentiality, 197

National security (*cont.*):
  freedom of expression, 197
  proportionality, 31
Nationality, determination of, 34
Nazis, 13
Negligence,
  HIV infection, 86, 131, 132–3
  legal aid, 44
  medical, *see* Medical negligence
  police, 100–1, 120, 139
Netherlands,
  horizontal application of human rights
    standards, 67
New Zealand,
  Bill of Rights, 58, 66–7
  damages, 86
  horizontal application of human rights
    standards, 66–7
  International Covenant on Civil and
    Political Rights, 66
"Newspaper rule", 15
NHS Trust,
  public authority, 105n
Nitrate concentrations,
  environmental rights, 173
Noise,
  aircraft, 91, 165, 179–80, 181
Nuclear testing, 34, 168
Nuisance,
  confidentiality, 185, 186
Nuremberg trials, 3

Obscene books,
  seizure, 99
Offices,
  home, respect for, 17, 91
Opportunity, loss of,
  damages, 81
Oral hearing, right to 33, 38,
  see also Fair and public hearing

Parental punishment,
  inhuman or degrading treatment or
    punishment, 62
Parliament,
  safeguarding rights through, 1, 4
  sovereignty, 5, 53, 59
Particulars of claim,
  claim, bringing and defending Convention,
    105–12
Passing-off, 97
Patents,
  peaceful enjoyment of possessions, 18, 96
  property rights, 18
Peaceful enjoyment of possessions,
  Anton Pillar orders, 19
  army occupation of property, 83–84
  company shares, 18

compulsory purchase, 174–5
contract, 94
control, 18–19, 172
damages, 83–4
debts, ownership of, 18
definition of possessions, 95–6
economic torts, 97
economic value, 18
environmental rights, 171–5
  availability of compensation, 172
  combination of Articles, claims under a,
    172–3
  control and possession distinguished, 172
  nitrate concentrations, 173
  planning decisions, 171–3
  "possessions", 171–2
  qualified right, 171
established economic interest, 96
examples, 18
"fair balance" test, 19
food safety emergency control orders, 96
freehold, acquisition of, 37
freezing order, 19
generally, 18–19
goodwill, 18
home, respect for, 91
international law, 18
judgment debts, 96
leases, 96
licences, 96
Mareva injunctions, 19
patents, 18, 96
peaceful enjoyment, 18
planning blight, 174–5
planning decisions, 171–3
police, 99
possessions, meaning of, 18, 95–6, 97, 171–2
public interest, deprivation in, 18, 171
qualified right, 171
search order, 19
shares, 96
unlawful interference with goods, *see*
  Unlawful interference with goods
Pepper v Hart, rule in, 74
Persistent vegetative state, persons in, 119
Personal injury cases,
  access to court, 46–7, 145–7
  clinical negligence, 135–57
    access to court, 145–7
    detention, persons in, 145
    equality of arms, 147–9
    experimental medical treatment, 144–5
    generally, 135
    inhuman or degrading treatment or
      punishment, 135, 144–5
    medical records, 156–7
    physical integrity, 155
    privacy, right to, 154–5

public hearing, 151–3
relevant articles, 135–45
representation, 147–9
right to life, *see under* Right to life
video surveillance, 155–6
"within a reasonable time", hearing,
    153–4
detention, persons in, 145
equality of arms, 147–9
inhuman or degrading treatment or
    punishment, 135, 144–5
legal aid, 45, 46
limitation period, 8, 149–51
medical records, 156–7
physical integrity, 155
public hearings, 151–3
representation, 147–9
right to life, *see under* Right to life
video surveillance, 155–6
Photographs,
police taking, 99
private life, interference with, 99
Physical integrity,
medical negligence, 155
personal injury cases, 155
Pig farms, 166
Planning,
blight, 174–5
damages, Strasbourg, 77
environmental rights, 77, 171–3
peaceful enjoyment of possessions, 171–3
public rights, 36
Police, 97–101
arbitrary detention, 98
arrest, 98
    force used on, 98
    statement of reasons for, 98
CCTV, use of, 99
civil actions against, 97–9
correspondence, respect for, 98–9
detention, 97–8
duty of care owed by, 101
effective remedy against, 97
fair and public hearing, 101
false imprisonment, 98
family life, right to private, 97, 98, 99
fingerprints, taking, 99
force used on arrest, 98
home, respect for, 97
ill-treatment and liberty and security of the
    person, 14
immunity from action, 15, 100–1, 180
inhuman or degrading treatment or
    punishment by, 97, 98
insulting language used by, 98
interception of communications, 137
interviews, information obtained during,
    188–9

intimate samples taken by, 99
investigative work, 100–1, 120, 139
lawyer, access to, 98
legal aid to bring claims against, 31, 41
liberty and security of the person, right to,
    14, 97–8
mock executions, 98
negligence, 100–1, 120, 139
peaceful enjoyment of possessions, 99
photographs taken by, 99
private life, interference with, 97, 98, 99
promptly brought before court, person must
    be, 98
proportionality, 31
right to life and, 97
riot, shots fired during, 98
search powers, 98
sensory deprivation, 98
suicide, liability for, 217
surveillance, 99
suspect's rights, 98–9
torture, 98
Political asylum,
inhuman or degrading treatment or
    punishment, 13
Pollution,
environmental rights, 165–7
right to life, 10
Positive obligations,
Convention rights, 60–1
Possession proceedings, 93
discrimination, 93
fair and public hearing, 93
home, respect for, 93
homosexuality, 93
Possessions, peaceful enjoyment of, *see*
Peaceful enjoyment of possessions
Press Complaints Commission Code of
Practice, 185
Presumption of innocence, *see* Innocence,
presumption of
Prevention of terrorism,
declaration of incompatibility, 75–6
Primary legislation,
conflicts, no resolution possible, 8
protection for, 5, 8
Prisoners,
family, right to found, 231
Privacy law, 59
development by courts, 57
see also Confidentiality; Family life, right to
    private; Home, respect for; Private life,
    interference with Private family life,
    Private parties, Family life, right to
    private; Home, respect for; Private life,
    interference with,
Private life, interference with,
access to personal information, 194–5

Private life, interference with (*cont.*):
  AIDS, 131–2, 192
  AIDS, disclosure of status, 131–2, 192, 193, 194
  business information/premises, 82
  care, disclosure of documents relating to, 82
  CCTV use, 99
  confidentiality, *see under* Confidentiality
  damages,
    Human Rights Act 1998, 84
    Strasbourg awards, 82
  defence, 115
  disclosure of private information, 192–4
  environmental rights, 160, 164–71
  fingerprints, 99
  HIV status, disclosure of, 131–2, 192, 193, 194
  interception of communications, 191–2
  intimate samples, 99
  medical records, 125, 126
  mental patients, 110–11, 115, 229–30
  particulars of claim, 110–11
  photographs, 99
  physical integrity of body, 110n, 155
  police, 97, 98, 99
  psychiatric reports, 193
  searches by officials, 82
  sexual abuse, 82
  sexual relationships, 123
  surveillance, 99, 194
  video surveillance, 155–6
  see also Family life, right to private; Home, respect for
Private parties,
  exclusion, 57
  horizontal effect of HRA, *see* Horizontal application of human rights standards
  International Convention on the Elimination of all forms of Racial Discrimination, 63
  International Covenant on Civil and Political Rights, 63
  private bodies, 105n
Privilege,
  defamation, 202, 203, 204
  fair trial guarantees, 14–15
  legal professional, *see* Legal professional privilege
  litigation, 188, 193
Prohibition, 8
Property rights, *see* Peaceful enjoyment of possessions
Proportionality,
  access to court, 30
  access to court, restrictions on, 37
  application of doctrine, 25–6
  environmental rights, 170, 171
  essence of right, 31

  fair trial guarantees, 30
  importance, 25
  importance of doctrine, 17, 26
  legal aid, 45
  meaning, 25–6, 31
  medical records, confidentiality of, 26
  mental patients, detention of, 214–15
  national security, 31
  police, 31
  qualified rights, 25–6
Protection of property, *see* Peaceful enjoyment of possessions
Psychiatric reports,
  private life, interference with, 193
Public authority,
  categories, 7, 105n
  courts, 7, 16, 57–8
  defence, 112
  definition, 7, 11, 56, 57, 137–8, 212
  directly affected by, 105
  doctors, 137–8
  examples, 7, 105–6n
  hospitals, 105n, 137
  hybrid bodies, 7, 105n, 112n, 137
  incompatible acts of, *see* Incompatible acts
  judicial bodies, 7, 16
  judicial review of acts of, 8
  liability, 7
  mental health, 212
  NHS Trust, 105n
  no public functions, bodies with, 7
  "obvious", 7, 105n, 112n, 137
  professional disciplinary bodies, 7
  tribunals, 7
  vertical application of HRA, 55–6
Public emergencies,
  inhuman or degrading treatment or punishment, 12–13
  right to life, 11
  torture, 12–13
Public hearing, *see* fair and public hearing
Public interest,
  confidentiality, 187–8
Public international law,
  challenges under Convention, 61
Public law,
  fair trial guarantees, 14
  margin of appreciation, 24
Public morals, protection of,
  margin of appreciation, 30
Public rights, 33–4
  fair and public hearing, 36
  planning applications, 36

Qualified rights, 20–6
  access to court, 29, 36, 146
  correspondence, respect for, 20
  fair trial guarantees, 29

family life, respect for, 20
freedom of assembly, 20
freedom of association, 20
freedom of expression, 20, 195–6
freedom of religion, 20
home, respect for, 20
"in accordance with the/prescribed by law",
    20, 21–2
justification, 21
liberty and security of the person, right to,
    19, 50, 97–8, 115n
margin of appreciation, 22–4
"necessary in a democratic society", 22–3
peaceful enjoyment of possessions, 171
"pressing social need", 25
proportionality, 25–6
telephone tapping, 21–2
Wednesbury unreasonableness, 24

Race discrimination,
    Constantine case, 1–3
    damages, 2–3
    see also Discrimination
Radiation exposure, monitoring of,
    medical negligence, 142–3
Rape,
    damages, Strasbourg, 79
Reasons for decisions, 16
Records, medical, 125–6, 156–7
Refuse, refusal of grant to dump, 81
Religion, freedom of, *see* Freedom of religion
Remand in custody for accused, 14
Remedial Order,
    effect, 75
    failure to make, 75
    grant, 75
    making, 8, 75
    no duty to make, 75
    procedure, 8, 75
    see also Declaration of incompatibility;
        Remedies
Remedies, 71–87
    Access to Justice reforms, 73
    aggregate of national remedies, 72–3
    arguable case,
        Article 13, 72
        Human Rights Act cases, legal aid for, 43
    Article 13, 72–4
    certiorari, 8
    damages, *see* Damages
    declaration of incompatibility, *see*
        Declaration of incompatibility
    declarations, 8
    "effective remedy", 72–4
    homosexuality, 74
    Human Rights Act 1998, 8
        scope, 8
    injunctions, 8, 71

legal aid, 73
mandamus, 8
new, 71–2
Pepper v Hart, rule in, 74
prohibition, 8
public law awards, 71
subordinate legislation, breach of, 71
Sweden, 72
Turkey, 73
Repairs,
    landlord and tenant, 91
Representation, *see* Legal representation
Reproductive technology,
    family, right to found, 130–1
Respect for family life, home and correspon-
    dence, *see* Correspondence, respect for; Family
    life, right to; Home, respect for
Retroactive criminal offences and punishment,
    freedom from, 16
    absolute rights, 19
    landlord and tenant, 92–3
Right to life, 11–12
    abortion, 68, 122, 123
    absolute right, 11, 19
    AIDS, 132
    allocation of medical resources, 124–5,
        138–41
    chemical hazards, 143, 163
    chronic illness, treatment of, 124
    clinical negligence, *see* medical negligence
        below
    construction by European Court of Human
        rights, 10
    damages, Strasbourg, 78
    deliberate act, causing death by, 121
    discrimination in health care provision, 125
    environmental circumstances, 120
    environmental rights, 162–4
    European Court of Human Rights,
        jurisprudence of, 11–12
    euthanasia, 121
    executions, 120
    fetus, of, 122, 123, 232–4
    full enjoyment, pollution free water and air
        for, 10
    importance of right, 11–12, 136
    India, 10
    inquests, 129
    IRA shootings in Gibraltar, 12
    Kurdish minorities in Turkey, 12
    life support systems, 119–20, 121
    medical negligence, 135, 136–43
        allocation of resources, 124–5, 138–41
        banning drugs, 142
        Bolam test, 140, 213, 215
        chemical hazards, 143
        chronic illness, treatment of, 124
        domestic law, 140–1

Right to life (*cont.*):
  medical negligence (*cont.*):
    duty of public authorities, 137
    effect of finding of negligence, 141
    freedom of expression and, 143
    health and safety, 141–2
    importance of Convention, 136
    information provision by health
       authority, 142
    lack of resources, 124–5, 138–41
    positive obligations, 136–7, 138, 139, 141
    public authorities, 137
    qualifications to right, 136
    radiation exposure, monitoring of, 142–3
    real and immediate risk to life, 138, 140
    resources, 124–5, 138–41
    scope of Article, 136
    smoking, 141–2
    vaccinations, 138
    vicarious liability, 140–1
  mental health, 210, 216–17
  mental patients, 216–17
  omission, causing death by, 121
  permissible deprivation of life, 12
    absolutely necessary, 12
  persistent vegetative state, persons in, 119
  personal injury cases 135, 136–43, *see also*
     medical negligence *above*
  physical life, restricted to, 10
  police negligence, 97, 120, 138, 139
  pollution, 10
  positive obligation, 120, 124, 136–7, 138,
     139, 141
  provision of medical treatment, 120–1,
     124–5
  public emergencies, 11
  qualifications to right, 11, 135, 136
  reasonable protection, 121
  terminally ill patients, 121
  United Kingdom, ruling against, 12
  vaccinations, 120, 132, 138
  war, 11, 135
Riot, shots fired during, 98

Safeguarding rights,
  common law, 1, 3
  method, 1
  Parliament, 1, 4
  traditional approach, 3
SAS Gibraltar shootings, 78
Search order,
  peaceful enjoyment of possessions, 19
Searches by officials,
  police powers, 98
  private life, interference with, 82
Security for costs, 49
Security of the person, right to, *see* Liberty and
     security of the person, right to

Seizure,
  obscene books, 99
  police powers, 98
Self-incrimination privilege, denial of,
     damages, Strasbourg, 77
Sensory deprivation,
  inhuman or degrading treatment or
     punishment, 98
  police, by, 98
Servitude, freedom from, 13
Sexual abuse,
  damages, Strasbourg, 82
  horizontal application of human rights
     standards, 62
  limitation period, 150
  mentally handicapped persons, 62, 110n
  private life, interference with, 82
Sexual relationships,
  abortion, 123
  family life, right to, 16, 123
  private life, interference with, 16, 123
Shares,
  peaceful enjoyment of possessions, 96
Slavery, servitude or forced or compulsory
     labour, freedom from, 13
  absolute right, 19
Social insurance,
  civil rights and obligations, 34, 36
Solitary confinement, 98
  Ireland, 98
South Africa,
  environmental rights, 160
  horizontal application of human rights
     standards, 66
Sovereignty of Parliament, 5, 53, 59
Speculative fee agreements, *see* Conditional fee
     agreements
Speech, freedom of, *see* Freedom of
expression
Statutory construction, 6–7
  basic rule of interpretation, 6, 75, 97
  declaration of incompatibility, *see*
     Declaration of incompatibility
  effect of provisions, 6–7
  generally, 5–6
  implied repeal, doctrine of, 6
  Pepper v Hart, rule in, 6
  power of courts, 6
  pre-1998 legislation, 6
  responsibility of courts, 6
  subordinate legislation, 6
Sterilization,
  incompetent adults, 123
  mental patients, 108n, 123, 212–13
  minors, 123
  without consent, 108n, 123
Sterilisations,
  family life, right to found, 123

Subordinate legislation,
  Human Rights Act 1998, 58, 59
  statutory construction, 6
Surveillance,
  family life, right to private, 99
  harassment, 156
  insurance company, by, 194
  police, 99
  private life, interference with, 99
  video, 155–6
Suspect's rights,
  liberty and security of the person, right to,
    98
  see also Detention; Police
Sweden,
  remedies, 72

Telephone tapping, 21–2
Terrorism,
  inhuman or degrading treatment or
    punishment, 13
  torture, 13
Terrorism, prevention of,
  presumption of innocence and, 8
  reverse onus provisions, 8
Thai Trading agreement, 46
Torts,
  confidentiality, 186
  economic, 97
Torture,
  absolute right, 12–13, 19
  assault, 13
  corporal punishment, 13
  definition, 13
  freedom from, 12–13
  police, 98
  public emergency, 12–13
  terrorism, 13
  third party carrying out/threatening, 13
  war, 12–13
  see also Inhuman or degrading treatment or
    punishment
Trade union membership,
  freedom of association, 17
  horizontal application of human rights
    standards, 62
Translators, 32, 210
Trespass,
  confidentiality, 185
  effect of HRA on claims involving, 95–6
  public interest justification, 94
Trial, *see* Access to court; Fair hearing,
  right to; Fair trial guarantees ;
  Legal aid
Tribunals,
  decisive proceedings, 127
  fair and public hearing, 127–9
  incompatible acts, 7

legal aid for hearings, 44
medical, 127–9
public authority, 7
tribunal established by law, right to
  independent and impartial, 16
Turkey,
  damages for inhuman and degrading
    treatment, 79
  Kurdish minorities and right to life, 12
  remedies, 73

UN Human Rights Committee,
  discrimination, interpretation of ICCPR on,
    63
Unborn children,
  abortion, 68, 122, 123
  Caesarean, forced, 122
  conflicting rights of mother, 123
  deportation affecting, 122
  margin of appreciation, 122
Unfair dismissal application,
  access to court, 41
  legal aid, 41
United States,
  Bill of Rights, 65
  defamation, 65
  horizontal application of human rights
    standards, 65
Unjust enrichment,
  confidentiality, 186
Unlawful interference with goods, 95–7
  compensation, 95
  conversion, 95
  definition of possessions, 95–6
  food safety emergency control orders, 96
  justification for interference, 95
  peaceful enjoyment of possessions, 95–7
  possessions, meaning of, 95–6
  see also Peaceful enjoyment of possessions

Vaccinations, 120, 132, 138
Vertical application of human rights
    standards,
  application of HRA, 55–6
  definition, 55
  generally, 53
  meaning, 54–5
  State actors, 55
Vexatious applications,
  legal aid, 42
Vicarious liability,
  claim, bringing and defending Convention in
    domestic proceedings, 109n
  medical negligence, 140–1
"Victims",
  right to sue under 1998 Act, 7
Video surveillance, 155–6
Vote, right to, 14

War,
  inhuman or degrading treatment or
    punishment, 12
  right to life, 11, 135
  torture, 12–13
Waste management licences, 177
Waste treatment plants, 165–6

Wasted costs orders, 49–50
Wednesbury unreasonableness,
  qualified rights, 24
White Paper,
  Rights Brought Home, 56, 74
Wrongful means, causing loss by, 97

Printed in the United Kingdom
by Lightning Source UK Ltd.
101173UKS00001B/78